P9-EDR-576

4900
AP 26 '94
LIBRARY
ASIS
1655 N.FORT MYER DR.
ARLINGTON, VA 22209
HV
6115
.U55
1993

Understanding and Preventing Violence

Albert J. Reiss, Jr., and Jeffrey A. Roth, Editors

Panel on the Understanding and Control of Violent Behavior
Committee on Law and Justice
Commission on Behavioral and Social Sciences and Education
National Research Council

NATIONAL ACADEMY PRESS
Washington, D.C. 1993

National Academy Press • 2101 Constitution Avenue, N.W. • Washington, D.C. 20418

NOTICE: The project that is the subject of this report was approved by the Governing Board of the National Research Council, whose members are drawn from the councils of the National Academy of Sciences, the National Academy of Engineering, and the Institute of Medicine. The members of the committee responsible for the report were chosen for their special competences and with regard for appropriate balance.

This report has been reviewed by a group other than the authors according to procedures approved by a Report Review Committee consisting of members of the National Academy of Sciences, the National Academy of Engineering, and the Institute of Medicine.

This project was sponsored by the National Science Foundation, the National Institute of Justice, and the Centers for Disease Control.

Library of Congress Cataloging-in-Publication Data

Understanding and preventing violence : panel on the understanding and
control of violent behavior / Albert J. Reiss, Jr., and Jeffrey A.
Roth, editors.
p. cm.
Includes bibliographical references and index.
ISBN 0-309-04594-0
1. Violence—United States. 2. Violence—United States—
Prevention. 3. Violent crimes—United States. I. Reiss, Albert
J. II. Roth, Jeffrey A., 1945-
HN90.V5U53 1993
303.6—dc20 92-32137
CIP

Copyright 1993 by the National Academy of Sciences. All rights reserved.

Printed in the United States of America

First Printing, November 1992
Second Printing, April 1993

PANEL ON THE UNDERSTANDING AND CONTROL OF VIOLENT BEHAVIOR

Albert J. Reiss, Jr. (Chair), Department of Sociology, Yale University
David P. Farrington (Vice Chair), Institute of Criminology, Cambridge University
Elijah Anderson, Department of Sociology, University of Pennsylvania
Gregory Carey, Institute of Behavior Genetics, University of Colorado
Jacqueline Cohen, School of Urban and Public Affairs, Carnegie Mellon University
Philip J. Cook, Institute of Policy Sciences, Duke University
Felton Earls, Department of Behavioral Sciences, Harvard University
Leonard Eron, Department of Psychology, University of Illinois
Lucy Friedman, Victim Services Agency, New York
Ted Robert Gurr, Department of Government and Politics, University of Maryland
Jerome Kagan, Department of Psychology, Harvard University
Arthur Kellermann, Emergency Department, Regional Medical Center, Memphis, and Department of Internal Medicine and Preventive Medicine, University of Tennessee
Ron Langevin, Juniper Associates Psychological Services, Toronto, and Department of Psychiatry, University of Toronto
Colin Loftin, Institute of Criminal Justice and Criminology, University of Maryland
Klaus A. Miczek, Department of Psychology, Tufts University
Mark H. Moore, Kennedy School of Government, Harvard University
James F. Short, Jr., Social and Economic Sciences Research Center, Washington State University
Lloyd Street, College of Human Ecology, Cornell University
Franklin E. Zimring, Law School, University of California, Berkeley

Jeffrey A. Roth, Principal Staff Officer
Neil Alan Weiner, Senior Research Associate
Maryellen Fisher, Senior Project Assistant
Teresa Williams, Senior Project Assistant

COMMITTEE ON LAW AND JUSTICE
1990-1991

Stanton Wheeler (Chair), School of Law, Yale University
Joan McCord (Vice Chair), Department of Criminal Justice, Temple University
Robert Boruch, Graduate School of Education, University of Pennsylvania
José Cabranes, U.S. District Judge, New Haven, Connecticut
John Coffee, Columbia University School of Law
Philip J. Cook, Institute of Policy Sciences, Duke University
David P. Farrington, Institute of Criminology, Cambridge University
Robert Kagan, Center for Law and Society, University of California, Berkeley
Mark H. Moore, Kennedy School of Government, Harvard University
Albert J. Reiss, Jr. (ex officio), Chair, Panel on the Understanding and Control of Violent Behavior
John Rolph, The Rand Corporation, Santa Monica, California
Ellen Schall, National Center for Health Education, New York
Jerome Skolnick, School of Law (Jurisprudence & Social Policy), University of California, Berkeley
Lloyd Street, College of Human Ecology, Cornell University
Neil Vidmar, School of Law, Duke University
Barbara Yngvesson, School of Social Science, Hampshire College

Jeffrey A. Roth, Principal Staff Officer
Maryellen Fisher, Senior Project Assistant

Contents

TABLES AND FIGURES

Tables

Figures

The National Academy of Sciences is a private, nonprofit, self-perpetuating society of distinguished scholars engaged in scientific and engineering research, dedicated to the furtherance of science and technology and to their use for the general welfare. Upon the authority of the charter granted to it by the Congress in 1863, the Academy has a mandate that requires it to advise the federal government on scientific and technical matters. Dr. Frank Press is president of the National Academy of Sciences.

The National Academy of Engineering was established in 1964, under the charter of the National Academy of Sciences, as a parallel organization of outstanding engineers. It is autonomous in its administration and in the selection of its members, sharing with the National Academy of Sciences the responsibility for advising the federal government. The National Academy of Engineering also sponsors engineering programs aimed at meeting national needs, encourages education and research, and recognizes the superior achievements of engineers. Dr. Robert M. White is president of the National Academy of Engineering.

The Institute of Medicine was established in 1970 by the National Academy of Sciences to secure the services of eminent members of appropriate professions in the examination of policy matters pertaining to the health of the public. The Institute acts under the responsibility given to the National Academy of Sciences by its congressional charter to be an adviser to the federal government and, upon its own initiative, to identify issues of medical care, research, and education. Dr. Kenneth I. Shine is president of the Institute of Medicine.

The National Research Council was organized by the National Academy of Sciences in 1916 to associate the broad community of science and technology with the Academy's purposes of furthering knowledge and advising the federal government. Functioning in accordance with general policies determined by the Academy, the Council has become the principal operating agency of both the National Academy of Sciences and the National Academy of Engineering in providing services to the government, the public, and the scientific and engineering communities. The Council is administered jointly by both Academies and the Institute of Medicine. Dr. Frank Press and Dr. Robert M. White are chairman and vice chairman, respectively, of the National Research Council.

CONTENTS: VOLUMES 2-4

Preface

In some 200 years of national sovereignty, Americans have been preoccupied repeatedly with trying to understand and control one form of violence or another.

Most periods of our history bear witness to substantial collective violence. On the road to collective bargaining and peaceful picketing, there was much violent conflict. The more rural settlements around mines were often the scene of bloody conflict, and urban industrial conflict carried with it violence on the picket lines and the destruction of company property. Perhaps the major success story in control of collective violence is the substitution of peaceful for violent means in resolving conflicts between labor and management.

Urban riots are part and parcel of our history from late colonial times. In the latter half of this century, ethnic and racial tensions have erupted in urban riots, destroying life and neighborhoods of some of our major cities. Responding to urban riots in the summer of 1967, President Lyndon Johnson appointed the National Advisory Commission on Civil Disorders (known as the Kerner Commission after its chair, Illinois Governor Otto Kerner), which issued its report in 1968. The report focused both on how local community and national action can deal with immediate responses to riot and on long-range prevention through the reduction of inequality in housing, education, welfare, and employment.

Much collective violence is systematically organized. Organized crime, especially that arising from conflict over the control of illegal territorial markets, has been a continuing preoccupation of national, state, and local government. The National Commission on Law Observance and Enforcement (known as the Wickersham Commission after its chair) was established by President Herbert Hoover to inquire into the lawlessness and violent and organized criminal activity associated with Prohibition. Most of its recommendations went unheeded, owing in part to the repeal of Prohibition. More recently violent criminal activity has been linked to labor racketeering and to the control of illegal trafficking in drugs. State and federal legislative hearings are held repeatedly on organized criminal activity and a number of federal executive agencies, such as the Drug Enforcement Agency, have been created to investigate and control it.

The assassination of President John F. Kennedy again dramatically raised the question of why do Americans so often resort to violent means. Quite apart from the joint executive and legislative inquiry into that tragic event, President Lyndon Johnson established (by Executive Order #11412 on June 10, 1968) the National Commission on the Causes and Prevention of Violence (known as the Eisenhower Commission after its chair, Milton S. Eisenhower), with the express mandate "to investigate and make recommendations with respect to: (a) the causes and prevention of lawless acts of violence in our society, including assassination, murder, and assault; and (b) the causes and prevention of disrespect for law and order, of disrespect for public officials, and of violent disruptions of public order by individuals and groups." James F. Short, Jr., a member of this panel, served as a codirector of research for the Eisenhower Commission. The research staff commissioned and coordinated 13 published reports, including 2 on historical and comparative perspectives on violence in America, to which Ted Robert Gurr of this panel contributed significant effort. There were volumes on the causes and consequences of violence, assassination and political violence, firearms and violence, the politics of protest, the media and violence, and selected incidents of riot as well as major issues in law and order, such as justice and inequality.

Other studies that arose out of concern with what often appeared to be waves of violent crime focused attention on one or more presumed causes. Often singled out was the role of mass media and communication on social behavior, especially on aggressiveness and violent behavior and the role of pornography in violent behavior. A Commission on Obscenity and Pornography (with William B. Lockhart as its chair) was appointed in summer 1968, and in spring 1969, by congressional request, the Department of Health, Education, and Welfare appointed a Scientific Advisory Committee on Television and Social Behavior under the general auspices of the surgeon general. Each group issued a number of technical scientific reports as well as a general report. Readers of these reports are faced, as were commission and committee members, with conflicting evidence and findings of small, if any, impact.

Clearly, public concerns and scientific inquiry on aggressive and violent behavior and its causes have fueled public policy debates on the control of violence for much of the twentieth century. One might understandably ask, then, what was the rationale underlying the establishment of the Panel on the Understanding and Causes of Violent Behavior.

The panel was set up by the Commission on Behavioral and Social Sciences and Education (CBASSE) of the National Research Council in response to the expressed interest of three federal agencies. The National Science Foundation's Program on Law and Social Sciences sought a review of current knowledge on the basic causes of violent behavior and recommendations about priorities in funding research in the future. The two other government agencies were primarily interested in an assessment of what was known about how to prevent and control violent behavior. The National Institute of Justice sought advice on how to prevent and control violent crimes committed by individuals and small groups, such as adolescent gangs, and the Centers for Disease Control's Injury Control Division sought advice that would assist them in setting priorities in preventing injuries and deaths from violent behavior. To ensure that these goals were met, the panel membership includes persons with a primary interest in the prevention and control of violent behavior.

CBASSE's Committee on Law and Justice had major responsibility to help to shape the specific mandate of the panel. They concluded that all previous assessments were undertaken in response to rather specific concerns and events, such as urban riots, or with specific questions, such as whether the portrayal of violence in the mass media causes people to behave in violent ways, or whether pornography causes sexual violence, or how much can one reduce violent injury and death from weapons with more restrictive gun control. Although each of the major studies had produced significant reviews of what was known about violent behavior, no comprehensive assessment had been attempted by a scientific panel. Moreover, previous assessments rested largely on reviewing the scientific work in only one or two social science disciplines; none had made a significant attempt to review what was known in the biomedical and biobehavioral disciplines. To chart effectively the future course of research on violent behavior and to draw implications from past research, the perspectives and models on violent behavior of the biological, psychological, and social sciences should be integrated. An overarching concern was in the development of science policy: the panel's work should contribute to setting priorities for future allocation of research and evaluation resources on the prevention and control of violent behavior. Accordingly, it undertook a review of current programs and expenditures of all major federal agencies that funded research or programs on violent behavior and enunciated a science policy perspective that might guide them in future funding.

Early on the panel recognized the extraordinary breadth of the topic of the understanding and control of all violent behavior. Given the major reviews undertaken by all the previous commissions and committees on violence and more recent scholarly work, it elected to restrict its focus largely to the understanding and control of violent behavior that was, at law, criminal behavior and the ways that biobehavioral, social, and psychological scientific research provided theoretical and empirical work relevant to its understanding and control. The panel narrowed further its focus by excluding collective violence on the grounds that previous reviews seemed to cover quite adequately what was known about collective violence and that later scholarly work offered no basis for questioning their findings. On similar grounds it decided to summarize what was known about the history of violence only in twentieth-century America.

Several interesting and certainly related topics are also excluded from the focus on interpersonal and small group violence or given very limited treatment. One is intrapersonal violence—forms of harm such as suicide and self-mutilation—which could be included on grounds that an understanding of violence against the self is theoretically linked to violence against others. The treatment of violence of custodians and their wards is given limited treatment in the panel's report, as is the treatment of police and citizen violence, owing to the circumstance that the panel lacked comprehensive contemporary reviews of research and our commissioned papers provided little coverage of these forms of violence. Also excluded is ethology: much work has been carried out on nonhuman animal behavior that is considered analogous to human aggressive and violent behavior and that appears quite relevant for an understanding of human aggression and interpersonal violence. Especially noteworthy are the many biobehavioral and behavioral studies undertaken with primates.

The panel also regrettably had to exclude a systematic review of cross-cultural research and of national studies that would lead to a genuine comparative approach to the understanding and control of violent behavior. It is to be hoped that this lack can be remedied by greater support of comparative national and cross-cultural violence research by federal agencies and private foundations.

Given the absence of a review of both ethological and cross-cultural research on violent behavior, the panel recognized that it could not satisfactorily deal with some questions concerning the causes of violent behavior and of violent crime. Accordingly, it focused more on issues and problems in understanding and control and on setting forth a model to guide interdisciplinary understanding of violent behavior and its control.

To carry out its task the panel relied in the first instance on a number of review papers prepared by staff and members of the panel. In addition, it commissioned a large number of reviews, many of which were selected for publication in three volumes supplementary to this report. These papers are the responsibility of the individual authors and do not necessarily represent the views of the panel. They were valuable resources for the panel and are published because it is believed they will prove likewise to individual scholars seeking reviews of the scholarly contributions on a given violence topic. The panel is grateful to the authors and to those who prepared comments at our Symposium on Understanding and Preventing Violence.

The biographical sketches of the panel members are presented in Appendix C. The diversity of their backgrounds is readily apparent. With such diversity, disagreement was not uncommon. Yet a consensus on recommendations was achieved, and differences in reaching consensus about the weight of the evidence or the strength of a particular explanatory model were usually resolved. Perhaps part of that lies in the linguistic properties of the English language: its reservoir of qualification seemed ample to cover most disagreements.

The panel is especially grateful to Jeffrey Roth, study director for the panel. His administrative skill and understanding of the Byzantine ways of the federal bureaucracy and of the NAS-NRC were matched with an extraordinary skill in drafting significant sections of the panel's report and critical assistance in the review of its entirety. For a time the panel had the services of Neil Weiner, and drew on his extensive knowledge of the literature. He also was helpful in assembling statistical profiles for the report.

The panel owes much to Maryellen Fisher, who prepared many of the charts and graphs and who shepherded the report through its many clerical phases. They are especially grateful to Christine McShane for turning the polyglot of disciplinary panelists toward a single voice and for clarification of obfuscation.

The panel is grateful to a number of consultants who provided material on specialized topics: James Alan Fox, Jack Levin, Kathleen Pike, Adrian Raine, Lisa Stolzenberg, and Cathy Spatz Widom. It is also grateful to the following people for their generous assistance of various kinds: Carolyn Rebecca Block, Richard Block, Barbara Boland, Andrea Cummings, Joseph DeBold, Rosemary Erickson, Jeffrey Fagan, Lois Fingerhut, David Goslin, Lawrence Greenfeld, Gary Kleck, Markku Linnoila, Elaine McGarraugh, W. Walter Menninger, Alan Mirsky, Glenn Pierce, Richard Rau, Dennis Roncek, Lawrence W. Sherman, Henry Steadman, Bruce Taylor, Lynn Warner, Donald West, Renee Wilson-Brewer, and the staff members of federal violence research sponsoring agencies who prepared responses to our survey.

The panel is grateful for the support, patience, and understanding of its sponsors and their liaison representatives to the panel: the National Science Foundation and its director of Law and Social Sciences, Felice Levine; the National Institute of Justice and Richard Linster, its director of research, and Christy Visher, liaison to the panel; the Centers for Disease Control and Mark Rosenberg, director of its Division of Injury Control, and James Mercy, liaison for that division.

Albert J. Reiss, Jr., Chair
Panel on the Understanding
and Control of Violent Behavior

Summary

In cities, suburban areas, and even small towns, Americans are fearful and concerned that violence has permeated the fabric and degraded the quality of their lives. The diminished quality of life ranges from an inability to sit on the front porch in neighborhoods where gang warfare has made gunfire a common event to the installation of elaborate security systems in suburban homes where back doors once were left open. Children in urban schools experience violence on the way to school and in the school building itself. Surveys show that large percentages of the population fear even walking in their neighborhoods at night. The nation's anxiety on the subject of violence is not unfounded. In 1990, more than 23,000 people were homicide victims. Violent deaths and incidents that result in lesser injuries are sources of chronic fear and a high level of concern with the seeming inability of public authorities to prevent them.

In 1988 the National Academy of Sciences was asked by a consortium of federal agencies—the National Institute of Justice, the National Science Foundation, and the Centers for Disease Control—to assess the understanding of violence, the implications of that understanding for preventive interventions, and the most important research and evaluation needed to improve understanding and control of violence. In response, the Academy created the Panel on the Understanding and Control of Violent Behavior. This volume presents the panel's findings, conclusions, and recommendations; Volumes 2, 3, and 4 contain the background papers the panel commissioned to facilitate its work.

The panel adopted as its definition of "violence": *behaviors by individuals that intentionally threaten, attempt, or inflict physical harm on others.* Death is the basis for defining the most serious violent crime—murder. However, with murder as with lesser acts of violence, the definition masks enormous diversity in underlying behaviors that cause death: shootings by robbers, intrafamily murders, minor disputes that turn violent, sexual attacks, and gang killings. This diversity is also masked in statistical classifications of nonfatal violent crimes such as assault, robbery, and forcible rape. Even greater diversity is seen in violent behaviors that may not be counted as crimes, such as school fights, violence among prison inmates, and violence in the home.

Other violent events involve large collectives: wars, state violence, riots, and some activities of organized crime. The panel did not attempt to analyze such collective violence in this report.

MEASURING VIOLENCE

Violent behaviors that society identifies as crimes are counted more completely and classified more accurately than those that are not. Three national measurement systems are of primary importance in counting crimes and their victims. The National Crime Survey (NCS) asks all persons age 12 and over in a national sample of households to recall and describe recent nonfatal victimizations. The Uniform Crime Reporting (UCR) system records basic information about crimes detected by or reported to police, supplementary information about homicides, and descriptions of arrestees. Homicide data are also tabulated annually from death certificates by the National Center for Health Statistics (NCHS) vital statistics program.

While murders are counted rather accurately, counts of nonfatal violent crimes are incomplete. Gaps and discrepancies occur because victimizations may not be recognized as crimes, because embarrassment or psychological stigma inhibits reporting, because victims are sometimes reluctant to involve authorities, because their consequences may not be thought worth reporting as crimes, and because of discretion in classifying and counting violent events.

Moreover, definitions of violent events as criminal or not change over time and differ among segments of society. Data are even less adequate for violent acts that authorities and the public are coming to recognize as serious crimes. Recent attention to bias crimes, for example, highlights the inadequacy of crime information on violence motivated by differences in ethnic status, religion, and sexual preference. A 1990 law requires modification of the UCR to improve statistics on bias crimes. Similarly, physical and sexual assaults against women and children by intimates and acquaintances are now increasingly recognized and reported as crimes. If all such events were included in official counts of assaults and rapes, those counts would increase substantially.

PATTERNS AND TRENDS

Nearly one-third of the 19 million crime victimizations reported to the NCS in 1990 involved violence. The prototype violent crime is an assault. Aggravated assaults—those with weapons or causing serious nonfatal injury—accounted for nearly 300 of every 1,000 violent victimizations. Less serious simple assaults accounted for more than 500. Robbery accounted for most of the rest. Forcible rapes accounted for about 20 in every 1,000; fewer than 4 in every 1,000 violent victimizations resulted in death for the victim.

These basic patterns raise several questions:

Is the United States More Violent Than Other Societies?

In general, the answer is yes. Homicide rates in the United States far exceed those in any other industrialized nation. For other violent crimes, rates in the United States are among the world's highest and substantially exceed rates in Canada, our nearest neighbor in terms of geography, culture, and crime reporting. Among 16 industrialized countries surveyed in 1988, the United States had the highest prevalence rates for serious sexual assaults and for all other assaults including threats of physical harm.

Is the United States More Violent Today Than Ever Before?

No. The national homicide rate has peaked twice in this century; each peak was followed by a decline. The first peak was in the early 1930s and the rate then fell for the next 30 years. More recently, the national homicide rate began to increase in 1973 and peaked between 1979 and 1981, declining until 1984 and 1985. The homicide rate has since increased and is now at about its 1980 level. Historical data suggests that certain cities may have experienced still higher homicide rates during the nineteenth century. What is true is that, as a result of population growth, today's homicide rates per 100,000 residents produce total numbers of homicides that are high by historic standards. Levels of nonfatal violent crimes also rose during the late 1980s, although there is less consistency in trends across cities. Only for aggravated assault do 1990 rates exceed 1980 rates in cities of all sizes.

Who Is at Greatest Risk of Violent Victimization and Death?

Demographic minorities. In 1990, blacks were 41 percent and Hispanics 32 percent more likely than whites to be victims of violent crime. Ethnic differences combine with age and gender patterns so that recently young black males have been about 20 times more likely than older white females to be victimized. Homicide rates are also highest for minorities: the black rate is 5 times the white rate, and rates for Native Americans about double the rate of the entire population.

Death rates from natural causes are generally low for young persons. Correspondingly, accidents and homicides become leading causes of death at younger ages. However, because minority homicide risks are high at all ages, only about one-fourth of the lifetime homicide risk for black and white males and females is experienced before the twenty-fifth birthday. American Indian males also have higher homicide victimization rates than white males, but they are more concentrated at later ages.

What Are the Consequences of Violent Crimes?

Although the public naturally focuses on death or injury as the outcome of violent crime, injury occurs in only about one-third of violent crimes. Most injuries are minor with only about half requiring any medical treatment and 4 percent requiring an overnight hospital stay. The victim is killed in fewer than 4 of every 1,000 violent crimes. However, the fact that 23,000 people died as a result of homicide in 1990, and that these deaths occurred in only a small percentage of violent encounters, should emphasize the magnitude of the total violence problem.

Even when death or injury is avoided, losses to victims and society are sizable: an estimated average cost of $54,000 per attempted or completed rape, $19,200 per robbery, and $16,000 per assault. About 15 percent of these costs are financial—victims' monetary losses, society's costs for lost productivity, emergency response, and administration of compensation. Roughly 85 percent reflects values imputed for nonmonetary losses, such as pain, suffering, the risk of death, psychological damage, and reduced quality of life. Responses to violence by law enforcement, criminal justice, and private security agencies add additional costs. Additional losses, which have not been estimated but are very visible, include the destruction of families and neighborhoods; the fortification of schools, homes, and businesses; and the deterioration and abandonment of community resources such as parks and playgrounds.

WHO COMMITS VIOLENT CRIMES?

We know less about the perpetrators of violent crimes than about their victims. However, we do know that offenders and their victims share similar demographic profiles. That is, they are overwhelmingly male (89% of all those arrested) and are disproportionately drawn from racial and ethnic minorities. Arrestees for violent crimes are somewhat older than victims. Men in the 25-29 age range were more likely to commit violent crimes in 1988 than any other age group. Perpetrators were acquaintances of their victims in a majority of simple assaults, forcible rapes and homicides, but in only 38 percent of aggravated assaults and 26 percent of completed robberies.

One quarter of nonfatal violent victimizations are committed by multiple offenders; almost half of robberies involve co-offenders, whereas forcible rapes and simple assaults are generally solitary crimes (only 8% of rapes and 19% of simple assaults involve more than one assailant). About 8 percent of robberies involve groups of four or more.

ARE VIOLENT CRIMES THE WORK OF "VIOLENT CAREER CRIMINALS"?

No. While a few individuals commit violent crimes frequently, they account for a small share of total violence in the United States. Despite occasional media reports to the contrary, "serial murderers" are responsible for only about 1 or 2 percent of homicides in any year. Most recorded violent crimes occur in the course of long, active criminal careers dominated by property offenses, so that arrests for violent crimes account for no more than 1 in 8 of all arrests in European and American cohorts whose records have been analyzed. The general pattern is that while few offenders begin their criminal careers with a violent crime, most long arrest records include at least one. It is inaccurate, however, to portray this as an "escalation" from property to violent crimes.

More generally, predictions of future violent behavior from past arrests are highly inaccurate.

What Effect Has Increasing the Prison Population Had on Levels of Violent Crime?

Apparently, very little. However, the question cannot be answered unambiguously. While average prison time served *per violent crime* roughly tripled between 1975 and 1989, reported levels of serious violent crime varied around the level of about 2.9 million per year. Estimates of the crime control effects of incarceration—by isolating violent offenders from potential victims in the community and by deterring others from committing violent crimes—are necessarily imprecise. However, if tripling the average length of incarceration per crime had a strong preventive effect, then violent crime rates should have declined in the absence of other relevant changes. While rates declined during the early 1980s, they generally rose after 1985, suggesting that changes in other factors, including some of those discussed in Part II of this report, may have been causing an increase in potential crimes.

Why did average prison time served per violent crime increase so substantially between 1975 and 1989? Experience varied somewhat by crime type and state, but the data point to general increases in both the average time served if incarcerated and the chance of imprisonment if arrested.

There is currently active discussion by public officials of further increases in prison sentences as a means of crime control. Analyses suggest that a further increase in the average time served per violent crime would have an even smaller proportional incapacitation effect than the increase that occurred between 1975 and 1989. According to the best estimates available to us, a 50 percent increase in the *probability of incarceration* would prevent twice as much violent crime as a 50 percent increase in the average term of incarceration. Achieving such an increase in certainty would, however, require substantial improvement in crime reporting and investments in police investigation and prosecution.

This analysis suggests that *preventive* strategies may be as important as criminal justice *responses* to violence. The success of preventive strategies depends, however, on understanding how individual potentials for violent behavior develop, of what circumstances are conducive to violent events, and of what social processes foster violence. While the complex interactions among these processes are still poorly understood, careful evaluations of promising interventions are contributing knowledge that increases the ability to prevent violence.

INDIVIDUAL POTENTIALS FOR VIOLENT BEHAVIOR

Psychosocial Perspectives

Aggressive childhood behaviors correlate with elevated potentials for adult violent behavior. However, of young children who display aggressive behavior patterns, little is known about why a few become violent adults while most do not. The distinguishing factors may be related to socioeconomic status because adult violent behavior is so much more concentrated than aggressive childhood behavior in lower-income neighborhoods. Identifying the relevant characteristics of communities, families, and persons should be of highest priority in future research.

Factors associated with aggressive behavior provide a useful starting point. Modern psychological perspectives emphasize that aggressive and violent behaviors are *learned* responses to frustration, that they can also be learned as instruments for achieving goals, and that the learning occurs by observing models of such behavior. Such models may be observed in the family, among peers, elsewhere in the neighborhood, through the mass media, or in violent pornography, for example.

Research suggests that several early childhood behaviors may be predictive of adult violent behavior. Sociable, spontaneous, and relatively fearless behavior in early childhood (an uninhibited or fearless temperament) may be a risk factor for later aggression and violence, especially in children with low socioeconomic status, whereas fearfulness may act as a protective factor against aggression. Temperament may explain why only a proportion of children from high-risk homes and neighborhoods develop antisocial or violent behavior.

Adult violent offenders tend to have shown certain personality features as children. They are high on hyperactivity, impulsivity, and attention deficit, tend to be restless and lacking in concentration, take risks, show a poor ability to defer gratification, and have low empathy. They also tend to have particularly low IQ scores. Other predictors in children, their families, and surroundings include abnormally frequent viewing of violence on television, bullying in the early school years, harsh and erratic discipline, abuse or neglect, lack of parental nurturance, low income in large families, criminal behavior by family members, early-grade school failure, peer rejection, poor housing, and growing up in a high-crime neighborhood.

Among protective factors that appear to reduce the chance of childhood aggressive behavior are a shy temperament, high IQ, being firstborn, and a small, stable family characterized by low discord.

Preventing Childhood Aggressive Behavior

Interventions that have shown some success in reducing children's aggressive behavior include:

- social learning and cognitive behavioral interventions with elements that emphasize the undesirability of aggression, nonaggressive methods of solving interpersonal problems, social skills training, and watching television programs that emphasize prosocial behavior and
- interventions such as tutoring by peers or specially trained high school students to reduce early-grade school failure.

Evaluations of these interventions with young children require long-term follow-ups to see if they reduce violent behavior at later ages. Psychosocial preventive interventions will be more successful if implementation involves parents, teachers, and significant others in the community.

Sexual Violence

Many psychosocial, biological, and cultural phenomena have been suggested as potential causes of sexual violence, by which we mean the threat or use of physical force either to coerce another person to submit to sexual behavior or to produce sexual excitement or release in the perpetrator. Incidents of sexual violence are more difficult to count and analyze than are most other violent incidents.

Under our definition, sexual violence includes a wide range of acts. Societal responses to those acts—as criminal, deviant, or culturally acceptable—have varied over time and across cultures. Response also hinges on circumstances. Where it is clear that the act is not consensual—as in assaults on strangers or children—it is usually treated as criminal or deviant. Most violent sex acts, however, involve acquaintances or intimates, and here the designation as violent depends on whether the act occurred under coercion or freely given consent. Consent can be interpreted differently by one or both of the participants and may be exceedingly difficult for a third party to ascertain.

Attempts to explain sexual violence, especially against strangers, have usually centered on individual differences. Among those that are not supported by available evidence are mental retardation, epilepsy, XYY or XXY chromosomal syndromes, and the use of pornography portraying consenting adults. Individual characteristics that may be involved and should be more thoroughly investigated include exposure to abnormally high testosterone levels during fetal development, abnormal testosterone levels and functioning, and genetic processes. In addition, studies of known sex offenders suggest that the following characteristics may be predictive: psychosocial and neurobiologic factors with respect to aggression generally, sexual abuse during childhood, chronic alcohol abuse, and the use of pornography that depicts violent attacks on women. Finally, clinical research suggests that a contributing factor may be violent sexual preferences, learned through experiences around the time of puberty, in which sexual arousal and release provide the reward for fantasies about violent acts. However, research on these characteristics is not conclusive as they are not found in all identified sexual assaulters and their prevalences among sex offenders have not been compared with those in the general population.

Of the available preventive interventions, behavioral treatment of offenders using aversive stimuli such as electric shock has shown mixed results, and several states have banned this approach. Assertiveness training, anger management, life skills training, and relapse prevention are more widely used but have rarely been rigorously evaluated outside institutions. Situational prevention strategies suggest installing video cameras, alarms, and emergency telephones in high-risk locations for sexual violence against strangers.

Explanations offered for sexual violence against acquaintances and intimates tend to emphasize beliefs about appropriate sex roles that encourage sexual violence. Although some surveys report that disturbingly high proportions of males as young as junior high school age subscribe to various justifications for forcible rape, the causal implications are unclear because there is no available evidence on whether men who engage in violent sexual behavior hold these attitudes more widely than men who do not.

Promising strategies for reducing the level and harms of sexual violence against acquaintances include socializing males about nonviolent, fulfilling sex roles and responsibilities toward women, teaching females ways to recognize the risks and to protect themselves, separating offenders and the intimates they repeatedly attack (e.g., by incarcerating offenders or sheltering victims outside the home), and repairing the physical and psychological consequences of sexual assault victimization. Systematic evaluations are needed of interventions that implement these strategies.

Violence in Families

Intrafamily violence is substantially underreported—because of traditional privacy surrounding family life, because the member composition of what makes up a family is changing, because the psychological trauma involved inhibits reporting, and because authorities have only recently begun to treat it as a crime. Nevertheless, about 6 percent of violence victims who reported to the NCS in 1990 were attacked by members of their own family—somewhat less than two-thirds were simple assaults (Bureau of Justice Statistics, 1992:Appendix 3, Table 3). The nature and severity of attacks differ significantly by sex, age, and relationship. Women are the most frequent victims of simple assaults, with divorced, separated, and cohabiting women at greatest risk. Intrafamily violence accounted for at least 18 percent of all homicides in 1990 (Federal Bureau of Investigation, 1991:13). With respect to homicide, although women are at greater risk of spousal homicide than men, a majority of family homicides do not involve spouses. Fathers, sons, and especially brothers are more likely to be killed by family members than their female counterparts.

Violence toward children includes homicides, as well as physical and sexual assaults, for which national incidence and prevalence estimates are not regularly published. Children under age 4 are more likely to be killed than older children. Infants and small children are more likely to be killed by their mothers than their fathers. Female children are three times as likely as males to be sexually abused. Black children are more than 1.5 times as likely to be physically abused, and 5 times more likely than white children to die of physical abuse or neglect. Rates of abuse—physical and sexual—are 6 times higher for children in families with income under $15,000 than for other children.

Assaults of family members are more than twice as likely as violence between strangers to occur as part of a chronic pattern. Four commonly suggested causes of family violence are chronic alcohol use, social isolation of the family, depression, and some intergenerational mechanism through which a high potential for violent behavior is transmitted from parents to children. However, better research is needed to determine whether alcohol use and depression are causes or effects of such behavior, and whether the intergenerational transmission occurs as a direct effect of victimization or through some more complex mechanism that is common to both abuse and neglect.

Systematic evaluations of preventive interventions for intrafamily violence have begun to occur. Visiting nurse programs appear to have some potential to reduce the prevalence of child abuse and should be tested further. With respect to police responses to partner assault, randomized experiments have not consistently shown arrest to have a deterrent effect. There is a general lack of systematic evaluations of nonpolice preventive interventions, and there are no comparisons of police with nonpolice preventive interventions in partner assaults.

The substantial amount of violence inflicted in domestic situations should encourage the allocation of resources to comparative tests of existing and new interventions that show promise of reducing domestic violence. These include alcohol abuse treatment and anger management training for assaulters, practical assistance and training in shelters to help repeat victims become self-sufficient, and criminal justice interventions such as restraining orders and nonincarcerative sanctions for assaulters.

Biological Perspectives on Violent Behavior

The psychosocial development of individual potentials for aggressive and violent behavior is potentially influenced by genetics, by neurobiologic characteristics, and by consumption of alcohol and other psychoactive drugs.

Genetic Influences

Strong evidence from Scandinavian studies points to genetic influences on antisocial personality disorder in adults, a diagnostic category that includes persistent assaultive behavior. Evidence of a genetic influence specific to violent behavior is mixed, however, and neither relationship has been studied in U.S. samples. If genetic predispositions to violence are discovered, they are likely to involve many genes and substantial environmental interaction rather than any simple genetic marker.

By themselves, genetic influences cannot explain either short-run temporal fluctuations in violence rates or variation in rates among countries. Genetic processes may, however, account for individual or family-level deviations from aggregate patterns within a society.

Neurobiologic Processes

Neurobiologic processes are the complex electrical (neurophysiological) and chemical (neurochemical and neuroendocrine) activities in specific brain regions that underlie all externally observable human behaviors. For at least five reasons, neurobiologic research on violent behavior should be expanded and integrated with research on the psychosocial and macrosocial causes of violence. First, specific neurobiologic "markers" for an elevated violence potential may eventually be discovered, most likely in neurological responses to external stimuli. Second, preventable neurobiologic abnormalities—due to inadequate prenatal care, childhood head injuries, and exposure to neurotoxins such as lead—may increase the risk of school failure and of poor peer and other interpersonal relationships that are empirically linked to subsequent aggressive behavior. Third, knowledge of the neurological activity that underlies violent behavior could assist efforts to develop pharmacological interventions that prevent violent behavior by some individuals, without undesirable side effects. Fourth, the use of psychoactive drugs, especially alcohol, may alter some individuals' neurobiologic functioning in ways that make violent behavior more likely. Fifth, recent improvements in the technology for measuring neurobiologic responses hold out the prospect for adding more precise information with fewer risks and burdens on research subjects.

To date, no known neurobiologic patterns are precise and specific enough to be considered reliable markers for violent behavior, whether sexually related or not. However, findings from animal and human studies point to several features of the nervous system as promising sites for discovering such markers and designing preventive therapies.

Knowledge of the neurological underpinnings of violent behavior is, quite properly, limited because more precise measurement techniques tend to impose greater burdens and risks on research subjects. Decisions to undertake specific research projects should balance these burdens against the value of the information sought and the likelihood of success. Research using animal subjects is a means of obtaining insights that may apply to violent human behavior without engaging human subjects, especially when the work is based on multiple species, including nonhuman primates, in both laboratory and seminatural settings. As with human subjects, each animal study should be designed to inflict the least possible stress and harm on subjects without invalidating scientific protocols.

Brain Dysfunctions Brain dysfunctions that interfere with language processing or cognition are especially common in conduct-disordered children, early school failures, delinquents, criminals and diagnosed psychopaths—populations with elevated risks of committing violent acts. At least three causes of these dysfunctions are preventable: exposure to lead; head injuries; and expectant mothers' use of alcohol, cocaine, opiates, or tobacco during pregnancy. Although not normally thought of as violence prevention programs, efforts to reduce these risks could have significant long-term payoffs in reducing future violent behaviors.

Alcohol, Other Psychoactive Drugs, and Violence Potentials Long-term heavy alcohol use is a predisposing factor for violent behavior at least for adults who showed both chronic aggressive behavior and alcohol abuse in childhood or early adolescence. Adult problem drinkers are more likely to have histories of violent behavior, but alcoholics are not more prevalent among violent offenders than among other offenders.

Other psychoactive drugs have different predisposing links to violent behavior depending on the amount and pattern of use. Taking marijuana or opiates in moderate doses temporarily inhibits aggressive and violent behavior; withdrawal from opiate addiction, however, may lead to heightened aggressive and defensive reactions. Chronic use of opiates, amphetamines, marijuana, and PCP increases the risk of violent victimization by altering the nervous system in ways that occasionally disrupt social communications, but it has not been pharmacologically linked to any increased potential for violent behavior. Long-term frequent use of amphetamines, LSD, and PCP has changed a few individuals' neurochemical functioning in ways that induced violent outbursts, but examples are extremely rare except among users with preexisting psychopathology. No evidence has yet established direct neurobiologic links between violent behavior and acute or chronic use of powdered cocaine. However, more research is urgently needed on the pharmacological effects of smoked cocaine or "crack," which enters the brain more directly.

While the pharmacological effects of alcohol and other drug use on violent behavior have been fairly well established, their role in violence also depends on the situational and social context in which they are commonly used. While these relationships are less precisely understood, ethnographic research on alcohol use suggests both that its role in violence depends on drinkers' expectations and on cultural norms—even binge drinking is commonly observed in some non-European cultures without violent aftermaths. For illegal psychoactive drugs, the illegal market itself accounts for far more violence than pharmacological effects. Research also points to occasional violence in the course of obtaining money to buy drugs, and an unknown amount of violence occurs, especially in families, in disputes over expenditures, time spent away from home, and other indirect consequences of drug and alcohol use.

SOCIAL PROCESSES AND VIOLENT CRIME

Interaction effects are important in understanding how social processes affect violent crime. For example, ethnicity and socioeconomic status (SES) appear to interact: at low SES levels, blacks are more likely to be homicide victims than whites; but at higher SES levels the differential attenuates or disappears. What social factors account for the variation? For at least 50 years, sociologists have pointed to three structural factors—low economic status, ethnic heterogeneity, and residential mobility. Subsequent research has supported these findings and refined them. This work points to:

- *concentrations* of poor families in geographic areas and greater income *differences* between poor and nonpoor (income inequality);
- measures associated with *differential social organization* such as population turnover, community transition, family disruption, and housing/population density—all of which affect a community's capacity to supervise young males; and
- indicators of *opportunities* associated with violence (e.g., illegal markets in drugs and firearms).

In addition, some individual-level risk factors for violent crimes point to possible community-level causes. Ineffective parenting, drug use, school failure, and a poor employment history are all more likely to occur in communities in which illegal markets are nearer at hand than are prenatal and pediatric care, good schools protected from violence, and legitimate employment opportunities. Communities that present different distributions of occasions for learning violent behaviors can be expected to produce quite different distributions of developmental sequences.

There is a critical need to understand how these risk factors interact. For example, there are poor communities with low levels of violence. However, interactions between ethnicity and community characteristics are particularly hard to disentangle empirically because poor minorities are so much more likely than poor whites to be concentrated in communities in which a very high percentage of residents live below the poverty line.

Community Characteristics

Quantitative indicators of community disorganization include high housing density, high residential mobility, high percentages of single-parent families and the occurrence of neighborhood transitions—both economic decline and gentrification. These appear to account for more of the geographic variation in violent victimization rates than do measures of poverty and income inequality.

These indicators appear to reflect a breakdown of social capital—the capacity to transmit positive values to younger generations. This breakdown appears in such intangibles as parents' inability to distinguish neighborhood youth from outsiders, to band together with other parents to solve common problems, to question each others' children, to participate in voluntary organizations and friendship networks, and to watch neighborhood common areas. Single parents who work have less time for such activities and constant family turnover in large multidwelling housing units makes them more difficult to carry out. Many "old heads"—community elders who took responsibility for local youth—have left urban communities, and the status of those who remain is diminished by contrast with the rise of successful young entrepreneurs in illegal markets.

Social and Economic Structure and Organization

The economic, organizational, and social niches in which poor people tend to live are disadvantaged in ways that defy easy measurement. These include isolation from legitimate economic opportunities and from personal contacts with those who control resources in the larger society. Legitimate routes to social status, income, and power are often severely limited in these communities.

Structural economic changes of the last decade have reduced employment opportunities for low-income urban minorities and increased the numbers of such families living near or below the poverty level. There has been an exodus of economically stable and secure families, which contributes to the decline of institutions of socialization and informal control. Measuring the causal influence of these trends is difficult for many reasons—including the fact that high levels of violence themselves may encourage the most stable families to leave the central cities.

Community Culture

Ethnographic studies of urban communities, primarily black and Hispanic, provide important hypotheses about how local cultures that support violence develop as a by-product of individuals' and groups' efforts to maintain and increase their social status.

First, if success in illegal markets requires violence, then violence levels may increase as illegal markets assume a more central role in the community's economy. Second, violence levels may increase as traditional community elders lose status to successful criminals. Third, as success in illegal markets transforms the symbols of social status to expensive material possessions, potentially violent disputes over those status symbols may increase. Fourth, because disputes in illegal markets cannot be settled through formal mechanisms, an increase in illegal marketing activity may increase levels of dispute resolution through violent means involving firearms, especially while informal "rules of the game" develop. Fifth, when law-abiding members of a community lose faith that public authorities can or will maintain order, many feel compelled to arm themselves for self-protection.

The best tests of these hypotheses would involve interventions that reduce the size and centrality of illegal markets in urban economies, that restore or enhance the social status of traditional community leaders, that increase the salience of social status symbols other than material goods attained through criminal activity, and that enhance the ability of public authorities and community-based institutions to cope with community problems and maintain order. The challenges lie in designing and implementing such interventions, in adapting them to the ethnic and cultural diversity of the communities, and in evaluating them.

Gangs and Violence

Gang diversity makes generalizations about their role in promoting or inhibiting violence difficult. Not all gangs regularly participate in violence or drug distribution. For those that do, intergang violent behavior serves similar purposes to interpersonal violent behavior: protecting reputation, resources, or territory. Such gangs may reward members who demonstrate prowess in intragang fighting. Gang violence associated with crack markets is widely perceived to have increased during the 1980s. Again, however, the patterns are not uniform. Research in New York, Los Angeles, and Miami found gang members less likely than other hard-core delinquents to be crack dealers. Research is needed to understand more about the roles of gangs in encouraging or mediating violent behaviors among adolescents.

THE CIRCUMSTANCES OF VIOLENCE

A promising approach to the understanding, prevention, and control of violence—a perspective with roots in both criminology and public health—is to focus on the places where violence occurs. The incidence of violent events varies widely in space—by city, neighborhood, and specific address. The greatest variation is found across locations within cities; for example, although 97.8 percent of all Minneapolis addresses generated zero robbery calls to police in 1986, 8 generated more than 20 calls each.

The violence potential of a situation depends on risk factors in both encounters and places. Examples of hazardous encounters in the community include disputes, illegal drug transactions, and robberies. Among the characteristics of encounters that affect the *probability* of a violent event are the nature of preexisting relationships among the participants, the degree to which communications are impaired by alcohol or other psychoactive drugs, and the proximity of an individual who could intervene. The presence of firearms potentially modifies both the probability and the severity of a violent event.

Some violent events arise out of behavioral interactions or exchanges: threats and counterthreats, the exercise of coercive authority, insults and retorts, weapons displays. Violent exchanges and responses to the exercise of authority can accompany encounters between police and citizens, and inmates and custodians in prisons and jails. The dynamics of these exchanges in high-risk encounters are only partially documented, but they can be expected to differ across ethnic and socioeconomic cultures and to depend on the visibility of encounters to public view. Improved understanding of these dynamics could lead to preventive interventions to modify high-risk encounters.

Illegal Markets as High-Risk Settings

It is not surprising that illegal markets are high-risk settings for violence. Illegal markets include those for drugs, firearms, and illegal services such as prostitution and loan-sharking. Physical and organizational structures of the markets may influence the degree of violence. A few ethnographic studies suggest that violence in prostitution, for example, is greater in settings over which the seller has less control over others' access. Thus "call-girl" operations are apparently less violent than open-air streetwalking, but more violent than houses of prostitution. Similarly, in drug markets, runner-beeper drug delivery systems may entail less violence than open-air markets, while heavily fortified crack houses may experience still less risk. But the hypotheses remain to be tested.

The effects of various enforcement strategies on the level of violence associated with illegal markets need additional study.

Firearms and Violent Events

Mortality rates from firearm violence are high in the United States compared with other countries and rising, especially among young black males. The nature of the causal relationship between the availability of firearms and mortality rates from firearm violence, especially involving handguns and so-called assault weapons, is a matter of intense public interest and often emotional debate.

Available research does not demonstrate that greater gun availability is linked to greater numbers of violent events or injuries. However, what is clear is that gun-inflicted injuries have more lethal consequences than injuries inflicted by other weapons. This suggests that making guns less available in high-risk situations (e.g., in the hands of unsupervised juveniles and others barred from legal gun markets, in homes with histories of family violence, in "fighting bars") might reduce the number of homicides.

Educational, technological, and regulatory strategies can be devised with the objectives of changing how handguns are used and stored, changing their allocation from higher-risk to lower-risk segments of the population, reducing their lethality, or reducing their numbers. For any of these policies to reduce homicides, two conditions must be met: the policy must reduce violent uses of at least some types of guns and they must not be replaced with more lethal weapons.

Over 80 percent of the firearms used in crimes are reportedly obtained by theft or through illegal or unregulated transactions. Therefore, while public debates continue over the wisdom of new regulations for firearms, we believe that priority should be placed on evaluating the effects of three strategies for enforcing existing laws governing the purchase, ownership, and use of firearms:

- disrupting illegal gun markets using both the centralized and street-level tactics currently in use for disrupting illegal drug markets;
- enforcing existing bans on juvenile possession of handguns; and
- community-oriented or neighborhood-oriented police work involving close coordination with community residents and community-based organizations to set enforcement priorities and to assist in enforcement and thereby to reduce perceived need for individual gun ownership.

A STRATEGY FOR IMPROVING THE UNDERSTANDING AND CONTROL OF VIOLENCE

Multiple factors, including those summarized in Table S-1, have been found to correlate with the probability of violent events. The correlations are low by conventional standards, inconsistent across settings, and usually specific to particular types of violent events. The causal mechanisms that underlie the correlations are not well understood. Nonetheless, awareness of these factors does suggest opportunities for understanding and preventing particular types of violent events.

The array of potential intervention sites for violent interpersonal events is very broad, ranging from neurobiologic processes to external conditions such as access to lethal weapons and the social structure of nonviolent opportunities for advancement. In considering each site, a systematic problem-solving strategy of innovation—diagnosing specific violence problems and designing preventive interventions, evaluating them, using the results to refine them, and replicating the evaluation—offers the greatest potential of improved understanding and control. Even this approach, which is commonplace in public health and medical science, cannot be expected to rapidly reduce overall violence levels. However, sustained collaborations of this sort by practitioners, evaluators, and basic scientists can be expected to yield significant inroads against specific forms of violence on which they are focused.

TABLE S-1 Matrix for Organizing Risk Factors for Violent Behavior

Units of Observation and Explanation	Proximity to Violent Events and Their Consequences		
	Predisposing	Situational	Activating
Social			
Macrosocial	Concentration of poverty Opportunity structures Decline of social capital Oppositional cultures Sex-role socialization	Physical structure Routine activities Access: Weapons, emergency medical services	Catalytic social event
Microsocial	Community organizations Illegal markets Gangs Family disorganization Preexisting structures	Proximity of responsible monitors Participants' social relationships Bystanders' activities Temporary communication impairments Weapons: carrying, displaying	Participants' communication exchange
Individual			
Psychosocial	Temperament Learned social responses Perceptions of rewards/penalties for violence Violent deviant sexual preferences Cognitive ability Social, communication skills Self-identification in social hierarchy	Accumulated emotion Alcohol/drug consumption Sexual arousal Premeditation	Impulse Opportunity recognition
Biological	Neurobiologic[a] "traits" Genetically mediated traits Chronic use of psychoactive substances or exposure to neurotoxins	Transient neurobiologic[a] "states" Acute effects of psychoactive substances	Sensory signal-processing errors Interictal events

[a]Includes neuroanatomical, neurophysiological, neurochemical, and neuroendocrine. "Traits" describes capacity as determined by status at birth, trauma, and aging processes such as puberty. "States" describes temporary conditions associated with emotions, external stressors, etc.

RECOMMENDATIONS

The panel found that a substantial knowledge base exists regarding some aspects of violent events and behaviors and that certain areas of knowledge are expanding rapidly. However, we were frustrated to realize that it was still not possible to link these fields of knowledge together in a manner that would provide a strong theoretical base on which to build prevention and intervention programs. For that reason, our recommendations primarily concern the research needed to improve our understanding of mechanisms at the individual, group, and community level and evaluations of the interventions that appear most promising.

To make progress in the understanding, prevention, and control of violent behavior, we call for a balanced program of efforts with short-term and long-term payoffs:

(1) problem-solving initiatives of pragmatic, focused, methodologically sound collaborative efforts by policy makers, evaluation researchers, and basic researchers.

(2) modifying and expanding national and local violence measurement systems for diagnosing particular violence problems and measuring the effects of interventions designed to solve them.

(3) programs of research projects in areas that have been largely neglected by federal violence research sponsors.

(4) the multicommunity research program described in Chapter 3, which is intended to expand society's capacities to understand and to modify community-, individual-, and biological-level processes that influence individuals' potentials for violent behavior.

The problem-solving initiatives and research programs in neglected areas can fairly quickly make incremental contributions to the understanding, prevention, and control of violent behavior. The improvement of violence measurement systems and the multicommunity research program, while requiring longer initial investment periods, will lay the groundwork for better diagnosis and understanding of violence in this country and for the design of more effective intervention programs.

PROBLEM-SOLVING INITIATIVES

In the next few years, sustained collaboration by policy makers, disciplinary researchers, and evaluation researchers in these areas could make major cumulative contributions to better understanding of specific violence problems and of interventions that may prevent and control them.

Recommendation 1: We recommend that sustained problem-solving initiatives be undertaken in six specific areas for which systematic intervention design, evaluation, and replication could contribute to the understanding and control of violence:

(a) intervening in the biological and psychosocial development of individuals' potentials for violent behavior (Chapter 3), with special attention to preventing brain damage associated with low birthweight and childhood head trauma, cognitive-behavioral techniques for preventing aggressive and violent behavior and inculcating prosocial behavior, and the learning of attitudes that discourage violent sexual behavior;

(b) modifying places, routine activities, and situations that promote violence (Chapter 3), with special attention to commercial robberies, high-risk situations for sexual violence, and violent events in prisons and schools;

(c) maximizing the violence reduction effects of police interventions in illegal markets (Chapters 4 and 6), using systematic tests and evaluations to discover which disruption tactics for the illegal drug and firearm markets have the greatest violence reduction effects;

(d) modifying the roles of commodities—including firearms, alcohol, and other psychoactive drugs—in inhibiting or promoting violent events or their consequences (Chapters 4, 5, and 6), with special attention to reducing weapon lethality through public education and technological strategies; ascertaining patterns of firearms acquisition and use by criminals and juveniles; ascertaining and modifying the pharmacological, developmental, and situational processes through which alcohol promotes violent behavior; pharmacologically managing aggressive behavior during opiate withdrawal; ascertaining whether smoking cocaine promotes violence through special pharmacological effects; and reducing drug market violence by reducing demand for illegal psychoactive drugs;

(e) intervening to reduce the potentials for violence in bias crimes, gang activities, and community transitions (Chapter 3); and

(f) implementing a comprehensive initiative to reduce partner assault (Chapters 3 and 5), including risk assessment; experimentation with arrest, less expensive criminal justice interventions, public awareness campaigns, batterers' counseling programs, alcohol abuse treatment for perpetrators, and family services; and further analyses of the relationships between women's shelter availability and assault and homicide rates.

Improving Statistical Information Systems

Many questions of fundamental policy and scientific importance cannot be answered today, and emerging violence patterns and problems are sometimes slow to be discovered, because of basic limitations of the systems for gathering information on violence.

Recommendation 2: The panel recommends that high priority be placed on modifying and expanding relevant statistical information systems to provide the following:

(a) counts and descriptions of violent events that are receiving considerable public attention but are poorly counted by existing measurement systems. These include but are not limited to intrafamily violence; personal victimizations in commercial and organizational robberies; violent bias crimes; and violent events in schools, jails, and prisons;

(b) more comprehensive recording of sexual violence, including incidents involving intimates, incidents of homicide and wounding in which the sexual component may be masked, and more complete descriptions of recorded events;

(c) baseline measurements of conditions and situations that are thought to affect the probability of a violent event (e.g., potentially relevant neurological disorders, arguments between intoxicated husbands and wives, drug transactions, employees handling cash at night in vulnerable locations);

(d) information on the treatment of violence victims in emergency departments, hospitals, and long-term care facilities; links to data on precipitating violent events; and development of these data as a major measurement system;

(e) information on long- and short-term psychological and financial consequences of violent victimization and links to data on violent events;

(f) measurements of violence patterns and trends for small geographic and jurisdictional areas, as baselines for measuring preventive intervention effects; and

(g) information system modifications to record more detailed attributes of violent events and their participants, in order to facilitate more precise studies of risk factors for

violence and evaluations of preventive interventions to reduce it.

Classification and measurement of sexual violence present special problems. Because violent sexual behaviors are diverse, better classification is essential for advancing its understanding and control. Classifications should be designed to facilitate effective treatment. Moreover, to reverse a long-standing pattern in classification research, special priority should be placed on improved classification of men who commit violent sexual acts against intimates. These men appear to be underrepresented in institutional samples of sex offenders.

Research in Neglected Areas

Seven research areas have been largely starved of resources for decades while applicable theory, measurement, and methodology have advanced. As a result, substantial and rapid progress can be expected from relatively small-scale research in the neglected areas.

Recommendation 3: We call for new research programs specifically concerned with the following areas:

(a) nonlaboratory research on the instrumental effects of weapons on the lethality of assaults, robberies, and suicide attempts (Chapter 6) ;

(b) integrated studies of demographic, situational, and spatial risk factors for violent events and violent deaths (Chapter 3);

(c) comparative studies of how developmental processes in ethnically and socioeconomically diverse communities alter the probabilities of developmental sequences that promote or inhibit violent behavior (Chapter 3);

(d) systematic searches for neurobiologic markers for persons with elevated potentials for violent behavior (Chapter 3);

(e) systematic searches for medications that reduce violent behavior without the debilitating side effects of "chemical restraint" (Chapter 3);

(f) integrated studies of the macrosocial, psychosocial, and neurobiologic causes of sexual and other violence among strangers, intimate partners, and family members (Chapters 3 and 5); and

(g) studies of violent behavior by custodians against wards (Chapter 3).

Multicommunity Longitudinal Studies

There is a need now to lay the basic research groundwork for the next generation of preventive interventions.

Recommendation 4: The panel calls for a new, multicommunity program of developmental studies of aggressive, violent, and antisocial behaviors, intended to improve both causal understanding and preventive interventions at the biological, individual, and social levels (Chapter 3).

This multicommunity study would include initial assessments, follow-ups, and randomized experiments for two cohorts in each community—a birth cohort and a cohort of 8-year-olds. Compared with other programs of longitudinal studies, this one would be distinguished by the combination of:

(1) specific emphasis on the relationships between aggressive and violent behavior, including social-level influences on those behaviors;
(2) a multicommunity design to facilitate more extensive study of cultural and biosocial influences, both on developmental sequences and on intervention effects;
(3) neurobiologic measurements that are as specific for relevant hypothesized processes in the brain as is ethically and technically feasible;
(4) designs that facilitate analyses of protective and aggravating conditions and factors in families, peer groups, schools, and communities;
(5) randomized tests of interventions that, on the basis of causal understanding at the social, psychological, and biological levels, show promise of fostering the development of prosocial behavior and inhibiting the development of potentials for violent behavior;
(6) oversampling of high-risk categories and special efforts to minimize attrition by study subjects in those categories; and
(7) cross-validation of official record and self-report versions of violent events.

The Level of Research Support

In addition to recommending priority areas for research, the panel also finds that research and evaluation funding should be increased if the important opportunities for studying and preventing violence are to be exploited. We surveyed federal agencies

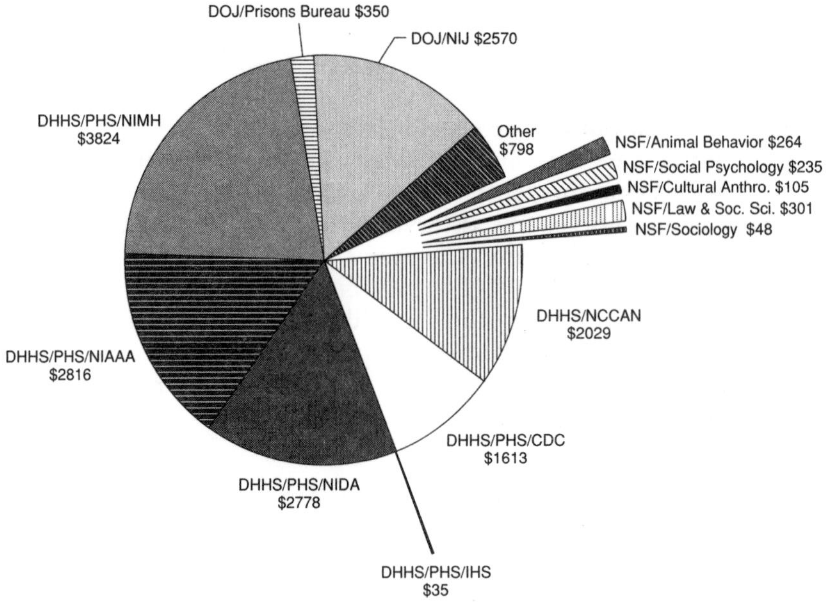

FIGURE S-1 Federal support of violence research, fiscal 1989, by agency.

and identified about $20,231,000 in intramural and sponsored violence research in fiscal year 1989. While that amount may sound large, it amounts to only $3.41 per 1988 event of violent victimization, and is only a tiny fraction of the estimated average cost imposed on society by each violent event.

As Figure S-1 shows, the Department of Health and Human Services (DHHS) provides the majority of federal violence research support, yet a large number of agencies contribute significant funds. The structure offers support for diverse approaches, but it also creates difficulties. In particular, the fragmentation and segmentation of sponsorship makes it difficult to initiate and maintain projects with a broad, comprehensive orientation to violence. Because most federal support is for two years or less, the problem is especially acute for interdisciplinary projects that require long-term commitments of large annual amounts. The segmentation also creates gaps into which important research topics without visible constituencies can fall. The science policy problem is to modify the existing structure in ways that preserve diversity while increasing interdisciplinary work, the coordination of research funding, and increased support of long-term research projects.

The report discusses options that might be employed to achieve these goals. Regardless of the approach chosen, the panel urges that the following principles apply: broad mandates that encompass basic and applied research; maximum feasible independence from political forces in setting its research agenda; and a commitment to diversity and collaboration across the social, behavioral, and biological sciences, evaluation research, and policy analysis.

REFERENCES

Bureau of Justice Statistics
1992 *Criminal Victimization in the United States, 1990.* Washington, D.C.: U.S. Government Printing Office.
Federal Bureau of Investigation
1991 *Uniform Crime Reports for the United States: 1990.* Washington, D.C.: U.S. Government Printing Office.

Part I
Violent Human Behavior

1

The Diversity of Violent Human Behavior

On December 26, 1990, the *New York Times* printed this account of nine homicides on Christmas Eve and Christmas Day in New York City (Finder, 1990):

> A 31-year-old immigrant from Ethiopia with a load of Christmas packages was shot and killed in the driveway of his house in Far Rockaway, Queens, on Christmas Eve. . . . Mr. Berhane Waldermarian, the police said, appeared to be the victim of a failed robbery attempt. He was approached by two men, one carrying a shotgun, in front of his home at 1423 McBride Street late Monday evening. He put down his Christmas packages and was shot once in the stomach. The men fled without taking anything. . . . He died at St. John's Hospital at 12:35 a.m. yesterday.
>
> Belinda Jackson, a 20-month-old girl, died of "multiple trauma" early Monday evening at Bronx-Lebanon Hospital, the police said. Her mother, Ruby Jackson, of 1691 Davidson Avenue in the Morris Heights section of the Bronx, was charged with homicide yesterday. . . . The child appeared to have been struck in the head with a sharp object.
>
> Maria Martinez, 67 years old, of 1652 University Avenue in the Morris Heights section of the Bronx, died several hours after she was punched in the face by her son, Heriberto Altreche. The incident occurred at 8:50 p.m. Monday during an argument at a family Christmas gathering. . . . Mr. Altreche, 37, also punched his sister, the police said. Mrs. Martinez died several hours later at Montefiore Hospital. Mr. Altreche was charged with assault for punching his

> sister. The police said they were awaiting autopsy results on Mrs. Martinez before deciding whether to file more charges.
>
> In another incident, at least two people were shot at 2:30 a.m. yesterday during a fight at a Christmas party at 2831 Valentine Avenue in the Bedford Park section of the Bronx. . . . An unidentified 34-year-old man was shot and killed and a 28-year-old man was wounded. Other people were shot at the party but fled, witnesses told the police. No arrests have been made.
>
> A cab driver was killed Monday night in a dispute with a customer over a fare at the Ging Chinese Restaurant at 94-03B 63rd Drive in Rego Park, Queens. . . . The driver, whom they did not identify, followed the passenger into the restaurant about 8:30 p.m. They argued and the driver was shot once in the head. The passenger fled and the driver died at 10:20 p.m. in Elmhurst General Hospital.
>
> Other slayings included that of a 33-year-old man, Ragip Mekuli, in the lobby of an apartment building at 3344 De Kalb Avenue in the Norwood section of the Bronx. The police said he was shot during a dispute with his brother-in-law, whom they did not identify, but who is being sought for questioning.
>
> Anthony Rodriguez, an 18-year-old Bronx man, was shot and killed on Monday night at Arthur Avenue and East 178th Street in the East Tremont section of the Bronx. Mr. Rodriguez, who lived at 1900 Belmont Avenue, was standing on the corner at 8:50 p.m. when two men dressed in black clothing and with black hoods fired a shot at him and missed, the police said. He ran down the street and was shot twice in the back. The suspects fled, and Mr. Rodriguez died at 9:40 p.m. at St. Barnabas Hospital.
>
> Detectives were also investigating two unidentified bodies. A man in his mid-20's was found at 2:55 a.m. yesterday near 150 Hope Street in an industrial area in the Williamsburg section of Brooklyn. His pants pockets had been turned inside-out and he had been shot many times in the back and buttocks, police said.
>
> In the second case, a man who had been shot in the head was found slumped over the steering wheel of a car at 11:30 p.m. Monday at the corner of Blake Avenue and Tapscott Street in the East New York section of Brooklyn. . . . No arrests have been made, the police said.

Crime statistics use a single phrase to describe this array of tragic deaths: murder and nonnegligent manslaughter. That category also includes many other kinds of killings, and many other kinds of circumstances. Although these violent events are lumped together for purposes of measuring and counting, each differs in its details.

The questions surrounding such violent events are many. How

were alcohol and drugs involved? Which killings resulted from disputes over the marketing of illegal drugs? In the case of shootings, how were the weapons acquired? Why did a Christmas Eve robbery attempt end as a homicide? What could motivate a mother to beat her infant daughter to death? Were the victims who were killed by nonfamily members acquainted with their killers? Could the intervention of others have averted it? How can one respond to the living victims?

The questions provoked by these violent deaths could well be asked about thousands of violent events that occur every day all over the country. Is life in the United States more violent than ever before? Is New York (or Atlanta or Detroit) a more dangerous place to live than the suburbs, the country, or a small city? Who bears the greatest risk of becoming a victim of violence, and can anything be done to avoid it? What kind of people commit violent acts? What do we know at this point about why? What do the circumstances surrounding violent events tell us?

These kinds of questions are asked every day by the people who are touched by a violent event or news of one. Similar questions are asked by law enforcement agents and others who investigate crimes and by those whose job is to intervene in the lives of offenders, victims, and their families. The panel has considered these and other questions in seeking to prevent and understand violent criminal behavior and how to control it and its consequences.

THE SEARCH FOR UNDERSTANDING AND STRATEGIES FOR PREVENTION AND CONTROL

Two concerns animate a search for the causes of violence. The principal scientific goal is to understand violent behavior in terms of the same concepts that attempt to explain other human behaviors. The principal policy goal is to find better ways to prevent and control violence. To name a cause of violence is often to suggest something about who or what should be held accountable for it, or even about what actions show some promise of preventing it in the future.

Despite limitations of research studies, much has been learned about the causes of violence and from evaluations of interventions to prevent and control it. This report points to many findings about what causes violent behaviors and about how they respond to pharmacological, developmental, criminal justice, and public health interventions.

Biological, medical, epidemiological, and social scientists have all contributed to the understanding of violence. Each discipline offers explanations of certain violent behaviors. In turn, these partial explanations point to different opportunities for interventions to prevent violent behaviors or ameliorate their consequences. But it is mistaken to view these explanations as mutually exclusive alternatives that suggest competing strategies. Rather their diversity suggests a rich array of complementary partial solutions to different aspects of a complex problem.

Full understanding of the causes of violence will not be achieved in the foreseeable future—nor is that understanding necessary in order to make progress in reducing violence. A successful intervention at just one point in a long causal chain can prevent some events or reduce their consequences, for example, emergency medical services keep some serious injuries from becoming deaths.

This principle is of course not unique to violence. For example, the incidence of AIDS is being reduced by intervening in the behaviors through which the HIV virus is transmitted (Coyle et al., 1991). These interventions are taking place at several levels: in subcultures (e.g., prostitutes and homosexuals), in the environment (e.g., by providing sterilized needles to intravenous drug users), and by changing individual behaviors (e.g., safe sex practices). In this way, prevention is coming about without full understanding. And independent of these preventive efforts, it is anticipated that biological research will lead to understanding cellular-level processes and to a vaccine—an alternative preventive tactic.

So too in the case of violence. Awareness of the diversity of violence and the complexity of its causes expands awareness of opportunities for intervention. Because the interactions across levels of explanation are understood so incompletely, awareness of intervention opportunities rarely translates into universal prescriptions for preventing violence. Rather, we recommend programs of well-controlled evaluations of interventions—suggested by existing knowledge and refined over time by altering the interventions and replicating the evaluations—as a means of improving prevention and control while accumulating understanding of causes. Later in this volume, we call for several such programs focused on specific components of "the violence problem."

THE PANEL'S APPROACH

The strategy of focusing on specific components is not unlike that taken by scientists investigating cancer—a label that, like violence, applies to diverse phenomena. This strategy has led to carcinoma-specific recommendations such as sunscreens to reduce the risk of skin cancer and high-fiber diets to reduce the risk of colon cancer.

For the diverse events labeled "violent," many classification schemes are possible. The choice of a scheme should depend on its purpose. Different classification systems may be needed to understand violent or aggressive acts by human as compared to nonhuman primates, for example. Similarly, useful classifications for the clinical treatment of people who have behaved violently differ from classifications used to prescribe criminal sanctions.

Rather than seeking a single classification system for violence, a preferable strategy involves different classification systems for causal explanation, for prevention, or for interventions that meliorate their consequences.

While the preferred strategy involves multiple classification schemes, much of what is known about violent events is based on records classified for the purposes of criminal justice agencies. The categories of behavior used in those data are based largely on violations of the criminal law, and a wide range of violent behaviors fall within each category. Because we must depend on research using these categories, most empirical findings concern categories that lump together diverse behaviors. This limits our knowledge of how to understand, prevent, and control each behavior. Preventing the death of either Mr. Waldermarian or Belinda Jackson would have required different tactics, neither of which is likely to be discovered through analyses of some aggregate "homicide." We therefore, in later sections of this volume, call for greater disaggregation in the measurement of violence.

Definition of Violence

The panel limited its consideration of violent behavior to interpersonal violence, which it defined as *behavior by persons against persons that intentionally threatens, attempts, or actually inflicts physical harm*. The behaviors included in this definition are largely included in definitions of aggression. A great deal of what we believe about violence is based on psychosocial research on aggressive behaviors (Dollard et al., 1939; Berkowitz, 1962; Eron, 1987, 1990; Eron et al., 1971), and there is substantial stability in aggressive behavior from infancy to adulthood though its forms change. That is, children who show aggressive behavior at age 8 are more likely than others to exhibit delinquent, criminal, or violent behavior in adolescence and adulthood (Olweus, 1979; Farrington, 1989, 1991). Little is known, however, about what distinguishes aggressive children who grow up to commit violent acts from those who do not. Later in this volume, we call for a large-scale longitudinal study of the factors—in communities, peer groups, families, and the individuals themselves—that influence this outcome.

The panel chose to concentrate primarily on the behavior of individuals and small groups rather than on the behavior of large collectivities, for three reasons. First, within the past 25 years at least half a dozen major reports have given substantial attention to collective violence, and it appeared that little new knowledge might be added by another similar effort (President's Commission on Campus Unrest, 1970; Winslow, 1972). Second, incidents involving individuals and small groups account for the vast majority of violent interpersonal acts in the United States, and the consequences of these acts are of major policy interest to public health and criminal justice agencies. Third, the panel sought to understand violent behavior by bringing together basic knowledge from the biobehavioral and social sciences; these converge most clearly at the individual and group process levels rather than the collective behavior level.

The panel's definition deliberately excludes consideration of human behavior that inflicts physical harm unintentionally. Generally, traumatic injuries and deaths in this circumstance are classified as unintentional (Committee on Trauma Research, 1985), even when they occur as a result of corporate policies (e.g., to expose workers to toxic chemicals) that increase the risk of injury or death for some category of persons. Also excluded are certain behaviors that inflict physical harm intentionally: violence against oneself, as in suicides and attempted suicides; and the use of violence by state authorities in the course of enforcing the law, imposing capital punishment, and providing collective defense.

One implication of our limited scope is that we do not consider the important question of why some violent behaviors are criminalized while others are not. Historically, for example, attempted suicide was criminalized in most Western countries until the early twentieth century—1960 in England (Hart, 1968). Violence against spouses is still in the process of becoming treated as criminal.

We recognize that understanding will be enhanced in future research by studying a broader range of violent behavior using classes based on behavioral rather than legal categories. Currently, however, there are severe empirical limitations to such work, since many of the data on violent behavior come from data collection systems that derive from the criminal law, especially those grounded in law enforcement and criminal justice discretionary decisions about behavior and events. Alternative systems of data collection, such as emergency and continuing medical treatment of injuries, capture more noncriminal violence and they are underutilized (Mercy and Houk, 1988). However, they also currently have severe limitations for a behavioral approach to violence because they include little if any information on the perpetrators and surrounding circumstances—information that is useful for understanding violent events but irrelevant to the objectives of physicians and emergency response teams.

Our definition of violence also excludes events such as verbal abuse, harassment, or humiliation, in which psychological trauma is the sole harm to the victim. However, especially in the context of violence in the family and sexual violence, we do attend to the psychological consequences of threatened physical injury.

Diversity in Perspectives

Four public institutions are concerned more or less directly with violence or its consequences and bring a variety of resources and problem-solving techniques to the problem of violence. They also generate and use different kinds of knowledge about it.

The criminal justice system focuses primarily on detecting violations of the criminal law and dealing with adult violators. Criminal justice agencies generate data and utilize research on such topics as the detection of offenders, arrests, criminal justice decision making, and the crime control effects of criminal justice sanctions. Recently, criminal justice interest has broadened to the management of programs for remediating certain consequences of violence (e.g., victim compensation, counseling rape victims), and crime prevention programs (e.g., neighborhood watch).

The juvenile justice system, traditionally concerned with preventing juvenile delinquency through early interventions, has moved closer to the adult criminal justice model in recent decades. Research intended for use by juvenile justice authorities is still most likely to focus on early detection, prevention, and treatment of delinquency than on the narrower included problem of violent behavior.

Systems that provide social services and treat mental health, alcohol abuse, and drug abuse are also concerned with violent behavior. In this area the emphases are on the prediction of dangerousness based on individual behaviors and diagnoses and on the management of patients' violent behavior. This work emphasizes the underlying neuroanatomical, neurophysiological, neurochemical, and behavioral mechanisms; the links through those mechanisms to the presenting problem; and interventions with those mechanisms to manage violent behavior. Monahan and his network of collaborators (1990) are currently assessing this work and have concluded that the data from risk assessment research do not provide much useful information on the risk of violence for the mentally disordered.

In the past decade, the public health system has begun to apply its traditional public education, assessment, and prevention principles in new initiatives to prevent intentional injuries and deaths. The public health approach seeks to locate populations at risk of intentional injury and to reduce risks by modifying the hazard, reducing the harm associated with the hazard, or repairing the harm more effectively. Compared with the approaches of the other institutions, the public health system gives less attention to the development, motivation, punishment, or rehabilitation of persons who commit violent acts and more attention to identifying and modifying elements of situations that surround violent events. It also stresses the roles of the public—as potential victims or as members of community-based organizations—in protecting the public health. And it stresses the role of emergency medical services in reducing the loss of life from violent events.

The Role of Values

Research findings, policy choices for the control of violence, and public values are inevitably intertwined. Policy advocates can be expected to selectively publicize findings that support their positions and the methodological flaws in studies that produce contradictory findings. So long as the policy-making arena resembles a free market of ideas, all perspectives are represented and the accumulation of evidence and resolution of scientific disputes at least raise the level of public policy debate.

Unfortunately, new scientific evidence about the causes of violence or about the effectiveness of some intervention might also be rejected merely because its implications conflict with citizens' ethically charged beliefs about such matters as personal responsibility, social justice, and biological determinism. Many people are more attached to their personal values than to their beliefs about causes of violence. In effect, people use their convictions about policy to judge the accuracy of findings and the effectiveness of interventions, rather than the other way around. People's convictions may even cause them to oppose undertaking particular studies. Violence control policy is therefore less innovative and effective than it should be, and knowledge of how to control violence is less advanced than it could be because some important questions are never investigated and because experience with some preventive interventions never accumulates.

PLAN OF THE REPORT

Chapter 2 reports patterns and trends in violence and in the characteristics of its victims and perpetrators.

In Part II, we look behind patterns and trends to summarize what is known about the connections between violence and risk factors that conventional wisdom considers to be causes of violent events. Evidence about these connections is drawn from basic research and from evaluations of experience with interventions to modify the factors.

Chapter 3 presents overviews of aggressive and violent behavior from three perspectives: the biological, the psychosocial, and the social context of surrounding communities. We then turn to specific factors that are currently receiving public attention as possible causes of violence. Chapter 4 examines alcohol and other psychoactive drugs, Chapter 5 discusses violence in families, and Chapter 6 considers firearms.

Part III is concerned with the development of strategies for preventing and reducing violence and for advancing its understanding. Chapter 7 begins by examining the nation's experience between 1975 and 1989 to consider the effectiveness of greater use of incarceration as a means of violence control. Then, as an aid to thinking about a broader array of interventions to prevent and control violence, the panel proposes a matrix for classifying the factors discussed in Part II. The matrix groups risk factors according to their temporal proximity to the violent behavior: predisposing factors, situational elements, and triggering events; it then arrays them across individual and social levels of description. Lacking a testable general theory of violence, we use the matrix merely to highlight the rich array of targets for interventions to prevent and control violence. It ends by explaining the value of careful evaluations as a means of simultaneously advancing the basic understanding of violence and the capacity to prevent and control it.

Finally, Chapter 8 presents the panel's views on science, policy, and violence control and proposes other areas that are ripe for improving intervention strategies. In it the panel makes four recommendations for advancing the understanding of violence as a basis for more effective prevention. One of these, a multicommunity longitudinal study, is intended to advance the integrated understanding of violence causes at the biological, individual, community, and microsocial levels.

REFERENCES

Berkowitz, L.
1962 *Aggression: A Social Psychological Analysis.* New York: McGraw-Hill.
Committee on Trauma Research
1985 *Injury in America.* Washington, D.C.: National Academy Press.
Coyle, Susan L., Robert F. Boruch, and Charles F. Turner, eds.
1991 *Evaluating AIDS Prevention Programs, Expanded Edition.* Washington, D.C.: National Academy Press.
Dollard, J., N. Miller, O. Mowrer, and R. Sears
1939 *Frustration and Aggression.* New Haven: Yale.
Eron, L.
1987 The development of aggressive behavior from the perspective of a developing behaviorism. *American Psychologist* 42:435-442.
1990 Understanding Aggression. Presidential Address. World Meeting of ISRA. Unpublished, June 12, 1990.
Eron, L.D., L. Walder, and M.M. Lefkowitz
1971 *Learning of Aggression in Children.* Boston: Little Brown.
Farrington, D.P.
1989 Early predictors of adolescent aggression and adult violence. *Violence and Victims* 4:79-100.
1991 Childhood aggression and adult violence: Early precursors and later-life outcomes. Pp. 5-29 in D.J. Pepler and K.H. Rubin, eds., *The Development and Treatment of Childhood Aggression.* Hillsdale, N.J.: Erlbaum.
Finder, Alan
1990 9 are killed in disputes or at parties over the Christmas holiday. *New York Times*, December 26, p. B1.
Hart, H.L.A.
1968 *Punishment and Responsibility.* Oxford: Oxford University Press.
Mercy, J.A., and V.N. Houk
1988 Firearm injuries: A call for science. *New England Journal of Medicine* 319(19):1283-1285.
Monahan, John
1990 Research Network on Mental Health and the Law: Continua-

tion Proposal for Phase II Support and Proposal for a Phase I-Phase II Transition Period. October 11.

Olweus, D.
1979 Stability of aggressive reaction patterns in males: A review. *Psychological Bulletin* 86:852-875.

President's Commission on Campus Unrest
1970 *The Report of the President's Commission on Campus Unrest.* Washington, D.C.: U.S. Government Printing Office.

Winslow, Robert W.
1972 *Crime in a Free Society. Selections From the President's Commission on Law Enforcement and Administration of Justice, the National Advisory Commission on Civil Disorder, the National Commission on the Causes and Prevention of Violence, and the Commission on Obscenity and Pornography.* Encino, Calif.: Dickenson Publishing Company.

2
Patterns of Violence in American Society

The mass media daily trumpet the most recent violent events in the world, and violence is an essential ingredient for many viewers of video screen drama. News of a relatively few violent crimes attracts a disproportionate amount of media attention compared with the more numerous violent events that are known only to the families, friends, and acquaintances of particular victims and perpetrators. Accounts of the more dramatic episodes of actual homicides, rapes, and robberies command special attention, as do the shootings of well-known people, gangsters, and police officers. To what extent do the violent criminal events reported in the media represent national patterns of violence in everyday life? How do patterns of violence in the nation today compare with patterns in other countries and at other times?

This chapter describes patterns discernible in violent behavior and trends in its occurrence or reporting, focusing on comparative levels of violence, the risks of becoming a victim of violence, the characteristics of violent offenders, and the circumstances surrounding violence.

DIFFICULTIES OF MEASUREMENT

There is no single way to define, classify, and measure the domain of violent events, because each counting system involves some evaluation of people's observations and reports of what they perceive as violent events. Any set of crime statistics, therefore, is based on events that are defined, captured, and processed by some institutional means of collecting and counting. Violent events that are socially constructed as crimes consequently are counted more accurately and completely than those that are not. In addition, society's interpretation of violent events as crimes changes over time and differs across segments of the population.

There is no national profile of all the violent events with which this panel was concerned. Rather, three nationwide measurement systems count and classify various components. We describe the strengths and limitations of these national systems here, and then indicate the variety of subnational data bases that are used in violence research.

First, for events that police classify as crimes, the Uniform Crime Reports (UCR) system collects basic information about the most serious crime committed. The UCR also records supplementary information about the circumstances of homicides and basic descriptions of arrestees. Second, for homicides, data are also tabulated annually from death certificates by the National Center for Health Statistics (NCHS). Third, for nonfatal violent victimizations, the National Crime Survey (NCS, later, the National Crime Victimization Survey) is a primary data source. The survey periodically asks national samples of all persons in households who are age 12 and older to recall and describe their recent victimizations. Survey questions are worded so as to direct respondents' attention to events that they personally regard as crimes.

The task of describing the national pattern of violence from these three systems is complicated by the fact that they differ in terms of (1) the domain of events that they attempt to capture, (2) the unit of count on which their statistics are based, (3) the timing of the counting and tabulation, and (4) the sources of discretion and error in recording and counting events. Table 2-1 provides a summary comparison of these characteristics of the three systems. To help readers interpret national data with the appropriate caution, we summarize these differences and their implications before reporting what is known about national patterns and trends. The difficulties of measuring violence are explained more fully in Appendix B.

Differences in Domain

Both NCS and UCR data produce national counts of three types of nonfatal violent crimes: forcible rape,[1] robbery, and aggravated

TABLE 2-1 Comparison of Violence Measurement Systems

System Characteristic	National Crime Survey	Uniform Crime Reports	National Mortality Statistics
Source	• Sample of U.S. households	• Incident reports of participating police agencies	• Death certificates
Domain	• Nonfatal violent victimizations of persons aged 12+	• Violent crimes known to police including homicides and violence during crimes against organizations	• Homicides
Unit of Count	• Most serious victimization during event	• Most serious crime during event	• Deaths
Timing	• Events occurring in 6-month reference period • Published annually with 10- to 12-month lag	• Collected contemporaneously • Published annually	• Collected contemporaneously • Published annually, with 2-year time lag
Sources of Discretion/ Error	• Respondent recall, construction as victimization, and choice to recount • Interviewer judgment • Agency rules for counting	• Victim/witness decision to report to police and discretionary police detection • Police determination that crime occurred • Counting rules	• Medical examiner judgment

assault. Both count attempted as well as completed crimes. However, within each type, the two sets of statistics are not strictly comparable because they capture different categories of event. The NCS is designed to record nonfatal victimizations of persons age 12 and over. Of these events, the UCR records only those incidents that become known to police as crimes—some 40 to 50 percent, according to NCS estimates. However, as shown in the figure, UCR counts include police-recorded incidents of two categories of events that fall outside the NCS domain: crimes against children younger than 12 and robberies of organizations. Simple assaults, the largest and least serious category of violent victimizations in NCS data, are not counted as index crimes by UCR.

Homicides are counted in both UCR and NCHS national mortality statistics. Usually, UCR homicide counts are slightly smaller than NCHS counts; homicides that occur outside police jurisdictions (e.g., in prisons) account for some of the discrepancy.

No national system reports threats to commit violent acts.

Differences in Unit of Count

Our concern is with violent events, but a single violent event may include both a number of violent crimes and a number of offenders and their victims. Differences between the NCS and UCR units of count in these events must be considered in interpreting the two sets of statistics.

The event described in Chapter 1 involving Mr. Waldermarian, for example, in which an attempted robbery ended in a shooting death, is counted only as a homicide by UCR (because UCR counts only the most serious crime in the event) and is uncounted by NCS because the victim's death eliminates him from the sample frame. Thus, the attempted robbery is also omitted from both systems. However, if the event involved multiple offenders, both of whom were later arrested, the event would be represented twice in arrest statistics.

A related discrepancy occurs, for example, in a robbery of multiple victims simultaneously. The UCR counts such a robbery as a single crime, as does NCS in its estimated count of incidents.[2] NCS victimization counts are weighted, however, to reflect multiple victimizations.

Differences in Timing

The systems that measure violence also differ in terms of their timing relative to the events they measure. Crimes are recorded in UCR more or less as they occur. Statistics are published annually with a lag of about six months. In contrast, NCS interviews take place throughout the year, with the respondents asked to recall all victimizations they experienced during the preceding six months, and data preparation and publication require about a year. Therefore, at times some events represented in the most recent NCS report have occurred at least a year before some events counted in the most recent UCR report. Not only does this discrepancy complicate comparisons of trends in the two series, but the comparative recency of UCR data tends to give them more visibility in the eyes of the public and policy makers. National mortality statistics are published with a lag of approximately two years.

Sources of Discretion and Error

The statistics produced by all three systems reflect not only actual events but also the discretion of the authorities that collect and publish the data. With homicide, for example, the systemic differences noted above probably account for some of the discrepancy between UCR and NCHS homicide counts. But even the NCHS counts are influenced by medical examiners' complex and subtle judgments, which are themselves subject to error.

Counts of nonfatal violent events are affected by the interactions of errors and discretion by both the statistical agencies and the victims of violence. Reporting a victimization to an NCS interviewer requires the respondent to accomplish a series of tasks: recall the event, recognize it as a victimization, decide whether it occurred during the six-month reference period, and decide whether it is worth mentioning, given the effort and possible embarrassment or fear that describing it to the interviewer may entail. In turn, the interviewer makes judgments about how to record the responses, and the Census Bureau and the Bureau of Justice Statistics set rules for interpreting, coding, and tabulating the recorded information. Before a violent event is counted in UCR statistics, it must have been reported to or discovered by a police agency, where someone is responsible for following a fairly detailed set of instructions for counting the crimes that occurred during the event. Thus, in both sets of data, complex activities are translated into statistics of violent events.

One clear example of how judgments affect national profiles involves what NCS classifies as "series victimizations." Whenever a respondent recalls more than three fairly similar victimizations and is unclear about the precise number or details of each one, the policy is to publish series victimization statistics separately from the annual statistics, ascribing the characteristics of the most recent victimization to all events in the series. Each event in the NCS series would be counted in UCR statistics provided that the police had knowledge of the incident.

This NCS policy for reporting of series victimizations is probably the most appropriate, given existing knowledge about recall of series victimizations. While the count of single victimizations underestimates total victimizations by at least 9 percent, any arbitrary rule for combining series and single victimizations would significantly raise the count. Counting each series victimization as three incidents (the minimum threshold for designating a series victimization) would increase the total by 28 percent, and weighting each reported series by the respondent's estimate of the count in the series would increase it by a factor of 10. Moreover, assuming that all victimizations in a series are identical to the last one introduces anomalies, especially when very small numbers of respondents report series victimizations of a given type.

The social construction of crime—the informal rules of society and the official policies of organizations that designate some acts but not others as crimes—no doubt affects national statistics on violent crime, but these effects have not been measured. As explained further in Appendix B, one effect of recent changes in the position of women in society has been to criminalize sexual and physical assaults against women in the eyes of many. Therefore, more NCS female respondents than in the past can be expected to construe assaults by their husbands and "date rapes" by acquaintances and intimates as victimizations that should be mentioned to an NCS interviewer. There has also been considerable moral and legal pressure for police agencies to treat more acts of domestic violence as criminal assaults, which would be counted in UCR statistics. Without knowing how widely these attitudes have spread, how significantly embarrassment and fear of retribution still inhibit women from reporting such incidents to NCS interviewers and to police, and how responsive police agencies are to such reports, we cannot know how much of the recent rise in overall assault rates is due to these changes in social construction.

Two comparisons explained more fully in Appendix B indicate that even after reporting a forcible rape, robbery, or assault to the police, some respondents fail to recount them to NCS interviewers. First, the UCR forcible rape count substantially exceeds the number that "should" have been reported, according to NCS data on the number of forcible rapes and the fraction of these reported to police. Second, while intensive "reverse-record comparisons" between NCS and UCR records in two jurisdictions found, as expected, that many violent victimizations reported to NCS interviewers had not been reported to police, they found, for example, that nearly half the aggravated assaults reported to San Jose, California, police were not reported to NCS interviewers. Reiss (1985:166-167) computed a crude estimate that the true San Jose aggravated assault rate was approximately double the NCS rate and triple the rate estimated from police reports.

One type of violence that is especially poorly counted is assaults of children by their parents. Some of these go unrecognized because they are socially construed as discipline rather than violence. The NCS counts such incidents only if the victim is aged 12 or older and overcomes the fear and embarrassment associated with recounting the event to an interviewer. A UCR record would require either a self-incriminating parental report to police or a report by a courageous victim, other family member, or an institutional official. The current institutional system for reporting and counting such incidents relies largely on reporting by school, social service, or medical professionals, who may miss physical evidence on many parts of the child's body, who often have no basis for judging whether an assaultive injury was inflicted by a parent or by another family member, and who may justifiably anticipate a confrontation and potential legal action if they report their suspicion.

In recent years, the NCS has begun publishing special tabulations of intrafamily violent victimizations. However, the counts are lower than counts based on several special-purpose surveys conducted since 1975. National estimates based on these surveys are discussed in Chapter 5.

Secondary Information

The primary violence measurement systems also differ in terms of the secondary information they record and report beyond occurrence of a violent event. The NCS reports information on characteristics of the victim, preexisting relationships between the victim and offender, the victim's perceptions of offender characteristics, and the aftermath of the victimization (e.g., extent of injury and financial loss, reporting of the victimization to the police). The NCS data on victim ethnic status are limited, however, and are collected according to current Census Bureau definitions. The program has only recently begun calculating separate victimization rates for Hispanics, and the national sample is too small to compute stable estimates for Native Americans or Asians. Because the NCS sample is designed to produce statistically efficient national estimates, it cannot produce reliable estimates for states or local jurisdictions.

For nonfatal violent crimes, the UCR program currently reports no information beyond occurrence of the event and place of occurrence in the years for which national data are available.[3] The Supplementary Homicide Reports tabulate limited additional information on victims' and offenders' demographic characteristics (if the offender is known), on victim-offender relationships, on circumstances of the event (e.g., committed in the course of a crime), and on the type of weapon. Because this information is tabulated before extensive police investigation in a coding scheme that does not accommodate multiple circumstances or relationships, its validity has been questioned. For city and suburban arrestees, UCR arrest reports tabulate gender and ethnic status (using the categories whites, blacks, Native Americans, and Asians/ Pacific Islanders, with no separate category for Hispanics). As a census of all crimes and arrests, the UCR program publishes crime and arrest statistics for states and localities with their own police agencies.

Subnational Data Bases

Quantitative research on the causes of violence uses not only these national data bases, but also other data that describe subnational areas or selected samples of individuals. Examples of subnational data bases in government agencies include: individual arrest records maintained by police departments and reports of child abuse maintained by local authorities. Individual investigators also assemble research data bases in a variety of ways—by collecting new data (e.g., surveys of violence in the home, longitudinal data on individuals' violent crimes and related life events), by coding data from agency record systems (e.g., hospital emergency department injury admissions, police incident reports), or by linking aggregate-level data (e.g., merging murder statistics and socioeconomic statstics at the census tract level). These kinds of data, and their strengths and limitations for research purposes, are discussed throughout the rest of this book, in conjunction with the findings from research in which they are used.

Recognizing the limitations of existing national measurement systems, this chapter describes patterns and trends in violence.

Although our national systems of measuring and counting violent crimes are imperfect and not entirely comparable, they can answer a number of basic questions.

COMPARATIVE LEVELS OF VIOLENCE

Common perceptions are that American society is more violent than most societies, that it is more violent today than ever before, and that violence is ever increasing. The facts are, unfortunately, more complex and simple generalizations are quite misleading.

Historical Trends in Homicide

Violent crime rates have fluctuated considerably throughout this century. The homicide rate has peaked twice; each peak was followed by a decline. From 1900 to the early 1930s, there was a substantial increase in homicide. The rate then fell for the next 30 years, to reach a low in the early 1960s. A rise in the 1960s and 1970s peaked in 1980 and was followed by a decline in the early 1980s and higher rates since 1985. The 1990 homicide rate reported by UCR (9.4 per 100,000 population) is somewhat below that of the two previous peaks in the twentieth century (a mean of 9.5 in 1931-1934 and 10.4 in 1979-1981) (Holinger, 1987).

Substantial differences in gender and ethnic homicide victimization rates have persisted since the late nineteenth century. Fragmentary evidence for the nineteenth century and more substantial time series for the twentieth show that nonwhite men and women have always been more likely to be murdered than white men and women (see Figure 2-1; Holinger, 1987). Although the ratio of black to white homicide rates varies from 1910 onward, in any year the ratio has never been lower than 5 to 1, and in the 1950s and 1960s the ratio was as great as 11 to 1 (calculated by Gurr, 1989, from Holinger, 1987); in 1989 the ratio was roughly 7 to 1.

The homicide pattern for blacks has diverged historically from that for other immigrants to the United States. In the nineteenth and early twentieth centuries, first-generation European immigrants to U.S. cities had generally higher homicide rates than those of the native-born white population (Lane, 1979; Monkkonen, 1989). Although it is difficult to trace the ethnic status of their descendants in contemporary America, the available evidence points to few, if any, differences in homicide rates of later generations of these European immigrant populations (Gurr, 1989).

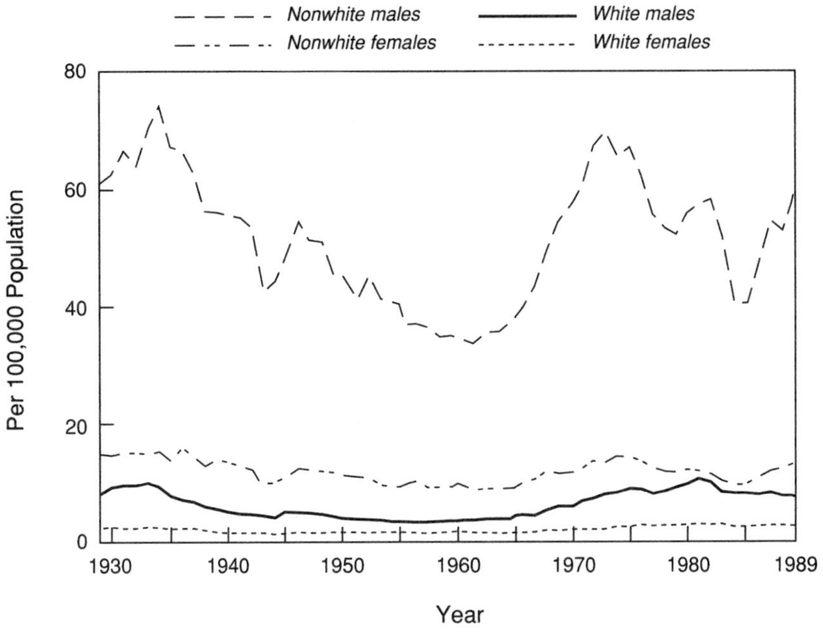

FIGURE 2-1 Age-adjusted homicide rates, by sex and race, United States, 1929-1989. SOURCE: Adapted from Holinger (1987)

The historical evidence for blacks suggests that their homicide victimization rates in the twentieth century are generally above those in the nineteenth century. Fragmentary data for some eastern U.S. cities suggest that, from 1860 to 1910, the ratio of black to white homicides varied between 2 and 3 to 1. After 1910, when more complete data are available, the ratio is greater. The 1931-1934 overall peak coincided with peaks for both white and black males. However, the 1979-1981 peak followed a tripling of the white male rate over the preceding three decades; the rate for black males had peaked about a decade earlier and, except for occasional year-to-year deviations, continued to fall until the mid-1980s. The explanation for this historical divergence for blacks may involve the residential segregation and the structure of opportunities for occupational and social mobility that blacks have experienced. According to a recent review (Jencks and Mayer, 1990), however, available evidence does not permit us to separate the effects of family, school, and neighborhood.

Trends since 1979-1981 in homicide and nonfatal violent crime rates are examined in more detail later in this chapter.

INTERNATIONAL COMPARISONS

Despite national differences in counting systems, it is clear that the developed nations of the world vary substantially in their rates of violent crime. The United States has significantly higher rates for most violent crimes than almost all other developed nations. The more serious the crime, the greater the difference between the U.S. rate and those of other developed nations.

Comparisons among countries are most valid for the crime of homicide (Figure 2-2). Based on reporting to the World Health

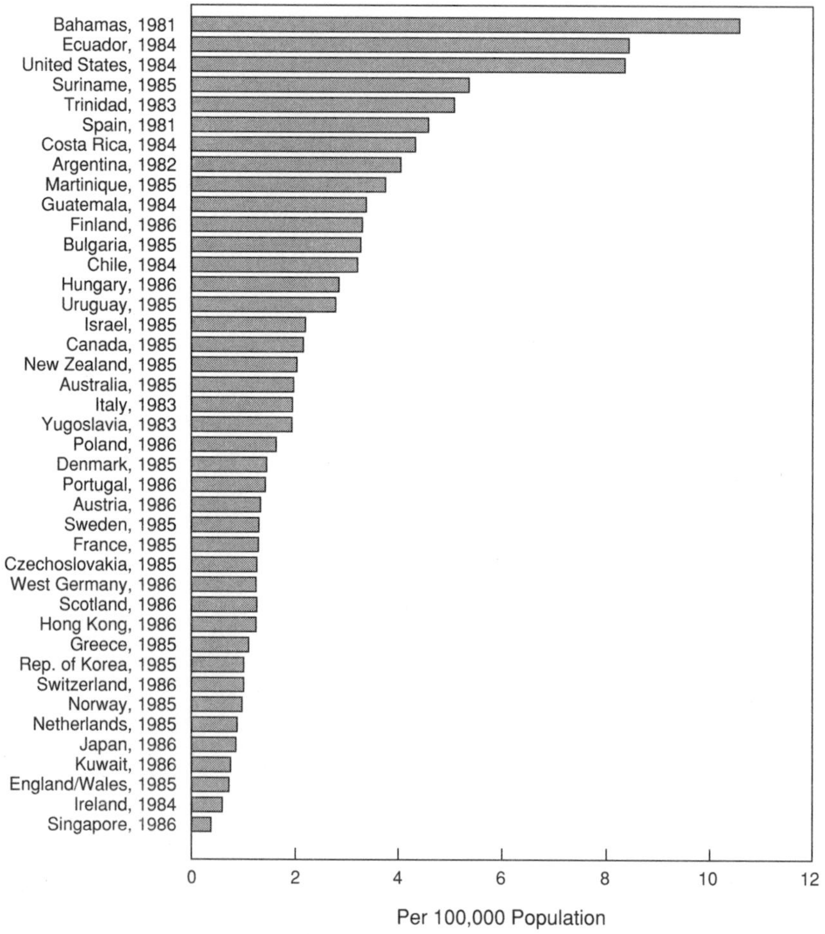

FIGURE 2-2 Crude homicide rates for selected countries, most recent year for which data are available. Data from the World Health Organization, 1987.

Organization during the period 1981-1986, the homicide mortality rate in the United States (8.3 per 100,000 population in 1984) was exceeded only by rates in the Bahamas and Ecuador and was nearly twice that of any European nation. Spain had the next highest rate, 4.3. Most European and British Commonwealth countries report rates on the order of 1 to 2 per 100,000. It is worth noting that recent U.S. homicide mortality rates for whites exceed the overall rates for developed countries generally; however, we do not have comparable homicide rates for nonminority populations in those countries.

For nonfatal violence, detailed comparisons are hampered by differences in the ways that countries define violent crimes, victims report crimes to the police, and police detect them and follow information, reporting, and counting practices. In an effort to achieve greater comparability, an International Crime Victim Survey was undertaken by telephone in 1989 (van Dijk et al., 1990). It allows comparisons between the United States and 15 other countries for the violent crimes of robbery, forcible rape, and assaults. However, because of small samples and low response rates, the data are more useful for relative rankings of countries and ranges of difference among them than for precise statistical comparisons. For robbery, the 1988 personal prevalence victimization rates were highest in Spain and the United States. For serious sexual assaults (forcible rape, attempted rape, indecent assaults), the United States had the highest prevalence rate, with Canada, Australia, and West Germany also reporting rates well above those of most of the other countries.

Assaults show a somewhat different pattern, perhaps owing to the nature of the question asked to elicit responses. The differences among countries were less marked; the rates for Australia and Canada were close to those of the United States.

What is puzzling in these data is that the homicide rates of the respective countries do not seem closely related to their assault rates. Especially noteworthy are the relative high rates of assault with force of the Netherlands and West Germany compared with their very low homicide rates. Some of the difference may be due to country differences in the ownership of handguns, which have greater lethality in assaults. Household possession of handguns was substantially greater in the United States than in any European country—a reported rate of 29 percent compared with less than 7 percent in any other country surveyed except Switzerland.

The United States has considerably more serious violent crime than does Canada, a country that classifies most offenses under rules comparable to ours. Although violent crime has been increasing in both countries since 1960, substantial differences persist between the rates reported by the UCR for both countries. The 1988 U.S. rate for homicide was four times that of Canada; the U.S. rate for robbery was two and a half times that of Canada. For 1982, the last year for which Canadian data are available, the U.S. rate for forcible rape was on the order of three times that of Canada. A satisfactory explanation of these disparities would have to take into account differences in the composition and distribution of the population as well as differences in culture and firearm availability.

VIOLENT CRIME IN THE UNITED STATES

How much crime is violent? The technical problems discussed above preclude any precise estimate of how much of all crime in the United States is violent. We report below some crude estimates, which are useful mainly to establish relative magnitudes among the types of crime and to discern overall trends. Comparisons focus primarily on the 1990 reporting year, the latest available at this writing.

National Estimates

In 1990 the National Crime Survey reported an estimated 34,403,610 personal and household crime victimizations.[4] Of these, 17 percent were attempted or completed violent crimes—8 percent if one excludes simple assault.[5] In considering only the 18,984,120 attempted or completed *personal* victimizations reported, about 32 percent were violent—just over 6 million. Of these, just over half were simple assaults, the least serious violent offense (Bureau of Justice Statistics, 1992:Table 1a).

The bulk of personal victimizations reported are theft from persons, which includes larceny with and without contact with the victim.[6] Together with the violent act of simple assault,[7] these nonviolent thefts constitute the large majority of personal victimizations.

In 1990 UCR estimated that the nation's police departments received reports of 14,475,600 index crimes, excluding arson; of these, about 1.8 million, or 13 percent, were attempted or completed violent crimes.[8] Police departments report a smaller proportion of all offenses as violent than the NCS reports, excluding simple assault (13 compared with 15 percent). This is in part due to the fact that victims were somewhat more likely to report property crimes than crimes of violence to the police. In 1988 victims reported a higher fraction of household victimizations of burglary, household larceny, and motor vehicle theft (40 percent) than violent personal victimizations (36 percent) to the police (Bureau of Justice Statistics, 1990:Table 92).[9]

Prototype Pattern

The NCS program reported 6,008,790 violent victimizations in 1990, and the UCR program counted 1,820,127 violent index crimes reported to police agencies. Despite their differences, the prototype violent event that emerges from the two systems is an assault, either aggravated or simple (Table 2-2). Of the violent victimizations, aggravated and simple assault account for nearly 8 of every 10. By excluding homicide from the UCR and simple assault from the NCS counts to achieve rough comparability, aggravated assaults account for almost 6 of 10 violent crimes reported in both systems. Robbery, which is an assault or threat of assault for the purposes of taking valuables, accounts for most of the rest—which means that at least 9 of every 10 acts reported as violent crimes or victimizations in the United States are either assaults or robberies. Sexual assaults account for most of the remaining violent offenses, and homicides account for just over 1 percent—23,438 of the violent crimes counted by the UCR.

As we said earlier, estimates of the frequency of criminal events are influenced by the decisions of victims and witnesses to report them, of officials to process them, of police detection practices, and of institutions to devise rules for counting them. Just how closely institutional reporting accords with the occurrence of events is a matter of disagreement, but, for example, it seems clear that murders are counted far more accurately than forcible rapes. Despite the errors, we can conclude that generally in 1990, the more serious the violent crime, the fewer the occurrences recorded. Historically, societal sanctions for crimes yielded the rank order of seriousness reflected in the rows of Table 2-2: murder, forcible rape, robbery, aggravated assault, simple assault. The UCR column of the table illustrates the inverse seriousness/frequency relationship for the four most serious violent crime types. The NCS column illustrates it for forcible rape, robbery, aggravated assault, and simple assault victimizations. In both columns, less serious acts are reported more frequently than more serious acts.

Historically, completed crimes have been considered more seri-

TABLE 2-2 Offense and Victimization Rates for Violent Crimes, United States, 1990

Type of Violent Crime	UCR Offenses[a]		NCS Victimizations[b]		
				Rate per 100,000	
	Number	Rate per 100,000 Persons	Number	All Persons	Age 12 & Older
All violent crimes	1,820,127	731.8	6,008,790	2,415.9	2,956.0
All violent crimes, excluding simple assault	1,820,127	731.8	2,880,660	1,158.2	1,417.1
All violent crimes, excluding simple assault and homicide	1,796,689	722.4	2,880,660	1,158.2	1,417.1
Murder and nonnegligent manslaughter	23,438	9.4	—	—	—
Forcible rape	102,555	41.2	130,260	52.4	64.1
Forcible rape[c]		(80.0)		(104.7)	(123.5)
Robbery	639,271	257.0	1,149,710	462.3	565.6
Aggravated assault	1,054,863	424.1	1,600,670	643.6	787.4
Simple assault	—	—	3,128,130	1,257.7	1,538.9
Total persons US	248,709,873				
Total persons, age 12 and older			203,273,870		

[a]Source: Federal Bureau of Investigation (1991:Table 2).
[b]Source: Bureau of Justice Statistics (1992:Table 1a).
[c]Forcible rape rates calculated for female population only (Federal Bureau of Investigation, 1990:Appendix III p. 329; Bureau of Justice Statistics, 1992:Table 5).

ous than attempted crimes, and crimes that involve weapons or cause injury are considered more serious than those that do not. Table 2-3 distinguishes between completed and attempted victimizations and reports the counts of assaults and victimizations that involve weapons and injuries. With a few exceptions, the data in the table conform to the expectation that less serious victimizations occur more frequently than more serious acts.

The greater frequency of completed than attempted robberies appears to contradict expectations regarding frequency and seriousness; in 1990 the NCS reported more than twice as many completed robberies as attempted ones. However, this proportion may not reflect the true pattern of occurrence. Attempts may be reported less frequently to NCS interviewers, even if they occur more frequently. Evidence on school crime and other studies suggests that attempted as well as actual robberies of children under age 12 and of schoolchildren at all ages are quite common. An alternative conjecture is that a higher proportion of all forcible rapes and robberies may be brought to completion because the victim is more compliant when the apparent risk is greater in these crimes and less likely to take forcible means of resistance.

Research is needed to learn more about the relationships that link reporting and self-protective behavior to characteristics of violent events for all violent crimes. Especially for the crimes of forcible rape and robbery, such studies should investigate how victim compliance under threat affects injury, completion, and reporting rates.

The various types of assault show the expected inverse relationship between frequency and seriousness. In 1990, 67 percent of assaults were attempts. Of all aggravated and simple assaults, 46 percent were attempted simple assaults without a weapon and without injury; 21 percent were attempted aggravated assaults with a weapon, but without injury; 20 percent were simple assaults with injury; and 13 percent were aggravated assaults with injury (Bureau of Justice Statistics, 1992:Table 1a). Assaults with injury are least frequently reported; attempted simple assaults without a weapon and without injury constitute almost half of all reported assaults.

Violent victimizations are more likely than nonviolent ones to involve multiple simultaneous victims. Therefore, on average, every 100 aggravated assault victimizations occurred in 80 events and every 100 simple assaults in about 90 events.

TABLE 2-3 Number and Percent Distribution of Victimizations, by Sector and Type of Crime, 1990

Sector and Type of Crime	Number	Percentage of Crimes Within Sector	Total Persons
Personal sector	18,984,120	100.0	203,273,870
Crimes of violence	6,006,790	31.7	
Completed	2,421,530	12.8	
Attempted	3,587,260	18.8	
Rape	130,260	0.7	
Completed	62,830	0.3	
Attempted	67,430	0.4	
Robbery	1,149,710	6.1	
Completed	800,510	4.2	
With injury	286,020	1.5	
From serious assault	123,740	0.7	
From minor assault	162,280	0.9	
Without injury	514,480	2.7	
Attempted	349,190	1.8	
With injury	110,380	0.6	
From serious assault	43,930	0.2	
From minor assault	66,440	0.4	
Assault	4,728,610	24.9	
Aggravated	1,600,670	8.4	
Completed with injury	627,000	3.3	
Attempted with weapon	973,660	5.1	
Simple	3,128,130	16.5	
Completed with injury	931,170	4.9	
Attempted without weapon	2,196,960	11.6	
Crimes of theft	12,975,320	68.3	
Completed	12,154,550	64.0	
Attempted	820,760	4.3	
Personal larceny with contact	637,010	3.4	
Purse snatching	165,490	0.9	
Completed	124,010	0.7	
Attempted	41,470	0.2	
Pocket picking	471,520	2.5	
Personal larceny without contact	12,338,319	65.0	
Completed	11,559,010	60.9	
Less than $50	4,592,470	24.2	
$50 or more	6,452,940	34.0	
Amount not available	513,590	2.7	
Attempted	779,290	4.1	

Consequences of Violent Crime

The major consequences of violence involve physical injury, psychological consequences, monetary and other costs, and lethality (the probability of death). There are no national data on psychological consequences, and those on economic costs are limited. Even the information on physical injury is limited since there is no assessment of the injury independent of the victim's self-report on the kind of injuries and the kind of medical treatment obtained for them.

Physical Injury

Physical means of violence include a person's body (hands, fists, feet), instruments such as firearms and knives, flammable liquids and explosives, poisons, and animals (such as attack dogs). Physical injury can range from minor harm, such as bruises, lacerations, and scrapes, to death.

During 1990, the NCS reported that the victim sustained some physical injury in 33 percent of robbery and assault victimizations (Bureau of Justice Statistics 1992:Table 80). The rate of physical injury was somewhat greater for aggravated (39%) than simple (30%) assault and for completed (36%) than attempted (32%) robberies.

The Bureau of Justice Statistics (1989a:Table 4) reported the distribution of injury severity and level of medical care received by injured victims for violent crimes in the United States, aggregated for the years 1979 to 1986.[10] The bulk of the injuries—83 percent—were considered minor in severity. Over half—52 percent—did not require any medical treatment. One-fifth required hospital care, but only 4 percent required an overnight stay. In any given year, only a small proportion of those with an overnight stay required more than a single day of hospitalization. Nevertheless, of the injured 1990 victims, 38 percent received hospital care for physical injuries from violent crime. Of the injured, 23 percent were hospitalized for less than a day, 7 percent were hospitalized from one to three days, and 8 percent for four days or more (Bureau of Justice Statistics, 1990:Table 88).

Costs

Physical and emotional trauma are usually assessed initially in terms of medical standards of physical or emotional impairment. Subsequently, these traumas and resulting impairment may be evaluated in monetary terms, as the cost of rehabilitation. Physical injury imposes costs on the injured person of emergency and continuing medical treatment. Violent deaths impose economic and psychological costs on surviving family members and loved ones. An impaired capacity to work, to continue in school, or to maintain one's quality of life are less often recognized, but consequential, costs of violent victimization. Loss of property in violent crimes is another way in which violence imposes economic harm.

Cost estimates prepared for the panel are $54,100 per attempted or completed forcible rape, $19,200 per robbery, and $16,500 per assault (Cohen et al., Volume 4). We emphasize that these estimates involve assumptions about what costs to include, who bears them individually and collectively, and the value of a life lost. Only about 15 percent of these costs are monetary, for such things as money losses, lost productivity, emergency medical services, and administration of compensation; 85 percent are imputed costs for nonmonetary losses such as pain, suffering, psychological damage, and the risk of death or reduced quality of life.

There are additional costs to society arising from the discretionary collective response to violent victimization. Law enforcement, adjudication, victim services, and correctional expenditures add thousands of dollars of cost to each criminal event. These costs are estimated by Cohen et al. (Volume 4).

Less direct consequences of violence may be delayed or cumulative. The stress induced by violent acts, especially when repeated within an intimate relationship, may culminate in severe emotional trauma or physical illness. Stresses may also accumulate for communal organizations. Although the cumulative effects of violent crime on neighborhood cohesion and public services are not easily measured, they are substantial for some communities. Delayed effects occur in even less obvious ways. The intergenerational transmission of violent behavior by physically abusive parents, siblings, and caregivers, for example, is a delayed cost, as new generations of violent persons inflict physical harm on their families and others in the community.

Lethality

Violent crimes vary considerably in their lethality—the probability that they will cause the victim's death. There are no routine published estimates of lethality because, as we explained above, the counts of homicides and victimizations come from different sources. Nevertheless, by combining UCR estimates of the fraction of homicides that occur in crime-related circumstances with NCS counts of violent victimizations, the panel calculated a crude estimate of lethality: in 1990, about 1 in every 257 violent victimizations was fatal to the victim. This estimate reflects an increase from about 1 in every 287 in 1988.

Homicide occurs more frequently in conjunction with some crimes than others. Rough estimates combining the same data sources are that death occurred in about 1 in every 500 forcible rapes and robberies, 1 in every 120 assaults with injury, and about 1 in every 400 arsons. These 1990 estimates are roughly unchanged from 1988 and, for forcible rape and robbery, are approximately the same as 1987 estimates prepared by Cohen et al. (Volume 4).

VICTIMS OF VIOLENCE

Although the rhetoric of campaigns against violence suggests that victims and offenders are distinct populations, in fact there is great similarity in their demographic profiles. Generally, both groups—those at the highest risk of violent offending as well as those at highest risk of violent victimization—tend to be young, black males of low socioeconomic status who live in the nation's central cities. The most insightful explanations of this victim-offender overlap are based on studies of local communities and samples of individuals, which we discuss in Chapter 3. Victim characteristics are discussed in this section, and offender characteristics in the next.

RISKS OF VIOLENT VICTIMIZATION

What is the risk of becoming a victim of a violent crime? We generally lack the information to calculate national estimates of risks that are contingent on the prior states, activities, and conditions that theory or practical experience suggests as possible causes of violence. Evidence about such determinants of risk, which is usually developed in special studies of small samples, is discussed in later chapters. Here we focus on the most commonly available national estimates of risk: rates for demographically defined subpopulations.

The annual risk of becoming a victim of personal violence—of homicide, forcible rape, robbery, or assault—is well below that of victimization from property crimes. As judged by victim reports to NCS, the risk of becoming a victim of personal violence in 1990 was 1 in 34 for people age 12 and older. That risk is less than half the risk of becoming a victim of a personal theft, which was 1 in 16 in 1990 for people age 12 and older (Bureau of Justice Statistics, 1992:Table 1a). In 1990 the risk of household victimization through burglary, household larceny, or motor vehicle theft was 1 in 6 households (Bureau of Justice Statistics, 1992:Table 1a).

For many purposes, the lifetime risk of violent victimization would be a more informative description than the annual risk for any single age range. The Bureau of Justice Statistics, drawing on the annual prevalence rates from the National Crime Survey, estimated that about 83 percent of the people now age 12 will be violently victimized in their lifetimes (Koppel, 1987). There is good methodological reason to conclude that this is a substantial overestimate (Lynch, 1989). However, because information is unavailable on the proportion of victims in any year who have also been victimized in previous years, we were unable to determine the degree to which it is overestimated. The panel recommends that ways be developed to measure the lifetime risk of nonfatal violent victimizations, especially risks of injury by serious assault, for different groups of people in the population.

Homicide

Usable estimates of lifetime risk have been calculated for homicide (Loftin and Wiersma, 1991). In 1987 and 1988, the *annual* risk of becoming a victim of a homicide was about 1 in 12,000, although by 1990 it had risen close to 1 in 10,600. The *lifetime* risk of being a homicide victim is of course much greater (Figure 2-3). Of the six demographic subgroups shown in the figure—male and female whites, blacks, and American Indians—black males are at the highest lifetime risk: 4.16 per 100 black males, which is equivalent to a 1 chance in 24.1 of dying by homicide. American Indian males are also at high risk (1.75 per 100 American Indian males, 1 chance in 57), as are black females (1.02 per 100 black females, 1 in 98.1). For white males and females and for American Indian females, chances of dying by homicide are substantially less than 1 in 100.[11]

This figure also makes clear that, despite media attention to the killings of adolescents and young adults, *less than one-fourth of one's lifetime homicide risk is experienced before the twenty-fifth birthday.* For five of the six subgroups (the exception is

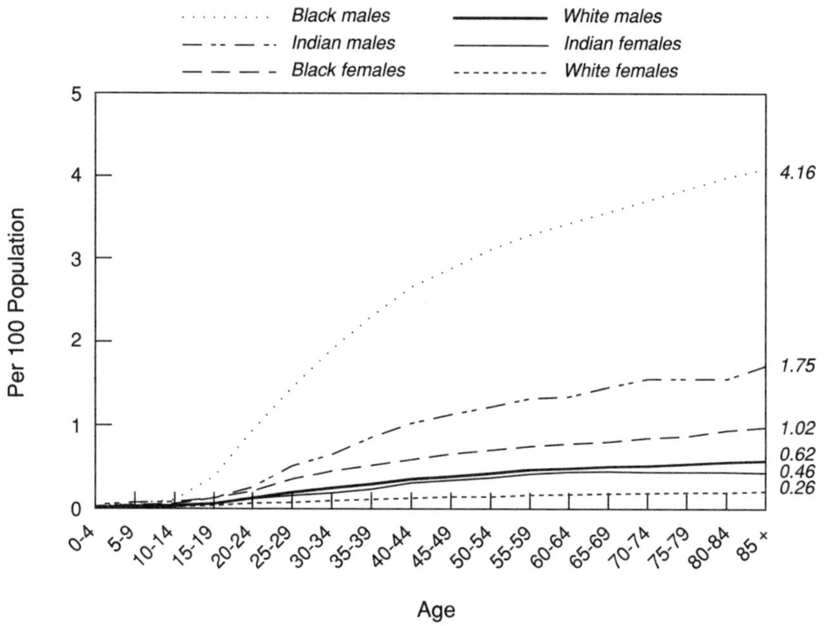

FIGURE 2-3 Cumulative homicide rate in five-year age intervals by race and gender, 1987.

American Indian males), the ratio of homicide risk by age 24 to lifetime risk lies in a narrow range, between 0.21 and 0.26. Murders of American Indian males occur later in life on average; the corresponding ratio is only 0.14.

Recent media attention has focused on homicides of young black males. The rate for black males ages 15-24 rose during the late 1980s, approaching levels not observed since a previous peak around 1970 (see Figure 2-4). However, Figure 2-3 makes clear that, although a sizable fraction of black males die of murder by age 24, the high homicide rate for young black males must be viewed in light of the high homicide rate for black males at *all* ages. One major unresolved question is why the homicide death rate is so high for blacks at all ages, especially black males (see Griffin and Bell, 1989). Another is to understand why, for this age category, the trends for black and white males have moved in different directions during several periods since 1940, as Figure 2-4 shows. We return to these issues in the context of firearms in Chapter 6 and in terms of community-level factors in Chapter 3.

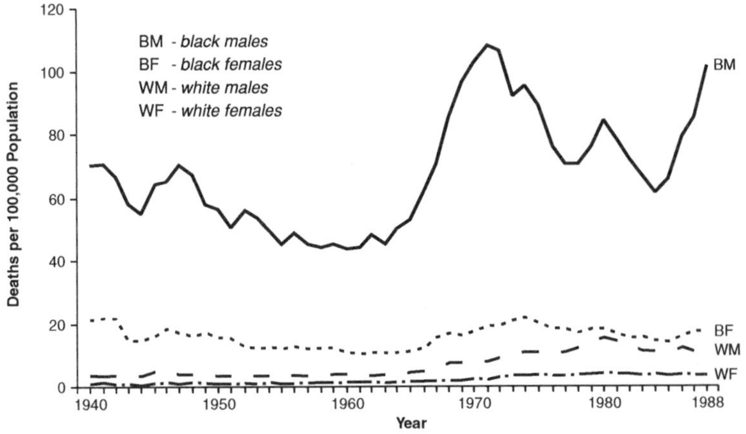

FIGURE 2-4 Homicide rates, persons ages 15-24 years, by race and sex, 1940-1988.

There is considerable variation in homicide mortality by gender and age. In 1988, for example, the homicide mortality rate ranged from 4.2 for females to 14.2 for males, and from 5.3 for whites to 34.4 for blacks. The variation by age and sex within these groups was, for example, from 2.7 for black males age 5 to 9 to 128.2 for black males age 20-24. The range for white males was from 0.8 for age 5 to 9 to 14.6 for white males 20-24 (National Center for Health Statistics, 1991).

The UCR Supplementary Homicide Report discloses that most victims in single offender-single victim homicides are slain by an offender of the same ethnic status:[12] 86 percent of white victims and 93 percent of black victims in 1990. In this kind of homicide, only 6 percent of black victims were slain by white offenders and 12 percent of white victims were slain by black offenders (calculated from Federal Bureau of Investigation, 1992:11).

Multiple homicides by one offender in a single event (so-called mass murders) account for only a very small proportion of all homicides. Similarly, in projecting from data on homicides by known offenders, instances of serial homicide by one offender also appear to be quite infrequent—on the order of 1 percent of all homicides, according to estimates prepared by Fox and Levin for the panel (J. Fox and J. Levin, personal communication, 1990).

Importance of Homicide as a Cause of Death The major causes of traumatic death in the United States are accidents, suicide, and homicide. Of these, homicides contribute the smallest number: from 1945 to 1988, the risk of death by homicide was about two-thirds that of death by suicide, one-third the risk of death by motor vehicle accident, and about one-fourth the risk of death by all other accidental causes. As Table 2-4 indicates, however, the overall homicide death rate per 100,000 population has increased since 1950, while the suicide rate has remained roughly constant and the motor vehicle accident death rate has decreased.

Overall, in the United States, homicide accounts for about one-fifth of all deaths due to suicide, homicide, and motor vehicle accidents. Adjusting annual death rates by age,[13] however, discloses significant variations in risk by gender and ethnic status. In the United States, the relative risk of death by motor vehicle accident varies primarily by gender, and the risks of homicide and suicide vary primarily by ethnic status.

Table 2-4 shows that, among black males and females, homicide (and legal intervention) is the leading cause of death by traumatic means, whereas among white males and females, homicide is substantially less common than the other causes. For both whites and blacks, the age-adjusted traumatic death rates are three to four times greater for males than for females; although the male-female differences fluctuate over time, the differences between black males and females are greater than those between white males and females. Blacks are more likely to be victims of homicide; whites are more likely to be victims of suicide.

Years of Potential Life Lost Although homicide accounts for a relatively small proportion of deaths each year, a different calculation of its cost tells a somewhat different story. Figure 2-5 shows the years of potential life lost before age 65 (YPLL) (Haenazel, 1950) to death from traumatic causes, heart disease, and malignant neoplasms (i.e., cancers).[14] Because homicide victims are younger on average than suicide victims, total YPLL for both causes of death are nearly identical, even though the homicide death rate is only 75 percent of the suicide death rate. For analogous reasons, the homicide YPLL is more than 40 percent of the YPLL for heart disease and about 36 percent of the YPLL for malignant neoplasms, despite much larger differences in death rates.

Other Sources of Violent Death

Comparisons of homicides with other sources of violent death beyond the panel's scope provide another perspective for our find-

TABLE 2-4 Age-adjusted Death Rates for Selected Causes of Death: United States, Selected Years by Gender and Ethnic Status (per 100,000 resident population)

	Year						
Cause	1950[a]	1960[a]	1970[a]	1980[a]	1987[a]	1988[b]	1989[b]
All ethnic status and both genders							
Homicide and legal intervention[c]	5.4	5.2	9.1	10.8	8.6	9.0	9.4
Suicide	11.0	10.6	11.8	11.4	11.7	11.4	11.3
Motor vehicle accidents	23.3	22.5	27.4	22.9	19.5	19.7	18.9
White male							
Homicide and legal intervention	3.9	3.9	7.3	10.9	7.7	7.7	8.1
Suicide	18.1	17.5	18.2	18.9	20.1	19.8	19.6
Motor vehicle accidents	35.9	34.0	40.1	34.8	28.4	28.5	26.8
Black male							
Homicide and legal intervention	51.1	44.9	82.1	71.9	53.8	58.2	61.5
Suicide	7.0	7.8	9.9	11.1	12.0	11.8	12.5
Motor vehicle accidents	39.8	38.2	50.1	32.9	28.5	29.6	29.4
White female							
Homicide and legal intervention	1.4	1.5	2.2	3.2	2.9	2.8	2.8
Suicide	5.3	5.3	7.2	5.7	5.3	5.1	4.8
Motor vehicle accidents	10.6	11.1	14.4	12.3	11.4	11.6	11.5
Black female							
Homicide and legal intervention	11.7	11.8	15.0	13.7	12.3	12.7	12.5
Suicide	1.7	1.9	2.9	2.4	2.1	2.4	2.4
Motor vehicle accidents	10.3	10.0	13.8	8.4	8.7	9.2	9.1

[a]Source: Adapted from U.S. Department of Health and Human Services (1990:Table 23, p. 121-122).
[b]Source: National Center for Health Statistics (1991:Part A).
[c]Legal interventions includes injuries inflicted by the police or other law enforcing agents including military on duty in the course of arresting or attempting to arrest law breakers, suppressing disturbances, maintaining order, and other legal actions including legal execution.

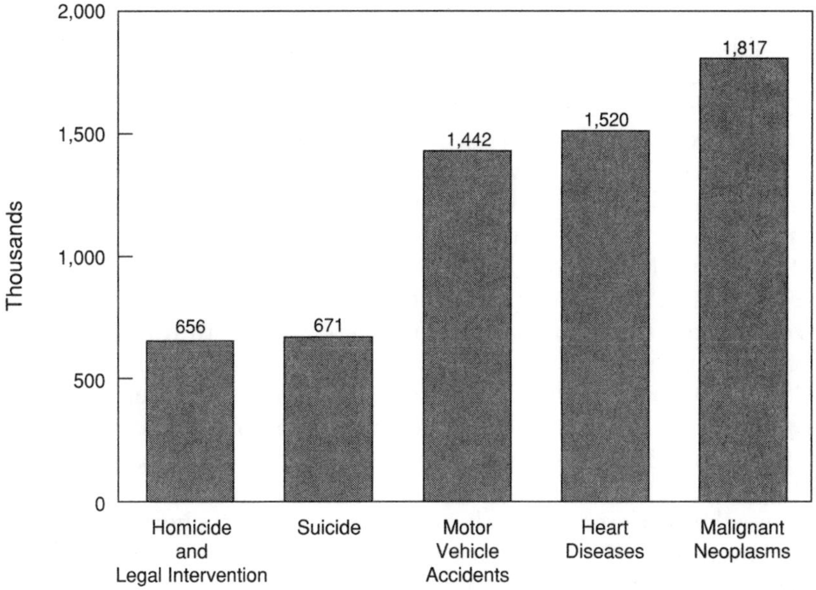

FIGURE 2-5 Total years of potential life lost for selected causes of death, 1987.

ings. Every year a relatively small number of deaths are classified as justifiable homicides—persons killed in self-defense or the justifiable defense of others. And periodically the casualties of military actions are a major cause of violent injury and death. Estimated American battle deaths for the Korean conflict are 34,000; for the Vietnam conflict, 47,365 (Bureau of the Census, 1990:Tables 556 and 557). In a year of intense conflict, the number of deaths in battle can equal or exceed those by homicide. In 1968, for example, the year when casualties in the Vietnam conflict were greatest, there were 14,623 American battle deaths and 13,648 reported deaths from murder and nonnegligent manslaughter in the continental United States (Bureau of the Census, 1990).[15]

Other Violent Crimes

For violent crimes that do not end in death, Table 2-2 shows that victimization rates from the two major reporting sources were substantially different in 1990. The aggregate rate for violent victimizations calculated from the NCS count was more than triple the UCR count of violent crimes known to the police. Previously discussed differences in the way the two systems classify and count violent crimes—especially the counting by NCS of events not reported to police and of simple assault—largely account for these discrepancies.

Two differences in the rates are especially noteworthy. The rate for forcible rape reported in the NCS, although greater than that reported by UCR, is well below what one would expect, given the rates at which forcible rape victims identified by NCS claim to have reported their victimizations to police. Research reviewed by Loftin and MacKenzie (1990) and others suggests that the NCS rate is an underestimate, perhaps because victims—even some who have reported the crimes to the police—may be inhibited by fear or embarrassment from discussing their victimization with the NCS survey interviewers. Also, they may not characterize forced intercourse by intimates as a victimization to be reported. The UCR is also likely to undercount incidents involving intimates and appears to undercount forcible rape attempts.

The other difference worth noting is that for robbery and aggravated assault in 1990, the ratios of UCR to NCS counts are about 7 percentage points higher than the fractions of NCS respondents who claim to have reported those crimes to the police. The "excess" UCR counts are probably explained by the broader coverage of UCR—commercial robberies and victimizations of children younger than 12 that are outside the NCS scope.

Individual Risks of Nonfatal Violent Victimizations

In this section we examine how the risks of violent victimization differ according to people's age, gender, ethnic status, marital status, and socioeconomic status. Two- and three-way associations for age, gender, and ethnic status suggest that the relationships among these factors are generally additive (Sampson and Lauritsen, Volume 3). For some subgroups of the population, the relative risk of violent victimization is higher than expected because of interaction effects. Age has the largest independent effect, followed by gender; ethnic status has the smallest effect of the three.

The rates reported are based on statistical information for the 1990 National Crime Survey (Bureau of Justice Statistics, 1992) unless another source is specified.

Age

Age is one of the most important single predictors of an individual's risk of violent victimization (Hindelang et al., 1978). The annual risk of victimization by violent crime peaks at age 16 to 19 for both men (95 per 1,000 population) and women (54 per 1,000) and declines substantially with age, to 3-4 per 1,000 at age 65 and older. This declining risk of victimization by age holds for the major violent crimes of forcible rape, robbery, aggravated assault, and simple assault, with substantially higher rates below than above age 25. Although the risk of violent victimization is highest at the younger ages, there is evidence that juvenile victimization is less likely to involve serious injury (Garofalo et al., 1987).

Gender

Except for forcible rapes and partner assaults, the risk of a woman becoming a victim of a violent crime is lower than that of a man. Among all female murder victims in 1990, however, 30 percent were slain by husbands or male friends compared with 4 percent of male victims killed by wives or women friends (Federal Bureau of Investigation, 1992:13). The lifetime risk of homicide is three to four times greater for men than for women. Gender differences are much smaller for robbery (Bureau of Justice Statistics, 1992:Table 3).

Women are substantially less likely than men to report being victims of aggravated or simple assault or attempted assault with a weapon. The risk of injury for assault victims is somewhat greater for women than men (38 per 1,000 for women and 30 for men). Women have a higher rate of both simple and aggravated assault by relatives than do men. Their vulnerability to assault by relatives is greater for simple than aggravated assault: the 1990 rate of simple assault by relatives was six times greater for women than men; the rate for aggravated assault was only roughly twice that for men (Bureau of Justice Statistics, 1992:Appendix V).

The reported forcible rape rate for women[16] in 1990 was 1.0 for every 1,000 women age 12 and over (Bureau of Justice Statistics, 1992:Table 3), well below their rates of aggravated assault (4.5) and simple assault (12.7). Female children are three times more likely than male children to be sexually abused (Sedlak, 1991:5-7).

Ethnic Status

Americans of minority status are at greater risk of victimization by violent crime than are those of majority status. The overall 1990 violent victimization rate reported by the NCS was 39.7 for blacks and 37.3 for Hispanics compared with a rate of 28.2 for whites (Bureau of Justice Statistics, 1992:Tables 6 and 8).

Simple assaults are a substantially larger proportion of all violent crimes for whites (56%) than for blacks or Hispanics (35%), but the risk of simple assault is about the same for these ethnic groups (16 per thousand whites, 14 for blacks, 13 for Hispanics). Excluding simple assaults from the violent crime rate, the rate of violent crime (forcible rape, robbery, and *aggravated* assault) for blacks and Hispanics is roughly twice that of whites—13 for whites, 26 for blacks, 24 for Hispanics. For reasons discussed early in this chapter, it is not possible to report victimization rates for other ethnic groups.

As noted above, blacks, especially black males, are disproportionately the victims of homicide. Although variations have occurred over time in rates by ethnic status and sex, black rates of homicide have exceeded white rates since at least 1910. In 1990 half of all homicide victims were black, and blacks were homicide victims at a rate six times that of whites (Federal Bureau of Investigation, 1992). Several studies using subnational data have found that the black-white homicide differential is attenuated substantially at high income levels. We discuss this interaction, and others that may help to explain this differential, in Chapter 3.

American Indians and Alaska natives are also at greater risk of homicide than are white Americans, though exact comparisons are lacking. In a recent special report, the Indian Health Service (1991) placed their age-adjusted rate at 14.1 per 100,000 in 1988—above that for the total population at 9.0 but half the 28.2 rate for all groups other than white. According to the Indian Health Service (1988:Chart 4.21) the rate for Native Americans has substantially exceeded the white rate, but has not exceeded the rate for the entire nonwhite population, since at least 1955.

Socioeconomic Status

Family income,[17] the primary indicator of socioeconomic status measured by the NCS, is inversely related to the risk of violent victimization. In 1988 the risk of victimization was 2.5 times greater for individuals in families with the lowest income (under $7,500) as the highest ($50,000 and over). Of all violent crimes, this negative relation is strongest for robbery.

The net effect of family income is less than that for age, gender, race, and marital status (Sampson and Lauritsen, Volume 3). Its contribution relative to these other factors may be negligible; consequently it remains unclear just how much and in what ways poverty contributes to the risk of violent victimization—an issue we take up in Chapter 3.

VIOLENT OFFENDERS

There is more uncertainty about the perpetrators of violent crimes than about their victims because of measurement errors in arrest records and sampling errors in surveys of offenders' self-reports. Because the two data sources are subject to different sources of error, one can be fairly confident about conclusions on which they converge. The panel cautions readers against interpreting annual statistics on arrestees as an indicator of the distribution of the people actually committing crimes: because persons arrested more than once in any year are disproportionally represented in arrest statistics, there are doubts that the arrest population is representative of the offender population.

Personal Characteristics

Ethnic Status

Blacks are disproportionately represented in all arrests, and more so in those for violent crimes than for property crimes. In terms of violent crimes, blacks constitute 45 percent of all arrestees. They are most overrepresented in the most serious violent crimes of homicide, forcible rape, and robbery (Table 2-5). Particularly striking is their substantial overrepresentation in the crime of robbery, a crime that is both a person and a property crime.

Other minorities are also overrepresented among all arrestees and among those arrested for violent crimes. Particularly striking is the relatively high representation of American Indians and Alaska natives, especially for aggravated and other assaults, given their proportions in the U.S. population (Federal Bureau of Investigation, 1990:Table 38).

It is not possible to calculate annual arrest rates for violent crimes for most demographic categories; however, rates of arrest can be calculated separately for whites, blacks, and others.[18] Thus: 1 white was arrested for every 576 whites in the population; 1 black for every 94 blacks; and 1 "other" for every 739 "others." This arrest rate for violent crimes is about six times greater for blacks than whites. However, because data are not available on repeat arrests during the year, these arrest incidence figures do *not* reflect the annual prevalences of arrest for the different subgroups.

TABLE 2-5 Percentage Distributions of All Persons Arrested for Violent Crimes, by Ethnic Status, 1990

	Ethnic Status				
Offense Charged	White American	Black American	American Indian or Alaskan Native	Asian or Pacific Islander	Total
Murder and nonnegligent manslaughter	43.7	54.7	0.7	0.9	100.0
Forcible rape	55.1	43.2	0.8	0.9	100.0
Robbery	37.7	61.2	0.4	0.8	100.0
Aggravated assault	59.9	38.4	0.9	0.8	100.0
Other assaults	64.1	33.9	1.2	0.8	100.0

Source: Federal Bureau of Investigation (1991:Table 38).

Gender and Age

Men make up 89 percent of all people arrested for violent crimes (Federal Bureau of Investigation, 1991:Table 37). Women accounted for only 10 percent of all arrestees for murder and nonnegligent manslaughter, 8 percent of those for robbery, and 1 percent of arrestees for forcible rape. They accounted for a higher proportion of those arrested for assaults: 13 percent for aggravated assault and 16 percent for simple assaults.

In 1990, arrestees for violent crimes were somewhat older on average than victims, with more falling in the age range of 25-29 than in any other. The age distribution for female arrestees is similar to that for males. Males under age 18, who constituted 16 percent of the U.S. population in 1988, represented roughly comparable portions of male arrestees for murder and nonnegligent manslaughter (14%), forcible rape (15%), aggravated assault (14%), and other assault (15%); they were overrepresented among arrestees for robbery at 24 percent (Federal Bureau of Investigation, 1990:Table 34).

The only major gender-age interaction of note is that the male arrest rate declines beginning at ages 45-49, while the female arrest rate remains fairly constant after age 45. After age 65, the female arrest rate approaches half that of males with both rates at their lowest for any age—comparable to their arrest rate for murder at age 14 and under. Figures 2-6A, B, C, and D present 1988 gender and age profiles for people arrested for violent crimes.

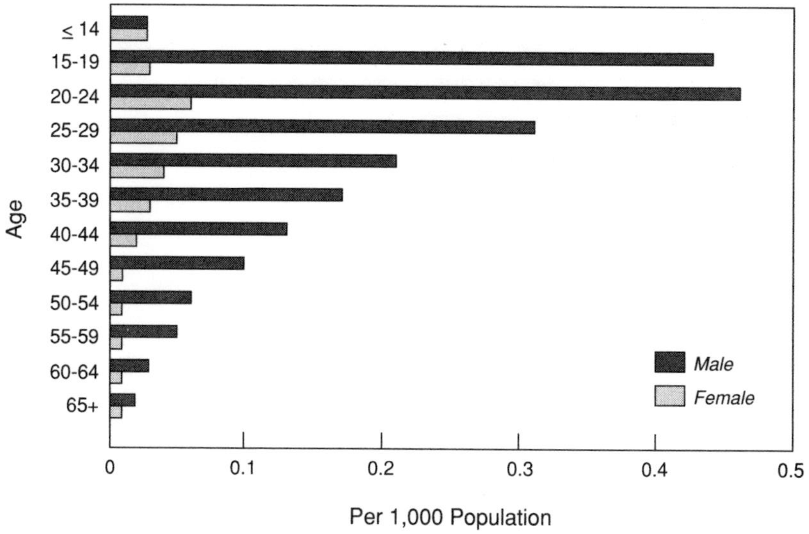

FIGURE 2-6A Arrest rates for murder and nonnegligent manslaughter, 1990.

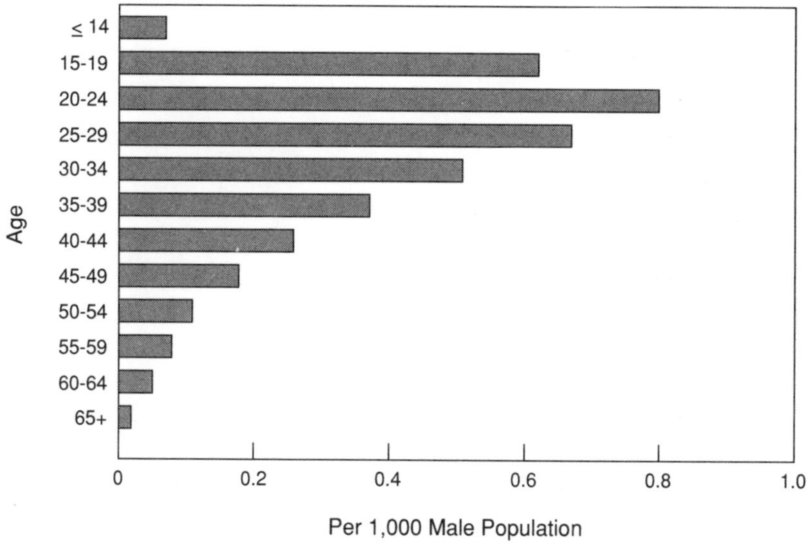

FIGURE 2-6B Arrest rates for forcible rape, 1990. For females, there are too few cases cited to be reliable.

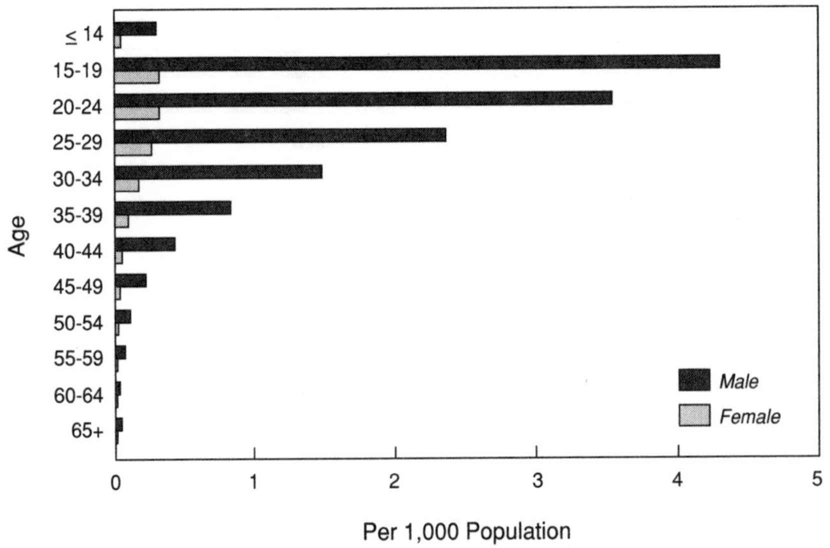

FIGURE 2-6C Arrest rates for robbery, 1990.

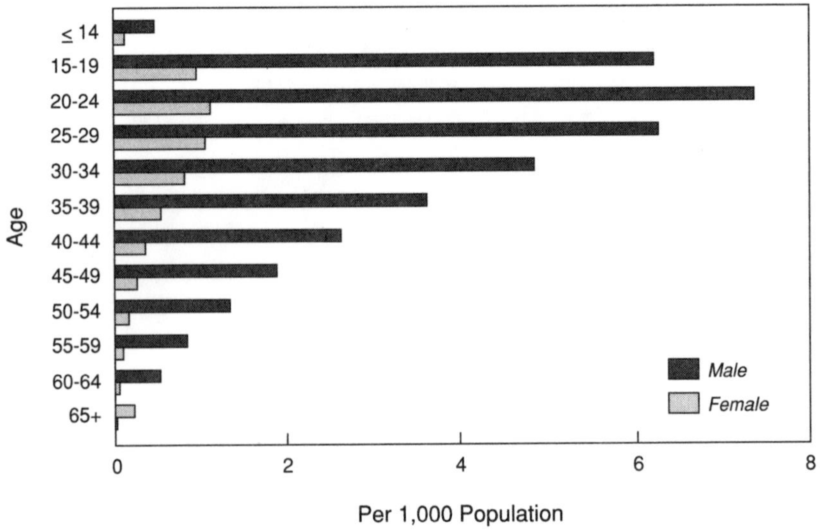

FIGURE 2-6D Arrest rates for aggravated assault, 1990.

PATTERNS OF OFFENDING

Violent Co-offending

Nearly three-fourths of all violent crimes are committed by lone offenders. Forcible rape was most likely to be committed alone: in 1990 only 12 of every 100 forcible rapes involved co-offenders. Robbery was most likely to be committed with others: in 1990 about 48 of every 100 completed robberies involved co-offenders.

Although the majority of violent crimes involve a single offender, co-offending substantially increases the number of people involved in violent victimizations. For example (using Figure 2-7 and Bureau of Justice Statistics, 1992:Table 70), for every 100 completed robberies, there will be a minimum of 182 offenders. That means that 182 people would have to be apprehended to clear all 100 robberies by arrest. Because a fair number of these offenders are also involved in other robberies or/and in other offenses with other co-offenders, they are linked in a much larger offending

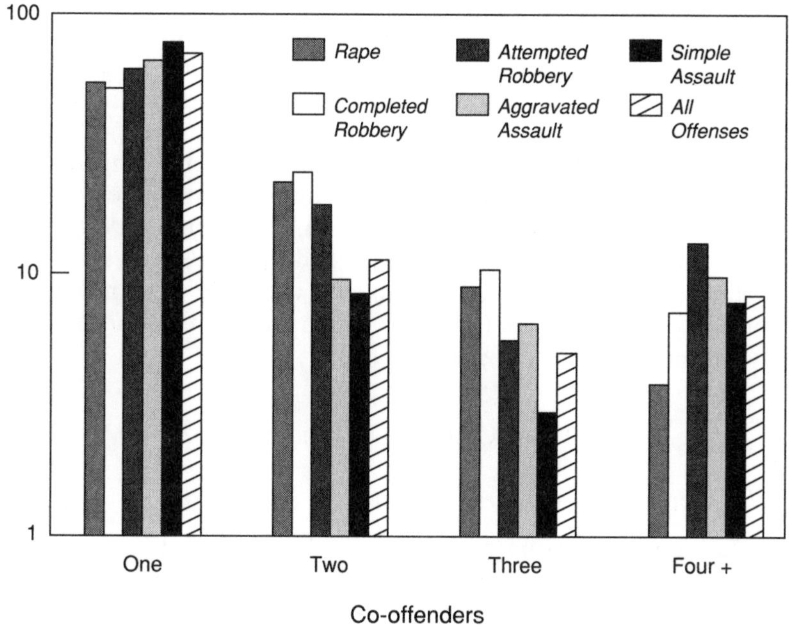

FIGURE 2-7 Violent crimes: percentage distribution of co-offenders by type of offense, 1990.

network that recruits and selects offenders (Reiss and Farrington, 1991).

Criminal Careers

A question asked by policy makers and others is whether criminals specialize in committing violent crimes or if "careers" in crime show a pattern of escalation from nonviolent to violent crimes. If either of these situations were the case, it would have implications for the effectiveness of selective incarceration strategies to reduce levels of violence. The evidence, however, shows otherwise.

Studies of various American and European cohorts have found that no more than 1 in 5 persons ever arrested had an arrest for a violent crime. Furthermore, such arrests were likely to be embedded in long careers dominated by arrests for nonviolent crimes, so that arrests for violence accounted for no more than 1 in 8 of all arrests in the group studied (see for example Farrington, 1991). There is a clear tendency for adult criminals to specialize in various kinds of property crimes or in various kinds of violent crimes rather than to switch between the two types (Blumstein et al., 1986; Farrington et al., 1988).

Although few criminal careers begin with a violent crime, most lengthy careers contain at least one. This pattern is sometimes erroneously interpreted as evidence of escalation from nonviolent to violent crime, or as a demonstration that certain arrest patterns predict subsequent violent crimes. In fact, by most measures, predictions of future violent behavior from arrest records have proven highly inaccurate (Monahan, 1988; Piper, 1985). This is true in part because officially recorded violent crimes are committed largely in the course of lengthy, versatile criminal careers rather than by specialized violent career criminals who could be easily targeted in a strategy of incarceration.

Victim-Offender Relationships

Overlap Between Offenders and Victims

National-level estimates are available on social and personal relationships between victims and offenders that may affect the distribution and consequences of violent events. By social relationship, we mean whether the offender and victim are of the same or different categories—defined in such terms as gender, ethnic status, and sexual preference. By personal relationship we mean the connections between victim and offender as *individuals*—strangers, drinking partners, lovers, spouses, custodian and inmate, and others.

Social Relationships

Clear-cut statements can be made about social relationships defined in terms of characteristics such as gender and ethnic status, which are easily observable and traditionally recorded in counting systems. When characteristics are more ambiguous, there is greater error in classification. As an example of the latter, violent bias crimes, which have recently attracted substantial public attention, are subject to greater error in reporting.

Gender Violence frequently crosses gender lines. Sexual assaults are disproportionally committed by males against females. Homicides by both men and women are more likely to involve male victims. Assaults, in contrast, are more likely to involve an offender and a victim of the same gender. Like assaults against women generally, cross-gender violence has more serious consequences for female victims. Readers are referred to Chapter 3 and Kruttschnitt (Volume 3) for a discussion of sexual violence and Chapter 5 for a discussion of family violence.

Ethnic Status For violent crimes that involve blacks and whites, one can construct a "chance-encounter" race mix by assuming that each individual's chances of violent offending and victimization are independent of race, so that the probability of any offender-victim race combination depends only on the prevalence of each race in the U.S. population. In these hypothetical circumstances, 78 percent of all violent events would involve a white offender and victim, 21 percent would cross racial lines, and only 1 percent would involve a black offender and victim.

According to the 1987 National Crime Survey (calculated from Bureau of Justice Statistics, 1989b:Table 43), in single-offender victimizations, whites assault whites at about the chance-encounter rate, blacks assault whites at about 72 percent of that rate, and whites assault blacks at about 56 percent of the chance-encounter rate. In contrast, blacks assault blacks at about 800 percent of the chance-encounter rate.

Violent Bias Crimes One type of violent behavior that has been recently defined in the criminal law is referred to as *hate* or *bias* crimes. Bias crimes are distinguished from other crimes by the presumed role of social relationships in their motivation. The Hate Crime Statistics Act of 1990 requires the UCR program to begin counting bias crimes and specifies that violent attacks, intimidation, arson, and property damage "that manifest evidence of prejudice based on race, religion, sexual orientation, or ethnicity" are all considered to be violent bias crimes. New state and local statutes that prescribe enhanced sentences for bias crimes define them in fairly similar terms.

Documenting and analyzing patterns of violent bias crimes is difficult, because these crimes are sometimes hard to recognize. Absent such signals as graffiti, organizational identity, or lifestyle of victims, classifying some violent act as a bias crime makes it necessary to determine the perpetrator's motivation—a difficult task subject to uncertainty, especially when the prejudice serves only to aggravate a conventional robbery with a gratuitous shooting, beating, or mutilation, for example.

The available statistics have generally been developed by advocacy organizations. Such organizations often lack the resources and infrastructure for regularly counting incidents and classifying them according to rigorous criteria but, by increasing awareness of bias crimes, they may encourage the designation of ambiguous events as bias crimes. Thus, for example, Montgomery County, Maryland, reported 196 bias crimes during 1989. This count constitutes between 14 and 81 percent of various advocacy groups' recent *national* counts (compiled by Ellis, 1990, for the panel), a share that is severely disproportionate to Montgomery County's 0.2 percent share of the U.S. population.

Most of the available data do not distinguish between violent and nonviolent bias crimes. An exception is a synthesis of 10 available victimization surveys of gay men and lesbians (Berrill, 1990). Between 24 and 48 percent of the gay men and lesbians surveyed reported having been threatened by violence related to their sexual orientation at some time in their lives. Similarly, between 9 and 23 percent reported having been punched, hit, or kicked, and between 4 and 10 percent reported having been assaulted with a weapon. In most of the surveys, the victimization rates for gay men exceed the rates for lesbians by factors of 2-4 to 1—slightly greater than the difference by gender for assault victimization in the general population, according to the National Crime Survey (Aurand et al., 1985; Gross et al., 1988).

Personal Relationships

About half of all homicide victims are murdered by neither intimate family members nor total strangers, but rather by people with some kind of preexisting relationship: friends, neighbors, casual acquaintances, workplace associates, associates in illegal activities, or members of their own or a rival gang (Table 2-6). The high prevalence of such preexisting relationships between victims and their killers suggests that most people's fears of being killed by strangers overestimate the risk; by the same token, people underestimate the probability of being killed by someone with a close or a known relationship to them.

As discussed earlier in this chapter, women face only about one-third the homicide risk faced by men (4.2 and 14.2 per 100,000, respectively). However, among homicide victims, women are about four times as likely as men to have been killed by intimate partners, and 50 percent more likely to be killed by other family members.

For violent crimes that do not end in death, a preexisting relationship between victim and offender is less likely, yet there is variation by type of crime. Of all nonfatal violent crime types, forcible rapes are most likely to involve intimates or acquaintances (61%), and attempted robbery is least likely (14%).

COMMUNITY VARIATIONS IN VIOLENT CRIME

Community characteristics affect the probability of violent crime. In this section we examine data describing variation in the rates of specific crime types over time, by community size, and from area to area within cities.

Variation by Community Size

The size of a community is related to its rate of violent crime. In line with many people's perceptions, smaller cities and rural and suburban areas on average have lower rates than larger cities and metropolitan areas. Figure 2-8A shows aggregate UCR violent crime rates from 1973 to 1990 for cities of different sizes. In general, the smaller the place, the lower the rate of violent crime. By 1990, the aggregate rate varied from 359 per 100,000 residents for cities with less than 10,000 population to a rate of 2,243 for those in cities with a million or more. Although not shown in the figure, outer suburban county areas not included in other groupings and rural counties were relatively safe places: in 1990, the com-

TABLE 2-6 Distribution of Homicides by Victim, Sex, and Relationship, for Events with Known Relationship Type

Relationship of Victim to Offender	Male Victims (%)		Female Victims (%)		All Victims (%)		
	Pierce[a] (N=9,274)	Warner[b] (N=1,354)	Pierce[a] (N=3,428)	Warner[b] (N=411)	Pierce[a] (N=12,702)	Warner[b] (N=1,765)	Maxfield[c] (N=139,593)
Intimate partner	9.1	9.7	38.9	36.0	17.2	15.8	18.2
Spouse	4.3	2.2	22.3	11.7	9.2	4.4	10.4
Common-law spouse	0.9	1.2	2.6	6.1	1.4	2.3	2.1
Other	3.9	6.3	14.0	18.2	6.6	9.1	5.7
Other family	10.9	8.5	16.2	16.1	12.3	10.3	11.6
Parent/stepparent	1.9	1.2	3.3	3.2	2.3	1.7	2.4
Child/stepchild	3.3	2.9	7.3	5.6	4.4	3.5	3.9
Sibling	2.1	1.3	1.6	1.7	2.0	1.4	1.8
Other	3.6	3.1	4.0	5.6	3.7	3.7	3.5
Other nonstrangers	58.9	60.6	32.7	35.6	51.8	54.8	46.9
Friend	9.0	11.1	4.1	6.3	7.7	10.0	5.3
Acquaintance/ Other known	49.9	49.5	28.6	29.3	44.2	44.7	41.6
Co-offenders	—	17.1	—	7.4	—	14.2	—
Gang	—	2.1	—	0.0	—	1.6	—
Legitimate business	—	1.8	—	1.8	—	1.8	—
Other	—	0.2	—	1.9	—	0.6	—
Stranger	21.2	21.4	12.2	12.4	18.8	19.3	23.1
Total known relationships	100.1	100.2	100.0	100.1	100.1	100.1	99.8
Percent unknown in original tabulation	30.2	4.4	27.3	1.9	29.4	3.8	28.6

[a]Tabulations of 1987 Supplementary Homicide Reports, prepared for the panel by Glen Pierce. Excludes 30.2% of male-victim and 27.3% of female-victim homicides with unknown victim-offender relationship.

[b]Tabulations prepared for the panel by Lynn Warner from sample of homicide cases adjudicated in 1988. Excludes 4.4% of male-victim and 1.9% of female-victim cases with unknown victim-offender relationship.

[c]Maxfield (1989) computed from Table 2, tabulation of 1976-1985 Supplementary Homicide Report, excludes 28.6% of cases with unknown victim-offender relationship.

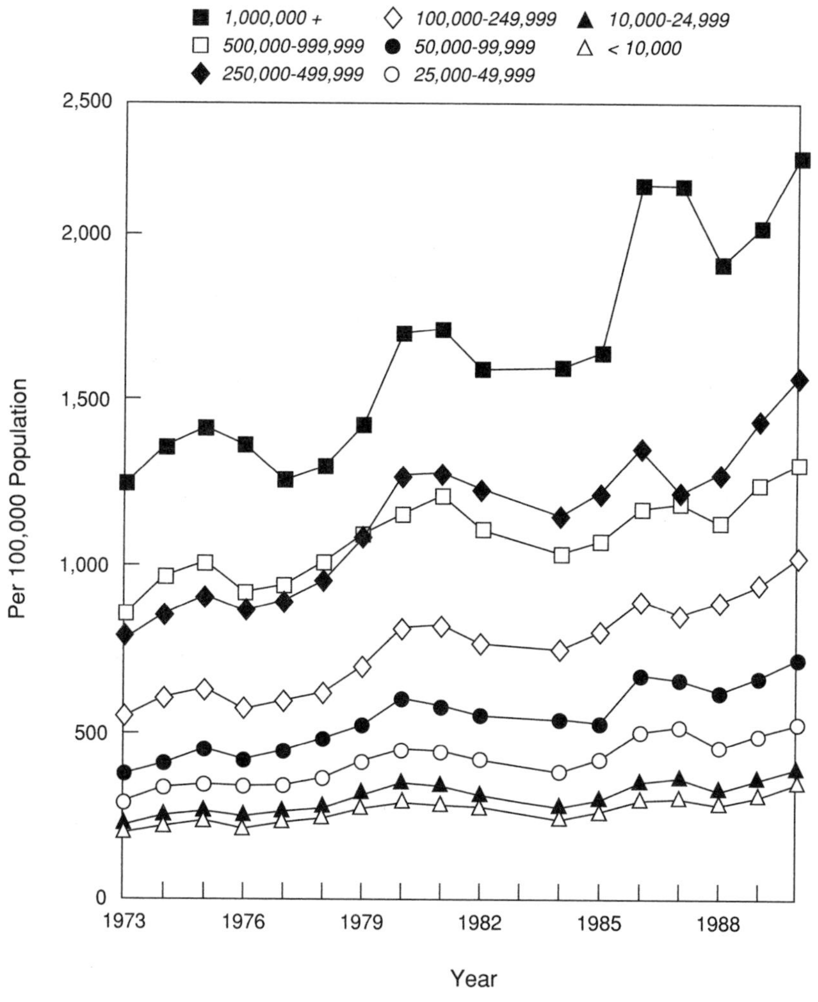

FIGURE 2-8A Total violent crime rate by city size.

parable crime rate in suburban areas was 450 per 100,000 population and in rural counties was 209—the lowest rate of all.

The figure also shows that, over a 17-year period, differences in the relative safety of communities of different sizes persisted through an overall increase in violent crime reported to the police. Annual changes in violent crime rates vary from year to year by size of community, yet overall the rise in rate is greater for large places than for small ones. Outer suburban and rural areas do not follow

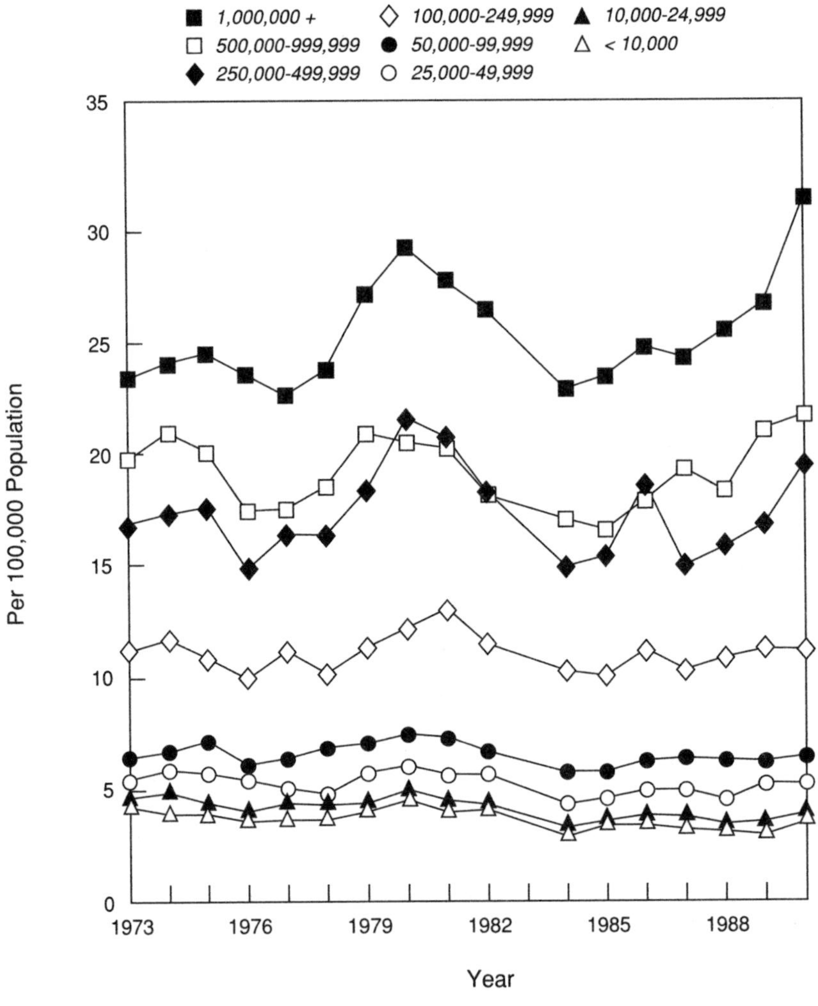

FIGURE 2-8B Murder and nonnegligent manslaughter rate by city size.

the pattern, however: the increase they have experienced is somewhat higher than that of cities with less than 25,000 residents.

In Figures 2-8B to 2-8E we present the rates of specific violent crimes over time for cities of different sizes. Forcible rape represents an exception to the general relationship between city size and crime rates—forcible rape rates in cities with populations between 250,000 and 999,999 exceed those in larger cities through almost the entire period. Otherwise, with occasional exceptions for a year or two, specific crime rates are highest for large cities and lowest for small cities.

Only assault and forcible rape rates have increased over time in cities of all sizes over the past 17 years. Homicide increases have been greatest in large cities, especially in recent years. In most size ranges, the rate for robbery was fairly stable, except for the increases in largest cities, especially since 1988. Just how much of these changes over time are due to changes in reporting behavior is unclear.

Homicide

The 15-year trends for homicide (Figure 2-8B) show roughly similar proportional fluctuations for cities of all sizes. The homicide rate rose to a peak in 1980 or 1981, then declined to a low in the mid-1980s. The rate has been rising since then, and at a somewhat greater rate for cities over than under 1 million.

By 1991 the homicide rate was approaching that for 1980-1981. The perception that recent homicide rates in the 1980s are the highest ever is unfounded. Of course, as the U.S. population increased over time, the annual *number* of homicides grew to historically high levels even with slightly lower *rates*.

Within any city size group, individual cities vary considerably in their annual homicide rate. Even some fairly sizable cities have no homicides in a given year. In Massachusetts in 1990, for example, 65 of the 86 cities with 10,000 or more population reporting to the UCR had no homicides. Two cities with over 100,000 residents—Scottsdale, Arizona, and Irvine, California—reported no homicides in 1990.

Forcible Rape

Because of UCR reporting practices, the reported rates for forcible rape are underestimated by at least a factor of two. Nevertheless, a striking feature of the forcible rape pattern is the relatively low rate for the largest cities, and its restricted range of variation by city size (Figure 2-8C).

The rate for each city size group differs significantly from that of the others but, unlike the pattern for all crimes, the annual rate does not vary directly with city size: among the three largest city size groups, those with 250,000 to 499,999 population have the highest rate and those with over 1 million the lowest. Annual variation in the rate differs somewhat from that for all vio-

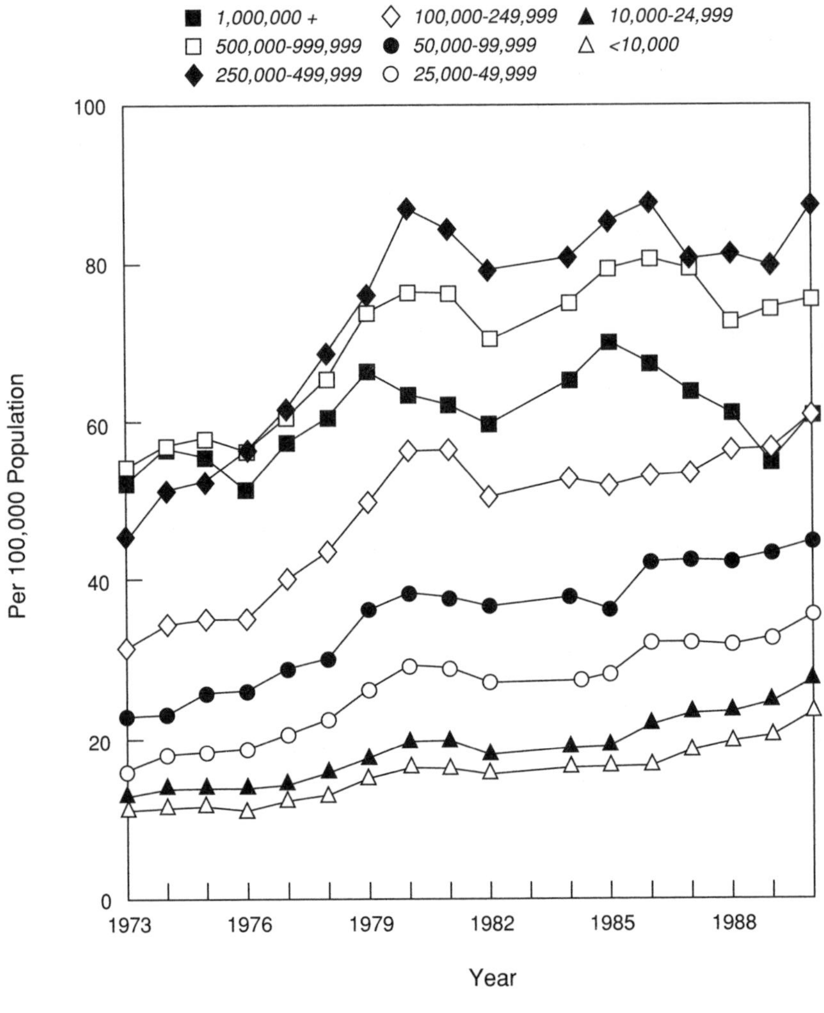

FIGURE 2-8C Forcible rape rate by city size.

lent crimes. In the 15-year period 1975 to 1990, there was a rise in the rate for all city size groups. In large cities, the fluctuations showed two peak periods followed by a decline. The short-term fluctuations around a rising secular rate in the large but not the smaller cities suggest there may be greater variation in reporting practices for the larger jurisdictions since it seems unlikely that such perturbations reflect changing local causal chains.

Cities of all sizes showed an increase over time in the forcible rape rate from 1975 to 1990. For cities with less than 250,000 population, the rate in 1990 was equal to or above that of the peak rate for the 15-year period. For the cities with 250,000 or more, the 1990 rate was still below the peak period. What is surprising is that after 1975 the rate for large metropolitan cities was significantly below that of cities between 250,000 and 1 million and remained so to 1990. Indeed, cities in the size group 250,000 to 500,000 generally showed the greatest annual increase.

Although direct evidence to account for this pattern of variation is lacking, some of the rise seems attributable to changes in the willingness of women to report forcible rape to the police and to changing practices of police departments in sympathetic processing of forcible rape victims (see Chapter 3).

Robbery

The basic pattern of variation by city size for robbery is similar to that observed for all violent crime combined (Figure 2-8D). What is most striking is the substantial variation at the beginning and the end of the 15-year period. The range in 1990 was from a low of 49 in cities under 10,000 to a high of 1,138 in cities over 1 million. Rural counties (not included in the figure) reported a rate of only 16 per 100,000 inhabitants. What is also apparent is that the cities of more than 1 million have rates substantially above that of even the next largest cities. This difference prevailed throughout the period, and in 1990 the range was from around 600 for cities of between 250,000 to 1 million to 1,138 for cities over 1 million. Clearly, *the nation's eight largest cities in 1990—New York, Los Angeles, Chicago, Philadelphia, Houston, Detroit, San Diego, and Dallas—are far more dangerous as measured by robbery incidents than are smaller metropolitan central cities on average.*

What may seem somewhat surprising is that, despite fluctuations in the robbery rate from 1973 to 1990 for each of the city size groups, the trend is distinctly upward only for the cities with more than 1 million and those with 100,000 to 250,000 population. Other trend lines are fairly flat.

Aggravated Assault

The rates for aggravated assault have increased in cities of all sizes since 1973 (Figure 2-8E). The rates peaked in 1980 for all groups, declined slightly, then rose to new highs in 1990. By 1990

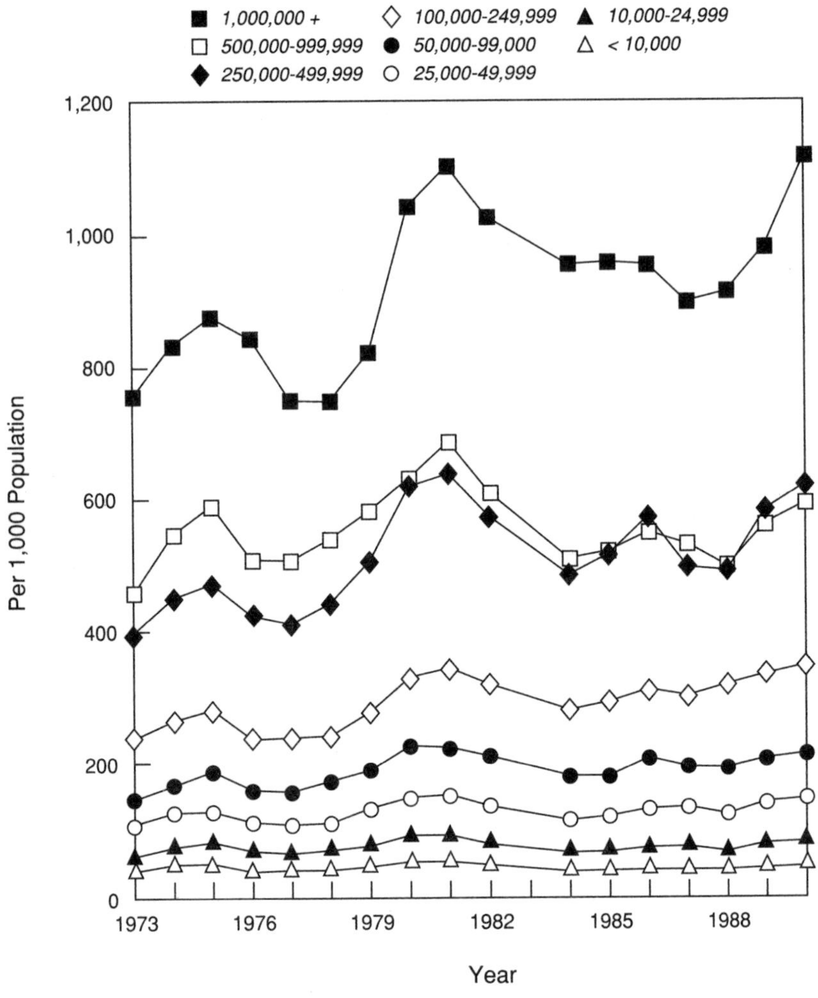

FIGURE 2-8D Robbery rate by city size.

the range of rates had widened substantially—from lows of 282 and 283, respectively, for cities with under 10,000 and 10,000 to 25,000 population to a high of 1,011 for cities of over 1 million. There was, on the whole, a fairly steady increase in the aggravated assault rate.

Worth noting is the fact that the aggravated assault rate was greater in cities of 250,000 to 500,000 than in cities of 500,000 to 1 million population. Indeed, over time, the aggravated assault rate of cities in the quarter to half million size diverged from that

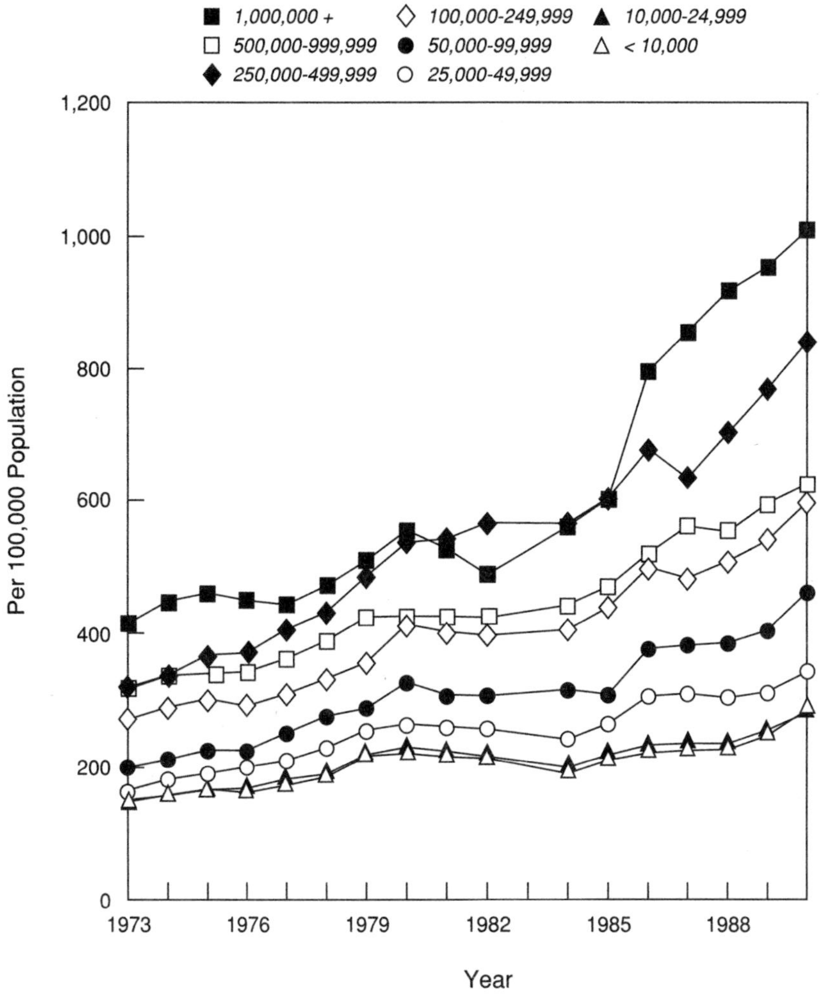

FIGURE 2-8E Aggravated assault rate by city size.

for other cities over 100,000. This class of cities does not generally fit the pattern of a direct relation between city size and violent crime. Why these 32 cities should experience higher aggravated assault rates than all but our largest central cities is unclear. Their rate of 842 in 1990 was well above the rate of 602 for cities of 100,000 to 250,000 and that of 621 for cities of 500,000 to 1 million. Not surprisingly, the lowest rate of aggravated assault—164 per 100,000 population in 1990—is reported for the rural counties.

Variation Within Cities

Violent crime rates vary, not only according to community size and over time, but also from neighborhood to neighborhood within cities. This spatial distribution of violent crime within cities can be dramatic, equaling and sometimes far exceeding the variation across city-size groups. Where one lives within even the highest crime rate cities affects one's risk of violent victimization more than the size of the city. Figure 2-9 is a map of census tracts in the city of San Diego, indicating the rate of violent crime in each tract during the second quarter of 1991. While 7 census tracts recorded less than 1 violent crime per 1,000 population, 1 reported 300.

Several clusters of adjacent San Diego tracts have roughly the same crime rates. Not surprisingly, higher rates generally occur in the central business district; however, these rates are difficult to interpret because the population of residents is smaller than the population of people at risk, who include many who commute there from outside the city or from other areas of the city. Rates are also high in low-income residential communities compared with those in above-average income communities.

There is considerable evidence that residents perceive crime in terms of its spatial distribution and community organization (Warr, Volume 4). People's perceptions of the relative safety of different neighborhoods largely match the reality, leading them to prefer some neighborhoods to others and to avoid stopping or staying in areas they perceive as violent. They are also aware that in daily living the risks of victimization change as they move from one area to another—from home to work, from home to play, or obtaining business or professional services (see Figure 2-10).

DATA NEEDS

Examination of the systems for counting and classifying violent behavior leads to the inescapable conclusion that our present official and unofficial systems of counting and classifying violent criminal behavior result in a substantial underestimation of both the kind and the amount of violent behavior. Our official systems for collecting information on crimes largely fail to collect information on intrafamily violence. The systems also undercount most nonfamily crimes in which the victim survives. There appears to be less underestimation for armed robbery than for assaults. Both sexual assaults and interpersonal assaults are substantially underreported in our official systems as evidence from

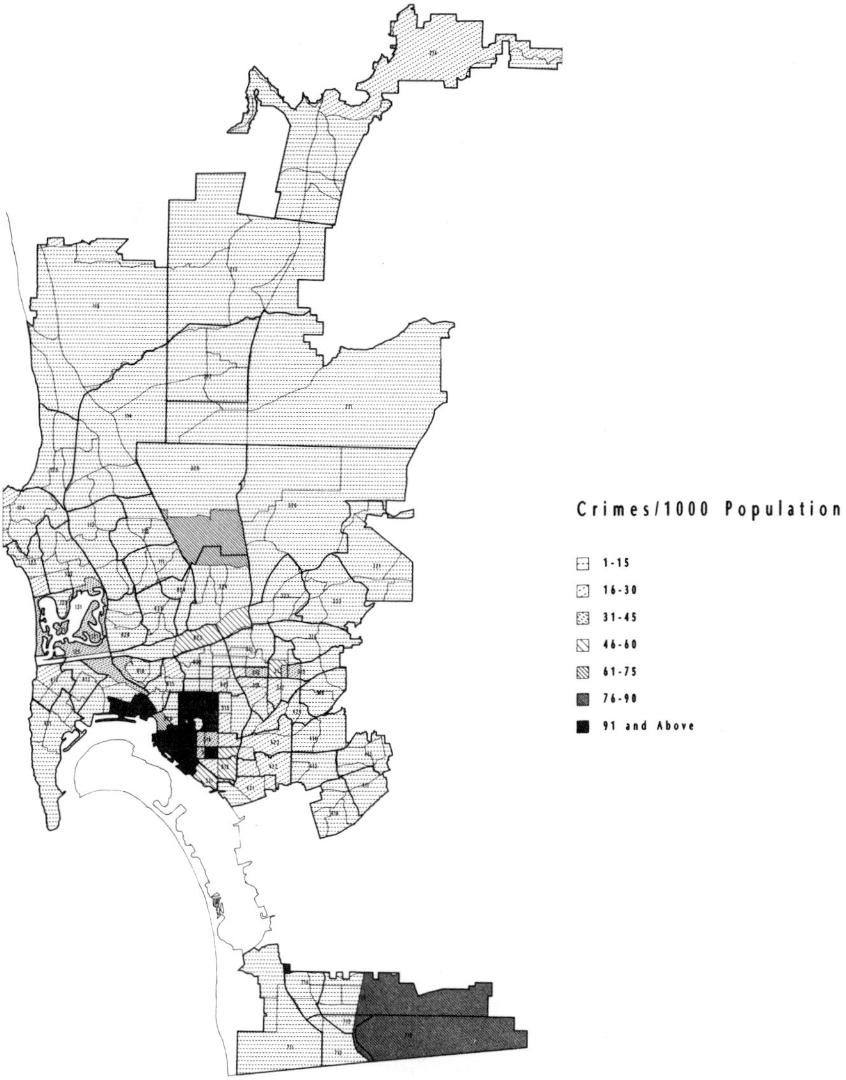

FIGURE 2-9 San Diego violent crime rate by census tract, 1991. Source: San Diego Police Department Crime Analysis Unit.

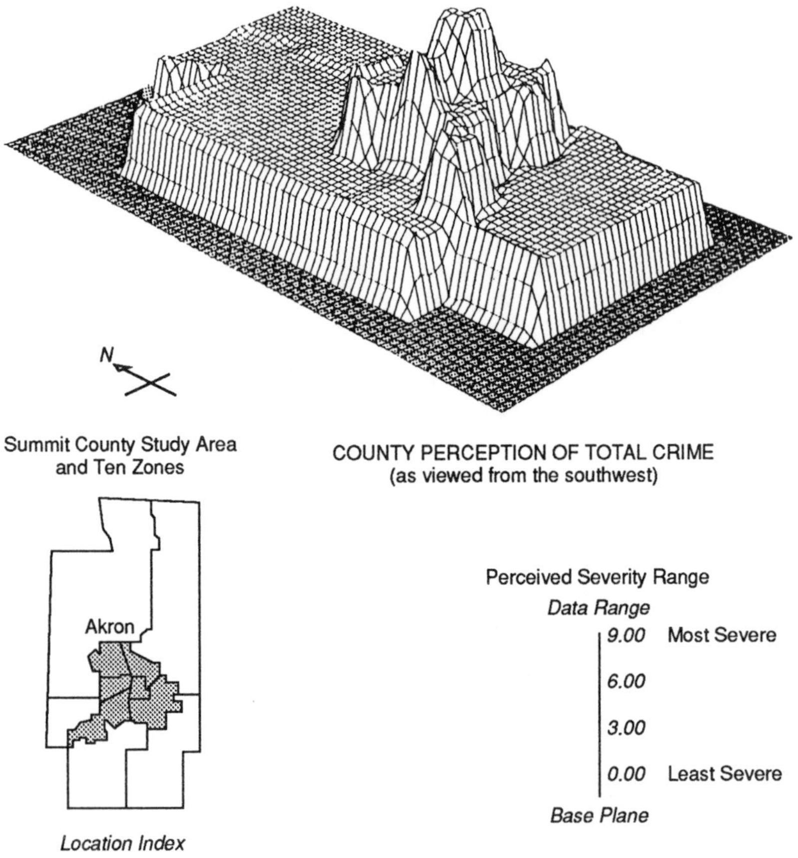

FIGURE 2-10 Contour map of perceptions in Summit County, Ohio. Source: Pyle (1980).

emergency treatment, other institutional records, and small sample surveys of selected populations (e.g., surveys of men and women for a city or college) make apparent.

As reflected in this chapter, there is a paucity of information about victimization risks for ethnic categories other than whites and blacks. The panel recommends that UCR, NCS, and NCHS explore and, to the extent possible, expand their capacities for collecting and reporting data for Hispanics, Asians, Native Americans, and other ethnic categories.

There is also a paucity of information on the consequences of victimization by violent crime. The NCS collects information on injury and property loss, but as Cohen et al. (Volume 4) explain, the information is insufficient to assess the overall cost consequences of violent crime. Moreover, there are few ways at present to merge information from diverse sources as, for example, from emergency or other medical treatment and crime victim data bases. The inability to merge data sources has implications not only for calculating the consequences and costs of crime but also for calculating conditional probabilities in the causal chain of crimes and their consequences. This lack of baseline conditional probabilities complicates the task of assessing the efficacy of interventions to prevent violent crimes or meliorate their consequences.

Available information on violent bias crimes lags far behind the pace of legislative initiatives in this area. In implementing the Hate Crimes Statistics Act of 1990, high priority should be given to supporting research on the following questions: (1) how various punishment schemes (e.g., increments to basic sentences) affect the incidence of violent bias crimes; (2) the psychological consequences of bias crime victimization; (3) individual risk factors for victimization among members of groups that are frequent objects of hate crimes; and (4) validation of hate violence counts obtained through the FBI's Uniform Crime Reporting Program and analytical comparisons with the counts obtained from other sources, such as advocacy groups and community-based organizations.

This chapter has pointed to various limitations of current information systems for measuring the national prevalence and incidence of violent crimes and their consequences, and for the victims of crimes. Those limitations imply a large number of recommendations, but the panel wishes to draw attention to five important information system needs at the local level to enhance our understanding of violent behavior and of interventions to control it.

(1) There is a pressing need for statistical information systems that link information on injuries and their treatment to information about the violent event. The development of emergency and trauma center information to make it relevant to violent crime should be a high priority. In addition, more information could be obtained from current hospitalization and medical treatment surveys, and more detail on the extent of injury could be recorded in NCS and in the new incident-based UCR program.

(2) There is an equally pressing need to develop information systems that will permit the calculation of probabilities of violent victimization conditional on circumstances. That information is useful public information for potential victims in assessing their personal risks, for researchers attempting to understand violent events, and for policy makers assessing the efficacy of

interventions to prevent violent crimes or meliorate their consequences.

(3) Present information systems provide only limited information on many types of violent victimization in which there is considerable public interest and which are the major focus of public policy. These include intrafamily violence, violent sexual assaults of men, women, and children, and the persons confronted and occasionally killed in the course of commercial robbery.

(4) Information on the consequences of violent crime and their costs is limited. There is almost no information on their cost to organizations and individuals. Efforts should be made to develop that information. At the present time there are no reliable ways to estimate the cost of the psychological consequences of crime such as fear of being victimized or the physical and psychological stress victims experience from past victimization. In addition, as Cohen et al. (Volume 4) conclude, there is little information on the nature and cost of victim services or of medical care.

(5) There is a need for more reverse-record checks and other comparative analyses of events that are captured in systems for counting violent crimes, victimizations, injuries, and deaths. Such studies will facilitate more accurate estimates of the undercounts of violence inherent in each system.

NOTES

1 UCR and NCS count only forcible rapes (rape by force), excluding statutory rapes (Federal Bureau of Investigation, 1974:12; Bureau of Justice Statistics 1992:Glossary, p. 156).

2 Like the UCR, the NCS counts only the most serious event as an incident as defined by its hierarchy rules. Therefore, the assault of a victim during a robbery will be counted as only a robbery victimization. Neither system, consequently, offers an estimate of all violent crimes committed during an event.

3 The UCR program is being changed to an incident-based reporting system, which will provide more information on victims and offenders and will also eliminate the hierarchy rule that counts only the most serious crime in a compound event.

4 The NCS classifies all victimizations as either personal- or household-sector victimizations. Burglary, household larceny, and motor vehicle theft are household-sector victimizations. Personal-sector victimizations are classified as crimes of violence (rape, robbery, and assault) or crimes of theft (personal larceny with contact and personal larceny without contact). NCS violent victimizations are only roughly comparable to UCR index crimes of violence, for reasons discussed earlier in this chapter.

5 The calculation excludes an estimated 3,128,130 simple assaults

for crude comparisons with UCR. Their exclusion reduces the number of violent victimizations from 6,008,790 to 2,880,660.

Aggravated assaults are attacks by one person on another for the purpose of inflicting severe or aggravated bodily injury. Attempts are included since it is not necessary that an injury result when a gun, a knife, or another weapon, including hands, fists, and feet, are used that could, and probably would, result in serious personal injury were the crime successfully completed. Both UCR and NCS classify injuries as serious when they result in broken bones, lost teeth, internal injuries, and loss of consciousness. The NCS also classifies any injury as serious if it requires two or more days of hospitalization.

6 Personal larcenies or personal crimes of theft include two subgroups. *Personal larceny with contact* involves personal contact between the victim and the offender and includes such crimes as purse snatching and pocket picking. *Personal larceny without contact* is theft of property of the victim without personal contact from any place other than the home or its immediate vicinity. The crime differs from household larceny only in the location in which the theft occurs.

7 The panel recognizes that the division between simple and aggravated assault involves considerable classification error and also that there are valid reasons for including simple assault as a violent crime, especially given its prevalence in domestic violence.

8 UCR violent index crimes are offenses of murder, forcible rape, robbery, and aggravated assault (Federal Bureau of Investigation, 1990:Table 1).

9 The inclusion of commercial and nonresidential offenses in the UCR but not the NCS also accounts for some of the difference, as it disproportionally increases the base for property crimes.

10 Because the Bureau of Justice Statistics (1989a) report is based on the National Crime Survey, it counts injuries only among surviving victims. Because death occurs in only about 1 percent of all victimizations involving injury, however, this statistical artifact has a negligible effect on the statistics reported here.

11 Loftin and Wiersma (1991) could not calculate risks for Hispanics because, at the time their data were collected, death certificates in only five states provided for that demographic category.

12 Single victim-single offender homicides account for only 54 percent of all homicides in which the ethnic status of victims was reported in 1990 (calculated from Federal Bureau of Investigation, 1990:11).

13 Age adjustment is a technique that applies the age-specific rates of a population to a standardized age distribution to eliminate the difference in observed rates that result from differences in population composition. For example, whites and females have lower infant mortality and longer life expectancies than blacks and males. Therefore, blacks and males are overrepresented in the ages of highest risk for criminality—a fact that would overstate gender/ethnic status homicide mortality differentials if no adjustment were made. Adjustment for age is usually done

to compare two or more populations at the same point in time or one or more populations at two or more points in time.

14 A commonly used measure of premature mortality due to a given cause of death is years of potential life lost (YPLL) before age 65. This measure is useful for comparing different causes of death in terms of premature mortality. However, blacks and males have shorter life expectancies than do whites and females, even when homicides are omitted from the calculation. Therefore comparisons by race and gender of YPLL before age 65 due to homicide overstate the relative premature mortality effects of homicide on blacks and males.

15 The reader should bear in mind that the young male adult military population exposed to battle deaths is also that most at risk of homicide. Hence the homicide rate for the resident U.S. population in war years will be below that expected for years when there are no battle deaths (Federal Bureau of Investigation, 1969:Table 1).

16 Until 1990, the NCS had reports of fewer than 10 sample cases of sexual assaults on males classified as forcible rape. The 1990 rate was reported as 0.2 per 1,000 males. There is a substantial underreporting of sexual assault on both males and females, but especially so for males at younger ages. Efforts should be made to secure more reliable measures of sexual assaults for both men and women at all ages.

17 Family income in the NCS includes the income of the household head and all other related persons residing in the same housing unit. The income of persons unrelated to the head of household is excluded (Bureau of Justice Statistics, 1990:Glossary).

18 Numerators are counts of violent crime arrests in Federal Bureau of Investigation (1992:Table 38). Denominators are estimated populations, 12 years of age and over by race in Bureau of Justice Statistics (1992:Table 6).

REFERENCES

Aurand, S.K., R. Adessa, and C. Bush
1985 Violence and discrimination against Philadelphia lesbian and gay people. (Available from Philadelphia Lesbian and Gay Task Force, 1501 Cherry Street, Philadelphia, PA 19102).

Berrill, K.T.
1990 Anti-gay violence and victimization in the United States: An overview. *Journal of Interpersonal Violence* 5(3, September):274-294.

Blumstein, A., J. Cohen, J.A. Roth, and C.A. Visher
1986 *Criminal Careers and "Career Criminals."* Vol. I. Washington, D.C.: National Academy Press.

Bureau of the Census
1990 *Statistical Abstract of the United States: 1990.* Washington, D.C.: U.S. Government Printing Office.

Bureau of Justice Statistics
1989a *Injuries From Crime: Special Report.* Washington, D.C.: U.S. Government Printing Office.
1989b *Criminal Victimization in the United States, 1987.* Washington, D.C.: U.S. Government Printing Office.
1990 *Criminal Victimization in the United States, 1988.* A National Crime Survey Report, December 1990, NCJ-122024.
1992 *Criminal Victimization in the United States, 1990.* Washington, D.C.: U.S. Government Printing Office.

Ellis, W.W.
1990 Bias Crime. Commissioned paper for the Committee on Research on Law Enforcement and the Administration of Justice, National Research Council.

Farrington, D.P.
1991 Childhood aggression and adult violence: Early precursors and later-life outcomes. Pp. 5-29 in D.J. Pepler and K.H. Rubin, eds., *The Development and Treatment of Childhood Aggression.* Hillsdale, N.J.: Erlbaum.

Farrington, D., H. Snyder, and T. Finnegan
1988 Specialization in juvenile court careers. *Criminology* 26:461-488.

Federal Bureau of Investigation
1969 *Uniform Crime Reports: Crime in the United States, 1968.* Washington, D.C.: U.S. Government Printing Office.
1974 *Uniform Crime Reporting Handbook.* Washington, D.C.: U.S. Government Printing Office.
1990 *Uniform Crime Reports: Crime in the United States, 1989.* Washington, D.C.: U.S. Government Printing Office.
1991 *Uniform Crime Reports: Crime in the United States: 1990.* Washington, D.C.: U.S. Government Printing Office.
1992 *Uniform Crime Reports: Crime in the United States, 1991.* Washington, D.C.: U.S. Government Printing Office.

Garofalo, J., L. Siegel, and J. Laub
1987 School-related victimizations among adolescents: An analysis of national crime survey narratives. *Journal of Quantitative Criminology* 3:321-338.

Griffin, Ezra E.H., and Carl C. Bell
1989 Recent trends in suicide and homicide among blacks. Special communication. *Journal of the American Medical Association* 282(16):2265-2269.

Gross, L., S. Aurand, and R. Adessa
1988 Violence and discrimination against lesbian and gay people in Philadelphia and the Commonwealth of Pennsylvania. (Available from Philadelphia Lesbian and Gay Task Force, 1501 Cherry Street, Philadelphia, PA 19102)

Gurr, T. R.
1989 Historical trends in violent crime: Europe and the United States.

In T.R. Gurr, ed., *Violence in America. Vol. 1: The History of Crime*. Newbury Park, Calif.: Sage Publications.

Haenazel, W.
1950 A standardized rate for mortality defined in units of lost years of life. *American Journal of Public Health* 40:17-26.

Hindelang, M., M. Gottfredson, and J. Garofalo
1978 *Victims of Personal Crime: An Empirical Foundation for a Theory of Personal Victimization*. Cambridge, Mass.: Ballinger.

Holinger, Paul C.
1987 *Violent Deaths in the United States: An Epidemiologic Study of Suicide, Homicide, and Accidents*. New York: Guilford Press.

Indian Health Service
1988 *Regional Differences in Indian Health*. Washington, D.C.: U.S. Department of Health and Human Services.
1991 *Regional Differences in Indian Health*. Washington, D.C.: U.S. Department of Health and Human Services.

Jencks, Christopher, and Susan E. Mayer
1990 The social consequences of growing up in a poor neighborhood. Pp. 111-186 in Laurence E. Lynn, Jr. and Michael G.H. McGeary, eds., *Inner-City Poverty in the United States*. Washington, D.C.: National Academy Press.

Koppel, Herbert
1987 Lifetime likelihood of victimization. Bureau of Justice Statistics Technical Report NCJ-104274. U.S. Department of Justice.

Lane, Roger
1979 *Violent Death in the City: Suicide, Accident, and Murder in Nineteenth Century Philadelphia*. Cambridge, Mass.: Harvard University Press.

Loftin, Colin, and Ellen J. MacKenzie
1990 Building National Estimates of Violent Victimization. Draft paper presented at the Symposium on the Understanding and Control of Violent Behavior. Destin, Fla. April 1-4.

Loftin, Colin, and Brian Wiersma
1991 Lifetime Risk of Violent Victimization from Homicide. Unpublished memo to the Panel on the Understanding and Control of Violent Behavior.

Lynch, James P.
1989 An evaluation of lifetime likelihood of victimization. *Public Opinion Quarterly* 53:262-264.

Maxfield, M.G.
1989 Circumstances in Supplementary Homicide Reports: Variety and validity. *Criminology* 27(4):671-695.

Monahan, J.
1988 Risk assessment of violence among the mentally disordered: Generating useful knowledge. *International Journal of Law and Psychiatry* 11:249-257.

Monkkonen, Eric H.
1989 Diverging homicide rates: England and the United States, 1850-1875. Pp. 80-101 in T.R. Gurr, ed., *Violence in America. Vol. 1: The History of Crime.* Newbury Park, Calif.: Sage Publications.

National Center for Health Statistics
1991 *Vital Statistics of the United States 1988. Volume II:Mortality.* Washington, D.C.: U.S. Government Printing Office.

Piper, E.
1985 Violent recidivism and chronicity in the 1958 Philadelphia cohort. *Journal of Quantitative Criminology* 1:319-344.

Pyle, G.F.
1980 Systematic sociospatial variation in perceptions of crime location and severity. Pg. 226 in D. Georges-Abeyie and K.D. Harries, eds., *Crime: A Spatial Perspective.* New York: Columbia University Press.

Reiss, A.J., Jr.
1985 Some failures in designing data collection that distort results. Pp. 161-177 in L. Burstein, H.E. Freeman, and P.H. Rossi, eds., *Collecting Evaluation Data: Problems and Solutions.* Beverly Hills, Calif.: Sage Publications.

Reiss, A.J., Jr., and D.P. Farrington
1991 Advancing knowledge about co-offending: Results from a prospective longitudinal survey of London males. *Journal of Criminal Law and Criminology* 82(2):360-395.

Sedlak, Andrea J.
1991 *National Incidence and Prevalence of Child Abuse and Neglect: 1988.* Washington, D.C.: Westat, Inc. (Revised September 5, 1991).

U.S. Department of Health and Human Services
1990 *Health United States, 1989.* Hyattsville, Md.: Public Health Service.

van Dijk, Jan J.M., Pat Mayhew, and Martin Killias
1990 *Experiences of Crime Across the World: Key Findings from the 1989 International Crime Survey.* Deventer, The Netherlands: Kluwer Law and Taxation Publishers.

Part II
Understanding Violence

3

Perspectives on Violence

In this chapter, we look behind patterns and trends to ask what explains them and how they might be altered. One starting point emphasizes that human behavior is shaped in part by long-term developmental processes through which children learn what events to anticipate, how to respond, and what the outcome will be. Children who learn that violent behavior "works" in families, on television, in violent pornographic literature, among peers, and in the community, it is argued, may have a greater potential to behave violently as adults.

This oversimplified psychosocial explanation ignores the fact that even if two individuals could be exposed to identical sequences of experiences as they developed, their potentials for adult violent behavior would differ because their nervous systems process information, recall experiences, and react to events differently. While heredity and the prenatal environment help shape an individual's nervous system by the time of birth, that system is constantly reshaped by experiences, by injuries, by temporary external influences such as stress or psychoactive chemicals, by hormonal activity, and even by violent behavior itself.

Even taken together, developmental and neurological explanations are incomplete. The mix of experiences during development—their violence content, the rewards and punishments for violent and nonviolent behavior, for example—is not the same in every family, school, or community. Quite apart from individuals' development, different communities and groups may reward or punish violence quite differently depending on its purpose, on the victim's ethnic status or sexual preference, and on his or her preexisting relationship(s) to the perpetrator(s). Places differ in terms of how frequently chance encounters offer the rewards or provocations that elicit violent behavior, how easily one can obtain lethal weapons, and how likely a passerby is to interfere in a violent encounter. To close another loop, however, neighborhoods also differ in terms of the risks they present to developing children's nervous systems in such forms as maternal drug use during pregnancy, head injuries to young children, and exposure to environmental toxins.

In short, research strongly suggests that violence arises from *interactions among* individuals' psychosocial development, their neurological and hormonal differences, and social processes. Consequently, we have no basis for considering any of these "levels of explanation" more fundamental than the others. Because existing studies rarely consider more than one of these levels simultaneously, very little is known about the relevant interactions. Therefore, we found it most convenient to discuss possible explanations and promising preventive interventions level by level, in the order used above.

First, we consider psychosocial explanations of violence, especially how early experiences and learning affect individuals' potentials for violent behavior, including sexual violence. Second, we look at violent behavior from a biological perspective, discussing underlying neuroanatomical organization; neurological activity—physiological, chemical, and hormonal; and the role of genetic transmission. Recognizing that both individual development and violent behavior occur at both levels simultaneously, we assess the prospects for reducing violence through various interventions.

We then turn to the larger social context of violence. Attempts to explain ethnic and socioeconomic patterns of violence bring us to consider the influences of family and social disorganization, opportunity structure, and community culture. A discussion of gang-related violence illustrates how these influences interact. We then look at specific circumstances in which violent events occur, focusing on places in the community and how they vary in violence rates. We consider preventive interventions, growing out of work in both criminology and public health, that are suggested by a focus on places and situations. We conclude the discussion of research findings by briefly considering violence in two special places: prisons and schools.

Recognizing how little is known about the relevant interactions between psychosocial, biomedical, and social influences on violence, we conclude this chapter by recommending a major longitudinal study to explore them. As a near-term means of simultaneously increasing understanding and improving violence control capacity, we recommend a series of violence problem-solving initiatives—programs that exploit both the scientific and the policy potential of rigorous evaluations—in Chapters 7 and 8.

VIOLENCE AND THE INDIVIDUAL

Psychosocial Perspectives

The research underlying psychosocial perspectives is concerned with the learning of aggressive or nonaggressive behaviors as responses to frustration or to ways of achieving desired goals, and the perceptual and cognitive processes through which individuals interpret their interactions with others and choose their responses.

As we note in Chapter 1, behavior described as aggression includes several violent behaviors. There is substantial stability in the potential for aggressive behavior from infancy through adulthood. A number of longitudinal studies show that children who show "aggressive" behavior at around age 8 are more likely than others to exhibit delinquent, criminal, or violent behavior in adolescence and adulthood (Olweus, 1979; Farrington, 1989, 1991). This continuity exists despite substantial changes in environment that usually occur in the late teenage years, as children leave schools, their parents' homes, and sometimes their communities (Olweus, 1984).

This behavioral continuity through environmental changes suggests strongly that individual differences associated with childhood aggressive behavior are also risk factors for adult violent behavior, although with weaker predictive power. Part of the stability and overlap in risk factors is explained by overlap between common definitions of aggression and our definition of violent behavior. For example, 5 of the 13 DSM-III-R (American Psychiatric Association, 1987) diagnostic criteria for conduct disorder are violent behaviors under our definition; other commonly used measures of aggression include fighting, and threats of violence, which also meet our standard for violence. But researchers measure aggression using a variety of criteria that do not fit our definition of violent behavior, such as interactions in preschool play groups, laboratory measures such as "hostility machine" use, vandalism, cruelty to animals, and verbal abuse of other children, for example (see Brain, Volume 2). Among children who exhibit aggressive behavior in childhood, the factors that distinguish the small number who go on to commit violent acts as adolescents or adults from the larger number who do not are not well understood. Identifying the distinguishing factors and explaining the processes through which they cause violent behavior remain fundamental questions for future research. Because aggressive behavior is easier to study than violent behavior, much of what we know comes from the psychological literature on aggression as it relates to violence.

Social Learning of Aggression and Violence

One explanation of aggressive and violent behaviors invokes the concepts of frustration, social learning, and information processing. More than 50 years ago Dollard et al. (1939) speculated that aggression was the consequence of frustration. Modern views emphasize that aggressive or violent behaviors are *learned* responses to frustration (Eron, 1990), that they can also be learned as instruments for achieving goals, and that the learning is facilitated by available models of aggressive or violent behavior.

In this framework, a child learns aggressive or violent behavior by observing or participating in situations in which violence occurs (e.g., instances of frustration, anger, opportunities for instrumental uses of aggression), by experiencing emotional states that are associated with violence, and by observing or experiencing sanctions (rewards and punishments) related to violent events. From early childhood, such occasions and their violent or nonviolent outcomes may be observed in the family, among peers, elsewhere in the neighborhood, or through the mass media. If such social learning inculcates aggression or violence as an appropriate response to frustration, anger, or opportunities, then the behavior may later be activated by cues such as frustration over school failure or loss of a competition, anger at another's behavior, or recognition of an opportunity to gain money by robbery, social status by fighting, or compliance with one's wishes by threats of violence.

Methods of Empirical Testing

Aggressive and violent behaviors in the community are usually analyzed using either cross-sectional data, comparing members of a sample at a single age or observation time, or longitudinal data, following a sample of individuals over time. In either case, data are collected on factors that are hypothesized to be relevant and on sample members' behavior, as measured by their self-reports, by officially recorded events such as arrests, or by the reports of third parties such as family members, peers, or teachers.

The merits of cross-sectional and longitudinal approaches, and of self-reports and official records, have been debated extensively (Weis, 1986; Farrington et al., 1986; Gottfredson and Hirschi, 1987; Blumstein et al., 1988). Because tests of many hypotheses require accurate recording of sequences of events and behaviors, longitudinal studies are usually the strongest approach. Where the hypothesized relevant factors can be manipulated (as is often the case), randomized experiments with longitudinal follow-ups are the method of choice. In any case, multiple outcome measures—based on self-reports, official records, and third-party reports—should be obtained and utilized.

In the sections that follow we discuss findings from research on aggressive and violent behavior, on violent sexual behavior, and on preventive interventions.

Aggressive and Violent Behaviors

Antecedents As explained in Appendix A, researchers have identified many correlates and antecedents of aggressive childhood behavior that are presumed to reflect psychosocial influences:

- in infancy: pregnancy and birth complications, low birthweight, and an uninhibited, fearless temperament;
- in the preschool years: fearless behavior, hyperactivity-impulsivity-attention deficit, restless behavior, and poor concentration;
- in the early school years: daring and risk-taking behavior, poor ability to defer gratification, low IQ, low empathy, and abnormally frequent viewing of violence on television;
- early family experiences: harsh and erratic discipline, lack of parental nurturance, physical abuse and neglect, poor supervision, and early separation of children from parents;
- early school experiences: school failure and interactions involving bullying and peer rejection; and
- factors associated with large low-income families, poor housing, criminal behavior by parents and siblings, and living in high-crime neighborhoods.

These are often presumed also to be risk factors for violent behavior. However, because the behavioral outcomes that are studied—aggression, delinquency, or crime, for example—are so broad, we cannot say with any precision how they are related to violent behavior. The nature of the relationships that have been found, however, suggest that any causal relationships to violent behavior are likely to involve complex interactions across levels of explanation. For example, as Denno (1990:10-11) explains, research prior to hers found that perinatal complications have a potentially strong link to intellectual deficits in poor environments but not in advantaged families, while measures of intellectual functioning have been empirically linked to delinquency or crime even when family socioeconomic characteristics are statistically controlled. Denno's own study (1990:78-81) links perinatal conditions to mental retardation at age 13-14 and mental retardation to the seriousness of delinquency—for females but not males.

Many risk factors that emerge during the preschool and early school years—fearlessness, attention deficit, inability to defer gratification, restlessness, and especially early school failure—are among the most robust predictors of childhood aggressive behavior. However, analyses of longitudinal data indicate that while IQ measured at age 8 appears to predict aggression at age 30, this relationship disappears when it is controlled for measures of aggression at age 8.

Violent events on television are one route through which social learning of aggressive behavior may occur. Some previous research reviews (e.g., Heath et al., 1989; Huesmann and Miller, in press) and a meta-analysis prepared for the panel (Comstock and Paik, 1990) conclude that frequent exposure to television violence is associated with more aggressive behavior by children and adults. However, there is debate about the underlying causal relationship. The correlations may reflect the joint effect of greater exposure to television violence and a heightened potential for violent behavior, both resulting from poor parental supervision. It may also be that children with a high potential for violent behavior select violent material to watch. There is also debate about the permanence of any direct effect, about the importance of whether the television violence is punished or rewarded, and about the behavioral effects of frustration that might be activated by compelling changes in children's television viewing patterns (see debate between Friedrich-Cofer and Huston, 1986; Freedman, 1986). Moreover, the effects of high levels of neighborhood violence may reduce the effects of viewing of television violence on children's potentials for violent behavior; we are aware of no research on this issue.

Violent offenders as measured by self-reports and official records of crimes are more likely than other adults to have experienced poor parental childrearing methods, poor supervision, physical abuse, neglect, and separations from their parents when they were children (Farrington, 1991). These experiences are commonly reported by violent sex offenders as well (Langevin et al., 1985).

School bullying is of interest both as a childhood aggressive behavior and as a precursor of adult violent behavior. Children who are rated "aggressive" by their peers at age 8 have significantly higher average levels of adult aggression, and the underlying causal relationship may involve peer rejection. Childhood aggressiveness has been cited as a common reason for peer rejection (Huesmann and Eron, 1986). However, conflicting findings exist (Cairns et al., 1988), and the role(s) of peer rejection in developing adult aggression is uncertain. Sorting out these relationships is important in choosing whether to try to prevent bullying, peer rejection, or both as approaches to preventing adult aggression.

Some factors appear to be protective, in the sense that they reduce the chance of aggressive behavior in individuals who would otherwise be at high risk. One protective factor, a high-income family, was already suggested as reducing the risk-increasing effects of perinatal complications. Other protective factors suggested by previous research include a shy temperament, high IQ, being firstborn, having a stable family, having affectionate caregivers, having parents who regularly attend religious services, and coming from small families characterized by low discord. As with adverse risk factors, however, these relationships have been observed with respect to aggressive but not violent behavior.

Preventive Interventions We reviewed evaluations of a number of preventive interventions that seek to alter the psychosocial risk factors listed above (see Appendix A). In careful evaluations, several interventions have shown some success in reducing children's aggressive behavior, but longer-term follow-ups are needed to see if they also prevent violent behavior at later ages. Some of the most promising programs are global, using multiple social learning and behavioral interventions simultaneously to emphasize several of the following: the undesirability of aggression; nonaggressive methods of solving problems; improved social skills; and improved television viewing habits (Guerra, 1990; Tremblay et al., 1991; Pepler et al., 1991). Other promising interventions have a single focus: social skills (Jones and Offord, 1989); or improved television viewing habits (Huesmann et al., 1983; Eron and Huesmann, 1984; Singer and Singer, 1981).

Several communities, including Oakland, California, and San Antonio, Texas, report success with a program for reducing early-grade school failure, one of the risk factors for aggression. The program involves daily tutoring of kindergartners by specially trained high school seniors and seems ripe for a carefully controlled evaluation.

Other behavioral approaches that warrant additional testing include parent training in consistent discipline (see review by Kazdin, 1985), combined parent and teacher training (Hawkins et al., 1991), preschool enrichment programs of the Head Start type (Berrueta-Clement et al., 1984), and school-based programs to combat bullying and reduce peer rejection (Olweus, 1991).

One preventive approach developed by the public health community was motivated in part by findings that most violent events are preceded by escalation from verbal conflict through insults and threats, and that the likelihood of escalation is increased by the presence of bystanders who do not attempt to mediate (see, e.g., Luckenbill, 1977; Steadman, 1982; Felson and Steadman, 1983). Using culturally specific role plays and other devices, the Boston Violence Prevention Curriculum was developed for use in tenth-grade health classes, to teach methods of interrupting escalation to violence. The curriculum emphasizes the undesirability of violent behavior, nonviolent responses to provocation, and mediation skills (Prothrow-Stith et al., 1987). A 10-site evaluation suggested some positive effects on knowledge and attitudes but little success in changing behavior (Spiro and DeJong, 1991). The lack of success may reflect the previously noted stability of aggressive behavior after middle childhood and the need to reinforce principles taught in school with experiences elsewhere in the community. A version of the program involving other community organizations is still being evaluated. Depending on the results of that evaluation, serious consideration should be given to developing and testing a revised version of the program, for use with children at around the third-grade level.

In general, research suggests that preventive interventions are more likely to be successful if they involve parents, peers, teachers, and significant others in the community, and if the intervention is adapted to the cultural norms of the target age, ethnic, and socioeconomic category. Interventions are likely to be more effective if they begin early—perhaps as early as the preschool years—and if they are based on clear theoretical models of aggression. Evaluations should test multiple interventions simultaneously, to compare their effectiveness in different populations, particularly with children of different ethnic statuses, socioeconomic statuses, and ages. Follow-up periods must be long enough to ascertain whether interventions in childhood prevent violent behavior as adults.

Violent Sexual Behavior

By *violent sexual behavior* we mean a threat or actual use of physical force that either coerces another person to submit to sexual behavior or leads to sexual excitement or release in the perpetrator. This definition includes a wide range of behaviors, and there is profound disagreement over whether the perpetrator of a violent sexual act is motivated by the power achieved through coercion, by the sexual excitement, or both. Designations of violent sexual behavior as acceptable, criminal, deviant, or the product of mental illness have varied over historical periods and across cultures. The designation has also hinged on circumstances. Where it is clear that informed consent could not have been given—acts against strangers or against children, for example—the acts are usually assumed to be criminal or deviant. For events involving intimates, the designation depends on whether both participants freely gave consent—a matter that may sometimes be ambiguous in one or both of their minds and, for some acts, may be exceedingly difficult for a third party to ascertain.

In studying sexual violence, the methods used to study other types of violence are especially difficult to implement. Because we do not yet know enough to identify categories of children at high risk for violent sexual behavior, it is difficult to design efficient samples for longitudinal study or for follow-ups intended to test the effectiveness of early preventive interventions. People may distort self-reports of violent sexual behavior because of embarrassment over discussing sexual behavior generally; however, persons with violent sexual preferences, by definition, are sexually aroused by contemplating or discussing both real and imagined violent events. Reports by victims and witnesses to sexual violence are subject to distortion because of emotional trauma over the events. In arrest reports, sexual motivation is sometimes disguised in certain cases of assault, homicide, and even burglary. All these kinds of reports are subject to error when the distinction between a violent and a nonviolent sexual event hinges on the issue of consent, which entails ambiguities and uncertainties.

A valuable behavioral measurement of violent sexual preference is phallometric measurement of arousal to violent sexual stimuli. However, sexual preference is not equivalent to sexual acting out. Moreover, while the accuracy of phallometric testing has been estimated at 85 to 90 percent in distinguishing between heterosexual and homosexual preferences, and 70 to 75 percent in distinguishing between preferences for children and adults, accuracy in distinguishing between preferences for violent and nonviolent sexual stimuli are considerably poorer (Murphy et al., 1986).

Research to date on violent sex offenders points to some of the same psychosocial and biological factors discussed earlier in this chapter with respect to aggressive and violent behavior generally: poor parental supervision; unstable family relationships; being abused or neglected as a child; abnormal functioning of sex hormones; and neurophysiological abnormalities in the temporal lobe of the brain. As discussed more fully in Chapter 4, perpetrators of sexual and nonsexual violence both share a tendency to have histories of alcohol abuse. Indeed, the criminal records of known violent sex offenders often contain notations of other crimes such as assaults, thefts, breaking and entering, and alcohol-related charges.

Because of the methodological problems mentioned above, the relationships of these factors and processes to sexual violence are generally less well understood than their relationships to violence generally. However, available findings are sufficient to rule out several simple causal relationships that have occasionally been suggested for violent sex offending: epilepsy, mental retardation, and some XYY or XXY chromosomal syndromes. In the paragraphs that follow we first discuss factors and processes that appear to operate differently with respect to sexual violence than to nonsexual violence, and then discuss prospects for treating violent sex offenders and preventing or mitigating incidents of sexual violence.

Deviant Sexual Preferences and Sex-Role Socialization Learning may be involved in one or both of two ways in the development of violent sexual behavior, which is usually studied using different samples and methods from those of other violent behavior. First, violent sexual preferences may be learned through experiences around the time of puberty, in which sexual arousal and release give the reward for fantasies about violent acts. Second, it may also be that, in the process of sex-role socialization, some children learn attitudes that facilitate violent sexual behavior toward women. Such attitudes include the general expectation that males are expected to behave aggressively while females behave passively and submissively (Baron and Straus, 1989; Cherry, 1983;

Russell, 1975; Weis and Borges, 1977), as well as beliefs that certain specific circumstances justify violent behavior against women (Burt, 1980; Check and Malamuth, 1983; and Kikuchi, 1988).

The available evidence is inconclusive on the role of sexual preferences as a cause of violent sexual behavior. As one would expect, phallometric tests of men in treatment have found rapists more likely than other men to respond to stimuli depicting rape, and child molesters respond more than others to stimuli depicting children. However, treatment populations may underrepresent men who sexually assault nonstrangers. Moreover, not even all sex offenders in treatment demonstrate deviant arousal patterns (Prentky, 1990), and there are no reliable estimates of the prevalence of men who are sexually aroused by violent fantasies or stimuli but never act on them.

The evidence is similarly inconclusive on the importance of sex-role socialization as a cause of sexual violence. Some surveys suggest widespread learning, by the early teenage years, of beliefs that are conducive to rape.[1] These findings are disturbing; however, their causal implications for violent sexual behavior are unclear. There is no available evidence on whether such attitudes are more prevalent among men who engage in violent sexual behavior than among men who do not. The theory of sex-role socialization does not attempt to explain violent sexual behavior against children, which is not justified by any widespread social belief system.

Pornography Some suggest that pornography encourages violent sexual behavior either by facilitating development of a deviant sexual preference for violence or by helping to inculcate beliefs about male-female sex roles that are conducive to violence (Dworkin, 1979; Morgan, 1980). Although the panel did not review the research on links between pornography and violence, a number of other scientific panels have investigated pornography and sexual violence, including the 1970 U.S. Commission on Obscenity and Pornography, the 1985 Special Committee on Pornography and Prostitution in Canada, and the 1986 U.S. Attorney General's Commission on Pornography. Scientific literature reviews prepared for these groups have generally concluded that, despite theoretical causal links, demonstrated empirical links between pornography and sex crimes in general are weak or absent. Studies of individual violent sex offenders have found no link between their offenses and their use of pornography; if anything, they do not appear to use pornography as much as the average male.

Researchers have explored the possibility that the use of pornography *with violent sexual or nonsexual content* may interact with other individual characteristics to elevate the risk of engaging in sexual violence (Donnerstein et al., 1987; Prentky, 1990). In several studies, pornography depicting either sexual or nonsexual violence against women aroused identified rapists more than nonrapists (Quinsey et al., 1984, cited in Prentky, 1990). However, both categories of subjects were also aroused by pornography that depicted consenting sexual activity. This suggests that any effect of pornography on the potential to rape may involve an interaction between violent content and some other characteristic(s) peculiar to rapists.

In short, we cannot rule out the possibility of a causal role for violent pornography. Research on this issue should be a high priority.

Sexual Abuse in Childhood Sexual abuse in childhood apparently has a very conditional causal relationship to subsequent violent sexual behavior, including child molestation (Prentky, 1990). Childhood sexual victimization is disproportionately common among child molesters, prostitutes, drug addicts, and criminals in general (Hanson and Slater, 1988). Yet prospective studies demonstrate that most victims of sexual abuse in childhood do not become child molesters (Finkelhor, 1984, cited in Prentky, 1990). Research suggests that sexual abuse in childhood plays a conditional role in a causal chain that leads to subsequent violence, depending on the precise nature of the event, the child's emotional reaction to it at the time, the emotional importance and trust that the victimized child had placed in the preexisting relationship to the molester, and the surrounding subcultural norms that reward or condemn sexual and other violent behavior (Prentky, 1990; Kaufman and Zigler, 1987; Browne and Finkelhor, 1986).

Mental Illness and Personality Disorders The relationships between violent sexual behavior and both mental illness and personality disorder are in question. Researchers consistently find that, although psychoses and major mental illnesses are rare among sex offenders, all diagnoses occasionally appear (Prentky, 1990). For perpetrators of sexual homicides, researchers such as Revitch (1965) and Dietz (1986) disagree on the prevalences of psychotic illnesses with hallucinations and/or delusions. Sex killers may be more prone to psychosis than are other individuals, although no particular diagnosis such as schizophrenia or psychopathy has been identified as characteristic. Although the term *psychopath* has sometimes been used as a label for those who commit sexual homicides, the term has been applied to a variety of different conditions over the years, and there is no scientific basis for considering psychopathy a specific adjunct of sexual homicide or of general sexual violence.

A number of studies have attempted to link specific personality characteristics to violent sexual behavior. Both lack of masculinity and extreme aggressiveness have been suggested as predictive characteristics. Current research, however, suggests that sex offenders who have been labeled as unassertive may be no different from offenders in general and that the label may reflect social class differences between prisoner and examiner rather than any inherent characteristic of sex offenders (Segal and Marshall, 1985). Antisocial personality is diagnosed in samples of sex offenders between 40 and 80 percent of the time (Prentky, 1990), and virtually all other psychopathologies co-occur at times. The personality profiles that are most common among sex offenders are also most common for general prison samples (see Megargee et al., 1988, cited in Chaiken et al., Volume 4).

Treatment Interventions Historically, the most common treatment for sex offenders has involved behavior therapy, and evaluations are largely limited to case studies in institutions. The majority of the reports available to this day are on homosexual men convicted of child molestation. The most common method of treatment has employed electric shock, paired with pictures of children, to reduce sexual arousal to children generally. The results have been mixed. In some states, the use of these techniques has been banned.

Initially, the claims of success were greater than they are today, but it is clear that behavioral techniques have an important role to play in the treatment of sex offenders. Other treatments, such as assertiveness training, anger management, life-skills training, and relapse prevention, are used more at present. Anger management appears to be an appropriate technique for dealing with both nonsexually and sexually violent individuals. The technique can help a person who is generally aggressive to deal with social problems. However, it has not been demonstrated that, in fact, such techniques can alter a long-term pattern of sexually aggressive behavior.

More fundamental issues have been raised about whether sex offenders are helped by any form of treatment. Clinicians and researchers are becoming increasingly aware that sex offenders are resistant to change. A primary factor in treatment plans now is to motivate the sex offender to change. Simpkins et al. (1989), for example, found that the more open the offender was about his sexual behavior, the more progress he made in treatment. However, substantial numbers of sex offenders deny that they have any sexual problem or resist treatment by noncompliance or dropping out.

Preventive Interventions Strategies for preventing sexual violence against acquaintances include educating boys and men about roles and responsibilities toward women, and teaching females about the dangers and how to protect themselves. However, these interventions have not been evaluated definitively for their potential to prevent sexually violent behavior. High priority should be given to conducting such evaluations.

Because the roles of sexual preferences and sex-role socialization as causes of violent potentials are still uncertain, and methods of changing them are still in development, we do not expect psychosocial interventions to reduce the incidence of sexual violence significantly in the short term. While more effective preventive interventions are being developed and tested, interim strategies for reducing the harm from sexual violence involve situational approaches to preventing events and tertiary prevention, which is intended to repair the consequences to the victim.

Situational approaches to prevention of sexual violence against strangers could operate by modifying places—for example, by installing emergency telephones and lighting, or by providing escort services. Alternatively, they could operate by altering routine activities. Examples of possible interventions for adult women include education to modify routine activities such as hitchhiking and walking alone in lonely areas, or to conceal status as single in public places. For reducing violence against child victims, training parents in how to choose caregivers and how to "street-proof" children and providing adult escorts all show promise. In this area, however, we lack systematic evaluations of effectiveness. Situational interventions for preventing nonsexual violence are discussed later in this chapter.

Yet another approach to intervention is to repair the consequences of sexual violence, which can include numerous physical and emotional symptoms. The most common forms of treatment for the psychological trauma that victims of sexual violence experience are crisis intervention counseling and psychotherapy/support groups. Other specific interventions to reduce fear and anxiety include systematic desensitization; stress inoculation training, combining education, relaxation training, and teaching of other coping skills; helping clients to identify cognitive distortions and maladaptive thought patterns and replace them with adaptive responses; and reducing the sexual anxieties and problems that the victim often experiences after a rape.

Although much of the research on these treatment strategies reports improvement in the victims, it is flawed by unclear criteria for inclusion, lack of control/comparison groups, and weak conceptualizations of treatment strategies with respect to the symptoms they target. Foa and her colleagues are currently conducting a large-scale outcome study, integrating various modalities discussed above, to identify the most effective forms of treatment.

Biological Perspectives

All human behavior, including aggression and violence, is the outcome of complex processes in the brain. Violent behaviors may result from relatively permanent conditions or from temporary states. Relatively permanent conditions may result from genetic instructions, from events during fetal or pubertal development, from perinatal accidents, or from brain trauma. Relevant temporary states may be brought on either by some purely internal activity (e.g., brain seizures) or through responses to external stressors, stimuli that produce sexual arousal, ingestion of alcohol or other psychoactive substance, or some other external stimulus. The possibility exists that some violent behavior may be prevented by modifying the precursors of the relevant neurological conditions and states.

Biological research on aggressive and violent behavior has given particular attention to the following in recent years:

(1) genetic influences;

(2) functioning of steroid hormones such as testosterone and glucocorticoids, especially their action on steroid receptors in the brain;

(3) functioning of neurotransmitters, particularly dopamine, norepinephrine, serotonin, acetylcholine, and gamma-aminobutyric acid (GABA);

(4) opioid and other neuropeptides;

(5) neuroanatomical abnormalities of certain brain morphologies;

(6) neurophysiological (i.e., brain wave) abnormalities, particularly in the temporal lobe of the brain;

(7) brain dysfunctions that interfere with language processing or cognition; and

(8) hypoglycemia and diet.

As we discuss in the following pages, correlations have been found between aggressive or violent animal or human behaviors and conditions or states in all these categories. However, interpreting these correlations is difficult. The interactions are complicated, precise measurement of brain activity is difficult, and violent behavior is rare, especially in the animal subjects used in much of the relevant research. The generalizability of experimental findings from other animal species to humans is not always straightforward, both because neurochemical functions vary across species[2] and because homologies are hard to draw between specific aggressive and predatory behaviors by animals and violent behaviors by humans. Most of the evidence concerning human subjects consists of correlations rather than experimental results. Causal interpretations are therefore tenuous. Not only are hormonal, neurotransmitter, and neurophysiological processes *involved in* violent and nonviolent behavior; these functions can be changed as *consequences of* violent behavior.

Given these difficulties, it should not be surprising that no patterns precise enough to be considered reliable biological markers for violent behavior have yet been identified. Researchers have, however, identified some particularly promising areas for further research that may eventually lead to nonintrusive diagnostic and prognostic indices of individuals' potentials for aggression and perhaps to preventive interventions without unacceptable side effects.

Many of these findings are summarized in the following pages. Pharmacological links between violent behavior and the use of alcohol and other psychoactive drugs are discussed in Chapter 4. More complete treatments and supporting citations can be found in Volume 2 of the panel's report. Existing findings leave open many questions that are important from scientific or policy perspectives, or both. Recommendations for research to fill these gaps appear in Chapter 8.

Genetic Influences

Correlations in studies of humans fairly consistently demonstrate genetic influences on individual potentials for antisocial behavior and juvenile delinquency (Bohman et al., 1982; Christiansen, 1977; Cloninger and Gottesman, 1987; Mednick et al., 1984). The role of genetic mechanisms in criminal and violent behavior has been examined in three studies of twins and adoptees, using data from Scandinavian countries (Bohman et al., 1982; Cloninger and Gottesmann, 1987; Mednick et al., 1984). These studies suggest at most a weak role for genetic processes in influencing potentials for violent behavior: the correlations and concordances of behavior in two of the three studies are consistent with a positive genetic effect, but are statistically insignificant.

The different findings with respect to the two categories of behavior raise the possibility that some genetic process that is relevant to violence may be concealed because violent behavior is rare and/or etiologically heterogeneous. In any event, the implications of these findings to violence patterns in the United States are uncertain because the measures of heritability derived from relatively homogeneous Scandinavian populations are not readily extrapolated to U.S. society.

By analogy, some evidence suggests that individuals may differ in their genetic predispositions to at least some forms of alcoholism (Cloninger et al., 1978; Plomin, 1989). That variation can be expected to have a greater effect on the distribution of alcoholism rates when alcohol is more readily available and inexpensive, and where alcoholism prevention programs are less successful, for example. Similarly, the effects of any variation in genetic predisposition to aggressive or violent behavior can be expected to depend on such factors as families' responses to aggressive behavior by their developing children, the availability of weapons, and the financial, social, and legal punishments and rewards for violent behavior.

Well-documented principles of behavior genetics have at least three implications for any genetic process that may be found in the future to affect potentials for violent behavior. First, any such process would have to involve many genes and substantial environmental variation, rather than any simple chromosomal syndrome that might be useful as a marker or risk factor. Second, because human gene pools change over periods of time measured in generations, and because gene pools within any country are so diverse, genetic processes *alone* cannot explain either short-run fluctuations in violence rates over time or variation in violence rates across countries. Third, in studies of psychological and social influences on violent behavior, the designs should collect the data on parents and siblings that are needed to control for confounding genetic influences, and greater use should be made of samples of twins, sibling pairs, and adoptees to develop a more precise understanding of the relevant genetic processes.

Over the past 40 years, occasional case studies of sexually deviant individuals and families have raised the possibility that some simple XXY or XYY chromosomal syndrome may transmit a potential for sexually violent behavior (Baker and Stoller, 1968; Baker et al., 1970; Bartlett, 1968; Pasqualini et al., 1957; see also reviews by Kessler and Moos, 1970; and by Owen, 1972). Case studies provide only weak tests of this hypothesis, and the panel is aware of no study using modern behavior genetic designs that has tested for genetic influences on sexual violence. In view of the general difficulties of establishing genetic relationships to rare behaviors that are also subject to environmental influences, however, it would be premature to rule out the possibility that some complex interaction involving multiple genes and life experiences may account for some instances of sexual violence.

In rodents, the successful establishment of aggressive and nonaggressive strains of a species, as well as comparisons across strains, demonstrates significant heritability of aggression (Carey, Volume 2). However, animal studies also show that tendencies toward aggression can be modified by experience, contextual cues, and the social environment.

Hormonal Mechanisms

Because testosterone is the principal androgenic hormone (i.e., the principal hormone in producing masculine characteristics), it has been more frequently studied in relation to sexual violence than to other violent behaviors. Studies find high prevalences of elevated testosterone levels in clinical samples of violent sex offenders, and there is some suggestion that this correlation increases with the violence of the crime. However, the correlation is probably confounded by alcohol abuse, which modifies testosterone levels in complex ways and is also associated with violent behavior.

Animal and human research suggests that prenatal and perinatal exposure to abnormal levels of androgenic hormones permanently alters the relationship between aggressive behavior and steroid hormones (see Brain, Volume 2, Tables 1, 3, and 4, for supporting citations). In female mice and rhesus monkeys, greater adult aggression has resulted from injections of testosterone during pregnancy or at the time of birth. Follow-ups of human children find that girls who were accidentally exposed to inappropriate androgenic hormones during fetal development display an unusually high long-term tendency toward aggression, while boys prenatally exposed to antiandrogenic steroids show decreased aggressiveness. It is not clear, however, whether the correlations in humans reflect direct hormonal influences on behavior or some psychosocial interaction involving peers' reactions to abnormal genital development caused by the abnormal hormone exposure.

Some correlations have been cited as suggesting that testosterone may promote immediate aggressive responses to provocative stimuli. However, these patterns are weaker in nonhuman primates than in lower animals, and weaker still in humans. Moreover, studies of humans provide fairly strong evidence of reverse causal relationships: that being subject to aggression or being defeated in competition decreases human androgen levels, and that winning a competition increases them (see, e.g., Brain, Volume 2).

Two kinds of studies offer evidence on how manipulations of hormone levels affect violent behavior. First, antiandrogen drugs show some promise as adjunct therapy for violent sex offenders, but the effect seems to depend more on reducing the sex drive than on dampening the violent behavior. Second, studies of the effects of administering synthetic derivatives of steroids (i.e., anabolic steroids) suggest that, despite occasional anecdotes concerning athletes in training, injections of anabolic steroids exert at most a weak influence accounting for little variation in violent behavior.

Recent studies suggest that the functioning of two other sex hormones—dehydroepiandrosterone sulfate (DHEAS) and luteinizing hormone—may be associated with unusual sexual behavior, including sexual violence.[3] These include both basal studies, which compare hormone levels in peripheral blood samples, and challenge tests, in which a hormone is injected to stimulate the brain and reactions are measured. Animal studies suggest that maximal information is extracted when one has both kinds of tests, because the interactions between resting levels and reactions to challenges are not yet well understood. The relationships between violent behavior and these sex hormones need more systematic investigation.

Neurotransmitters and Receptors

Of at least 50 known neurotransmitters, 4 have been studied most thoroughly in relation to aggressive behavior (primarily in animals, but occasionally in humans): dopamine, norepinephrine, serotonin, and GABA. Findings from these studies are reviewed in Volume 2, and the following discussion is based on those sources.

Among other neurological functions, dopamine activates neural processes for pleasure and reward; cocaine, amphetamine, and other psychoactive drugs stimulate these processes (see Chapter 4 for further discussion of drug effects on dopamine receptors). Although evidence from animal studies points to large natural changes in brain dopamine systems during and following aggressive and defensive behavior, there is no evidence on whether similar responses occur in humans. It is possible that the brain dopamine activity in animals is one of the rewarding aspects of aggression, but specific markers for dopamine involvement in any specific type of aggression are not available.

Antipsychotic drugs, especially those that antagonize the D2 subtype of dopamine receptor are frequently used to quell acute violent outbursts or as long-term "chemical restraint" for violence-prone persons confined in institutions. However, these drugs alter behaviors other than aggression and, as with cocaine and amphetamine, chronic use of these drugs produces an array of neurological problems (see Miczek et al., Volume 2, Chapter 3).

Norepinephrine transmission and its contribution to the "flight or fight" syndrome has been well documented for decades. Researchers have recently identified specific brain regions in which this activity takes place. Noradrenergic activity, however, occurs in conjunction with high levels of arousal generally, and no specific noradrenergic marker in any brain region has been identified for violent or aggressive behavior.

In the past dozen years the most significant clinical use of noradrenergic drugs has involved those that inhibit the activity of beta-type adrenergic receptors (beta-blockers). These drugs are used to manage violent behavior by hospitalized retarded, schizophrenic, and autistic patients. However, their aggression-reducing effect may occur through their actions on certain subtypes of serotonin receptors, and their behavioral effects are not specific to aggression. Clonidine, a drug that targets alpha-type adrenergic receptors, has been used to manage irritability, aggression, and defensive acts during withdrawal from addiction to alcohol, nicotine, and opiates.

Serotonin is the neurotransmitter that has been most intensively studied in animal and human research on violent behavior. Marked changes in serotonin synthesis, release, and metabolism have been observed in individuals of many nonhuman animal species that have repeatedly engaged in violent or aggressive behavior. But the substantial variation in serotonin functions across species makes extrapolations from one species to another, including humans, problematic.

Since the late 1970s, several researchers using human subjects have reported inverse correlations between serotonin concentrations in blood or spinal fluid and various measures of aggressive, impulsive, or suicidal behavior. Recent studies of Finnish males by Virkkunen, Linnoila, and associates (Virkkunen et al., 1989; Linnoila et al., 1989) find that a complex interaction among serotonin concentration, alcoholism, responsivity to glucose challenge (a test for hypoglycemia), and aspects of monoamine metabolism may be related to these behaviors. More generally, a number of correlative studies reviewed by Ellis (1991) suggest that low monoamine oxidase (MAO) blood concentrations may indicate elevated potentials for suicide, sensation seeking, impulsiveness, alcoholism, and criminality. More consistent replications and a better understanding of the relationship between measures in blood, spinal fluid, and relevant brain regions are needed before these factors can be accepted as biological markers for violent behavior.

Certain drugs that act on the serotonergic system have been found in animal trials to reduce aggressive behavior and to decrease anxiety in humans. Current clinical research with novel drugs acting on serotonin receptor subtypes promises to reveal specific antiaggressive effects in humans with fewer side effects. Beta-blockers and lithium may achieve their antiaggressive effects through action on these serotonin receptor subtypes.

GABA was long thought to act as a neurotransmitter that inhibited aggressive behavior in animals. The latest research finds that GABA activity has excitatory as well as inhibitory actions in many discrete brain regions, but no pattern provides a marker for aggressive or violent behavior in animals or humans.

The $GABA_A$ receptors are of particular clinical interest as the site of action for benzodiazepines, one of the most important antianxiety drugs used to reduce aggression and to sedate very agitated individuals. Evidence from animal and human studies documents the calming effects of these drugs for most persons. However, under certain conditions, these drugs occasionally lead to violent outbursts called "paradoxical rage." $GABA_A$ receptors are also one of the targets of alcohol action in the brain, and these receptors represent a promising site for pharmacological interventions to reduce alcohol-related violent behavior.

Neuroanatomical Abnormalities

Experiments involving electrical stimulation of specific brain regions in cats have established two distinct types of aggressive behavior, predation and affective defensive aggression (i.e., "rage"), which involve different circuits of neural activity. The limbic system and perhaps secondarily the cerebral cortex appear to modulate both types of behavior (see Mirsky and Siegel, Volume 2). These findings raise the possibility that a similar typology may apply to human aggression, perhaps involving the same neural pathways. However, concern for human subjects prevents researchers from using the techniques needed to assess how applicable neurological models of feline or other animal aggression are in classifying or explaining human aggression.

Available evidence from small samples of humans also points tentatively to structures in the limbic system, especially the amygdala and medial hypothalamus, as brain sites associated with certain violent behaviors. However, this evidence has been seriously questioned, in part because of the general difficulty of studying the limbic system directly. Perhaps more importantly, virtually all the human subjects were observed in the course of treatment for diagnosed brain abnormalities or for highly unusual histories of chronic unprovoked violent behavior. There is no sound basis for generalizing from either of these atypical groups to statements about brain regions that might be involved in violent behavior by persons in the general population.

Neurophysiological Abnormalities

Several studies suggest rare episodes of violence either before or between seizures associated with temporal lobe epilepsy (Mirsky and Siegel, Volume 2). However, the question remains unanswered as to whether patients with seizure disorders have greater or smaller potentials for violence than the general population. New, less intrusive brain imaging techniques may facilitate research that would provide better understanding of the brain structures involved in aggressive and violent behavior in the general population.

A link between abnormal, not necessarily violent, sexual behavior and brain disorders was suggested by Kolarsky et al. (1967), who found that among epileptics, unusual sexual behavior occurred more commonly when neurophysiological abnormalities appeared in the temporal lobe than in other sites. These findings were later supported by some studies of animals and, most recently, by studies using advanced tomographic techniques that found a high prevalence of temporal lobe impairment among humans who engage in sexually anomalous behaviors (Langevin, 1990). Preliminary research suggests that men with sadistic sexual preferences show temporal lobe anomalies more often than do other offenders. These correlations cannot be said to show either that temporal lobe abnormalities *cause* violent sexual behavior or that epilepsy is a risk factor for violent or nonviolent sex offending.

Other Brain Dysfunctions

Several kinds of indirect evidence suggest that abnormalities of brain functioning increase the risks of violent behavior, although no specific neurophysiological marker has yet been identified (see Mirsky and Siegel, Volume 2, on which the following discussion is based). First, a large number of studies indicate that neuropsychological deficits in memory, attention, and language/verbal skills—which sometimes follow from limbic system damage—are common in children who exhibit violent or aggressive behavior (see, e.g., Mungas, 1988; Miller, 1987; Piacentini, 1987; Lewis et al., 1988). While this correlation could reflect some direct relationship between limbic system damage and aggressive behavior, it is more likely to reflect less direct results of distorted social interactions with peers resulting from impaired communication skills, or to arise from frustration over the inability to compete successfully with peers in cognitive tasks.

Second, certain peripheral measures of nervous system activity such as heart rate and skin conductance have been found to differ on average between samples of normal controls and samples of criminals, delinquents, conduct-disordered children, and psychopaths (Kagan, 1989; Raine and Venables, 1988a; Raine et al., 1990a; Siddle et al., 1973; Wadsworth, 1976). Third, abnormal patterns of brain electrical activities—slow waves and the P300 component of event-related brain potentials—have been found in samples of incarcerated criminals and psychopaths (see, e.g., Williams, 1969; Hare, 1978; Raine and Venables, 1988b; Raine et al., 1990b). The appropriate interpretation of these patterns is not entirely clear because neither the samples nor the environments reflect the community. The findings, however, raise questions that can be more clearly resolved through research that uses new technology for brain scans, especially magnetic resonance imaging (MRI) and positron emission tomography (PET). Such research is expensive and subject to human subjects requirements.

From the standpoint of designing violence control interventions, perhaps the most useful information about brain dysfunctions and violent behavior is the extent to which they arise from social-environmental conditions. Some individuals' dysfunctions may well be a result rather than a cause of aggressive behavior: they may originate in head injuries inflicted by others in retaliation. However, research reviewed by Mirsky and Siegel (Volume 2, Table 13) points to the following environmental correlates of cognitive deficits, hyperactivity, and other precursors of violent behavior: exposure to environmental lead (e.g., in air contaminated by leaded fuels, from paint in older houses, from plumbing systems) and maternal use of opiates, cocaine, alcohol, and tobacco during pregnancy.

In addition to other likely benefits for children's health, interventions to reduce substance abuse by pregnant women and to reduce small children's environmental lead exposure should be considered potential long-range preventive interventions for violence. However, health education is frequently insufficient by itself to alter expectant mothers' behavior during pregnancy (Institute of Medicine, 1985).

Hypoglycemia and Diet

Several kinds of studies suggest possible relationships between aggressive behavior and sugar intake and metabolism, but the interpretation of findings is problematic (see more detailed reviews in Kanarek, Volume 2; Venables and Raine, 1987). For example, some studies find that interventions to reduce sugar consumption reduce antisocial behavior by institutionalized juvenile offenders, and some studies find correlations between sugar intake and hyperactivity in young children; however, the findings are inconsistent. Moreover, outside controlled settings, children's sugar intake may be related to family characteristics such as socioeconomic status and parental supervision, which are also correlated with aggressive behavior (see Kanarek, Volume 2).

Similarly, hypoglycemia (i.e., low blood glucose levels and associated behavioral symptoms) is relatively common in violent offenders (Virkkunen, 1986), and the peak time of day for assaults in prison coincides with the peak time for acute symptoms of hypoglycemia. Although these findings suggest that some relationship exists, they should not be interpreted as evidence of a direct causal link, because at least two alternative explanations cannot be ruled out. First, alcohol use increases susceptibility to hypoglycemia and is also related to the occurrence of violent events. Second, hypoglycemia has also been theoretically linked to both low heart rate and electroencephalogram (EEG) slowing, which are common among violent offenders.

Occasional claims have surfaced that various food additives (e.g., artificial colors or preservatives) are associated with hyperactivity or other precursors of violent behavior (see, e.g., Feingold, 1975). Although open trials in family settings tend to support these claims, carefully controlled double-blind experiments do not. Such relationships may exist, but they appear to affect at most a small fraction of preschool children.

Occasional studies have found correlations between violent behavior or nondisease mortality (including intentional injury) and cholesterol intake or levels. These findings are mixed and therefore inconclusive, and the studies have generally failed to control for other behavioral changes that may have accompanied changes in cholesterol intake (see Kanarek, Volume 2).

Some studies of rodents, cats, and humans suggest that nicotine temporarily reduces aggressive behavior. Of course, the potential use of nicotine to control such behavior should not be considered independently of the enormous health risks of tobacco smoking (Miczek et al., Volume 2).

Developmental and Biomedical Evaluation and Research Needs

We have presented a number of findings about the biological and psychosocial development of individual potentials for violent behavior. A number of questions that still remain unanswered either have been mentioned or are implicit in the discussion. We recapitulate them here.

Aggression and Violence

Our discussion of the psychosocial and biological development of potentials for violent behavior points to three promising intervention strategies that could begin at least in early childhood, and in one case before birth:

(1) prevention of brain injuries, substance abuse by pregnant women, exposure to lead, and other prenatal, perinatal, and postnatal events linked to brain dysfunctions that increase individuals' potential for aggression;

(2) cognitive-behavioral preventive interventions including parent training, school-based antibullying programs, social skills training, and interventions that stress the undesirability of aggression, teach nonviolent conflict resolution, and promote viewing of television programs that emphasize prosocial behavior; and

(3) prevention of school failure through preschool educational

enrichment and through kindergarten tutoring by specially trained high school students.

These strategies are complementary rather than mutually exclusive: each can be expected to prevent some children from developing potentials for violent behavior, but none will be universally effective. Long-term evaluation programs are needed to learn how to adapt these intervention modes to specific subpopulations of children and to specific types of aggressive and violent behavior.

Sexual Violence

Very little is known about how potentials for sexual violence develop, how violent sex offenders differ from the general male population in terms of either sexual preferences or socialization toward women, or how the occurrence and recurrence of violent sexual behavior can be prevented. We place particular priority on four sets of research questions:

(1) What are the roles of genetic-environmental interactions, sexual abuse in childhood, the learning of tolerant attitudes toward rape, and chronic alcohol abuse in the development of individual potentials for violent sexual behavior?

(2) What is the role of violent deviant sexual preferences in causing violent sexual acts? How do these preferences differ between samples of known violent sex offenders and other samples? What events produce these violent preferences? What role, if any, does violent pornography play in their development? Are there specific neurological, endocrine, or genetic markers either for them or for an elevated potential to act on them? What subpopulations, if any, would benefit from hormone therapy?

(3) What preventive and educational strategies show promise of reducing sexual violence involving intimates, acquaintances, or strangers?

(4) Several psychosocial interventions—relapse prevention therapy, assertiveness therapy, and anger management therapy—show some promise of changing some individuals' violent deviant sexual preferences, especially when combined with pharmacological interventions that reduce the intensity of the sex drive. Systematic evaluation is needed, involving randomized experiments where practicable,[4] to assess the effectiveness of these interventions in preventing the recurrence of sexually violent acts.

Improved classification and measurement are essential for making progress on these issues, but they present special problems in the context of sexual violence. Classification systems should be refined and improved to facilitate both better developmental understanding and more effective treatment. In addition, special priority should be placed on improved classification of violent sexual acts against intimates that do not routinely lead to institutionalization.

Advancing Biomedical Understanding

For many people, attention to genetic, neurophysiological, neurochemical, and neuroendocrine processes that underlie violent behavior raises concerns about the potential for ethically unacceptable future preventive interventions. The specters of eugenics, preemptive incarceration based on individuals' biomedical profiles, and maintaining classroom discipline with drugs that dull children's creativity are all occasionally raised. Actually, as we have explained in previous pages, better biomedical understanding of violence has added violence prevention to the list of justifications for rather benign interventions with families, such as teaching pregnant women to avoid drug use and new mothers to protect their children from head injuries, and interventions in communities, such as reducing children's exposure to lead.

A primary dilemma to accumulating better biomedical understanding is that less intrusive and more broadly accepted biomedical research methods tend to provide information that is more remote from the causative brain mechanisms. For example, analyzing urine or hair samples imposes negligible burdens on subjects, but the results confound relevant neurochemical processes with unrelated events that occurred long before or long after an episode of violent behavior. Sampling blood—a somewhat more intrusive procedure—eliminates some confounding influences, but abnormal blood concentrations of serotonin metabolites, for example, may reflect serotonin production, metabolism, or excretion effects *resulting from* violent behavior together with any other life events rather than any causal effect specific for violence. Spinal taps—an uncomfortable procedure that involves some risk—produce measures that mirror ongoing brain activity somewhat better, but they are unrelated to the initiation or termination of violent acts and cannot distinguish the brain region in which the activity occurred. Modern brain imaging techniques locate brain activity somewhat more precisely but demand several hours of subjects' time, involve the injection of radioactively labeled tracers into the bloodstream, and sometimes trigger claustrophobic episodes in some people.

Decisions to undertake specific research projects should balance the burden on subjects against the value of the information that may be obtained and the likelihood of success in obtaining that information. Clearly, for obtaining any given piece of information, less invasive procedures are preferred over more invasive ones. Among research projects that impose equal burdens on subjects, those that are intended to obtain more specific information about neurological or neuroendocrine functioning and behavior, or that study responses to demands and challenges, should be preferred over studies of more peripheral processes or of resting levels of chemicals or neurological activity. Specific challenge tests are needed to distinguish among current biomedical theories of aggressive and violent behavior, such as the serotonin deficit, imbalance in the autonomic nervous system, and a physiological basis of temperament—all of which have partial support, at least, from animal studies.

As an important source of information about the basic genetic, neurobiologic, developmental, and environmental factors that determine aggressive and violent behavior, proper use of animal models is a means of reducing research burdens on human subjects. The systematic study of animal models for adaptive, predatory, and pathological forms of aggressive behavior represents the primary means to gain insights into all the relevant neurobiologic mechanisms, including neurotransmitter systems and neurophysiological processes. In turn, these insights are a basis for exploring and designing effective interventions.

Extrapolations from animal models of aggression and violent behavior to the human condition need to take species differences into account. The most promising findings are based on work with several animal species, at least one of which ought to be a primate species. Particularly profitable lines of inquiry for animal models are those that focus on the individual organism, its genetic predispositions, its development, and its interactions with social units and environmental events.

The critical ethical dilemma of experimental research on aggression and violent behavior is the trade-off between experimental preparations with high realism and face validity versus the demand for protection of research subjects against stress and pain. It is unacceptable for experimental biomedical research with humans to achieve high face validity in studies of violent behavior. Therefore, it is necessary to develop and implement animal models, often as a means of building an empirical basis for subsequent research that places acceptable but nonnegligible burdens on human subjects. Each study of animal or human subjects needs to be designed to inflict the least possible stress and harm on the subjects without invalidating the information to be obtained.

VIOLENCE AND SOCIAL PROCESSES

Individuals, including those who behave violently, live and act in collective social units such as families, gangs, markets, voluntary organizations, and communities. People who commit crimes are influenced by a host of factors beyond their personal and family characteristics (Gottfredson and Taylor, 1986; Robins, 1978). How do social processes affect an individual's potential for violent behavior? In this section we draw on a diversity of research to discuss factors and processes in communities, neighborhoods, and other social units that are related to violent crime. We explore the links between poverty and violence, and the possible roles of culture in poor communities. The section closes with a discussion of recent research on youth gangs and violence, as an illustration of how collective social units both shape and are shaped by the communities of which they are a part.

We know a great deal more about the extent and nature of violence and related behavior *within* the individual and social levels of explanation than we do about relationships that cross those levels. Most studies focus on a single level of explanation, or on rates of violence for categories of individuals or areal units, rather than linking them. Although the lack of adequate data is responsible for this state of affairs, adequate theory to guide data collection and analysis is equally at fault. For these reasons, we must draw on a broad range of studies and on the most persuasive empirical findings and theoretical arguments concerning the manner in which different levels of explanation relate to one another.

How Do Ethnic Status and Poverty Affect Violence?

Chapter 2 explains that blacks, Hispanics, and American Indians are at greater risk than whites for becoming victims of violent crime. However, a look behind this simple pattern reveals a more complex picture.

The panel looked for evidence on violence rates for the smallest, most homogeneous areas for which data are available—census tracts.[5] Four studies were found in which the dependent variable was the homicide victimization rate and the independent variables were measures of the racial or ethnic composition and of the economic status of the census tract. The studies covered three cities in Ohio (Muscat, 1988), New Orleans (Lowry et al., 1988), Atlanta (Centerwall's, 1984 reanalysis of Munford et al., 1976), and Boston. All are epidemiological studies of recent vintage. Although these studies were not designed to answer the question we pose, are of uneven quality, and focus on different types of homicide, they are nevertheless the best evidence available.

In all four studies, there is an interaction between ethnic status and socioeconomic status. At low socioeconomic levels, blacks have much higher risks of becoming homicide victims than do whites. At higher socioeconomic levels, the difference between blacks and whites disappears and even reverses in one of the studies. Although the details of each study vary somewhat, the results are generally the same. The relationship is illustrated in Figures 3-1 and 3-2, which depict the New Orleans and Atlanta findings.

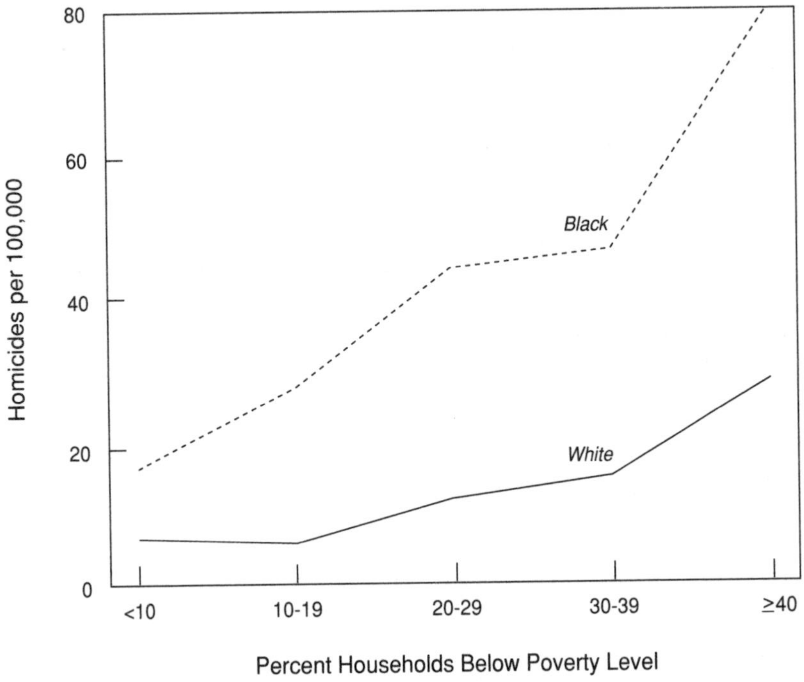

FIGURE 3-1 Mean annual homicide rate, New Orleans (1979, 1982, 1985, 1986).

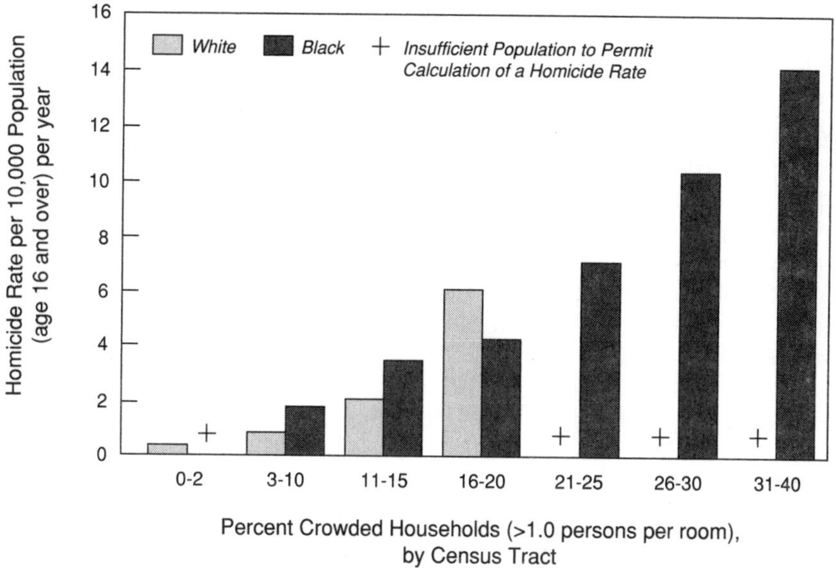

FIGURE 3-2 Intraracial domestic homicide rates, Atlanta, 1971-1972. SOURCES: Population data—1970 U.S. census; homicide data—Atlanta Police Department and Medical Examiner Offices, Fulton and DeKalb counties, Georgia.

Links Between Poverty and Violence

The interaction described above suggests that socioeconomic status, as measured using some indicator of poverty, is a useful starting point for understanding and controlling violence. More than 50 years ago, the classic work of Shaw and McKay (1942) on the ecology of crime and delinquency led to the conclusion that three structural factors—low economic status, ethnic heterogeneity, and residential mobility—resulted in the disruption of community cohesion and organization, which in turn contributed to variations in crime and delinquency among communities. This conclusion was buttressed by the fact that high rates of delinquency persisted in communities characterized by these factors over many years despite high population turnover in the communities, which changed the ethnic and racial character of their residents.

Researchers since then who have studied community-level variations have found associations between poverty and high rates of official delinquency (Gordon, 1967), but few studies focused specifically on violent crime. Those that did continued to find that homicides were disproportionately concentrated in areas of poverty (Bullock, 1955; Bensing and Schroeder, 1960; Beasley and Antunes, 1974; Mladenka and Hill, 1976). This pattern has held up regardless of which ethnic group occupied the poor areas. Three of these studies examined violent crime in Houston (Bullock; Beasley and Antunes; Mladenka and Hill). Like Shaw and McKay, each reported high correlations between violent crime rates and measures of poverty. Areas in Houston with high rates of violent crime were also characterized by high population density and a high proportion of black residents.

Recent research finds correlations between violence rates and many community characteristics that are distinct from, but related to, socioeconomic status: concentrations of poverty, residential mobility and population turnover, family disruption, high density in housing and population, features of local social organization (e.g., low density of friends and acquaintances, few social resources, weak intergenerational ties in families and communities, weak control of street-corner peer groups, and low organizational participation in community life), and opportunities associated with violence (such as gun density, drug distribution networks, and the location of nonhousehold activities conducive to violence) (summarized by Sampson and Lauritsen, Volume 3).

But finding statistical relationships between community characteristics and violence still does not explain how they are related to poverty and, in turn, how they increase violence. And it does not explain why race differences in violent crime rates tend to disappear when poverty is included as an explanation. In the next section we briefly review available findings that link violence rates not only to poverty levels in a community, but also to specific dimensions of poverty.

Dimensions of Poverty

One reason it is so difficult to disentangle the effects of race/ethnic status from community influences is because poor whites and poor blacks live in areas that are very different—economically and otherwise—making simple comparisons impossible. In 1980, for example, in the five largest U.S. cities, 85 percent of poor blacks lived in poverty areas, compared with only 30 percent of poor whites; nearly 40 percent of poor blacks lived in areas characterized by *extreme* poverty, compared with 7 percent of poor whites.

Another source of difficulty is that observed relationships between particular communities and violence, by race, necessarily reflect differences between communities that are not—and probably cannot—be accurately measured, statistically controlled, or otherwise fully taken into account. Compared with whites, the "ecological niches" in which poor blacks live are disadvantaged in ways that defy easy measurement, such as job quality, access to high-status social networks, and exposure to conventional role models (Wilson, 1987:58-60).

Despite these difficulties, in broad and summary terms the research finds that community influences often *combine with poverty and with one another* to produce high rates of violent crime. Although some studies report that the racial composition of communities has a direct effect on violence, virtually all studies report that the effects of race are also mediated by other factors, such as family structure and community change (Sampson and Lauritsen, Volume 3). When these factors are controlled statistically, the effects of race and ethnic status diminish or disappear altogether.

This argument, it should be emphasized, is not theoretically limited to black-white comparisons. More data and research have been devoted to such comparisons, in part because blacks are the largest ethnic/racial minority in the United States. To the extent that the community-level correlates of violence are found to characterize other ethnic and racial groups, the expectation is that they too will experience high rates of violence. Empirical evidence is lacking, in part because, as we note in Chapter 2, the relevant statistical systems have only recently begun to record other ethnic designations.

Community Characteristics Researchers have identified a number of community characteristics that are related to violence rates. For example, in studies of neighborhood rates of violent crime, measures of the density of multiunit housing, residential mobility, and the prevalence of disrupted family structures generally accounted for more variation than did measures of poverty and income inequality (Sampson, 1983, 1985, 1987). Another study, of 57 neighborhoods in three cities, found a similar link between levels of violence and residential mobility in poor, but not in affluent, neighborhoods (Smith and Jarjoura, 1988:40, cited in Sampson and Lauritsen, Volume 3). High population density was associated not only with high rates of violence but also with high rates of poverty, teenagers in the population, single-parent households, and nonwhite populations—all commonly found correlates of violence.

The interactions among these factors make it difficult to estimate their independent effects using data on a cross section of neighborhoods at a single point in time. However, in a study of changes in violence rates from 1970 to 1980 in 277 Baltimore neighborhoods, Taylor and Covington (1988) found sharp increases not only in areas that experienced increasing concentrations of people in poverty but also in neighborhoods in which gentrification improved housing characteristics and altered family composition. The suggestion that neighborhood change per se is associated with increased violence levels is consistent with the theory that disturbances in *social organization* of any kind are a factor in increasing neighborhood violence levels. In a study of changes in homicide rates in metropolitan areas and states from 1960 to 1980, Land et al. (1990) report similar findings for poverty, income inequality, and family disorganization.

Although it is difficult to isolate specifically how these factors affect individual behavior, including violence, the National Research Council's Committee on National Urban Policy marshaled impressive evidence that in recent decades poverty and its correlates have become increasingly concentrated in inner-city neighborhoods (Lynn and McGeary, 1990; McGeary and Lynn, 1988). This concentration has occurred through changes at the regional level—for example, migration from the South to certain northern cities, especially New York, Chicago, Philadelphia, Newark, and Detroit—and through changes in the structure of economic and other opportunities across neighborhoods within large- and medium-sized metropolitan areas (Wilson, 1991:2; Jargowsky and Bane, 1990:44-48).

Social and Economic Structure and Organization Several studies demonstrate the special vulnerability of urban minorities to fundamental economic changes in some cities and to population changes within specific communities (Wilson, 1987; Hagedorn, 1988; Sullivan, 1989; Anderson, 1990). Primary among these, Wilson argues, are "*structural economic changes*, such as the shift from goods-producing to service-producing industries, the increasing polarization of the labor market into low-wage and high-wage sectors, technological innovations, and the relocation of manufacturing industries out of the central cities" (1987:39).

The "concentration effects" of ghetto poverty have been a central focus of William Julius Wilson's (1987) work. One effect of the increased concentration, Wilson argues, has been the social isolation of inner cities from mainstream institutions. As the black middle class grew during the 1980s, many middle- and working-class black families found it possible to move out of the ghetto into areas with more desirable housing and other neighborhood amenities. In turn, their leaving removed an important "social buffer" that might have deflected "the full impact of the . . . prolonged and increasing joblessness that plagued inner-city neighborhoods in the 1970s and early 1980s" (Wilson, 1990:75).

Community residents left behind in areas of extreme poverty have experienced high levels of family disruption, poor access to prenatal and child care, and low infant birthweight—factors that earlier in this chapter we described as developmental precursors of aggressive and violent behavior. Recent research confirms their association with violence.

These same communities and families also experience high levels of family disruption via divorce, desertion, and female-headed families; the breakdown of community networks of informal social control (Wallace and Wallace, 1990; Sampson, 1985; Messner and Tardiff, 1986; Smith and Jarjoura, 1988; all reviewed in Sampson and Lauritsen, Volume 3); and changes in routine activities that increase their risks of violent victimization.

The breakdown of social organization is exemplified in Furstenberg's (1990) comparison of families in two poor Philadelphia communities. One is a black housing project in which parents characteristically practiced an individualistic style of parental management. Mistrust among neighbors was high, and "mothers complained of their inability to distinguish neighborhood youth from strangers, and they bemoaned the alienated sense in which local parents ignored the open misbehavior of youth in the community." Despite enormous expenditures of time and energy devoted to their children, "parents seemed unable to band together to solve common problems." The other community was white and poor, but was characterized by strong social networks among families, "even those with poor parenting skills" (p. 24). Here, the "high degree of observability keeps youth in check. The task of parents inside the home is reinforced by the support rendered by other parents outside the home" (p. 25). Sampson concludes that parenting is much more than the "individualistic process that contemporary society makes it out to be" (p. 26).

The link between levels of social organization and violence is also illustrated in a comparison of military and nonmilitary communities. For black males, the homicide death rate for soldiers was only 9 percent of the civilian rate for the same age category; the difference between military and nonmilitary whites was somewhat smaller (Rothberg et al., 1990). While this striking difference in the risk of homicide could be due to soldiers' higher levels of education, the researchers who conducted the study emphasize the control of violence by community regulation of lifestyle, noting the importance of both formal and informal regulations in controlling people's behavior.

The diminution of adults' ability to supervise children in their families and neighborhoods exemplifies a breakdown of what Coleman (1990) has called social capital—the quality of intergenerational relationships. Research is needed to test the lack of social capital as a causal factor in violence.

Community Culture Poverty, high turnover in population, and other features of socially disorganized communities affect community culture by impeding communication, erecting barriers to common values, and making effective collective action to achieve such values virtually impossible (Skogan, 1990). Under such circumstances in an isolated community, widely accepted cultural values become "unviable," and an oppositional culture may begin to shape what are considered to be appropriate standards of behavior (Anderson, 1978).

In Wilson's words: "As the basic institutions declined, the social organization of inner-city neighborhoods (sense of community, positive neighborhood identification, and explicit norms and sanctions against aberrant behavior) likewise declined. This process magnified the effects of living in highly concentrated urban poverty areas—effects that are manifested in ghetto-specific culture and behavior" (1987:138).

A vivid picture is provided by Elijah Anderson's ethnographic study of adjoining community areas in Philadelphia: Northton, a black community formerly of mixed socioeconomic status, now increasingly occupied by the ghetto poor, and The Village, a gentrifying mixed-race community. Anderson (1991) analyzed the complex oppositional culture—widely shared in some poor black communities—that has resulted from the unique historical circumstances, structural economic changes, and institutional failures experienced by the ghetto poor he has observed.

The street culture requires skills utterly unlike those required in the service economy. While workers employed in the old manufacturing economy could act tough and use coarse language, these behaviors limit opportunities for employment in the service economy.

Drugs exacerbate the problems. "The drug economy is in many ways a parallel, or a parody, of the service economy (with an element of glamour thrown in). Rival drug dealers claim particular street corners to sell their wares. Corners are literally bought and sold, and they belong to the one who has the power to claim the space for the time being; such claims may result in territorial disputes that are sometimes settled by violence. . . . For many young men the drug economy is an employment agency superimposed on the existing gang network. Young men who 'grew up' in the gang, but now are without clear opportunities, easily become involved; they fit themselves into its structure, manning its drug houses and selling drugs on street corners. With the money from these 'jobs,' they support themselves and help their families, at times buying fancy items to impress others" (Anderson, 1990:244).

The language of the street legitimizes and enhances involvement in the underground economy. Young people speak of crime as "going to work" and "getting paid" (see also Sullivan, 1989). Groups of young black males have been observed to chant "a beat, a beat, a beat" as they build themselves up to assault and robbery.

In another example of social capital deterioration, older people, even "old heads" who once sought to guide the young along conventional, law-abiding lines, feel threatened, let down, and compromised, and many are ambivalent about the criminal behavior of the young, as the following field observation suggests (Anderson, 1990:243):

> Outside the barbershop on a corner in Northton, old heads . . . steal a closer look at what "must be" a drug dealer. Self-conscious, they try to hide their interest, paying a kind of civil inattention to the show. Others, including a group of young boys nearby, have come over for a look at the "bad ride," but for them the driver is really the main attraction. He is a dealer. That is the way they make sense of the charismatic, close-cropped young black man literally "dripping with gold," dressed in his full urban regalia, including midnight blue Adidas sweat suit and new white sneakers. Rose-tinted glasses thinly shade his eyes. In a show of style, he profiles; lightly stepping into his Lincoln Town Car, he exhibits his cool. He sinks into the richly upholstered front seat, leans on the armrest, and turns up the stereo. His performance is all the more remarkable because of his youth (about twenty-one), which contrasts sharply with his expensive possessions. Local people are intrigued by this figure. Ambivalent, they recoil at his image, but they envy him just the same. The old heads feel especially conflicted; most definitely they condemn his car—which "he did not

have to work for." But secretly, some even admire him. He's "getting over," making it, though not in the right way, the way they were taught.

Among many poor blacks in the ghetto, ambivalence easily becomes alienation. A commonly voiced theme is "the Plan," encapsulating a host of issues and images that negatively affect the ghetto poor, including unemployment, police brutality, drugs, AIDS, incarceration, gentrification, and competing ethnic group businesses (Anderson, 1990). The Plan is discussed as a conspiracy engaged in by the wider community to commit genocide on the black community. It is systematically perpetrated by white officials and caretakers and, perhaps inadvertently, by some better-off blacks. Black-on-black crime is viewed as particularly strong proof of the conspiracy, because so little is done to curb it and to protect ghetto citizens. Incidents of unpunished police brutality in the black community are also taken as evidence. Institutions that most affect the life chances of the ghetto poor are profoundly distrusted, especially law enforcement, the business community, schools, public welfare, and city authorities.

Even those who do not espouse the genocide theory are affected by the siege mentality it engenders. They come to feel that, at the very least, the wider society intentionally disrespects blacks. Mutual suspicion and concern with respect pervade the ghetto poor community. Under such circumstances, social order becomes precarious. Because of concern for being "dissed" (disrespected), respect is easily violated. Because status problems are mixed with extreme resource limitations, people, especially young people, exaggerate the importance of symbols, often with life-threatening consequences.

These consequences are exacerbated by the widespread belief that authorities view black life as cheap, hardly worth their attention. This view is reinforced when black-on-white crime receives more attention by authorities and by the media than does black-on-black crime. The result is that people feel thrown back on their own limited resources. They arm themselves, take offense, and resist in ways that contribute to the cycle of violence.

Conclusions

Structural characteristics, such as the availability of legitimate and illegitimate job opportunities, and cultural characteristics, such as beliefs and values that are transmitted in families and neighborhoods, interact powerfully with individual and social factors to produce behavioral outcomes, among individuals and communities. The complexity of these relationships and their theoretical linkages defy simple characterization. We concur with the assessment of Jencks and Mayer (1990), who conclude: "We badly need better studies of neighborhoods' impact on teenage crime. We especially need studies that focus on the effect of very poor neighborhoods, including large public housing projects. We also need studies that follow families as they move in and out of very poor neighborhoods and examine how such moves affect teenagers' behavior" (p. 162).

We also need studies of the effects of crime on communities, including large public housing projects, and of community effects of population turnover in neighborhoods. As should be clear from the preceding discussion, communities vary in their ability to control violence, in the opportunities they present for crime and violent confrontations, and in the extent to which their local cultures encourage or discourage violence.

Youth Gangs and Violence: An Example of Social Processes at Work

Frederic M. Thrasher, the first social scientist to study gangs systematically, defined the gang as "an interstitial group originally formed spontaneously, and then integrated through conflict" (Thrasher, 1927:57). He discovered that gangs were to be found principally in the "interstitial areas," that is, the city's slums. From observation he concluded that the "ganging process is a continuous flux and flow, and there is little permanence in most of the groups" (p. 31). He went on to describe a variety of types of gangs, gang characteristics, and characteristics of individual members, and gang activities.

Since Thrasher's classic work, many definitions of gangs have been suggested. Most of these include some reference to the delinquent or other forms of socially disruptive behavior that are the objects of concern (Klein, 1971; Klein and Maxson, 1989; Hagedorn, 1988). Several classifications of gangs have been suggested (Cloward and Ohlin, 1960; Miller, 1975, 1980; Taylor, 1990a). All definitions of gangs include (or imply) common elements: gangs are groups whose members meet together with some regularity, over time, on the basis of group-defined criteria of membership and group-defined organizational characteristics. For our purposes, then, gangs are self-determining, non-adult-sponsored groups that demonstrate continuity over time.

When gang members become involved with others in the commission of violent acts, to the extent that these acts *develop out of gang interaction or are related to gang membership*, the behavior of such groups may be regarded as gang-related, even though they may involve few members of a gang. Defining *gangs* and *gang-related* in this way avoids the circularity of including in the definition the behavior that is to be explained. The definition excludes small groups that are organized only for the commission of crime, such as drug selling crews (Williams, 1989).

How prevalent are youth gangs? Again the definitional issue makes the question difficult to answer. In his report to the Violence Commission, Klein (1969) estimated that in the Los Angeles census tract with the most gang members "only 6 percent of the 10- to 17-year-old age bracket were gang affiliated" (p. 1445). This estimate may be low by our more inclusive definition, and it may not reflect current levels of gang involvement in some cities. Gangs appear to have proliferated since Klein's research, particularly in certain areas of large cities, and to have spread to cities that previously had no "gang problem." Spergel et al. (1989) placed 1987 gang membership in Los Angeles city and county at about 70,000, and recent police estimates approach 100,000.

We know that many gangs are extremely violent, yet violent behavior among even the most violent gangs is relatively rare. When violent episodes occur within or between gangs, or when gangs attack others or destroy property, some members typically do not participate. Moore's (1987) observation that levels of lethal violence among gangs in the 1950s and 1970s varied "from one clique to another within the same gang" (p. 218) seems to be equally applicable to contemporary gangs and to lesser forms of violence as well.

Explaining Violent Gang Behavior

The explanations of violent gang behavior can be organized roughly parallel to the individual-level and social-level explanations of violent behavior that we used earlier in this chapter. In the following pages, we first consider possible explanations in terms of individual gang members and then consider explanations in terms of the functions of violent behavior for the gang as a social unit. Finally, we then discuss explanations in terms of cultural and structural forces in the communities that gangs inhabit.

Violent Behavior by Individual Gang Members In terms of individuals, there is no reason to believe that learning processes differ between members of gangs and others. However, violent behavior is more prevalent among gang members than others of the same age and gender, and it often differs in other ways. Klein and Maxson (1989) suggest that homicides by gang members are not as closely related to intimate personal relationships as other homicides are, and that gang membership is often implicated in both homicide perpetration and victimization. Moreover, fighting between gangs has been observed to occur over extended periods (Schwartz, 1987) and to victimize persons who are not gang members, often inadvertently (Jankowski, 1991).

A study of high school students and dropouts in three cities found that higher percentages of gang members than others reported *participation* in delinquent behaviors (Fagan, 1990). And, despite the much higher involvement of males than females in law violation, "prevalence rates for female gang members exceed the rates for nongang males for all 12 behavior categories" (p. 12). Violent offenses among the behaviors studied included felony assault, minor assault, and robbery.

Of equal importance is that the *frequency* with which the violent offenders committed such offenses differed little by either gender or gang membership. Together with the universally observed variability of violent behavior among gang members, this finding strongly suggests that *similar processes produce frequent and persistent violent behavior among gang members and others alike.* Gangs exert important influences on violent behavior and on the communities in which they live. However, more general processes, at the individual and social levels of explanation, must account for individual and community violence—especially its frequency and persistence. Field research with gangs is one key to understanding the nature of these processes (Hagedorn, 1988; Jankowski, 1991; Moore, 1987; Vigil, 1988; Padilla, 1990).

As noted by Short (1991), Jankowski emphasizes the "defiant individualist character" of members of the gangs he observed, which includes such attributes as intense competitiveness, mistrust or wariness in dealings with others, self-reliance, and a survivalist orientation toward a hostile world (see also MacLeod, 1987; Hagedorn, 1988). One of the chief organizational problems for gangs is to reconcile the conflicting needs and demands of the defiantly individualist members of the group.

The Functions of Violence for the Gang Studies of young people in many cities and different time periods, using a variety of research methods, find that fighting with age peers, particularly among young males, is more characteristic of individuals and groups with lower socioeconomic status than among higher-status youth. Where gangs are most common, socialization into violence begins early in life. And *intragang* fighting is more common than is either *intergang* fighting or violent behavior directed outside the gang (Jankowski, 1991; Miller et al., 1961; Hagedorn, 1988). Sullivan (1989) found that fighting with age peers, often with serious consequences, occurred at an early age among white, Hispanic, and black youth gangs in Brooklyn. The experience gained in this way often was later applied to the "systematic pursuit of income" (p. 109). Most fighting among boys in their early and middle teens is about status (MacLeod, 1987; Horowitz, 1983; Short and Strodtbeck, 1965). For some, however, the scarcity of resources, the symbolic significance of some types of property, and the lack of access to legitimate means of acquiring it translate into violence at an early age.

Fighting within and between gangs, as well as attacks on others, often serves group purposes, such as demonstrating personal qualities that are highly valued by the gang or reinforcing group solidarity by disciplining individual members (Jankowski, 1991). Violent behavior by individual gang members is also heavily influenced by group values and the perceived requirements of group membership or status within the group. Gang conflict often occurs when a gang believes that its status or reputation, its turf, or its resources (e.g., its share of a drug market) are threatened by another gang. A member who feels his status within the gang threatened may react aggressively. The response may be direct, as in an attack on a threatening person, or indirect, as when a gang leader acts to reestablish his position by acting violently toward someone outside the gang in response to a perceived threat to his leadership (Short, 1990, 1991).

The interpersonal and group dynamics of such behavior are not well understood. A small research literature suggests that it is neither irrational nor entirely predictable solely on the basis of individual characteristics. Group processes such as those noted above are implicated in much violent behavior by gang members (Jankowski, 1991; Short, 1990; Farrington et al., 1981; Short and Strodtbeck, 1965). At this level of explanation, interpersonal relationships and group processes often interact to produce threats, insults, and conflicts that escalate to produce violent exchanges, even to the extreme of "victim-precipitated" homicides (Wolfgang, 1957; Schwartz, 1987).

Community Influences on Gang Violence Social forces that influence young people range from their families and communities to the global economy. Local neighborhoods and communities are especially important as the social settings that are most immediately experienced (Schwartz, 1987; Reiss and Tonry, 1986). To gang members, even the *meaning* of crime is shaped both by the neighborhood in which they spend their time almost entirely unsupervised by adults, and by the consumerist culture promoted in the media (Sullivan, 1989:249). Status threats are likely to be played out with violence within the gang milieu. Opportunities for violent behavior are greater in this context, especially for young people who have been socialized into violence or who lack the social skills to achieve status through nonviolent means. Adding to this context competition over drug markets produces an extremely volatile mix, which often results in violence.

Many of Thrasher's observations from the 1920s apply equally well to contemporary gangs. Most youth gangs are found in inner cities, in areas of poverty, physical deterioration, and institutional breakdown. Because racial and ethnic minorities tend to be concentrated in such areas, many—but not all—gangs are comprised of minority youths. These gangs are therefore subject to the cultural and structural forces that affect minority communities.

Cultural Influences Besides the cultures promoted in the media, some of the major influences on youth gangs in this country are immigration to the United States and the position of ethnic and racial minorities in this country and in local communities. Ethnic antagonisms are often a source of gang violence (Jankowski, 1991; Sullivan, 1989; Vigil, 1987; MacLeod, 1987; Moore et al., 1978; Short and Strodtbeck, 1965) and some ethnic traditions encourage violence (Chin, 1990; Vigil, 1988). The ethnic character of violence and of gangs reflects the ethnic composition of inner cities, as evidenced by the emphasis among Hispanic groups on honor (above references; Schwartz, 1987; Horowitz, 1983) and the violence associated with traditional tongs and triads of Chinese gangs (Chin, 1990). Other ethnic variations in gangs, and in violence, relate to the status of ethnic groups in U.S. society, local communities, and social settings as well as to ethnic traditions.

Much non-Hispanic white gang violence continues to be directed against minority youth, especially blacks (Jankowski, 1991; Sullivan, 1989), and at times against Hispanics and others (Moore, 1987). Jankowski observes that in largely Irish Boston communities a tradition of adult social and athletic clubs is an important factor in community acceptance of youth gangs. And in many Chicano communities of East Los Angeles, street gangs have become "quasi-institutionalized" since the 1930s and 1940s (Moore et al., 1978; Moore, 1987, 1991; Vigil, 1987).

Structural Influences Recent field studies of gangs report that many young men remain active in gangs rather than growing out of them, as was the case in the past. While marriage, family responsibilities, and jobs once were the normal route out of the gang, the scarcity of good, stable job opportunities now makes that progress elusive. Much recent research documents the decline in manufacturing jobs available in inner cities, the rise of a service economy that offers few opportunities for advancement, and an increasingly segmented labor force in which whites dominate higher-paying jobs while minorities are consigned to low-wage (often part-time) work, welfare, and the illegal economy. As noted earlier in this chapter, as more affluent and stable minority populations have moved out of poverty areas, the communities left behind have lost their most effective role models and institutional leaders (Anderson, 1990; Lemann, 1991).

The effects of these developments on gangs and gang violence are not clear. Some field research reports that the presence of older members in gangs has led to more rational pursuit of economic gain or to their transformation into groups organized solely for criminal purposes. This is particularly the case when gangs become heavily involved in drug distribution, in which case violence is likely to become more instrumental in character (Taylor, 1990a,b; Chin, 1990; Williams, 1989).

As noted above, the availability of attractive, conventional role models is reported to have declined. Many "old heads"—respectable and respected middle- and working-class adults who made it a point to advise young people as to acceptable conduct—have left these communities. Those who remain often find themselves ignored, disparaged, or threatened. Younger, flashier, and (at least temporarily) successful drug dealers now appeal to even younger youth (Anderson, 1990).

In Hispanic communities in East Los Angeles, "good" jobs that left the area as a result of economic shifts have been replaced by unstable, low-wage, and unsheltered jobs, much as has occurred in other cities. Immigrants from Mexico compete with gang members and others for these jobs. Older gang members who have not found stable conventional jobs, many of whom have been in and out of prison and whose family and community ties tend to be weak, hang around with younger gang members. The result, Moore reports, is that the gang is perpetuated as an agent of "street socialization" rather than becoming more integrated into conventional community life (Moore, 1991; see also Short, 1991).

Conclusion

The importance of local community cultures and structures of economic opportunity for understanding and controlling violent behavior can hardly be overestimated. Although important clues exist, the processes that result in individual violence, gang violence, and violence in large gatherings of mainly young people are a high priority for future research. Among the clues, the interaction of social factors and intergenerational relationships seems most promising. When communities are weakened by demographic and economic shifts that concentrate poverty and destabilize their institutions, conventional processes of socialization and control fail. When intergenerational relationships break down or are distorted by such developments, the likelihood that gangs will flourish and compete with one another, often with deadly consequences, is enhanced.

We do not consider in this report a number of important questions about youth gangs, on which there is substantial research and controversy. Among these questions are how and why gangs form, why youths join gangs, how gang presence and membership affect youths' development, how gangs differ from other youth groups, what nonviolent activities gangs engage in, and how to suppress gang activity. Distinctions between traditional youth gangs and drug distribution organizations, and the roles of both in drug market violence, are discussed in Chapter 4.

THE CIRCUMSTANCES OF VIOLENCE

To this point in this chapter, we have discussed individual and social processes that may contribute to a person's potential for violent behavior. A promising approach to the understanding and control of violence—a perspective with roots in both criminology and public health—is to focus on the places where violence occurs.

The incidence of violent events varies widely in space—by city, neighborhood, and specific address. For example, although 97.8 percent of all Minneapolis addresses generated zero robbery calls in 1986, 8 addresses generated more than 20 calls each (Sherman et al., 1989).

Individual- and aggregate-level violence risk measures have different implications for violence reduction strategies. Once a place with high *individual* risk (i.e., many violent victimizations per person at risk or, ideally, per person-hour at risk) is identified, private citizens have an incentive to reduce their own risk by avoiding the place, and business proprietors in the place have an incentive to "harden" it with guard dogs, private security, or various physical changes (Cook, 1986). But because of high daily traffic, some places like shopping centers with relatively low individual risks may have high *aggregate* risks (i.e., they account for a disproportionate share of violent victimizations in an area per year). In such places, the social benefits of violence risk reduction may exceed the total of all private benefits, and government interventions to reduce risks (e.g., by increasing police patrols or by making the place physically less conducive to violence) are sometimes warranted.

Planning intervention strategies oriented toward location begins with an understanding of the risk factors in places in the general community. We first consider what is known about how the probabilities and consequences of violent events in a place are related to the routine activities of people who inhabit it. We then consider risk factors for violence in various physical environments. We then consider violence in two special places—prisons and schools.

Routine Activities and High-Risk Encounters

According to "lifestyle" and "routine activities" theories, people's daily activities affect violent victimization rates by determining how often potential victims come together with potential perpetrators in places where no one is likely to intervene (Hindelang et al., 1978; Cohen and Felson, 1979). The evidence from American data for routine activities theory is largely indirect; "nighttime activity outside the home" is the most specific behavior that is statistically associated with higher rates of violent victimization. Most of the supportive evidence concerns personal characteristics that are presumed to be associated with activities that increase the chances of victimization: being a teenager or young adult, male, single, unemployed, and low-income—the last effect is especially strong for robbery and negligible for rape. These studies find blacks more likely than whites to be robbed, but no more likely to be assaulted.

Analyses of Canadian and British surveys, which record more details about respondents' activities, find higher risks of violent victimization correlated specifically with spending more nights per week out alone, greater frequency of drinking in pubs, and use of public transportation. We have no way of knowing whether these are also risk factors in the United States, which differs significantly in terms of the use of private transportation, access to neighborhood bars and other sources of alcohol and drugs, and racial composition.

Although these findings tempt one to suggest that limiting one's outside activities will also limit exposure to violent victimization, especially in bars or on public transportation alone at night, the evidence suggests that a more complex chain of events may limit the effectiveness of such a strategy in neighborhoods most vulnerable to violence. Some communities present higher risks than others because of the community-level characteristics discussed earlier (e.g., social disorganization, concentration of poverty) rather than any individual's characteristics or routine activities (Sampson and Wooldredge, 1987). Residents of high-risk neighborhoods do rearrange their routine activities because they fear victimization, according to hosts of studies reviewed by Cook (1986) and Warr (Volume 4), yet their efforts fail to offset the higher risk associated with their neighborhoods (Miethe and Meier, 1990).

The evidence is too fragmented, and the crime types analyzed to date are too broad, to conclude that community context and individual precautions interact as described here to determine violent victimization risks. Further work is needed to answer the practical question of what specific activities people should avoid, in which locations and at what times, to reduce their risk of violent victimization.

The Physical Environment

Research has identified only a few physical characteristics of residential and public places as unambiguously associated with the risk of violence (Sampson and Lauritsen, Volume 3; Taylor and Gottfredson, 1986). Public areas near apartment units, located in geographic areas with high rates of divorce and population turnover, are particularly dangerous (Sampson and Wooldredge, 1987). Such areas concentrate large numbers of adolescents, who are unsupervised while their single parents are at work. Because of the high population turnover, potential monitors are unlikely to know these children, and potential victims tend to be unknown to their attackers. Apartment housing areas, especially those on city blocks that are large in area and population, with high population density, and near public housing projects and high schools are also associated with high risks of violence (Beasley and Antunes, 1974; Mladenka and Hill, 1976; Roncek, 1981; Roncek and Faggiani, 1986; Sampson, 1983; Schuerman and Kobrin, 1986; Smith and Jarjoura, 1988).

One particularly dangerous place is the open-air drug market. Although there is no systematic geographic research on the spatial characteristics of drug markets (Harries, 1990), attributes of "desirable" drug markets have been identified (Garreau, 1988):

(1) easy on-off: a narrow one-way access road for automobile traffic, down which dealers can monitor arriving customers or marked police vehicles without being "blind-sided";
(2) wide-openness: multiple escape routes (e.g., through hallways, breezeways, or woods) behind sellers on the street; and
(3) barricades: obstacles to police cars and officers on foot weighed down by equipment, which are relatively surmountable by teenage boys.

During the 1970s, under the rubric of "defensible space," prescriptions for changing the physical environment were offered to reduce crime and violence (Newman, 1973a,b, 1975). Recommendations included physical barriers to transform large housing projects into clusters of smaller ones, design innovations to facilitate surveillance, intermingling residential areas with safe areas, and use of garden-style rather than high-rise apartment designs. A demonstration project in Hartford, Connecticut, experimented with physical changes designed to create symbolic entrances to the neighborhood and to close off side streets to through traffic (Gardiner, 1978).

Evaluations of these techniques indicate some success in reducing crime and especially fear of crime, at least in the short run (Newman and Franck, 1980, 1982; Fowler, 1981; Fowler and Mangione, 1981). But the desired effects failed to materialize in one multiethnic housing project (Merry, 1981a,b) and proved to be short-lived in the Hartford demonstration.

The reason for the inconsistent and temporary effects appears to be that crime and violence arise from interactions between the social environment and the physical environment, which cannot be controlled entirely through manipulations of the physical environment. The communal feeling of territoriality and mutual protection, on which the defensible space concept rests, apparently failed to materialize in the multiethnic housing project because of lingering anonymity and mistrust across ethnic groups. In Hartford, citizens' participation in neighborhood patrols and maintenance of the symbolic entrances fell off after an initial reduction in the fear of crime. To intruders bent on crime, this deterioration may well have signaled a decline in local guardianship and concern and therefore in the risk of detection by responsible monitors. These findings suggest that architectural innovations help cohesive communities to make dangerous places less so, but are insufficient in themselves to create long-term safety.

Architectural change is one of a number of surveillance techniques for crime prevention (Clarke, 1983). Another technique—reported to have limited success—is to increase traffic by responsible monitors through dangerous places.

Another approach is called "target hardening," with such devices as alarms, dogs, locks, etc. Clarke concludes that, although these have been successful in reducing property crimes such as thefts and burglaries, they have no clear-cut effects on violence risks.

A third type of prevention is called "environmental management" and includes techniques designed to make targets for instrumental violence less accessible or less attractive to would-be perpetrators. Exact-change requirements for passengers on New York City buses, for example, caused a substantial reduction in bus driver robberies (Chaiken et al., 1974) and airport screening procedures brought about a substantial reduction in skyjackings (Landes, 1978).

The most elaborate approach to situational interventions comes from the public health perspective. One example of a public health framework for controlling intentional (i.e., violent) injuries appears in Table 3-1. The framework addresses (1) primary prevention—prevention of the violent event, (2) secondary prevention—reduction of the harm caused by the event, and (3) tertiary prevention—repair of the harm. It draws attention to strategies that involve not only altering the behavior of perpetrators and victims but modifying hazards in the environment, such as weapons, architectural barriers, and valuables in the possession of a vulnerable robbery target.

Examples of primary prevention tactics include locating automatic teller machines in well-lit, high-traffic areas; limiting cash on hand in retail stores and posting signs to that effect; installing plexiglass shields for lone employees who must handle cash in public places, especially at night; and staggering school hours so that older children are in class while vulnerable younger children are walking to and from school. Secondary prevention tactics are

TABLE 3-1 Public Health Injury Control Framework

PRIMARY PREVENTION

1. Prevent creation of the hazard.
   - Avoid placing automatic teller machines in high-risk locations.
   - Restrict the sale of handguns.
2. Reduce the amount of hazard brought into being.
   - Limit cash on hand at convenience stores to less than $30.
   - Restrict the size of magazines in semiautomatic rifles.
3. Prevent the release of a hazard that already exists.
   - Equip police officers with firearms that have "user-specific" safeties.
   - Increase scene visibility for passerby or employee surveillance of high-risk locations.
4. Modify the rate of release of a hazard from its source.
   - Ban magnum charges in handgun ammunition to decrease muzzle velocities and wounding potential.
   - Ban automatic weapons and semiautomatic assault weapons.
5. Separate by time or space the hazard from the people to be protected.
   - Restrict knives and firearms from high-risk locations through use of metal detectors and other forms of weapons screening.
   - Release younger children from school 30 minutes before older children and stagger recess times.
6. Physically separate the hazard from people to be protected by barriers.
   - Install bullet- and knife-proof shields in cabs.
   - Install bullet-proof booths for clerks in all-night gas stations and high-risk convenience stores.

SECONDARY PREVENTION

7. Modify surfaces and basic structures to minimize injury.
   - Ban hollow point and explosive bullets to decrease injury severity.
   - Substitute plastic containers for glass containers in bars and at large sporting events.
8. Make the people to be protected more resistant to damage.
   - Equip all officers involved in law enforcement with bullet-proof vests.
   - Equip special high-risk police units with combat-style head protection and body armor.

TERTIARY PREVENTION

9. Begin to counter damage already done.
   - Adopt the enhanced 911 system on a universal basis.
   - Provide all paramedics and emergency medical technicians with special training in the management of penetrating injuries.
10. Stabilize, repair, and rehabilitate injured people.
    - Support a national system of trauma centers.
    - Promote a multidisciplinary approach to the treatment and rehabilitation of victims of violence, including psychological as well as physical care.

aimed at reducing the lethality of accessible weapons through such means as requiring the use of plastic rather than glass beverage containers in crowds; reducing access to firearms; providing bullet-resistant clothing to police and private security officers in vulnerable circumstances; and reducing available firepower through restrictions on muzzle velocity and hollow-point ammunition. Tertiary prevention tactics include enhanced emergency telephone service (which automatically displays to the dispatcher the address of the calling telephone); training emergency medical technicians on penetrating injuries; building trauma centers; and providing psychological and physical rehabilitation to victims of violence.

Convenience stores are a focus of private efforts to reduce violence. According to the National Institute on Occupational Safety and Health (NIOSH), retail trade is the highest-risk category for female occupational homicides (Bell, 1991). Most of them occur in the course of robberies, although customers' demands to violate age and time restrictions on beer and wine sales also trigger occasional high-risk encounters. Among the possible risk factors for occupational homicide identified by NIOSH (1992) are interaction with the public, the exchange of money, and evening employment as possible risk factors. Local passenger transportation and retail food sales are especially high-risk occupations. In Gainesville, Florida, over a five-year period, 96 percent of all convenience stores were reportedly robbed, compared with 36 percent of the fast food restaurants, 21 percent of the gas stations, and 16 percent of the liquor stores (Clifton, 1987).

A number of risk factors for convenience store robbery have been suggested, for example: (1) location on a low-traffic street near limited commercial activity (Duffala, 1976); (2) a small parking lot, longer operating hours, not offering gasoline service, and being located near socially disorganized neighborhoods (D'Allessio and Stolzenberg, 1990); and (3) operating with only one clerk in the store (Jeffery et al., 1987).

Interventions that have been implemented to prevent convenience store robberies include requirements to operate with two clerks, and a "robbery prevention package" adopted by the National Association of Convenience Stores. The package includes reducing the amount of cash available and posting signs to that effect; clearing the windows to make the cash register and safe visible to passersby; increasing lighting, inside and out; training employees in robbery prevention techniques; moving cash registers to more visible positions; and eliminating escape routes. As discussed in Chapter 7, evidence on the effectiveness of these interventions is inconclusive.

Violence in Special Places

Violence at a given level or severity is not equally problematic in all places. Social concern is greater in places where it impairs social functions that are especially important, or in places where the victims are legally required to be. Unfortunately, knowledge from research lags behind social concern in two such special places: prisons and schools.

Prison Violence

A fundamental question about prison violence is the extent to which inmates' violent behavior is imported from their lives in the community, learned in prison as a standard means of social interaction ("prisonization"), or triggered by prison conditions, such as frustration over the deprivation of accustomed privileges. Studies using institution-level data find some evidence that the deprivations associated with extraordinary crowding, long parole referral dates, and few visitors are associated with more assaults by inmates on one another and on staff. They also find some evidence of importation: prisons with greater numbers of inmates who behaved violently on the street experience higher levels of prison violence (Ellis et al., 1974; Gaes and McGuire, 1985).

We could find no strong empirical evidence that prisonization is a common cause of interpersonal prison violence. However, several ethnographic studies suggest that incarcerated street gang members import gang activities, including illegal markets, into the prison setting and tailor them to the special conditions there (Jacobs, 1977; Fleisher, 1989). Illegal markets in prison, like those in the community, operate under codes of conduct (enforced by violence) in the absence of legal systems for protecting franchise territories, resolving disputes, enforcing agreements, and recruiting employees (Fong, 1987; Moore et al., 1978; Toch, 1977). Studies also suggest that both gang violence and sexual violence in prisons seem to maintain the racial and ethnic affinities and rivalries for social dominance that characterize the inmates' home communities (Lockwood, 1980). We discussed gangs earlier in this chapter; Chapter 4 has a further discussion of illegal markets.

Social Control and Prison Violence In recent decades, two legal processes—the proliferation of determinate and mandatory minimum sentences and litigation over prison reform—have transformed the nature of social control mechanisms available to prison administrators. A vital policy question is whether these processes have aggravated or inhibited prison violence. In both cases, existing research provides no clear answers, and the ongoing nature of the legal processes both demands and facilitates studies of how they are affecting prison violence.

One could speculate that the predictability of determinate sentences would reduce prison violence by reducing frustration caused by uncertainty over release dates. Alternatively, one could speculate that a determinate or mandatory minimum sentence, by ruling out the chance of reducing time served through good behavior, removes a restraint on violent behavior. In an analysis of California prison experience in the mid-1970s with new mandatory minimum sentences (Forst and Brady, 1983) the results were mixed: an increase in inmates' assaults on one another and on staff, with and without weapons, but a decrease in prison homicides.

The rubric of prison reform covers a host of mechanisms available for social control of prisons that have been changed recently in many places by litigation, social activism, and new management structures (Barak-Glantz, 1981; Engel and Rothman, 1983; Flynn, 1976; Park, 1976; Rubel and Goldsmith, 1980; Toby, 1983a). Perhaps the most thoroughly studied reforms occurred in the Texas prison system, where the court decision in *Ruiz* v. *Estelle* (S.D. Texas, 1980) required changes to redress excessive crowding, excessive disciplinary force, the designation of selected inmates empowered to discipline other inmates, vague rules and arbitrary enforcement, inadequate health care, and inadequate fire and safety standards.

The mandated reforms were implemented in 1983, and the two in-depth studies document a clear pattern of decreased violence by staff and increased violence by inmates during the following two years (Marquart and Crouch, 1985; and Ekland-Olson 1986). Inexperienced staff were hired to fulfill some requirements, residual inmate resentment from the prereform period continued, inmates' urges to test the system in the wake of their new rights could have been anticipated, and the abrupt realignment of rights and responsibilities necessarily placed inmates and staff in unfamiliar social interactions. Research on Texas prison experience since 1985 could help to distinguish permanent from temporary effects.

A more encouraging view of the effects of innovation in correctional facilities is the experience with direct supervision in jails (Nelson, 1988). Direct supervision involves both design and management: replacement of standard cell rows or pods under remote surveillance with "living units" of approximately 50 cells clustered around a day room, with 24-hour management by officers located inside the unit. Direct supervision has usually been introduced as a means of personnel cost reduction rather than as a court-ordered reform; Nelson reports several examples of reduced inmate violence.

Influences on Prison Violence Situational influences on prison violence include crowding, the facility's conduciveness to monitoring, and the nature of interpersonal interactions. Individual influences include inmates' psychopathology and their concept of personal space.

Two distinct concepts of crowding are in use: (1) spatial density, the number of inmates per unit of area, and (2) social density, the number of inmates per partitioned unit. Increases in both spatial and social density (the latter measured by the use of dormitories) are associated with increases in inmate assaults on one another and on staff (Gaes, 1985). These measures have larger effects on crowding than do the proportion of young inmates or the rate of inmate turnover in the facility—two measures that are often linked to increased violence. However, none of the studies that Gaes reviewed have both facility-level and individual-level measures of crowding, so it is not clear whether inmates who live in less crowded circumstances are less likely than others to be perpetrators or victims of violence. Also, as documented by Ekland-Olson (1986), any violence reduction effect from a decrease in crowding may be offset at least temporarily by a breakdown of social control, as in the Texas case.

The location of a violent event can influence prison violence—especially the extent to which it can be monitored. One study finds, as expected, that assaults in prisons frequently occur in areas that are difficult to monitor (Atlas, 1983). However, many assaults also occur in well-supervised areas, such as detention and high-security areas. These findings are difficult to interpret: they may suggest that assaults are spontaneous, therefore not easily deterrable by monitoring. The rates may also be affected by variations in time spent in the well-monitored areas, or by the violence potentials of the populations assigned to the high-security areas.

Although sexual assaults in prisons are widely assumed to be commonplace, we could find little published systematic research on the subject (Prentky, 1990). Several unpublished studies report highly variable victimization rates, depending on the prison sampled, the definition used, and the reference period. This work suggests no particular risk factors.

Two psychological characteristics are specifically associated with violent behavior in prison. One is psychopathology; Toch (1989) notes cases of patterned violence, in which inmates regularly repeat a specific pattern of violent behavior. The other individual risk factor for fights and other violent behavior in prison is an exaggerated sense of social distance—their desired physical distance from others, which may be repeatedly violated in densely populated prisons (Walkey and Gilmour, 1984).

School Violence

Although 5.3 percent of all 1990 nonfatal violent victimizations of persons aged 12 and over reportedly occurred in school buildings, and another 4.5 percent on school property (Bureau of Justice Statistics, 1992), relatively few studies of school violence have been carried out. Until recently—as violence in urban schools has emerged as an issue in its own right—the focus in schools was on disruptive behavior, a category that ranges from talking in class to vandalism to violent behavior. As a result, far less is known about school violence than about prison violence, much of that knowledge simply confirms common sense expectations, and most of it is based on old data.

A special victimization survey sponsored by the National Institute of Education (NIE, 1978) reported far more school robberies than the National Crime Survey, a discrepancy that should be more fully explored and explained, since it could be due to errors in either survey. Violence rates in secondary schools are highest in school districts marked by higher crime rates and more street fighting gangs—an indication that the school reflects the community, and evidence that is consistent with the importation of violent behaviors into the school, by both students and intruders. According to an analysis of National Crime Survey data by McDermott (1979), the majority of violent victimizations of students and teachers were committed by strangers: more than 90 percent of reported rapes, 80 percent of robberies, and 60 percent of aggravated and simple assaults. While some of these could have been committed by fellow students who were previously unknown to the victims, some may also have been committed by intruders (Toby, 1983b).

The NIE study also reports higher rates of student violence in schools in which students perceive signs of ineffective social control: undisciplined classrooms, lax or arbitrary enforcement of school rules, and a weak principal. It is not clear whether the ineffective control gives a kind of permission that encourages violent behavior, or whether high violence levels create fear among authorities that undermines their will to impose discipline. Despite expectations that mandatory desegregation efforts might increase school violence either because of student frustration or because cross-area busing would increase anonymity, the NIE survey found no strong effect.

Finally, the NIE survey provides aggregate-level evidence that violence levels are related to students' attachments to the values that schools are intended to promulgate. In secondary schools, violence rates increased with the percentages of students who did not aspire to good grades, who did not view their curricula as relevant, and who did not believe that their school experience could positively influence their lives.

A MULTICOMMUNITY LONGITUDINAL RESEARCH PROGRAM

Earlier in this chapter, we surveyed knowledge about aggressive and violent behavior from three perspectives: psychosocial development, biomedical, and social. While each perspective has contributed findings with scientific and policy implications, these findings are pieces in a mosaic that is yet to be assembled. We cannot yet answer the question, How do psychosocial, biomedical, and social processes *operate and interact* to explain violence patterns in the United States today?

More specifically, many risk factors for aggression were listed earlier in this chapter, yet we do not know either which ones actually cause aggression or how they are related to subsequent violent behavior. Promising causal theories (e.g., shy versus uninhibited temperaments, social learning of aggression, serotonin deficits, neurologically based cognitive and attention deficits, attachment theory) that are discussed more fully in Appendix A and Miczek et al. (Volume 2, Chapter 6) have yet to be compared against one another in a common framework. Knowledge of the specific developmental sequences that link perinatal and preschool events, childhood aggression, and adult violence is still only approximate, fragmentary, and segregated from community and ethnic contexts. Better understanding of these sequences could improve the timing of interventions—perhaps in age ranges in which behavior is relatively malleable, or just before key developmental transitions that separate periods of relative behavioral stability.

As discussed earlier, there is a need to resolve conflicting findings about the interactions between bullying, peer relations, aggression, and violence. Because developmental studies rarely examine community influences or compare sequences across communities or ethnic categories, we do not know the extents to which the well-documented continuity in aggression reflects continuity in individuals versus the environment. Childrearing practices may have different effects in different communities or cultures, and protective factors at the community and family levels compensate for adverse circumstances at either level.

Even without this integrated perspective on violence, researchers and practitioners have designed interventions that succeeded in reducing aggressive or violent behavior—by small amounts, in selected samples, and in certain communities. As we recommend in Chapter 8, systematic programs to refine and evaluate these interventions should be launched immediately. Over the long term, however, designing more comprehensive violence prevention strategies requires better answers to the basic question posed above. With a 12- to 15-year perspective in mind, therefore, we call for a multicommunity longitudinal research program to investigate the psychosocial, biomedical, and social processes that explain: (a) why some children exhibit patterns of aggressive behavior at early ages while most do not and (b) why only a minority of aggressive children go on to commit violent acts as adults.

In principle, there has long been no reason why investigators, by combining community- and individual-level data, could not study how social structures and cultures interact with individuals' psychosocial development to influence their potentials for violent behavior. But such studies have rarely been carried out because of the substantial burdens they impose on data collection and on scholars' capacities to span competently the range of relevant theories and methods.

Longitudinal studies pose methodological and human subject problems not ordinarily encountered in experiments or cross-section surveys. These will require special attention in their design and implementation.

Methodological and measurement problems arise because of the length of time subjects are studied. Among these problems are selective attrition of subjects and locating subjects who move or change their names. Complex analytical issues arise in separating community context and change variables from individual-level variables.

Likewise, human subject issues are more complex. Some of the measures, particularly those relating to biomedical measures, may be viewed as particularly intrusive and raise questions about the conditions for informed consent. Similarly, there are issues of whose consent is required. For younger cohorts, parental consent is required, but is the consent of only one parent required when parental information pertains to both and at what age is the consent of the child to be obtained? There likewise are special issues of protecting confidential information, especially those relating to subpoena or when information is secured on physical and sexual abuse of subjects when there are legal reporting requirements.

Despite these difficulties, relevant longitudinal studies have occasionally been carried out with selected small populations; these are reviewed by Farrington, Tonry et al. (1991), and Appendix A. However, even taken together they fail to answer the basic question posed above for a variety of reasons. Many collected data too infrequently to describe event sequences in detail (Olweus, 1980; Magnusson and Bergman, 1988; McCord and McCord, 1956). Developmental data in several of the most important studies were collected several decades ago (e.g., McCord and McCord, 1956; Wolfgang et al., 1972; Huesmann and Eron, 1984) or in foreign countries (e.g., Moffitt and Silva, 1988; Farrington and West, 1990; Olweus, 1980; Kolvin et al., 1988; Magnusson and Bergman, 1988), so their findings may not apply to violence in today's urban American communities. Several recent longitudinal studies (Elliott et al., 1989; Huizinga et al., 1991; Loeber et al., 1991; and Thornberry et al., 1991) collected data at sufficiently close intervals in American communities; however, they do not focus on aggression and violence, and they do not cover the prenatal/birth-to-adult ages.

Perhaps the greatest difference between the program we recommend and previous longitudinal studies is that our recommended program would provide an unparalleled opportunity to examine the relationships between biomedical variables and violent behavior. As explained earlier in this chapter, modern research using animal and human subjects suggests links between violent behavior and variables ranging from exposure to alcohol and drugs in the uterus, to serotonin deficits, to neuroendocrine functioning, and to head injuries, for example. It is unlikely that any of these links constitutes a causal relationship in isolation. Longitudinal designs offer the opportunity to detect individual differences in these variables early in life, to examine their stability and change over time, and to ascertain how variation in them is related to variation in behavior. For behaviors such as aggression and violence, which are fundamentally influenced by development, tracking individuals over time represents an essential scientific strategy for discovering such relationships. Once discovered, the relationships may suggest ways, within strict ethical guidelines, to enhance the effectiveness of humane, beneficial, and minimally intrusive violence prevention strategies.

The logic behind the program we recommend follows from the discussions in this chapter of the development of aggression and violence, of relevant biological and psychosocial risk factors, and of promising preventive interventions. The program would involve studies in multiple communities that vary in their demographic and socioeconomic composition, their urban status, and their neighborhood and community organization (see this chapter for examples), to investigate how variations and change in these factors alter the probabilities of various developmental sequences. In each community, the proposed program calls for study of multiple cohorts from prenatal to adult, each selected to overrepresent high-risk categories. The major components are similar for each study: a comprehensive *initial assessment* of biological, temperamental, cognitive, and behavioral characteristics in members of each cohort; *longitudinal follow-ups* of "high-risk" and "normative" subsamples of each cohort, with at least annual data collection from multiple sources, to assess how the children's life courses and future behaviors are related to the characteristics and key life transitions measured; measures of community environments and changes in them; and *randomized experiments* to measure the effects of one or more promising preventive interventions on other high-risk and normative samples in each cohort. In 10 years, plus time for analysis of the data, this program would lay the groundwork for new approaches to violence prevention by enhancing our understanding of (1) biological and behavioral characteristics of infants that increase their risk of growing up to commit violent acts; (2) protective factors—conditions, events, and processes in families and communities that prevent the development of high potentials for violent behavior in high-risk individuals; and (3) preventive interventions grounded in knowledge of protective factors.

The three components are described in the following pages.

The Initial Assessment

In each study the initial assessment would collect a substantial amount of data, which could be used not only for analysis but also, if feasible, to subdivide each sample in each community into high-risk and normative subsamples. The specific criteria for defining the subsamples of cohort subjects should be developed as part of study design but should include behavioral indicators of temperament and cognition, and biomedical indicators.

To distinguish between "inhibited" and "uninhibited" temperament, batteries of behavioral measures can be applied as early as the age of 4 months. In the behavioral battery, the infant could be exposed to unfamiliar visual, auditory, and olfactory stimuli, and various changes are taken as measures of autonomic responsivity. Levels of motor activity and irritability would be quantified from videotapes. This battery would permit the detection of uninhibited infants who showed relatively low levels of motor activity and irritability in response to cognitive testing. In later cohorts, these measures could be augmented with parent, teacher, peer, and significant other ratings of aggressive behavior. Cognitive capacity can be measured by about the age of 4 years, using tests of the knowledge of letters and of numbers, and short-term memory for words.

The biomedical measures should be carefully selected according to the principles described earlier in this chapter. Under these principles, one category of data would include items that can be collected in simple interviews—family drug and alcohol use and aggressive behavior, alcohol and drug exposure in utero, exposure to heavy metals, and some head injuries, for example. These variables appear to be linked biomedically to the potential for violent behavior and, under strict confidentiality, the data can be collected without burden on study subjects. Not only could analyses of these simple biomedical measures provide promising leads, but also their inclusion in statistical models would improve estimates of how psychosocial influences and interventions affect potentials for violent behavior.

In a second category, certain noninvasive, low-cost, and reasonably accurate physiological measures—while not specific enough to identify the brain activity that links a violent act to a specific stimulus—can be used in a longitudinal design to establish predictive relationships. For example, saliva measures of gonadal and adrenal hormones offer reasonably accurate indicators of endocrine activity. In a longitudinal design, saliva measures could be used to trace the onset and progression of puberty. When linked to longitudinal data on peer interactions and behavior, the information could be used to estimate predictive relationships for violent behavior. Once established, such relationships might be used to identify categories of youth for whom social skills training or some other intervention might be especially effective in reducing chances of violent behavior.

Similar cases can be made for measuring evoked brain potentials, heart rate and heart rate variability, and galvanic skin responses because noninvasive procedures exist. While these are not very specific probes into cortical and autonomic system functioning, they place negligible risks and burdens on subjects. They can contribute to the testing of hypotheses about the arousability of the autonomic nervous system, lateralization of brain functions, and the presence of seizure activity. As with endocrine activity, analyses of repeated measures linked to records of behavior over time may reveal useful predictive relationships.

A third category of biomedical measurement techniques imposes nonnegligible burdens or risks on subjects. Among these, spinal taps and brain imaging techniques at the current state of image resolution measure brain activity too imprecisely and are too nonspecific to violent behavior, to warrant their inclusion in our proposed program. In contrast, pharmacological or endocrinological challenge tests offer the prospect of information about sensory thresholds and physical mobilization in stressful situations. Because neurological markers for violence potentials are likely to exist in such responses rather than in resting levels of chemicals or neurological activity, the challenge test methodology should be considered for inclusion in the program we recommend. However, to guard against problematic, potentially irreversible, side effects in the study subjects, only challenge tests that have been carefully explored and calibrated should be considered in this program. Among those that can be safely conducted, only those that test specific hypotheses about biomedical causes (e.g., a serotonin deficit, a neurologically based temperament) or that promise new preventive or therapeutic interventions should be included.

Longitudinal Follow-up

In each cohort, the longitudinal follow-up would involve annual contacts. Annual measurements in early cohorts should include the demographic characteristics, delinquent and criminal behavior, and drug and alcohol abuse of all household members; measures of the subjects' physical growth, minor physical anomalies, injuries, and illnesses; measures of subjects' development, including neuromotor performance, IQ, perception, communication skills, and temperament.

The annual measures should also attempt to capture family interaction patterns, such as family degree of organization, stability, bonding between children and parents, stimulation by caregivers, parental discipline and conflict management, and measures of physical, social, religious, and moral functioning in the family. They should also record important life events; characteristics of the community, neighborhood, day-care facilities; and, after school entrance, behavioral observations of teachers and peers. And they should record behaviors including aggression and its precursors, as well as interactions with peers, family members, and other caregivers.

For each of the preadolescent cohorts, the final assessment should emphasize outcome measures including parent, peer, and teacher reports of the child's aggressive behavior, laboratory assessments of the child's behavior with same-sex peers, and behavioral measures of autonomic responsivity.

For all later cohorts, we recommend annual collection of self-reports and official records of subjects' violent, antisocial, delinquent, and criminal behavior; behavioral indicators of temperament (e.g., impulsivity, attention deficit, risk taking); indicators of cognitive structure (e.g., hostile bias, perceptual accuracy, and realistic appraisal of behavioral consequences); indicators of cognitive functioning (e.g., intelligence, cognitive ability, academic attainment); indicators of commitment to the normative social structure (e.g., indicators of expected future achievements, of respect for community norms, of alienation from social norms); interactions with parents and peers; characteristics of family structure and family members' behavior; and work history.

The study design calls for studying the development of each cohort in different kinds of community environments. Although cohort subjects will initially be selected in different community environments, those environments will change as the subjects develop, and subjects and their families will change community environment. Consequently, it will be essential to track both changes in community environments and the environmental history of each subject. Among the community characteristics to be investigated that have been linked to risk of delinquent, criminal, and other kinds of violent behavior are the peer networks of neighborhoods (e.g., violent gangs); the kinds of illegal activity in the community (e.g., illegal drug markets); the opportunities for legitimate work and occupational mobility; the value and normative structure of the community; and the family structure of communities (e.g., proportion of children in single-parent households).

Analysis should focus on separating community- from individual-level effects.

Analyses of data from all cohorts would permit much more precise documentation than is currently available of how temperament affects developmental processes, and of how developmental processes and life events interact to determine the risk of aggressive behavior at all ages to adult status. In addition, the analyses would identify protective factors that prevent aggressive children from developing into violent adults.

Randomized Experiments

The randomized-experimental component of the proposed research is intended to compare preventive interventions such as the three categories mentioned earlier: prevention of relevant brain dysfunctions, cognitive-behavioral interventions, and prevention of early-grade school failure. We have in mind comparative assessments of intervention "packages," designed to answer two kinds of questions. First, how do the interventions in each package compare in their effectiveness at preventing high-risk children from developing aggressive or violent behaviors? Second, do the interventions provide other benefits to children, including those who are not classified as at high risk for violence? The latter question is important because it usually becomes necessary—both to broaden political support and to avoid stigmatizing high-risk children—to provide an intervention program to all children in a geographic area rather than to only a subset. To answer both questions, a classification rule would be needed to classify study subjects as high-risk or normative, but the interventions would be tested on both groups.

The study should also be designed to measure the effects of community-level interventions both on the cohort samples and on community violence levels. Possible interventions include parent education programs beginning at the prenatal stage, anti-violence campaigns by religious and community-based organizations, and efforts to limit exposure to violence in the media.

Outcome measures for evaluating the individual-level interventions should include, of course, measures of aggressive and violent behavior as reported by the study subjects, parents, peers, teachers, social workers, and, for the early cohort, juvenile justice authorities. Also, because demonstrating benefits beyond violence control will hasten public acceptance of programs, outcome measures should include other outcomes where specifically relevant to the intervention: reading and arithmetic ability, short-term memory, retention in school, educational achievement, television viewing habits, and substance abuse and sexual activity during adolescence.

NOTES

1 In a survey of 1,700 Rhode Island boys and girls in the seventh to ninth grades (Kikuchi, 1988), 20 percent answered that a male on a date had a right to sexual intercourse against the women's consent if "he spent a lot of money on her." Another study finds that about 55 percent of college males in a sample reported "some" or "higher" likelihood of raping someone in the future (Malamuth, 1981). Another reports that a majority of a sample of 598 men believed that rape reports usually result from a women's concealing a pregnancy or seeking reprisal against a man and endorsed other expressions of tolerance toward rape (Burt, 1980). Another study found that scores on an Attitudes Toward Women Scale were similar for incarcerated rapists, incarcerated nonsexual offenders, and nonoffenders with low socioeconomic status.

2 There is relative evolutionary constancy for acids, peptides, and steroids, their synthetic and metabolic enzymes, their receptors and messenger systems in mammalian nervous systems. However, there is considerable specialization in the functions of neurotransmitter systems across animal species. The most reliable information comes from studies comparing at least two species, one of which ought to be primate.

3 A study by Bain et al. (1987) found that pedophilic men manifest disturbances in the hypothalamic-pituitary axis and overrespond to injections of hormones that stimulate gonadal function. Bain et al. (1988) found abnormal levels of DHEAS in sexually aggressive men, but an ACTH challenge test was not significant.

4 We are aware of only one randomized experimental evaluation of a treatment program for violent sex offenders that involves follow-up outside an institutional setting. The Sex Offender Treatment and Evaluation Project (SOTEP), mandated and funded by the California state legislature, involved random assignment of volunteers to a relapse prevention program during the last 18-30 months of their prison terms. By 1989, 98 treatment and control subjects had been released to the community, and they are still being followed up. Since the intervention did not shorten participants' incarceration terms and provided treatment that was not otherwise available, the study did not increase danger to the community. Preliminary findings suggest that the relapse prevention program had some success (Miner et al., 1990).

5 Using census tracts has limitations: they are not individual level and therefore say nothing about the risks of an individual, black or white, with higher or lower status than his neighbors. But information from census tracts is better than information from states or metropolitan areas because tracts are more homogeneous.

REFERENCES

American Psychiatric Association
1987 *Diagnostic and Statistical Manual of Mental Disorders, DSM-III-R* (Third Edition, Revised). Washington, D.C.: American Psychiatric Association.

Anderson, E.
1978 *A Place on the Corner.* Chicago: The University of Chicago Press.
1990 *Streetwise: Race, Class, and Change in an Urban Community.* Chicago: The University of Chicago Press.
1991 Alienation and Crime Among the Ghetto Poor, prepared for the Panel on the Understanding and Control of Violence (unpublished).

Atlas, R.
1983 Crime site selection for assaults in four Florida prisons. *Prison Journal* 63:59-71.

Bain, J., R. Langevin, R. Dickey, and M. Ben-Aron
1987 Sex hormones in murderers and assaulters. *Behavioral Sciences & the Law* 5:95-101.

Bain, J., R. Langevin, R. Dickey, S. Hucker, and P. Wright
1988 Hormones in sexually aggressive men: I. Baseline values for eight hormones. II. The ACTH test. *Annals of Sex Research* 1:63-78.

Baker, H.J., and R.J. Stoller
1968 Sexual psychopathology in the hypogonadal male. *Archives of General Psychiatry* 18:631-633.

Baker, D., M. Telfer, C. Richardson, and G. Clark
1970 Chromosome errors in men with antisocial behavior: Comparison of selected men with Klinefelter's syndrome and XYY chromosome pattern. *Journal of the American Medical Association* 215(5):869-878.

Barak-Glantz, I.
1981 Toward a conceptual scheme of prison management styles. *Prison Journal* 61:42-58.

Baron, Larry, and Murray A. Straus
1989 *Four Theories of Rape in American Society.* New Haven, Conn.: Yale University Press.

Bartlett, D.J.
1968 Chromosomes of male patients in a security prison. *Nature* 219:351-353.

Beasley, R.W., and G. Antunes
1974 The etiology of urban crime: An ecological analysis. *Criminology* 11:439-461.

Bell, Catherine A.
1991 Female homicides in United States workplaces, 1980-1985. *American Journal of Public Health* 81(6):729-732

Bensing, R.C., and O. Schroeder
1960 *Homicide in an Urban Community.* Springfield, Ill.: Charles C Thomas.

Berrueta-Clement, J.R., L.J. Schweinhart, W.S. Barnett, A.S. Epstein, and D.P. Weikart
1984 *Changed Lives.* Ypsilanti, Mich.: High/Scope.

Blumstein, Alfred, Jacqueline Cohen, and David P. Farrington
1988 Longitudinal and criminal career research: Further clarifications. *Criminology* 26:57-74.

Bohman, M., C.R. Cloninger, S. Sigvardsson, and A.L. von Knorring
1982 Predisposition to petty criminality in Swedish adoptees: I. Genetic and environmental heterogeneity. *Archives of General Psychiatry* 39:1233-1241.

Browne, A., and D. Finkelhor
1986 Impact of child sexual abuse: A review of the research. *Psychological Bulletin* 99:66-77.

Bullock, H.S.
1955 Urban homicide in theory and fact. *Journal of Criminal Law, Criminology, and Police Science* 45:565-575.

Bureau of Justice Statistics
1992 *Criminal Victimization in the United States, 1990.* Washington, D.C.: U.S. Government Printing Office.

Burt, M.R.
1980 Cultural myths and support for rape. *Journal of Personality and Social Psychology* 38:217-230.

Cairns, Robert B., Beverley D. Cairns, Holly J. Neckerman, Scott D. Gest, and Jean-Louis Gariépy
1988 Social networks and aggressive behavior: Peer support or peer rejection? *Developmental Psychology* 24(6):815-823.

Centerwall, Brandon S.
1984 Race, socioeconomic status, and domestic homicide, Atlanta, 1971-2. *American Journal of Public Health* 74(8):813-815.

Chaiken, J.M., M.W. Lawless, and K.A. Stevenson
1974 The impact of police activity on subway crime. *Urban Analysis* 3:173-205.

Check, J.V.P., and N.M. Malamuth
1983 Sex role stereotyping and reactions to depictions of stranger versus acquaintance rape. *Journal of Personality and Social Psychology* 45:344-356.

Cherry, F.
1983 Gender roles and sexual violence. Pp. 245-260 in E.R. Allgeier and N.B. McCormick, eds., *Changing Boundaries: Gender Roles and Sexual Behavior.* Palo Alto, Calif.: Mayfield.

Chin, K.
1990 *Chinese Subculture and Criminality: Non-Traditional Crime Groups in America.* Westport, Conn.: Greenwood.

Christiansen, K.O.
1977 A review of studies of criminality among twins. In S.A. Mednick and K.O. Christiansen, eds., *Biosocial Bases of Criminal Behavior*. New York: Gardner.

Clarke, R.V.
1983 Situational crime prevention: Its theoretical basis and practical scope. Pp. 225-256 in M. Tonry and N. Morris, eds., *Crime and Justice: An Annual Review of Research*. Vol. 4. Chicago: University of Chicago Press.

Clifton, W., Jr.
1987 Convenience Store Robberies in Gainesville, Florida: An Intervention Strategy by the Gainesville Police Department. Gainesville, Florida Police Department, photocopy.

Cloninger, C.R., and Gottesman, I.I.
1987 Genetic and environmental factors in antisocial behavioral disorders. Pp. 92-109 in S.A. Mednick, T.E. Moffitt, and S.A. Stack, eds., *The Causes of Crime: New Biological Approaches*. New York: Cambridge University Press.

Cloninger, C.R., K.O. Christiansen, T. Reich, and I.I. Gottesman
1978 Implications of sex differences in the prevalences of antisocial personality, alcoholism, and criminality for familial transmission. *Archives of General Psychiatry* 35:941-951.

Cloward, R.A., and L.E. Ohlin
1960 *Delinquency and Opportunity*. Glencoe, Ill.: Free Press.

Cohen, L., and M. Felson
1979 Social change and crime rate trends: A routine activities approach. *American Sociological Review* 44:588-607.

Coleman, J.S.
1990 *Foundations of Social Theory*. Cambridge, Mass.: Harvard University Press.

Comstock, G., and Paik, H.
1990 The Effects of Television Violence on Aggressive Behavior: A Meta-analysis. Unpublished report to the National Academy of Sciences Panel on the Understanding and Control of Violent Behavior, Washington, D.C.

Cook, P.J.
1986 The demand and supply of criminal opportunities. In M. Tonry and N. Morris, eds., *Crime and Justice: An Annual Review of Research*. Vol. 7. Chicago: University of Chicago Press.

D'Allessio, S., and L. Stolzenberg
1990 A crime of convenience: The environment and convenience store robbery. *Environment and Behavior* 22(2):255-271.

Denno, Deborah W.
1990 *Biology and Violence: From Birth to Adulthood*. Cambridge: Cambridge University Press.

Dietz, P.E.
1986 Mass, serial, and sensational homicides. *Bulletin of the New York Academy of Medicine* 62:477-491.

Dollard, J., L.W. Doob, N.E. Miller, O.H. Mowrer, and R.R. Sears
1939 *Frustration and Aggression.* New Haven, Conn.: Yale University Press.

Donnerstein, E., D. Linz, and S. Penrod
1987 *The Question of Pornography.* New York: Free Press.

Duffala, D.C.
1976 Convenience stores, armed robbery, and the physical environment. *American Behavioral Scientist* 20:227-246.

Dworkin, A.
1979 *Pornography: Men Possessing Women.* New York: G.P. Putnam's Sons.

Ekland-Olson, S.
1986 Crowding, social control, and prison violence: Evidence from the post-Ruiz years in Texas. *Law & Society Review* 20(3):389-421.

Elliott, D.S., D. Huizinga, and S. Menard
1989 *Multiple Problem Youth: Delinquency, Substance Use, and Mental Health Problems.* New York: Springer-Verlag.

Ellis, D.
1991 Monoamine oxidase and criminality: Identifying an apparent biological marker for antisocial behavior. *Journal of Research in Crime and Delinquency* 28:227-251.

Ellis, D., H.G. Grasmick, and B. Gilman
1974 Violence in prisons: A sociological analysis. *American Journal of Sociology* 80:416-443.

Engel, K., and S. Rothman
1983 Prison violence and the paradox of reform. *Public Interest* 70-73:91-105.

Eron, L.D.
1990 Understanding aggression. Presidential address to the World Meeting of ISRA, Banff, Alberta, June 12.

Eron, L.D., and L.R. Huesmann
1984 The relation of prosocial behavior to the development of aggression and psychopathology. *Aggressive Behavior* 10:201-212.

Fagan, Jeffrey
1990 Social processes of drug use and delinquency among gang and non-gang youths. In C. Ronald Huff, ed., *Gangs in America.* Newbury Park, Calif.: Sage Publications.

Farrington, D.P.
1989 Early predictors of adolescent aggression and adult violence. *Violence and Victims* 4:79-100.
1991 Childhood aggression and adult violence: Early precursors and later-life outcomes. Pp. 5-29 in D.J. Pepler and K.H. Rubin,

eds., *The Development and Treatment of Childhood Aggression.* Hillsdale, N.J.: Erlbaum.

Farrington, David P., Leonard Berkowitz, and Donald J. West
1981 Differences between individual and group fights. *British Journal of Social Psychology* 20:163-171.

Farrington, David P., Lloyd E. Ohlin, and James Q. Wilson
1986 *Understanding and Controlling Crime: Toward a New Research Strategy.* New York: Springer-Verlag.

Farrington, D.P., and D.J. West
1990 The Cambridge study in delinquent development: A long-term follow-up study of 411 London males. Pp. 115-138 in H.J. Kerner and G. Kaiser, eds., *Criminality: Personality, Behavior, and Life History.* Berlin: Springer-Verlag.

Feingold, B.F.
1975 Hyperkinesis and learning disabilities linked to artificial food flavors and colors. *American Journal of Nursing* 75:797-803.

Felson, R.B., and H.J. Steadman
1983 Situational factors in disputes leading to criminal violence. *Criminology* 21(1, February):59-74.

Finkelhor, D.
1984 *Child Sexual Abuse: New Theory and Research.* New York: The Free Press.

Fleisher, M.
1989 *Warehousing Violence.* Newbury Park, Calif.: Sage Publications.

Flynn, E.E.
1976 The ecology of prison violence. In A.K. Cohen, G.F. Cole, and R.G. Bailey, eds., *Prison Violence.* Lexington, Mass.: Lexington Books.

Fong, R.S.
1987 A Comparative Study of the Organizational Aspects of Two Texas Prison Gangs: Texas Syndicate and Mexican Mafia. Ph.D. dissertation.

Forst, M.L., and J.M. Brady
1983 The effects of determinate sentencing on inmate misconduct in prison. *The Prison Journal* 63:101-113.

Fowler, F.G.
1981 Evaluating a complex crime control experience. In L. Bickman, ed., *Applied Social Psychology Annual.* Vol. 2. Hillsdale, N.J.: Erlbaum.

Fowler, F.G., and T.W. Mangione
1981 An Experimantal Effort to Reduce Crime and Fear of Crime in an Urban Residential Neighborhood: Reevaluation of the Hartford Neighborhood Crime Prevention Program. Draft executive summary. Cambridge: Harvard/Massachusetts Institute of Technology, Center for Survey Research.

Freedman, J.L.
1986 Television violence and aggression: A rejoinder. *Psychological Bulletin* 100:372-378.

Friedrich-Cofer, L., and A.C. Huston
1986 Television violence and aggression: The debate continues. *Psychological Bulletin* 100:364-371.

Furstenberg, Frank
1990 How Families Manage Risk and Opportunity in Dangerous Neighborhoods. Paper presented at the annual meeting of the American Sociological Association, Washington, D.C.

Gaes, G.G.
1985 The effects of overcrowding in prison. Pp. 95-146 in M. Tonry and N. Morris, eds., *Crime and Justice: An Annual Review of Research*. Vol. 6. Chicago: University of Chicago Press.

Gaes, G., and W.J. McGuire
1985 Prison violence: The contribution of crowding versus other determinants of prison assault rates. *Journal of Research in Crime and Delinquency* 22:41-65.

Gardiner, R.A.
1978 *Design for Safe Neighborhoods*. Washington, D.C.: U.S. Government Printing Office.

Garreau, J.
1988 The invisible hand guides D.C.'s visible menace: Street-corner drug trade provides a model of capitalism, say economists, police. *Washington Post*, December 12, pp. A1, A14-A15.

Gordon, Robert A.
1967 Issues in the ecological study of delinquency. *American Sociological Review* 32(6):927-944.

Gottfredson, Michael, and Travis Hirschi
1987 The methodological adequacy of longitudinal research on crime. *Criminology* 25:581-614.

Gottfredson, S.D., and R.B. Taylor
1986 Person-environment interactions in the prediction of recidivism. In R. Sampson and J. Byrne, eds., *The Social Ecology of Crime*. New York: Springer-Verlag.

Guerra, N.
1990 Social cognitive approaches to the prevention of antisocial behavior in children. Paper presented at the Workshop on Hostility and Sociability, Warsaw, Poland (September).

Hagedorn, J.
1988 *People and Folks: Gangs, Crime, and the Underclass in a Rustbelt City*. Chicago: Lakeview Press.

Hanson, R.K., and S. Slater
1988 Sexual victimization in the history of sexual abusers: A review. *Annals of Sex Research* 1:485-500.

Hare, R.D.
1978 Electrodermal and cardiovascular correlates of psychopathy. In

R.D. Hare and D. Schalling, eds., *Psychopathic Behavior: Approaches to Research.* New York: John Wiley & Sons.

Harries, K.D.
1990 *Serious Violence: Patterns of Homicide and Assault in America.* Springfield, Ill.: Charles C Thomas.

Hawkins, J.D., E. Von Cleve, and R.F. Catalano
1991 Reducing early childhood aggression. *Journal of the American Academy of Child and Adolescent Psychiatry.*

Heath, L., L.B. Bresolin, and R.C. Rinaldi
1989 Effects of media violence on children. *Archives of General Psychiatry* 46:376-379.

Hindelang, M., M. Gottfredson, and J. Garofalo
1978 *Victims of Personal Crime: An Empirical Foundation for a Theory of Personal Victimization.* Cambridge, Mass.: Ballinger.

Horowitz, Ruth
1983 *Honor and the American Dream.* New Brunswick, N.J.: Rutgers University Press.

Huesmann, L.R., and L.D. Eron
1984 Cognitive processes and the persistence of aggressive behavior. *Aggressive Behavior* 10:243-251.
1986 *Television and the Aggressive Child.* New York: Erlbaum.

Huesmann, L.R., and L.S. Miller
in press Long term effects of repeated exposure to media violence in childhood. In G. Comstock, ed., *Public Communication and Behavior.* Vol. 3. Orlando, Fla.: Academic Press.

Huesmann, L.R., L.D. Eron, R. Klein, P. Brice, and P. Fischer
1983 Mitigating the imitation of aggressive behaviors by changing children's attitudes about media violence. *Journal of Personality and Social Psychology* 44:899-910.

Huizinga, D., F. Esbensen, and A.W. Weiher
1991 Are there multiple paths to delinquency? Denver youth survey. *Journal of Criminal Law and Criminology* 82(1):83-118.

Institute of Medicine
1985 *Preventing Low Birthweight.* Washington, D.C.: National Academy Press.

Jacobs, James B.
1977 *Stateville: The Penitentiary in Mass Society.* Chicago: University of Chicago Press.

Jankowski, Martin Sanchez
1991 *Islands in the Street: Gangs and American Urban Society.* Berkeley, Calif.: University of California Press.

Jargowsky, Paul A., and Mary Jo Bane
1990 Ghetto poverty: Basic questions. Pp. 16-67 in Laurence E. Lynn, Jr., and Michael G.H. McGeary, eds., *Inner-City Poverty in the United States.* Washington, D.C.: National Academy Press.

Jeffery, C.R., R.H. Hunter, and J. Griswold
1987 Crime analysis, computers, and convenience store robberies.

Appendix D to Wayland Clifton, Jr., Convenience store robberies in Gainesville, Florida: An intervention strategy by Gainesville police department. Paper presented at the 1987 meeting of the American Society of Criminology, Montreal, November.

Jencks, C., and S.E. Mayer
1990 The social consequences of growing up in a poor neighborhood. Pp. 111-186 in L.E. Lynn, Jr., and M.G.H. McGeary, eds., *Inner-City Poverty in the United States.* Washington, D.C.: National Academy Press.

Jones, M.B., and D.R. Offord
1989 Reduction of antisocial behavior in poor children by non-school skill-development. *Journal of Child Psychology and Psychiatry* 30:737-750.

Kagan, J.
1989 Temperamental contributions to social behavior. *American Psychologist* 44:668-674.

Kaufman, J., and E. Zigler
1987 Do abused children become abusive parents? *American Journal of Orthopsychiatry* 57:186-192.

Kazdin, A.E.
1985 *Treatment of Antisocial Behavior in Children and Adolescents.* Homewood, Ill.: Dorsey Press.

Kessler, S., and R. Moos
1970 The XYY karyotype and criminality: A review. *Journal of Psychiatric Research* 17:29-34.

Kikuchi, J.J.
1988 Rhode Island develops successful intervention program for adolescents. *NCASA News* (Fall):26-27

Klein, Malcolm
1969 Violence in American juvenile gangs. Pp. 1425-1460 in Donald J. Mulvihill and Melvin M. Tumin, eds., *Crimes of Violence.* Vol. 13. Staff report submitted to the National Commission on the Causes and Prevention of Violence. Washington, D.C.: U.S. Government Printing Office.
1971 *Street Gangs and Street Workers.* Englewood Cliffs, N.J.: Prentice-Hall.

Klein, Malcolm, and Cheryl Maxson
1989 Street gang violence. Pp. 198-234 in Neil Alan Weiner and Marvin E. Wolfgang, eds., *Violent Crime, Violent Criminals.* Newbury Park, Calif.: Sage Publications.

Kolarsky, A., K. Freund, J. Machek, and O. Polak
1967 Male sexual deviation: Association with early temporal lobe damage. *Archives of General Psychiatry* 17:735-743.

Kolvin, I., F.J.W. Miller, M. Fleeting, and P.A. Kolvin
1988 Social and parenting factors affecting criminal-offence rates: Findings from the Newcastle thousand family study (1947-1980). *British Journal of Psychiatry* 152:80-90.

Land, Kenneth, P. McCall, and L. Cohen
1990 Structural co-variates of homicide rates: Are there any invariances across time and space? *American Journal of Sociology* 95:922-963.

Landes, W.M.
1978 An economic study of U.S. aircraft hijacking, 1961-1976. *Journal of Law and Economics* 21:1-32.

Langevin, R.
1990 Sexual anomalies and the brain. Pp. 103-113 in W.L. Marshall, D.R. Laws, and H.E. Barbaree, eds., *Handbook of Sexual Assault: Issues, Theories, and Treatment of the Offender*. New York: Plenum Press.

Langevin, R., J. Bain, M.H. Ben-Aron, R. Coulthard, D. Day, L. Handy, G. Heasman, S.J. Hucker, J.E. Purins, V. Roper, A.E. Russon, C.D. Webster, and G. Wortzman
1985 Sexual aggression: Constructing a predictive equation. A controlled pilot study. Pp. 39-76 in R. Langevin, ed., *Erotic Preference, Gender Identity, and Aggression in Men: New Research Studies*. Hillsdale, N.J.: Lawrence Erlbaum.

Lemann, Nicholas
1991 *The Promised Land: The Great Black Migration and How It Changed America*. New York: Alfred A. Knopf.

Lewis, D.O., J.H. Pincus, B. Bard, and E. Richardson
1988 Neuropsychiatric, psycho-educational, and family characteristics of 14 juveniles condemned to death in the United States. *American Journal of Psychiatry* 145:584-589.

Linnoila, M., J. DeJong, and M. Virkkunen
1989 Family history of alcoholism in violent offenders and impulsive fire setters. *Archives of General Psychiatry* 46:613-616.

Lockwood, D.
1980 *Prison Sexual Violence*. New York: Elsevier.

Loeber, R., M. Stouthamer-Loeber, W. Van Kammen, and D.P. Farrington
1991 Initiation, escalation and desistance in juvenile offending and their correlates. Pittsburgh youth study. *Journal of Criminal Law and Criminology* 82(1):36-82.

Lowry, Philip W., Susan Hassig, Robert Gunn, and Joyce Mathison
1988 Homicide victims in New Orleans: Recent trends. *American Journal of Epidemiology* 128(5):1130-1136.

Luckenbill, D.F.
1977 Criminal homicide as a situated transaction. *Criminal Homicide* (?):176-186.

Lynn, Laurence E., Jr., and Michael G.H. McGeary, eds.
1990 *Inner-City Poverty in the United States*. Washington, D.C.: National Academy Press.

MacLeod, Jay
1987 *Ain't No Makin' It: Leveled Aspirations in a Low-Income Neighborhood*. Boulder, Colo.: Westview Press.

Magnusson, D., and L. Bergman
1988 Individual and variable-based approaches for longitudinal research on early risk factors. In M. Rutter, ed., *Studies of Psychosocial Risk: The Power of Longitudinal Data.* Cambridge: Cambridge University Press.

Malamuth, N.M.
1981 Rape proclivity among males. *Journal of Social Issues* 37:138-157.

Marquart, J.W., and B.M. Crouch
1985 Judicial reform and prisoner control: The impact of *Ruiz v. Estelle* on a Texas penitentiary. *Law & Society Review* 19(4):557-586.

McCord, W. and J. McCord
1956 *Psychopathy and Delinquency.* New York: Grune and Stratton.

McDermott, M.J.
1979 *Criminal Victimization in Urban Schools.* Albany, N.Y.: Criminal Justice Research Center. (Analytic Report SD-VAD-8 1979.)

McGeary, Michael G.H., and Laurence E. Lynn, Jr., eds.
1988 *Urban Change and Poverty.* Washington, D.C.: National Academy Press.

Mednick, S.A., W.F. Gabrielli, and B. Hutchings
1984 Genetic influences in criminal convictions: Evidence from an adoption cohort. *Science* 224:891-894.

Megargee, E.I., M.J. Bohn, and J.L. Carbonell
1988 A Cross-Validation and Test of the Generality of the MMPI-Based Offender Classification System. Final report of National Institute of Justice grant no. 1596001138A1, Tallahassee, Fla.: Florida State University.

Merry, S.E.
1981a Defensible space undefended: Social factors in crime prevention through environmental design. *Urban Affairs Quarterly* 16:397-422.
1981b *Urban Danger: Life in a Neighborhood of Strangers.* Philadelphia, Pa.: Temple University Press.

Messner, S., and K. Tardiff
1986 Economic inequality and levels of homicide: An analysis of urban neighborhoods. *Criminology* 24:297-318.

Miethe, T., and R. Meier
1990 Opportunity, choice, and criminal victimization. *Journal of Research in Crime and Delinquency* 27:243-266.

Miller, L.
1987 Neuropsychology of the aggressive psychopath: An integrative review. *Aggressive Behavior* 13:119-140.

Miller, W.B.
1975 *Violence by Youth Gangs and Youth Groups as a Crime Problem in Major American Cities.* Washington, D.C.: U.S. Government Printing Office.

1980 Gangs, groups, and serious youth crime. Pp. 115-138 in D. Shichor and D. Kelly, eds., *Critical Issues in Juvenile Delinquency*. Lexington, Mass.: D.C. Heath.

Miller, Walter B., Hildred Geertz, and Henry S. G. Cutter

1961 Aggression in a boys' street-corner group. *Psychiatry* XXIV:283-298.

Miner, M.H., J.K. Marques, D.M. Day, and C. Nelson

1990 Impact of relapse prevention in treating sex offenders: Preliminary findings. *Annals of Sex Research* 3:165-185.

Mladenka, K., and K. Hill

1976 A reexamination of the etiology of urban crime. *Criminology* 13:491-506.

Moffitt, T.E., and P.A. Silva

1988 Neuropsychological deficit and self-reported delinquency in an unselected birth cohort. *Journal of the American Academy of Child and Adolescent Psychiatry* 27:233-240.

Moore, Joan W.

1987 Variations in violence among Hispanic gangs. Pp. 215-30 in Jess F. Kraus, Susan B. Sorenson, and Paul D. Juarez, eds., *Research Conference on Violence and Homicide in Hispanic Communities*. University of California, Los Angeles.

1991 Institutionalized Youth Gangs: Why White Fence and El Hoyo Maravilla Change So Slowly. Working Group on the Social and Economic Ecology of Crime and Drugs in Inner Cities, Social Science Research Council, unpublished.

Moore, J.W., with Robert Garcia, Carlos Garcia, Luis Cerda, and Frank Valencia

1978 *Homeboys: Gangs, Drugs, and Prisons in the Barrios of Los Angeles*. Philadelphia, Pa.: Temple University Press.

Morgan, R.

1980 Theory and practice: Pornography and rape. In L. Lederer and A. Rich, eds, *Take Back the Night: Women on Pornography*. New York: William Morrow and Company.

Mungas, D.

1988 Psychometric correlates of episodic violent behaviour: A multidimensional neuropsychological approach. *British Journal of Psychiatry* 152:180-187.

Murphy, W.D., M.R. Haynes, S.J. Stalgaitis, and B. Flanagan

1986 Differential sexual responding among four groups of sexual offenders against children. *Journal of Psychopathology and Behavioral Assessment* 8:339-353.

Muscat, Joshua E.

1988 Characteristics of childhood homicide in Ohio, 1974-84. *American Journal of Public Health* 78(7):822-824.

National Institute of Education

1978 *Violent Schools—Safe Schools: The Safe School Study Report to the Congress*. Washington, D.C.: U.S. Government Printing Office.

National Institute for Occupational Safety and Health
1992 Homicide in U.S. workplaces: A strategy for prevention and research. Washington, D.C.

Nelson, W.R.
1988 Cost savings in new generation jails: The direct supervision approach. *National Institute of Justice Construction Bulletin* (July).

Newman, O.
1973a *Architectural Design for Crime Prevention.* Washington, D.C.: U.S. Government Printing Office.
1973b *Defensible Space: Crime Prevention Through Urban Design.* New York: Macmillan.
1975 *Design Guidelines for Creating Defensible Space.* Washington, D.C.: U.S. Government Printing Office.

Newman, O., and K.A. Franck
1980 *Factors Influencing Crime and Instability in Urban Housing Developments.* Washington, D.C.: U.S. Government Printing Office.
1982 The effects of building size on personal crime and fear of crime. *Population and Environment* 5:203-220.

Olweus, D.
1979 Stability of aggressive reaction patterns in males: A review. *Psychological Bulletin* 86:852-875.
1980 Familial and temperamental determinants of aggressive behavior in adolescent boys: A causal analysis. *Developmental Psychology* 16:644-660.
1984 Development of stable aggressive reaction patterns in males. Pp. 103-137 in R.J. Blanchard and D.C. Blanchard, eds., *Advances in the Study of Aggression.* Vol. I. Orlando, Fla.: Academic Press.
1991 Bully/victim problems among schoolchildren: Basic facts and effects of a school based intervention program. Pp. 411-448 in D.J. Pepler and K.H. Rubin, eds., *The Development and Treatment of Childhood Aggression.* Hillsdale, N.J.: Erlbaum.

Owen, D.R.
1972 The 47, XYY male: A review. *Psychological Bulletin* 78(3):209-233.

Padilla, Felix
1990 Going to Work: The Entrepreneurial Side of the Gang. Unpublished manuscript.

Park, J.W.L.
1976 The organization of prison violence. In A.K. Cohen, G.F. Cole, and R.G. Bailey, eds., *Prison Violence.* Lexington, Mass.: Lexington Books.

Pasqualini, R.Q., G. Vidal, and G.E. Bur
1957 Psychopathology of Klinefelter's syndrome. *Lancet* 2:164-167.

Pepler, D.J., G. King, and W. Byrd
1991 A social-cognitively based social skills training program for aggressive children. Pp. 361-379 in D.J. Pepler and K.H. Rubin, eds., *The Development and Treatment of Childhood Aggression*. Hillsdale, N.J.: Erlbaum.

Piacentini, J.C.
1987 Language dysfunction and childhood behavior disorders. *Advances in Clinical Child Psychology* 10:259-285.

Plomin, R.
1989 Environment and genes. *American Psychologist* 44(2):105-111.

Prentky, R.A.
1990 Sexual Violence. Paper prepared for the Panel on the Understanding and Control of Violent Behavior, National Research Council. March 1.

Prothrow-Stith, D., H. Spivak, and A. Hausman
1987 The violence prevention project: A public health approach. *Science, Technology, and Human Values* 12:67-69.

Quinsey, V.L., T.C. Chaplin, and D. Upfold
1984 Sexual arousal to nonsexual violence and sadomasochistic themes among rapists and non-sex-offenders. *Journal of Consulting and Clinical Psychology* 52:651-657.

Raine, A., and P.H. Venables
1988a Skin conductance responsivity in psychopaths to orienting, defensive, and consonant-vowel stimuli. *Journal of Psychophysiology* 2:221-225.
1988b Enhanced P3 evoked potentials and longer P3 recovery times in psychopaths. *Psychophysiology* 25:30-38.

Raine, A., P.H. Venables, and M. Williams
1990a Relationships between CNS and ANS measures of arousal at age 15 and criminality at age 24. *Archives of General Psychiatry* 47:1003-1007.
1990b Relationships between N1, P300 and CNV recorded at age 15 and criminal behavior at age 24. *Psychophysiology* 27:567-575.

Reiss, Albert J., Jr., and Michael Tonry, eds.
1986 *Communities and Crime*. Chicago: University of Chicago Press.

Revitch, E.
1965 Sex murder and the potential sex murder. *Diseases of the Nervous System* 26:640-648.

Robins, L.N.
1978 The interaction of setting and predisposition in explaining novel behavior: Drug initiations before, in, and after Vietnam. In D.B. Kandel, ed., *Longitudinal Research on Drug Use*. New York: John Wiley & Sons.

Roncek, D.
1981 Dangerous places: Crime and residential environment. *Social Forces* 60:74-96.

Roncek, D., and D. Faggiani
1986 High schools and crime: A replication. *Sociological Quarterly* 26:491-505.

Rothberg, Joseph M., Paul T. Bartone, Harry C. Holloway, and David H. Marlowe
1990 Life and death in the U.S. Army. *Journal of the American Medical Association* 264(17):2241-2244.

Rubel, R.J., and A.H. Goldsmith
1980 Reflections on the rights of students and the rise of school violence. Pp. 71-79 in K. Baker, and R.J. Rubel, eds., *Violence and Crime in the Schools*. Lexington, Mass.: Lexington Books.

Russell, D.E.H.
1975 *The Politics of Rape: The Victim's Perspective*. New York: Stein & Day.

Sampson, R.J.
1983 Structural density and criminal victimization. *Criminology* 21:276-293.
1985 Neighborhood and crime: The structural determinants of personal victimization. *Journal of Research in Crime and Delinquency* 22(1):7-40.
1987 Personal violence by strangers: An extension and test of the opportunity model of predatory victimization. *Journal of Criminal Law and Criminology* 78: 327-356.

Sampson, R.J., and Wooldredge
1987 Linking the micro- and macro-level dimensions of lifestyle-routine activity and opportunity models of predatory victimization. *Journal of Quantitative Criminology* 3:371-393.

Schuerman, L., and S. Kobrin
1986 Community careers in crime. Pp. 67-100 in A.J. Reiss, Jr., and M. Tonry, eds., *Communities and Crime*. Vol. 8. in *Crime and Justice: A Review of Research*. Chicago: University of Chicago Press.

Schwartz, Gary
1987 *Beyond Conformity or Rebellion: Youth and Authority in America*. Chicago: University of Chicago Press.

S.D. Texas
1980 *Ruiz v. Estelle* 503 F. Supp. 1265.

Segal, Z.V., and W.L. Marshall
1985 Heterosexual social skills in a population of rapists and child molesters. *Journal of Consulting and Clinical Psychology* 53:55-63.

Shaw, C.R., and H.D. McKay
1942 *Juvenile Delinquency and Urban Areas*. Chicago: University of Chicago Press.

Sherman, L.W., P.R. Gartin, and M.E. Buerger
1989 Hot spots of predatory crime: Routine activities and the criminology of place. *Criminology* 27(1):27-55.

Short, James F.
1990 Gangs, neighborhoods, and youth crime. *Criminal Justice Research Bulletin* 5(4):1-11.
1991 Poverty, ethnicity and crime: Change and continuity in U.S. cities. (Review essay.) *Journal of Research in Crime and Delinquency* 28(4):501-518.

Short, James F., and Fred L. Strodtbeck
1965 *Group Process and Gang Delinquency*. Chicago: University of Chicago Press.

Siddle, D.A.T., A.R. Nicol, and R.H. Foggit
1973 Habituation and over-extinction of the GSR component of the orienting response in anti-social adolescents. *British Journal of Social and Clinical Psychology* 12:303-308.

Simpkins, L., W. Ward, S. Bowman, and C.M. Rinck
1989 The Multiphasic Sex Inventory as a predictor of treatment response in child sexual abusers. *Annals of Sex Research* 2:205-226.

Singer, J.L., and D.G. Singer
1981 *Television, Imagination, and Aggression: A Study of Pre-Schoolers*. Hillsdale, N.J.: Erlbaum.

Skogan, Wesley G.
1990 *Disorder and Decline: Crime and the Spiral of Decay in American Neighborhoods*. New York: Free Press.

Smith, D.R., and G.R. Jarjoura
1988 Social structure and criminal victimization. *Journal of Research in Crime and Delinquency* 25:27-52.

Spergel, Irving A., G. David Curry, Ruth Ross, and Ronald Chance, eds.
1989 Survey. National Youth Gang Suppression and Intervention Project. School of Social Service, University of Chicago.

Spiro, A., III, and W. DeJong
1991 Preventing Interpersonal Violence Among Teens: Field Tests and Evaluation of the Violence Prevention Curriculum for Adolescents. Final report for National Institute of Justice grant no. 87-IJ-CX-0009.

Steadman, Henry J.
1982 A situational approach to violence. *International Journal of Law and Psychiatry* 5:171-186.

Sullivan, M.
1989 *Getting Paid: Youth Crime and Work in the Inner City*. Ithaca, N.Y.: Cornell University Press.

Taylor, Carl S.
1990a Gang imperialism. Pp. 103-115 in C. Ronald Huff, ed., *Gangs in America*. Newbury Park, Calif.: Sage Publications.
1990b *Dangerous Society*. East Lansing, Mich.: Michigan State University Press.

Taylor, Ralph B., and Jeanette Covington
1988 Neighborhood changes in ecology and violence. *Criminology* 26(4):553-589.

Taylor and Gottfredson
1986 Environmental design, crime, and prevention: An examination of community dynamics. Pp. 387-416 in A.J. Reiss, Jr., and M. Tonry, eds., *Communities and Crime.* Vol. 8. Chicago: University of Chicago Press.

Thornberry, T.P., A.J. Lizotte, M.D. Krohn, M. Farnworth, and S.J. Jang
1991 Testing interactional theory: An examination of reciprocal causal relationships among family, school, and delinquency. Rochester youth development study. *Journal of Criminal Law and Criminology* 82(1):3-35.

Thrasher, Frederic M.
1927 *The Gang: A Study of 1,313 Gangs in Chicago.* (Abridged ed., 1963.) Chicago: University of Chicago Press.

Toby, J.
1983a Violence in school. Pp. 1-47 in M. Tonry and N. Morris, eds., *Crime and Justice: An Annual Review of Research.* Vol. 4. Chicago: University of Chicago Press.
1983b *Violence in School.* Washington, D.C.: National Institute of Justice, Research in Brief.

Toch, H.
1977 *Police, Prisons, and the Problem of Violence.* Chapter 4. Washington, D.C.: U.S. Government Printing Office.
1989 Violence in prisons. Pp. 267-285 in K. Howells and C.R. Hollin, eds., *Clinical Approaches to Violence.* New York: John Wiley & Sons.

Tonry, M., L.E. Ohlin, and D.P. Farrington
1991 *Human Development and Criminal Behavior: New Ways of Advancing Knowledge.* New York: Springer-Verlag.

Tremblay, R.E., J. McCord, H. Boileau, P. Charlebois, C. Cagnon, M. LeBlanc, and S. Larivee
1991 Can disruptive boys be helped to become competent? *Psychiatry.*

Venables, P.H., and A. Raine
1987 Biological theory. Pp. 3-28 in B. McGurk, D. Thornton, and M. Williams, eds., *Applying Psychology to Imprisonment: Theory and Practice.* London: Her Majesty's Stationery Office.

Vigil, James Diego
1987 Street socialization, locura behavior, and violence among Chicano gang members. Pp. 231-241 in Jess F. Kraus, Susan B. Sorenson, and Paul D. Juarez, eds., *Research Conference on Violence and Homicide in Hispanic Communities.* University of California, Los Angeles.
1988 *Barrio Gangs.* Austin, Tex.: University of Texas Press.

Virkkunen, M.
1986 Reactive hypoglycemia tendency among habitually violent offenders. *Nutrition Reviews* 44:94-103.

Virkkunen, M., J. DeJong, J. Bartko, and M. Linnoila
1989 Psychobiological concomitants of history of suicide attempts

among violent offenders and impulsive fire setters. *Archives of General Psychiatry* 46:604-606.

Wadsworth, M.E.J.
1976 Delinquency, pulse rate and early emotional deprivation. *British Journal of Criminology* 16:245-256.

Walkey, F., and D.R. Gilmour
1984 The relationship between interpersonal distance and violence in imprisoned offenders. *Criminal Justice and Behavior* 11(3):331-340.

Wallace, R., and D. Wallace
1990 Origins of public health collapse in New York City: The dynamics of planned shrinkage, contagious urban decay and social disintegration. *Bulletin of the New York Academy of Medicine* 66:391-434.

Weis, Joseph G.
1986 Issues in the measurement of criminal careers. Pp. 1-51 in A. Blumstein, J. Cohen, J.A. Roth, and C. Visher, eds., *Criminal Careers and "Career Criminals."* Vol. II. Washington, D.C.: National Academy Press.

Weis, Kurt, and Sandra S. Borges
1977 Victimology and rape: The case of the legitimate victim. Pp. 35-75 in D.R. Nass, ed., *The Rape Victim.* Dubuque, Iowa: Kendall/Hunt.

Williams, D.
1969 Neural factors related to habitual aggression: Consideration of those differences between those habitual aggressives and others who have committed crimes of violence. *Brain* 92:503-520.

Williams, Terry
1989 *The Cocaine Kids: The Inside Story of a Teenage Drug Ring.* Menlo Park, Calif.: Addison-Wesley.

Wilson, William Julius
1987 *The Truly Disadvantaged: The Inner City, the Underclass, and Public Policy.* Chicago: University of Chicago Press.
1990 Race-neutral programs and the democratic coalition. *The American Prospect* 1(Spring):74-81.
1991 Studying inner-city social dislocations: The challenge of public agenda research. *American Sociological Review* 56(February):1-14.

Wolfgang, Marvin E.
1957 Victim-precipitated criminal homicide. *Journal of Criminal Law, Criminology, and Police Science* 48(I):1-11.

Wolfgang, Marvin E., Robert M. Figlio, and Thorsten Sellin
1972 *Delinquency in a Birth Cohort.* Chicago: University of Chicago Press.

4

Alcohol, Other Psychoactive Drugs, and Violence

The connections between violence and alcohol and other psychoactive drugs—primarily opiates, cocaine, amphetamines, PCP, and hallucinogens—have rarely received much weight in developing national policy. Historically, mercantilist national ambitions, tariff revenue, presumed medical properties, the ethnic and social status of users, and moral assessments of alcohol and other drug use have played more prominent roles in formulating drug policy (Musto, 1973). Even today, despite anecdotal and research support for some connections between illegal drugs and violence, and despite reports of recent dramatic increases in drug-related violent deaths, violence remains a secondary consideration in formulating federal drug policy (White House, 1990).

Whether or not connections between drugs and violence are a matter of concern in formulating national policy on drugs, it seems important from the standpoint of policy on violence control to examine what is known about how violence is affected by the use of alcohol and other psychoactive drugs, by the marketing of illegal drugs, and by policy interventions to control those activities. From an intellectual perspective, studying how violence is related to psychoactive drugs is of special interest because it demonstrates so clearly the basic premise of Chapter 3—that violent events arise from interactions that cut across the biological, psychosocial, and macrosocial levels.

At the biological level, pertinent neurobiologic relationships have been discovered between certain psychoactive drugs (including alcohol) and violence, but certainly no basis for a blanket assertion that taking any of them causes people to behave violently. To start with, each of these drugs produces its own distinct array of biological changes; their effects on the body are not alike. For any drug, the particular changes depend on the acute dose level, the long-term pattern of drug use, and whether the concentrations in the brain and body are rising or falling. How these changes affect aggressive or violent behavior depend not only on interactions with endocrine, neurochemical, and genetic mechanisms, but also on interactions with processes at the micro- and macrosocial levels.

The link among alcohol, other psychoactive drugs, and violence turns out to be not an example of straightforward causation, but rather a network of interacting processes and feedback loops. In this chapter we examine patterns of violence related to the use of alcohol and other psychoactive drugs, evidence on the multiple connections that account for the relationship, and findings about the effects of interventions for controlling alcohol- and drug-related violence.

To study these relationships, one would like to manipulate the variables hypothesized to be causal and to measure the change in violent behavior. Efforts to adhere to this scientific ideal are properly constrained, of course, by technical and ethical limitations on measurement and manipulation. Therefore, quite different methods are used at different levels, and available methods are limited in terms of both the precision of statements that can be made and our confidence in them. In general, our statements become less precise and more speculative as the studied behavior more closely resembles human violent behavior in the community.

In contrast to pharmacological relationships, which are often studied in controlled experiments with human or animal subjects, evidence about social-level relationships between psychoactive drugs and violence is more fragmentary. It consists primarily of analyses of cross-sectional variation at different points in time (when different drugs were in vogue), a few ethnographic studies conducted during times of community transition, and facts about changes in particular communities at particular times. Necessarily, therefore, our arguments and conclusions at this level are more speculative than those at other levels.

With these cautions in mind, we turn now to a discussion of patterns of violence and the use of alcohol and other psychoactive drugs.

PATTERNS OF USE AND VIOLENCE

Alcohol

Situational Drinking

Most studies of alcohol use and violence focus on situational relationships between episodes of drinking and violent events; in general, pre-1981 studies find alcohol use by the perpetrator or the victim immediately before more than half of all violent events (Greenberg, 1981). More recent data confirm these findings: between 1982 and 1989, the prevalence of liquor use by offender or victim in Chicago homicides fluctuated between 32 and 18 percent, while the prevalence of other drug use rose only from about 1 to about 5 percent (Block et al., 1990).

The Drug Use Forecasting (DUF) program, in use in 22 cities, asks voluntary samples of felony arrestees whether they used alcohol within 72 hours before committing the crime for which they were arrested. During 1989, 59 percent of males and 53 percent of females arrested for violent Uniform Crime Reports index offenses reported such alcohol use. In a 1986 national survey of state prison inmates, the fraction who reported having used alcohol just before committing their crimes was smaller—about 33 percent for convicted rapists, robbers, and assaulters (Bureau of Justice Statistics, 1990:Table 14). The difference between arrestees and prison inmates would be expected if a disproportionate share of the alcohol-related incidents involved acquaintances who were reluctant to press charges and appear as witnesses.

These prevalence data are, of course, only suggestive. They are not sufficient to demonstrate that alcohol use increases the risk of violence. Greenberg's (1981) review found substantial alcohol involvement in nonviolent crimes as well as violent ones, and alcohol use prevalence rates in the DUF samples were nearly identical for violent and nonviolent offenses. Prevalence data are not sufficient to show that alcohol use or intoxication increases the general risk of violence. To test that hypothesis with prevalence data, one would need a benchmark: the fractions of people *not* involved in violence or crime while drinking—with appropriate adjustments for demographic characteristics of participants, time of day, day of week, and place of occurrence. The panel has been unable to locate or construct such benchmark prevalence data. However, an array of studies discussed later in this chapter finds connections between situational drinking and aggressive or violent behavior at the biological, social, and cultural levels.

Chronic Drinking

Only a few studies exist of the relationship between chronic drinking and potentials for violent behavior. In one sample of diagnosed alcoholics, 29 percent had a history of serious violence, including weapon use and inflicting injuries requiring medical attention (Shuckit and Russell, 1984). More importantly for our purposes, comparisons show that within otherwise comparable samples, problem drinkers are more likely than others to have histories of violence. In studies of prison inmates, those classified as "heavy" or "problem" drinkers had accumulated more previous arrests for violent crimes, were more likely to have been incarcerated for a violent crime, and reported higher average frequencies of assaults than did other inmates (see review by Collins, 1986). In a sample of Finnish juvenile delinquents, Virkkunen (1974) found an arrest rate for violent crimes of 22 percent for those who had also been arrested for drunkenness, compared with 12 percent for delinquents without a drunkenness arrest; a similar differential, 47 to 36 percent, was found for property crimes.

Studies of the prevalence of alcoholics among violent offenders indicate that alcoholism has been diagnosed in 20 to 40 percent of convicted murderers, 20 to 30 percent of convicted robbers, and 30 to 40 percent of convicted aggravated assaulters (Greenberg, 1981). These fractions are similar to those found among convicted property offenders.

Other Psychoactive Drugs

Compared with alcohol, there are relatively few sources of data on patterns of drug use and violence. These sources and studies provide the following picture:

(1) In 1989, 60 percent of arrestees for violent offenses tested positive for at least one illegal drug[1]—about the same fraction as those arrested for public order offenses, slightly less than those arrested for property crimes and sex offenses, and, as expected, far less than those arrested for drug offenses.

(2) Users of certain drugs[2] commit violent crimes at higher individual annualized frequencies than do nonusers, and violent crime frequency increases with drug use frequency.

(3) The risk of drug-related homicide varies *by place*—from perhaps 10 percent of all homicides nationwide, to a third or more in certain cities, to more than 70 percent in high-risk areas of some cities—as well as *over time,* in ways that vary from area to area.

Use Among Arrestees

Data on the prevalence of drug-positive tests among arrestees are available from the DUF program, in which samples of arrestees are voluntarily tested for 10 drugs other than alcohol (see note 1). In 1989, for males and females combined, 60 percent of arrestees for violent crimes tested positive for at least one of these drugs in 1989—just a few percentage points above the fraction who reported using alcohol. Higher drug-positive rates occurred among arrestees for public order offenses (62 percent), property and sex offenses (66 percent), and drug offenses (83 percent). Compared to male arrestees, the drug-positive rates for female arrestees were 3 to 6 percent lower for both violent and property offenses, about the same for drug offenses, and 7 percent higher for public order offenses including prostitution, for which drug use is prevalent. These 1989 drug-positive rates are 1 to 5 percent lower than 1988 levels for all crime-by-gender groups. They are toward the high end of a 1986 range reported for Washington, D.C., by Wish et al. (1986) and Toborg et al. (1986). By combining data for all (violent and nonviolent) felony arrests from the 22 cities, about 20 percent of all arrestees tested positive for two or more of the drugs.

By themselves, these figures are difficult to interpret. Because the urine samples are collected at the time of arrest, they convey little information about drug use at the time of the offense for persons who were not arrested at the scene—traces of drug use leave the body at different rates for different drugs. Even absent this problem, the lower prevalence of positive tests among arrestees for violent offenses compared with arrestees for other offenses would argue against the presumption that using psychoactive drugs causes violent offending. The presumption is further weakened by the conclusion of Chaiken and Chaiken (1990) that only small fractions of adolescent and adult drug users ever commit a "predatory" offense (i.e., robbery or other crime for gain). Finally, without baseline measures of the prevalence of drug users among community residents who are not arrested, one cannot assess how much more common drug use is among criminals than among others in the community.

Violence Frequencies

Studies of offender samples consistently find that users of certain illegal psychoactive drugs have higher individual annualized frequencies for such violent offenses as robbery, armed robbery, and assault than do nonusers of drugs (Blumstein et al., 1986; Chaiken and Chaiken, 1990; Cohen, 1986; Johnson et al., 1985). The relationship holds over a variety of definitions of drug use: heroin addiction and use (Ball et al., 1983; Chaiken and Chaiken, 1982); daily heroin and cocaine use; and multiple illicit drug use (Elliott and Huizinga, 1984). Because use of multiple drugs including alcohol is so common in offender populations (Wish and Johnson, 1986), available data do not permit us to relate differences in offending rates to specific drugs.

Elliott and Huizinga (1984) report the only evidence that partially conflicts with this general conclusion, based on respondents to the longitudinal National Youth Survey (NYS). In 1976, multiple illicit drug users in their sample reported an average robbery incidence (7.2 per person per year) more than double that for nonusers (3.1). In 1980 the relationship was reversed: multiple illicit drug users reported an incidence of only 6.4, compared with 13.1 for nonusers. As noted by Chaiken and Chaiken (1990), this may reflect decreased participation in robbery as sample members move out of the teenage years, or the possibility that subjects who are both multiple illicit drug users and robbers may drop out of the NYS sample over time—an indication of the importance of efforts to minimize attrition in longitudinal studies.

These descriptive patterns, of course, are not explanations. They are consistent with predatory offending to raise money for drugs, with individual differences or community characteristics that encourage high levels of both drug use and violent offending, and even with a pharmacological effect of drug use on behavior. These and other plausible explanations are considered later in this chapter.

Drug Use and Homicide Rates

Illegal psychoactive drug use and marketing are clearly implicated in a substantial share of urban homicides, but the relationship is far from the uniform, straight-line relationship claimed by some policy makers (Isikoff and Sawyer, 1990). Although estimating the fraction of all homicides classified as "drug related" involves judgments and approximations, two national estimates from the early 1980s are fairly consistent at 10 percent (Harwood et al., 1984) and 9 percent (Goldstein and Hunt, 1984) for 1980. Urban rates are higher and rose substantially during the 1980s (Goldstein, 1989).

Inciardi (1989) found substantial differences in homicide trends across six cities between 1985 and 1988-1989, as their local crack

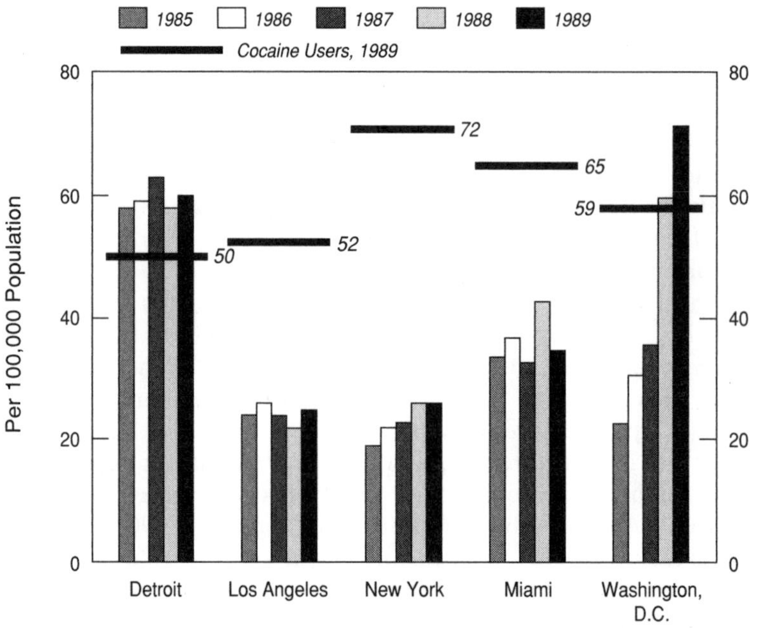

FIGURE 4-1 Homicide rates, 1985-1989; cocaine users among male arrestees, 1989. SOURCE: Compiled in Inciardi (1989).

epidemics unfolded. Homicide trends during those years varied from decreases in Detroit and Los Angeles to an increase of more than 350 percent in Washington, D.C. For the five DUF participants among the six cities compared by Inciardi, Figure 4-1 extends Inciardi's trends through the end of 1989 and relates them to DUF data on the fraction of 1989 male arrestees testing positive for cocaine, including crack. Neither the levels nor the trends of homicide rates in those cities show any consistent relationship to the prevalence of cocaine users among male arrestees. New York, with the highest cocaine prevalence of the five cities, and Los Angeles, with the second lowest, have the lowest homicide rates. The New York, Miami, and D.C. data resemble, if anything, an inverse relationship between homicide rates and arrestees' cocaine use. Clearly, the aggregate-level relationships between cocaine use and homicide trends defy simple straight-line description.

PHARMACOLOGICAL LINKS BETWEEN DRUG USE AND VIOLENCE

ALCOHOL

Experimental and ethological (i.e., seminatural setting) studies demonstrate that low acute doses of alcohol temporarily increase, and high doses temporarily decrease, aggressive behavior in many animal species, including fish, lower mammals, primates, and humans. The increased aggression is associated with the generally arousing effects of alcohol in the early phases of its action; what happens during the later phases, when dysphoric effects occur, has not been well studied (Babor et al., 1983).

Chronic alcohol administration to rats causes an increase in their rate of injurious aggression as a response to social provocations, and there is preliminary evidence of a similar pattern in primates. These patterns for other animals are consistent with those previously discussed for humans: high prevalence and incidence of violent crimes among diagnosed alcoholics, and a high fraction of alcoholics among violent offenders (Miczek et al., Volume 3).

Conventional wisdom sometimes explains these effects in terms of disinhibiting effects of alcohol that are presumed to release aggressive impulses from inhibition by the brain. Yet the evidence from three decades of studies of animals and humans clearly demonstrates that there is no simple dose-response relationship. Rather: "whether or not alcohol in a range of doses . . . causes a certain individual to act aggressively more frequently or even to engage in 'out of character' violent behavior depends on a host of interacting pharmacological, endocrinological, neurobiologic, genetic, situational, environmental, social, and cultural determinants" (Miczek et al., Volume 3). These relationships are discussed in the following pages, drawing heavily on comprehensive reviews by Miczek et al. (Volume 3) and Fagan (1990).

Endocrinological Interactions

Statistical associations between alcohol use and human sexual violence raise the possibility that alcohol consumption might stimulate violent behavior through the endocrine system. Actually, higher alcohol doses reduce testosterone concentrations through action on the testes and liver—a process that is incompatible with the presumption (Van Thiel et al., 1988). However, in experiments with rodents and primates, acute low alcohol doses were found to increase aggressive behavior in individuals who already had high blood testosterone levels by more than in other individuals, presumably as a result of testosterone action in the brain.

The fact that males are more likely than females to behave violently after consuming alcohol also suggests the possibility of an endocrinological interaction. However, no relevant experimental evidence exists, and correlational analyses suggest that the gender differential is likely to reflect social factors that lead males to expect greater aggression-heightening effects from alcohol than do females (Crawford, 1984; Gustafson, 1986a, b).

Neurobiologic Interactions

Many neurobiologic explanations have been offered for the effect of alcohol on the central nervous system. At least a few of these are consistent with nonexperimental evidence and relate specifically to aggressive or violent behavior, but none has been confirmed through experiments.

In one sample of violent Finnish alcohol abusers, abnormally low cerebrospinal fluid concentrations of the serotonin metabolite 5-hydroxyindoleacetic acid (5-HIAA) were correlated with poor impulse control (Linnoila et al., 1983; Virkkunen et al., 1989a, b). But this correlation could reflect either that poor serotonergic functioning interacts with alcohol to cause violent behavior, or that chronic alcohol abuse interferes with serotonergic functioning simultaneously with other effects on potentials for violent behavior. Low serotonin metabolism appears to be linked to a low response to glucose challenge tests in alcoholic violent offenders, suggesting a possible interaction among predispositions toward violent behavior, alcoholism, and hypoglycemia.

In recent animal experiments, pharmacologically blocking the $GABA_A$/benzodiazepine receptor complex inhibited several common behavioral effects of alcohol, including stimulating aggressive behavior in rats and monkeys (Weerts et al., in press). These findings suggest that the $GABA_A$/benzodiazepine receptor complex may be involved in the aggression-heightening effect of alcohol doses. Future studies of the $GABA_A$/benzodiazepine receptor complex need to examine its role in promoting human aggression under the influence of alcohol.

Some evidence also suggests alcohol is related to violent human behavior through effects on electrical activity in the brain. In one small sample of people who had committed a violent or antisocial act, alcohol doses produced an electroencephalogram (EEG) abnormality consistent with temporal lobe damage that is aggravated by the alcohol (Marinacci and von Hagen, 1972). A more recent study found a reduced P300 component of event-related potentials in violent but not nonviolent alcoholics (Branchey et al., 1988).

Genetic Interactions

There are consistent demonstrations of genetic bases for alcohol abuse (Goodwin, 1973) and for antisocial personality (Schubert et al., 1988), a psychiatric category for which some of the diagnostic criteria are violent behaviors. The fact that they frequently co-occur raises the possibility of some common elements in their genetic bases. Whether the two bases are independent or not is in controversy, with Cadoret et al. (1985) claiming independence and Cloninger et al. (1989) claiming a link for one subtype of alcoholic. One recent study (Grove et al., 1990) involved too small a sample to reach firm conclusions, and, surprisingly, the panel could find no relevant animal studies of this issue.

Other Psychoactive Drugs

Biological links between psychoactive drug use and violence differ by type of drug, amount, and pattern of use. Use of marijuana or opiates including heroin in moderate doses temporarily inhibits violent and aggressive behavior in animals and humans. In animals, withdrawal from opiate addiction leads pharmacologically to heightened aggressive and defensive actions that last beyond other physiological withdrawal symptoms. Although the same may be true of humans, performing comparable research on addicted human subjects is complicated by multiple pharmacological, conditioning, and social processes that are difficult to disentangle. Chronic use of opiates, amphetamines, marijuana, or PCP eventually alters the nervous system in ways that disrupt social communications—an effect that may increase one's involvement in altercations that escalate to violence.

Amphetamines, cocaine, LSD, and PCP resemble one another in terms of their pharmacological links to violent behavior. Small acute doses increase competitiveness, volubility, and other socially acceptable aggressive behaviors, but are not known to increase the risk of violent behavior. Higher doses seem to cause generally disorganized behavior, including occasional violent outbursts in a subset of individuals. Long-term frequent use may change the nervous system in ways that induce psychosis, and violent behavior sometimes occurs during drug-induced psychosis. But the frequency of such episodes varies from sample to sample and seems highest among drug users with preexisting psychopathology.

These findings are developed further in the following pages. (See Miczek et al., Volume 3, for more complete discussion and supporting citations.)

Opiates

Doses of morphine and other opium derivatives temporarily reduce aggressive behavior in animals and violent behavior in humans, according to a large number of studies. While occasional heroin use offers humans the feeling of well-being, chronic use affects mood and behavior in more complex ways. Chronic use reduces social interactions in animals and often leads humans to feelings of confusion, hostility, and suspicion; these in turn may increase the risk of violent behavior in future interactions.

Chronic use of opiates leading to addiction also modifies the neuroreceptors for opioid peptides—opiate-like chemicals produced within the body. Studies of rodents, cats, and primates in the last decade have shown that such long-term alteration impairs the animals' abilities to communicate while under stress. Extrapolating this relationship to humans, the addiction effect could disrupt individuals' social communications in ways that increase their risks of violent behavior or victimization during subsequent stressful interactions.

Animal studies over 25 years have demonstrated that withdrawal from opiates increases the probability of heightened aggressive and defensive acts that continue after other withdrawal symptoms have subsided. Studies of rodents indicate that brain dopamine and noradrenergic receptors undergo marked changes during withdrawal from opiates. This suggests that drugs such as clonidine may be useful in managing human aggression during withdrawal from heroin, and clinical evidence in humans provides some support.

Relationships involving opiate addiction, withdrawal, and violent behavior may be amplified by preexisting feelings of rage among heroin addicts. Elevated prevalences of these feelings in opiate addicts have led some to theorize that some persons may become addicted in the course of seeking relief from feelings of rage. A return of those feelings during withdrawal could precipitate violent behavior.

Amphetamines

Since the first amphetamine was synthesized in 1887, a number of varieties have been developed and used to fight fatigue, enhance endurance, suppress appetite, and alter moods. The class includes drugs such as *dextro-* and *levo*-amphetamine, and *d*-methamphetamine, which are available as appetite suppressants as well as illegally produced and distributed drugs such as "ice" (smokable methamphetamine), "eve" (MDA), and "ecstasy" (MDMA). Their effects on the nervous system and on violent and other behaviors have been studied using both animal models and human subjects and clearly depend on the level and long-term pattern of intake.

At acute low doses amphetamines increase aggressive and defensive behaviors in fish, pigeons, mice, rats, cats, and monkeys. This effect is most apparent during withdrawal from opiates and under habituation to aggression-provoking conditions, and enhanced aggressive behavior is most apparent in socially dominant animals. In humans, low amphetamine doses are associated with enhanced volubility and competitiveness but not necessarily with increased risk of violent behavior. Findings from clinical experience, laboratory experiments, and self-reports highlight the euphoria produced by low doses of amphetamines, but also note occasional cases of anxiety.

Although available data do not permit one to construct dose-response curves for amphetamine use by animals or humans, higher doses do not seem to simply amplify the behaviors observed at low doses. Rather, intermediate doses are associated with increased defensiveness and general disorganization of animals' social behaviors, including not only pursuit, threat, and attack, but also copulatory, maternal, and other social interactions. Analogously, human users display less impulse control at higher doses.

Chronic administration of amphetamines to animals causes social withdrawal and eventually heightened threat and defensive reactions. It is tempting to interpret these as analogues to paranoia and psychosis, which are well documented in human chronic amphetamine users and are sometimes accompanied by serious violent outbursts. While the occasional occurrence or seriousness of violent behavior during amphetamine-related psychosis is not in doubt, its prevalence varies across samples, ranging from perhaps 10 percent among chronic users in the general population to perhaps two-thirds among users with preexisting psychopathology. Thus, while chronic amphetamine use seems more closely related to violent behavior than is use of other psychoactive drugs, the strength of the relationship depends on the user's prior psychiatric condition.

The neurochemical mechanisms for amphetamine's effects on aggressive and violent behavior remain to be identified. While acute amphetamine doses mimic the effect of stressful external stimuli in releasing dopamine and norepinephrine within the brain, and some aspects of amphetamine psychosis are successfully managed by antipsychotic drugs that block dopamine receptors, these drugs do not reverse the disruption of social behavior, and massive incapacitating doses are required to decrease violent behavior associated with chronic amphetamine use.

Cocaine

The limited pharmacological and psychiatric literature has not yet established *direct* neurobiologic links between violent behavior and acute or chronic cocaine use. Chronic use in powdered or smokable ("crack") form sometimes leads to paranoid or psychotic states, in which violent or aggressive behavior may sometimes occur. Such cases were observed in 6 percent of all cocaine-related emergency department admissions in one hospital over a two-year period. However, another study reported no difference in the frequency of violent acts between institutionalized cocaine users and other inpatients. Information is urgently needed to determine whether the rapid access of smoked cocaine to the brain produces distortions in the perceptions of social signals and a particular propensity to engage in violent behavior.

In mice, rats, and monkeys, acute cocaine intake increases defensive reactions to stress but disrupts aggressive behavior. Even chronic cocaine treatment did not increase aggressive behavior in several species. Thus, the animal literature is quite consistent with the finding of Goldstein et al. (1989) that homicide arising from the pharmacological effects of cocaine is fairly rare.

Hallucinogens

The drugs in this category are chemically diverse. They include cannabis in various forms (marijuana, hashish, bang), phencyclidine, and LSD.

During the past two decades, five major scientific reviews of the research literature have concluded that violent human behavior is either decreased or unaffected by cannabis use. Similarly, studies of many animal species demonstrate that acute doses of THC, the psychoactive ingredient in marijuana, promote submissive and flight responses and, at least in large doses, inhibit attack and threat behavior. These effects persist during chronic administration to the animals.

According to clinical reports, violent behavior occurs at least occasionally in persons who are either under the influence of acute doses of phencyclidine (PCP, "angel dust") or experiencing psychosis brought on by long-term use of the drug. The frequency of such events among PCP users is unknown. No experimental studies of PCP and human violence have been conducted, and spontaneous PCP use usually accompanies use of alcohol or other drugs with confounding neurobiologic effects. Therefore, the pharmacological effects of human PCP use are not yet well understood, and specific drugs to control violent behavior that occurs under the influence of PCP are not yet available. In animal experiments, PCP doses have increased some aggressive behaviors under certain conditions; but the more uniform consequence is that the animals treated with PCP become the targets of aggression by other animals, presumably because the PCP triggers inappropriate social signals, provocative actions, and hyperactivity.

The pharmacological relationship between LSD and violent behavior was studied fairly intensively several decades ago. Studies of humans suggest that LSD use does not trigger violent behavior but does sometimes aggravate the effects of preexisting psychopathology, including violent outbursts. LSD doses have been observed to increase aggressive, defensive, and timid reactions in different animal species, suggesting a possible heightened sensitivity to social and environmental stimuli generally.

PSYCHOSOCIAL LINKS BETWEEN DRUG USE AND VIOLENCE

There is fairly strong evidence that individual differences beyond the biological processes discussed above intervene in the relationships between violent behavior and the use of alcohol and other psychoactive drugs. For example, the experimental statistics that demonstrate the basic alcohol dose relationship—heightened aggression at low doses and reduced aggression at high doses—demonstrate variation across individuals. At any dosage within the low-dose range, while most individuals are experiencing heightened aggression, a few are experiencing reductions. An analogous scattering of individual responses occurs in the high range.

Gender appears to be of fundamental importance in modifying the relationship between alcohol use and violent behavior. National surveys report that male drinking patterns are more likely than those of females to incorporate binge drinking and aggressive behavior, and that violent behavior while under the influence of alcohol is very rare among females (Blane and Hewitt, 1977; Cahalan and Cisin, 1976; and Gandossy et al., 1980, all cited in Fagan, 1990). Identifying the biological, expectational, and social factors that account for this differential behavior remains a question for future research.

Additional evidence of differences is the finding that individuals' histories of aggressive and violent behavior are a critical determinant of whether or not alcohol and psychoactive drug use increases those behaviors. The finding recurs in studies of animals (Pettijohn, 1979; Miczek and Barry, 1977) and of humans (Rydelius, 1988). In experimental studies of mice, rats, and monkeys, alcohol doses that more than doubled the average rate of threat and attack behavior in animals that had previously exhibited these behaviors had no effect in animals who had previously behaved in primarily submissive and defensive ways (Blanchard et al., 1987; Winslow and Miczek, 1985; DeBold and Miczek, 1985).

There is also correlational evidence from longitudinal studies of humans that the links between chronic alcohol use and aggressive or violent behavior remain fairly stable through the developing years into adulthood. Studies demonstrate that childhood aggression is a risk factor for both heavy drinking and violent behavior in young adulthood (Pulkkinen, 1983). McCord (1983, 1988) found that the combination of early childhood aggressiveness and alcoholism as an adult predicted high levels of violent behavior.

Studies framed within a medical model are consistent with these findings. Miczek et al. (Volume 3) point to two subcategories of dually diagnosed personality disorders that have been found to have elevated risks of violent behavior: alcoholics diagnosed as sociopathic (O'Leary et al., 1978; Yates et al., 1987) and individuals diagnosed with antisocial personality disorder who abuse both alcohol and other psychoactive drugs. The latter group may form a specific genetic subtype (Cloninger, 1987). Although questions have been raised about the validity of these diagnostic categories and the distinction between them, the findings are consistent with those of the longitudinal studies.

Identifying a link between specific childhood behaviors or personality disorders and adult violent behavior under the influence of alcohol or other drugs does not explain episodes of such behavior in adults without either of the disorders. Theoretical and clinical literature reviewed by Fagan (1990) points to specific emotions that often precede or accompany aggressive behavior—hate, rage, shame, guilt, helplessness, and dependence—and suggests that these may be related to the consumption of alcohol or other psychoactive drugs in any of several ways.

First, users may select specific drugs to dampen or intensify certain emotions. Wurmser and Lebling (1983, cited in Fagan, 1990) report case studies in which cocaine and Methedrine temporarily diminished feelings of helplessness and dependence; barbiturates and opiates reduced feelings of rage, despair, and loneliness; and stimulants, hallucinogens, and alcohol were used to dampen feelings of depression, guilt, shame, and helplessness. Second, social processes such as family arguments that are associated with substance abuse (e.g., spending too much money on alcohol or drugs) may trigger the violent behavior. Third, both the violence-related emotions and the substance abuse may grow out of some underlying developmental or family pathology. Possibilities found by Fagan (1990) in the literature include a divergence at some developmental stage between social expectations and personality development; and compulsive masculinity during adolescence, which could encourage displays of both drug use and aggressive behavior. There is no consensus as yet on any of these explanations for the co-occurrence of violent behavior and alcohol and drug abuse that is consistently found in longitudinal studies (McCord, 1983, 1988; Elliott and Huizinga, 1984).

SOCIAL-LEVEL LINKS BETWEEN DRUG USE AND VIOLENCE

Researchers have discovered a few characteristics of encounters involving the consumption of alcohol, and of the places in which they occur, that seem to increase the probability of a violent event. Although developing a risk profile for such encounters might be feasible using case control methods, the panel is aware of no such effort. Even less is known about encounters involving the *consumption* of illegal drugs because research access is difficult to obtain. Violence during encounters in the course of *marketing* illegal drugs is discussed in a later section of this chapter.

In an encounter between individuals, immediately prior consumption of alcohol, amphetamines, PCP, or cocaine disrupts behavior in ways that may increase the chance of disputes or aggravate their consequences: appraisal of the consequences of behavior, the sending and receiving of socially significant signals, and threat attribution. These disruptions can accelerate exchanges of threats and violent behaviors, which may help to account for the previously noted high prevalences of blood alcohol in both perpetrators and victims of violence.

In this section we discuss three categories of social-level interactions between violence and the use of drugs: (1) striking differences across cultures and subcultures in patterns of alcohol use and violence, which have not yet been explained in terms of specific cultural features; (2) indications of frequent serious violence associated with obtaining and distributing illegal drugs; and (3) fragmentary evidence that is consistent with less direct, more speculative links between violence and the distribution and use of illegal drugs.

Cultural Differences in Alcohol Use and Violence

In studies of cultural differences in patterns of alcohol use and violence reviewed by Miczek et al. (Volume 3) and Fagan (1990), positive associations between alcohol use and violence have been reported in many countries populated by Europeans and their descendants: Australia, Finland, Sweden, South Africa, Canada, and the United States. However, studies of non-European cultures do not uniformly find similar connections. In a review of ethnographic reports from 60 small-scale and folk societies, Schaefer (1973) reported that men frequently get drunk in 46 of them but routinely participate in drunken brawls in only 24. Similarly, MacAndrew and Edgerton's (1969) accounts of Western Hemisphere tribal societies reported that drinking parties transform members of the normally tranquil Abipone tribe into combative individuals but cause the normally aggressive, head-hunting Yurunas to withdraw socially.

Several explanations have been suggested for such differences (Fagan, 1990). First, some ethnographic reports attribute them to cultural norms or customs. For example, male members of the Camba tribe of subsistence farmers go on rum-drinking binges twice a month, but aggression during or between those periods is virtually nonexistent. In contrast, lethal knife fights are common during similar binges by Finnish Lapps, who are not abnormally violent when sober (Heath, 1983). Intoxicated Navajo fight almost exclusively with family members. And Plains Indian men are expected to fight when intoxicated as young men, yet older "family men" are expected to avoid violence when intoxicated. Despite these general tendencies, behavioral differences across individuals and situations within any single culture suggest that the cultural pattern explanation is incomplete.

Second, some cultures within larger societies may use intoxication to excuse or to embolden violent and other behaviors that are unacceptable to the larger societies. For example, the high rate of violent deaths and alcohol abuse among Native Americans has been interpreted as part of a coping strategy to deal with problems that arise during acculturation into white society (Westermeyer and Brantner, 1972; Seltzer, 1980). Studies of California gangs suggest that Hispanic and black gangs may use alcohol to achieve different behavioral states—Hispanic gang members seeking a rather frenzied *locura*, blacks seeking a reserved cool—both of which facilitate violent behavior (Vigil, 1987, 1988; Feldman et al., 1985, cited in Fagan, 1990).

Third, some studies suggest that the alcohol-violence connection in any culture depends on the stresses placed on members of that culture by the social structure. The aggressive drinkers among Naskapi men in northern Canada were reportedly the least successful iron miners—though the cause-effect relationship is unclear (Robbins, 1979, cited in Fagan, 1990). Gordon (1978, cited in Fagan, 1990) reported that Dominican immigrants to the United States brought their whole families, found greater economic opportunity, changed their drinking locations from bars to homes, and reduced their aggression. He found the opposite experience with drinking and aggression among Guatemalan men, who left their wives at home and lived without the company of women (Gordon, 1982, cited in Fagan, 1990).

Finally, the effects of alcohol on human behavior may be modified by expectations about those effects (Miczek et al., Volume 3; Levinson, 1983, cited in Fagan, 1990). As noted by Fagan (J. Fagan, personal communication, February 15, 1990), one ethnographic study suggests that even intoxicated people's behavior during encounters may be constrained by their awareness of social expectations. Over the course of an evening of drinking and socializing with four male adolescents, Burns (1980) reported them to be quiet and deferential when surrounded by their elders in a familiar neighborhood tavern, but more aggressive (including threats with a gun) in other surroundings. The causal mechanism may well be reciprocal. Burns speculated that his subjects' drinking heightened their aggressiveness, which caused them to search for locations more conducive to its expression, where in fact they did express it. There is a need for more rigorous research, involving larger samples, to test alternative explanations.

Clearly, patterns of drug and alcohol use and violent behavior differ across cultures and subcultures. But the patterns can apparently be modified, despite the difficulty of ascertaining what features of a given culture account for the pattern there.

Obtaining and Distributing Illegal Drugs

The illegality of some psychoactive drugs raises their street prices above the levels that would exist in an open market. The raised price is associated with two different kinds of encounters, each of which carries a risk of violence. First, some drug users commit robberies or burglaries[3] to obtain drugs or money for purchasing drugs. Second, the artificially raised prices create excess profits for drug dealers, which raises the stakes in disputes about marketing practices. Since these illegal markets are not subject to legal dispute resolution mechanisms, violence may be a first resort.

Goldstein et al. (1989) designated the first type of violence *economic* and the second *systemic*. To assess their relative frequency, he and his colleagues classified the police records of 414 homicides that occurred between March and October 1988 in selected precincts of New York City. They classified 53 percent of the homicides as drug related: 39 percent systemic, 2 percent economic, 8 percent due to the pharmacological effects of drugs, and 4 percent multiple cause.

This effort was valuable in demonstrating the difficulty of defining drug-related violence. It demonstrated that multiple factors interact in more complex ways than a simple classification scheme would suggest. Also, the researchers found that they applied the scheme quite differently than the police officers who had prepared the case reports—particularly in designating the "causal" factor(s). Officers and researchers both classified more drug-related events as "systemic" than any other category, but the officers used the "economic" category far more often than did the researchers (Ryan et al., no date). The inconsistency suggests that inferring causality in a particular case is difficult and subjective, especially when multiple causal factors are present in an event.

Economic Violence

In his analysis of New York City homicides, Goldstein et al. (1989) classified as economic only the 2 percent that occurred in the course of "economic crimes in order to finance costly drug use"—primarily robberies and burglaries. This figure understates the role of economics in drug-related violence for several reasons. First, the drug motivation for a robbery or burglary is often concealed, or at least slow in coming to light. Second, the classification excludes at least two kinds of economically motivated violence. Homicides in the course of illegal drug marketing to support drug use (e.g., a robbery of drugs from a dealer in which the user or dealer is killed) were counted as drug related but classified as systemic. But violence in the course of economic crimes with indirect drug-related motivation—a robbery to obtain grocery money after spending the intended grocery money on drugs—was not counted as drug related.

A body of research concurs that, except during withdrawal periods, heroin users in need of funds tend to avoid violent crimes if nonviolent alternatives such as burglary are available (Anglin and Speckart, 1988). Despite users' general aversion to violence, robbery by heroin users is common, and users are prevalent among robbers (Blumstein et al., 1986; Chaiken and Chaiken, 1990; Goldstein, 1989). Economic drug-related violence has been less clearly demonstrated among adult users of other illegal drugs, although Inciardi (1980) found similar patterns of robbery by young users of heroin and other illegal drugs.

In part, the lack of evidence reflects a scarcity of pertinent studies. However, the low prevalence of economic drug-related violence reported by Goldstein may also reflect access to other sources of income among users of cocaine and synthetic psychoactive drugs. Cocaine and crack dealing offer attractive alternatives to robbery or burglary as a means of financing purchases. Also, wholesalers distribute crack to street dealers on a consignment basis, and the negotiated reimbursement is usually set to allow for some personal use by the retailer. In addition, Reuter et al. (1990) estimated median earnings in 1985-1987 for street-level crack dealing in Washington, D.C., at $30 per hour—a supplement to legal income for more than two-thirds of the persons arrested for illegal drug sales during that period. The growth of earnings opportunities in crack marketing may help to explain the fact that, although sales and use of cocaine (including crack) in the District of Columbia grew rapidly between 1981 and 1987, the annual number of reported property crimes including robbery decreased by more than 20 percent, from 53,870 to 42,783.

In short, while economic drug-related violence is almost certainly more common than Goldstein's estimate of 2 percent would suggest, its importance is apparently specific to expensive dependence-producing drugs and therefore declining as smokable crack replaces heroin as the drug of choice, and crack selling becomes a source of substantial income.

Systemic Violence

Systemic drug-related violence can be expected to resemble violence associated with other illegal markets, such as prostitution, loansharking, alcohol during Prohibition, and black markets in other prohibited goods. It was the most common form of drug-related violence, according to Goldstein et al.'s (1989) analysis. Available knowledge about the circumstances surrounding systemic violence comes mostly from ethnographic or interview studies (Johnson et al., 1985; Fagan, 1989; Hamid, 1990; Bourgois, 1989; Mieczkowski, 1989; Chin, 1990).

Systemic drug-related violence takes three distinct paths. Organizational systemic violence includes territorial disputes with rival organizations over drug distribution rights; the enforcement of organizational rules, such as prohibitions against drug use while selling or trafficking; battles with police; punishment of individual officers, informers, or antidrug vigilantes; and efforts to protect drugs or sellers. Of these, territorial disputes were found most common in both the Goldstein and the Chin studies.

Transaction-related systemic violence includes robberies of drugs or money from the seller or the buyer during a transaction, assaults to collect debts, and the resolution of disputes over the quality or quantity of drugs or over paraphernalia ownership or rights. Both the New York City studies report that of these, robberies of dealers and assaults to collect debts are more common than the other circumstances listed here. Another common violence provocation in illegal drug marketing, termed "messing up the money," occurs when a lower-level dealer fails to return the agreed-upon amount of money after disposing of his drug consignment. Because the discrepancy may occur through personal consumption, theft or loss of the drugs, robbery or personal use of the money, or other illegal acts, the resulting dispute can rarely be settled with evidence and often leads to violence.

Systemic violence involving third parties can involve bystanders to drug disputes; participants in related illegal markets such as protection rackets, firearms, and hired "enforcement"; and prostitutes who also sell or use crack. This kind of violence is especially difficult to study safely, so little is known about it. Sherman et al. (1989) found that, although shootings of bystanders increased in four large cities between 1977 and 1988, they accounted for less than 1 percent of all 1988 homicides in those cities, and drug market conflicts were only one of several causes of bystander shootings.

Data on the frequencies of these subcategories of systemic violence are fragmentary and subject to question. There is need for more systematic counting of their occurrences and analysis of the frequency of their occurrence in different settings.

Social and Indirect Drug-Related Violence

To this point, our discussion of social-level links between illegal drugs and violence has been limited to purchases and distribution. Social interactions that are less obviously drug related may also be involved, as well as the interaction of technological change in illegal drug marketing with broader socioeconomic trends.

First, illegal drug markets are magnets for risk-seeking persons carrying weapons and valuables and for potential victims. It seems clear that violent drug market participants behave violently outside the drug market as well (Inciardi, 1989; Fagan and Chin, 1989a,b, 1991). While the extent to which violent participants select themselves into drug market locations is unclear, ethnographic studies demonstrate that the markets create opportunities for violence that are only indirectly related to drug marketing. Sellers carrying drugs and buyers carrying money are attractive targets for robbery. Weapons brought to the marketplace out of fear are readily accessible during disputes over nondrug matters. Female buyers, whose drug habits may have drawn them into prostitution, are targets for sexual assaults. In general, greater numbers of market participants make these and similar violence opportunities more common. However, findings about prostitution operations suggest that off-street marketing environments—through appointments with beepermen or in crack houses—may reduce the hazards of drug transactions.

Second, disputes over the consequences of drug use can involve violent events that are related only indirectly to the use or sale of drugs and so may not be classified as drug related. This possibility was illustrated above by a robbery of grocery money to replenish funds spent on illegal drugs. In-depth interviews or ethnographic observation may be needed to discover the drug connection in some disputes that turn violent—over strained family finances, too many nights away from home, careless job or school performance, or other problems that may or may not be consequences of drug use. The incidence of violent events with a hidden connection to illegal drugs is unknown.

Third, there is reason to ask how youth gangs and systemic drug-related violence are related. It seems unlikely that the nationwide explosion of crack-related violence is accounted for by long-standing youth gangs with violent traditions that have adopted crack dealing as a new source of funds (Klein et al., 1988; Inciardi, 1989). Rather, the perceived increase in gang-related crack violence during the 1980s appears to result from a combination of real and artifactual causes. Apparently, some traditionally violent youth gangs in some cities did turn to crack sales as a source of income. Elsewhere, profit-seeking organizations selling crack sprang up, and researchers and criminal justice officials categorized them together with traditional youth gangs despite their distinct orientation. However, some of the perceived increase in crack-related violence was apparently artifactual—attributable to the activities of gang members acting on their own or to coincidences between independent trends in crack sales and in gang violence. The diversity noted by Fagan (1989) suggests that as a means of reducing violence, selective attention to the specific gangs that have a history of violence may be more effective than general attention to crack-selling gangs on the supposition that they are likely to be involved in violence.

A fourth possibility is a breakdown of violence-inhibiting social control mechanisms in the communities that surround illegal drug markets. The violence surrounding crack may be related to large-scale social changes that have interacted with the economic, social, and organizational context of crack marketing and use (J. Fagan, personal communication, February 15, 1990; Fagan and Chin, 1989a). In contrast to earlier times, crack and cocaine marketing during the 1980s became a highly decentralized and visible activity in neighborhoods that lacked legitimate economic opportunities. The boundary between sellers and users disappeared, and easy unregulated access into the market at all levels replaced the stable system whose complex rules and territorial franchises had been enforced by crime organizations (Johnson et al., 1985, 1990; Sampson, 1987; Adler, 1985; Murphy et al., 1989).

Outmigration of stable families and individuals with ties to the legitimate economy had already weakened neighborhood social controls against violence. The few remaining "old heads" who had acted as community social monitors lost respect because of their reduced economic status and became too intimidated by the crack market participants to exercise their moral authority (Anderson, 1990). The emergence of visible, violent crack markets hastened these processes and further weakened social inhibitors of violence in *all* contexts, including the drug market (Hamid, 1990; Goldstein et al., 1987). In this view, removing drug markets is useful as an intervention to control violence only to the extent that their elimination facilitates restoring social institutions and legitimate economies in the afflicted communities.

Although empirical tests of this theory against alternatives are virtually impossible to carry out, individual-level studies by Fagan and Chin (1989a,b, 1991) seem to rule out some alternative explanations—some "new breed" of violent juveniles, or more violent rules in crack markets than in other contemporary drug markets—at least in certain areas of New York City. Their findings are consistent with the possibility that other factors—perhaps community-level social and economic processes—account for the variation in violence levels related to crack distribution.

These relationships are extremely difficult to verify and measure. But even though they are speculative, raising them as possibilities seems preferable to discounting them as possible explanations of the perceived rise in "drug-related violence." In raising them, we hope to stimulate research that would test these hypotheses more rigorously and estimate their empirical significance more precisely. Such findings would contribute to more informed development of policies for controlling drug-related violence.

INTERVENTIONS TO REDUCE DRUG-RELATED VIOLENCE

The preceding discussions suggest four kinds of interventions that should be considered for reducing levels of violence related to alcohol and other psychoactive drugs:

(1) biological interventions: through pharmacological treatments to reduce craving for illegal drugs or to manage heightened tendencies toward aggressive behavior associated with alcohol and the withdrawal stage of heroin use;

(2) developmental interventions: through cognitive-behavioral interventions intended to prevent children from initiating use of psychoactive drugs;

(3) individual-level interventions for adults: to incarcerate drug-

using offenders and to terminate or reduce drug use through a variety of treatment techniques; and

(4) community-level interventions: increases in alcohol excise tax rates, and police tactics intended to disrupt illegal drug markets.

The following pages review available evidence on the effectiveness of these intervention strategies in reducing levels of drug-related violence.

Biological Interventions

For most illegal psychoactive drugs, the strongest links to violence are through users obtaining the money needed to purchase illegal drugs and through violence associated with drug distribution. The most effective pharmacological intervention into these links is likely to be therapeutic medication that reduces craving for drugs. For heroin users, methadone and LAAM have long been used for this purpose; on average, heroin-dependent persons have better outcomes, in terms of drug use and other criminal behavior, when they are treated with methadone than when they are not (Gerstein and Harwood, 1990:153). For other illegal psychoactive drugs, no therapeutic medication to reduce drug craving is currently in widespread use. The most promising avenues of research for developing such medications involve blockers of dopamine and norepinephrine receptor subtypes.

Because alcohol use and heroin withdrawal are associated with heightened tendencies toward aggression by some individuals, medications that target specifically the violence-promoting effects of these substances would be useful. However, they do not currently exist and, as far as we know, are not under development. In animal studies, clonidine has been found to reduce aggressive behavior during withdrawal from heroin, and clinical trials should be mounted to test its effectiveness for humans in withdrawal. Since it seems fairly clear that the $GABA_A$/benzodiazepine receptor complex is one site involved in the aggression-promoting effects of alcohol, development of a medication to block that action appears to be a promising strategy for reducing alcohol-related violence. Because alcohol affects so many biological processes, other sites should be explored as well.

As noted by Miczek et al. (Volume 3), long-term basic research is needed to identify categories of individuals in whom psychoactive drugs do promote violent behavior, attending to pharmacological conditions at the time of the violent act; individuals' physiological and psychological characteristics; their genetic, developmental, and social backgrounds; and prevailing social conditions. Research on possible violence-promoting effects of smoking crack cocaine should also receive high priority.

Developmental Interventions

Based on the preceding discussion, successful substance abuse prevention during childhood shows promise of reducing violence levels through two distinct routes. First, interventions that discourage alcohol use may prevent alcohol-related violent behavior, especially by aggressive children who may later enter one of two high-risk dual diagnosis categories: (a) alcoholic/sociopathic and (b) antisocial personality disorder coupled with abuse of both drugs and alcohol. Second, because violent events occur so frequently in illegal drug markets, successful drug abuse prevention may eventually reduce violence levels by reducing the number and size of these markets.

The most common strategy for substance abuse prevention to date has involved school-based programs intended to discourage 11- to 14-year-olds from taking up the use of tobacco, alcohol, marijuana, and other drugs. The general approach is to teach youngsters not only the health effects and other consequences of using these substances, but also techniques for resisting peer pressure to use them. Variations have been developed that begin education as early as kindergarten. Also, at least two programs, DARE in Los Angeles and SPECDA in New York City, have brought police officers into the classrooms to help in teaching (DeJong, 1986).

In an assessment of available evidence from evaluations of the effectiveness of community-based and school-based drug abuse prevention programs, the National Research Council (Gerstein and Green, 1992) concluded that some interventions have succeeded in delaying initiation of tobacco, alcohol, and marijuana use among youth. To the extent that these substances are stepping stones to other psychoactive drugs, some prevention strategies may also help to reduce the number of users or delay the onset of use of these other illegal drugs. Despite the number of rigorous evaluations of preventive interventions over the years, the overall effectiveness of these strategies in reducing psychoactive drug use has yet to be documented. Evaluating the effectiveness of community-based and school-based interventions in reducing illegal drug use and its contribution to violent behavior should be a high priority.

Individual-Level Interventions for Adults

Incarceration of Drug-Using Offenders

The strategy of selectively longer incarceration terms for convicted offenders with histories of drug use (and other characteristics associated with higher offending frequencies) was considered in depth by the Panel on Research on Criminal Careers (Blumstein et al., 1986). Despite drug users' higher average frequencies of violent crimes such as robbery and assault, that panel concluded that such selective strategies would have minimal effects on violent crime levels without massive increases in prison populations. No recent findings suggest a contrary conclusion.

Because arrestees with drug use histories are more likely to be rearrested before trial if released on financial or nonfinancial conditions, a plausible related strategy is to make drug use monitoring through urinalysis a condition of pretrial release, with positive test results considered grounds for returning the defendant to jail. A randomized experimental test of this strategy in the District of Columbia offered only statistically insignificant evidence that negative urine tests predict lower pretrial rearrest rates,[4] but failure to show up for the test was a strong positive predictor of pretrial rearrest for new crimes.

Substance Abuse Treatment

After working primarily with heroin addicts from the 1960s until the early 1980s, residential therapeutic communities have extended their programs to cocaine abusers over the past decade. Their approach—a highly structured residential process of resocialization, behavior modification, progressive responsibility, and planned reentry into the community—is perhaps the treatment most widely applied today to drug abusers with serious criminal histories. Randomized experiments have so far proven impracticable as a means of evaluating the effectiveness of such programs, so the best available evidence is based on nonrandomized studies of persons seeking admissions. The Institute of Medicine (IOM) concluded that clients of therapeutic communities show less criminal activity during treatment and after discharge than before admission, and that the minimum retention period needed to obtain this benefit is at least 3 months, with further improvement through 12-18 months (Gerstein and Harwood, 1990:15).

For drug abusers in prison, drug abuse treatment usually consists of individual or group psychotherapy a few times a week with no postrelease follow-up. Not surprisingly, such treatment is not sufficiently intense to demonstrate effectiveness in changing violent, criminal, or drug use behavior following release. However, a few programs—Stay'n Out (in a New York prison), Cornerstone (in the Oregon State Hospital), and the California Civil Addict Program—combine elements of therapeutic communities in institutions with coordinated postrelease follow-up in the community. The IOM committee concluded from well-controlled prospective evaluations that, for inmates who complete them, these programs significantly reduce rearrest rates (Gerstein and Harwood, 1990:17).

Community-Level Interventions

Increasing Alcohol Excise Taxes

A National Research Council study panel saw "good grounds for incorporating an interest in the prevention of alcohol problems into the setting of tax rates on alcohol" (Moore and Gerstein, 1981:114). An analysis by Cook (1981) for that panel found evidence suggesting that state-level rates of liquor consumption, and consequently auto fatalities and cirrhosis deaths, were reduced by increases in alcohol excise tax rates. We know of no similar analysis of how alcohol tax rates are related to violence rates. However, given the links between alcohol and violence, we believe that such an analysis should be carried out and its results considered in public debates about violence control policy. Moreover, changes in alcohol taxes and other control policies present opportunities to evaluate their effects on violence levels.

Police Disruption of Illegal Drug Markets

To disrupt active drug markets, police currently use three primary strategies alone or in combination: (1) targeted undercover operations to remove sellers or buyers from the scene; (2) highly visible sweeps or crackdowns, sometimes billed as "taking back the neighborhood"; and (3) cooperation with local community residents and organizations in antidrug efforts.

Undercover tactics for street-level drug market disruption include the "buy-bust," in which the undercover officer buys illegal drugs and then (with assistance) arrests the seller, and the "reverse sting," in which the undercover officers pose as dealers, sell illegal drugs or an imitation, and arrest the buyer. In one evaluation, the use of undercover tactics in Birmingham, Alabama, may have produced a delayed decrease in violent crimes reported to the police. However, the effect is uncertain because the experimental controls broke down (Uchida et al., 1990).

Drug-related police crackdowns are intended to achieve additional disruption through the high visibility associated with police saturation of a small target area. Crackdowns in Lynn and Lawrence, Massachusetts, New York City, Philadelphia, Oakland, California, and Washington, D.C., have been studied in some depth (Kleiman, 1986; Uchida et al., 1990). In the short run, these crackdowns reduced the volume of illegal drug sales on the streets in the targeted area. However, there is controversy over the extent to which the crackdowns merely moved the drug markets off the street into less visible locations in high-rise housing projects, displaced robberies and burglaries to surrounding areas, and accelerated a downward trend in the homicide rate that was occurring throughout the city at the same time. The evaluators of the Oakland effort made perhaps the only supportable generalization, that success in police crackdowns requires three interrelated elements: a highly committed police department, a receptive community, and a drug market that is not yet too firmly entrenched (Uchida et al., 1990).

Currently, three comprehensive evaluations of how police activity affects drug trafficking and violent crime are under way in Pittsburgh, Kansas City, and Jersey City, under the National Institute of Justice Drug Market Analysis Program. With the aid of geocoding, the program will permit geographic analysis of police activity, drug marketing, and violent crime levels, so that both local and displacement effects can be observed.

Police cooperation with the community in disrupting illegal drug markets includes meetings with community groups, interviews with citizens to inform them about early signs of developing drug markets and a telephone hotline for reporting suspicions, and distributions of leaflets about illegal psychoactive drugs and markets. This variety of community-oriented policing requires a major reorientation of police priorities that permeates through all ranks from the chief down to patrol officers. In one attempt to evaluate community cooperation as a drug market disruption tactic using a pretest/posttest design, the intervention was delivered in a disjointed and inconsistent way and failed to demonstrate any effects on robberies or violent crime, relative to a control beat (Uchida et al., 1990).

RESEARCH AND EVALUATION NEEDS

This chapter has discussed findings about a number of links between violence and psychoactive drugs including alcohol. While progress has been made in understanding those links and using them to reduce violence, much remains to be done. We consider the following areas to be most important in future research and evaluation programs:

(1) developing medications to reduce drug craving and to reduce the aggression-promoting effects of alcohol use;
(2) male-female differences in the link between alcohol use and violent behavior;
(3) other individual differences—behavioral, genetic, and neurological—that distinguish people who behave violently while drinking alcohol from those who do not;
(4) relating different combinations of multiple psychoactive drug use pharmacologically to aggressive and violent behavior in humans and other animals;
(5) relating the various methods and patterns through which users commonly take psychoactive drugs to their patterns of violent behavior—in particular, ascertaining whether the rapid access of smoked "crack" cocaine to the brain produces perceptual distortions or violent behaviors that do not occur with powdered cocaine;
(6) genetic processes that may influence the relationship between chronic alcohol abuse and aggressive or violent behavior in humans and other animals;
(7) relationships between levels of violence related to illegal drug distribution and demographic and socioeconomic processes in the surrounding communities;
(8) the incidence of violence that is indirectly related to alcohol or other drug use through incidents such as arguments over debt repayments, over the use of family money, and over time spent away from home;
(9) profiles of the prevalence of alcohol and other psychoactive drug use by time of day and day of week, and by demographic and socioeconomic categories, as benchmarks for analyzing their causal role in violent events; and
(10) evaluations using randomized experiments to test how the following approaches to reducing drug consumption affect violence levels: community- and school-based substance abuse prevention programs, urinalysis monitoring of drug-positive arrestees for violent offenses during pretrial release, substance abuse treat-

ment for incarcerated drug-using violent offenders with coordinated postrelease follow-up in the community, and police disruption of illegal drug markets in cooperation with local community-based organizations.

NOTES

1 The urine specimens are tested for cocaine, opiates, marijuana, PCP, methadone, benzodiazepine (Valium), methaqualone, propoxyphene (Darvon), barbiturates, and amphetamines. Samples are collected at the time of arrest on a voluntary basis; an average of 80 percent of arrestees voluntarily cooperate. Test criteria are set to detect use of most drugs in the preceding 24 to 48 hours, but marijuana and PCP can be detected for several weeks after use.

2 Among studies of this relationship, many group all illegal drugs together. Those that distinguish among drugs usually list cocaine, heroin, amphetamines, barbiturates, and hallucinogens other than marijuana (Elliott and Huizinga, 1984).

3 Burglaries entail a risk of violence if the burglar encounters an occupant of the property.

4 Data from the experiment can be used to study how pretrial rearrest probability is related to positive test results because, according to Toborg et al. (1986), pretrial release was rarely revoked following a positive test result or even failure to show up for testing.

REFERENCES

Adler, P.A.

1985 *Wheeling and Dealing: An Ethnography of an Upper-Level Dealing and Smuggling Community*. New York: Columbia University Press.

Anderson, E.

1990 *Streetwise: Race, Class, and Change in an Urban Community*. Chicago: The University of Chicago Press.

Anglin, M.D., and G. Speckart

1988 Narcotics use and crime: A multisample multimethod analysis. *Criminology* 26(2):197-233.

Babor, T.F., S. Berglas, J.H. Mendelson, J. Ellingboe, and K. Miller

1983 Alcohol, affect, and the disinhibition of verbal behavior. *Psychopharmacology* 80:53-60.

Ball, J.C., J.W. Schaeffer, and D.N. Nurco

1983 The day-to-day criminality of heroin addicts in Baltimore—A study in the continuity of offense rates. *Drug and Alcohol Dependence* 12:119-142.

Blanchard, R.J., K. Hori, and D.C. Blanchard

1987 Ethanol effects on aggression of rats selected for different levels of aggressiveness. *Pharmacology Biochemistry and Behavior* 27:641-644.

Blane, H.T., and E. Hewitt
1977 Alcohol and Youth: An Analysis of the Literature, 1960-75. Final report prepared for the National Institute on Alcohol Abuse and Alcoholism, contract no. ADM 281-75-0026. Rockville, Md.: U.S. Public Health Service.

Block, C.R., R.L. Block, M. Wilson, and M. Daly
1990 Chicago Homicide From the Sixties to the Nineties: Have Patterns of Lethal Violence Changed? Paper presented at the meetings of the American Society of Criminology, Baltimore, Md., November 5.

Blumstein, A., J. Cohen, J. Roth, and C. Visher, eds.
1986 *Criminal Careers and "Career Criminals."* Washington, D.C.: National Academy Press.

Bourgois, Philippe
1989 In search of Horatio Alger: Culture and ideology in the crack economy. *Contemporary Drug Problems* 16(Winter):619-649.

Branchey, M.H., L. Buydens-Branchey, and C.S. Lieber
1988 P3 in alcoholics with disordered regulation of aggression. *Psychiatry Research* 25:49-58.

Bureau of Justice Statistics
1990 *Criminal Victimization in the United States, 1988.* A National Crime Survey Report, December 1990, NCJ-122024.

Burns, T.F.
1980 Getting rowdy with the boys. *Journal of Drug Issues* 10:273-286.

Cadoret, R.J., T.W. O'Gorman, E. Troughton, and E. Heywood
1985 Alcoholism and antisocial personality. *Archives of General Psychiatry* 42:161-167.

Cahalan, D., and I. Cisin
1976 Drinking behavior and drinking problems in the United States. In B. Kissin and H. Begleiter, eds., *The Biology of Alcoholism.* Vol. 4. New York: Plenum.

Chaiken, J., and M. Chaiken
1982 Varieties of Criminal Behavior. Santa Monica, Calif.: Rand.
1990 Drugs and predatory crime. Pp. 203-239 in M. Tonry and J.Q. Wilson, eds., *Drugs and Crime (Crime and Justice: A Review of the Literature, Vol. 13).* Chicago: University of Chicago.

Chin, K.
1990 *Chinese Subculture and Criminality: Non-Traditional Crime Groups in America.* Westport, Conn.: Greenwood.

Cloninger, C.R.
1987 Neurogenetic adaptive mechanisms in alcoholism. *Science* 236:410-416.

Cloninger, C.R., S. Sigvardsson, S.B. Gilligan, A.-L. Von Knorring, T. Reich, and M. Bohman

1989 Genetic heterogeneity and the classification of alcoholism. Pp. 3-16 in E. Gordis, B. Tabakoff, and M. Linnoila, eds., *Alcohol Research from Bench to Bedside.* Binghampton, N.Y.: Haworth Press.

Cohen, J.

1986 Research on criminal careers: Individual frequency rates and offense seriousness. In A. Blumstein, J. Cohen, J. Roth, and C. Visher, eds., *Criminal Careers and "Career Criminals."* Vol. 1. Washington, D.C.: National Academy Press.

Collins, J.J., Jr.

1986 The relationship of problem drinking to individual offending sequences. In A. Blumstein, J. Cohen, J.A. Roth, and C.A. Visher, eds., *Criminal Careers and "Career Criminals."* Vol. 2. Washington, D.C.: National Academy Press.

Cook, P.J.

1981 The effect of liquor taxes on drinking, cirrhosis, and auto accidents. Pp. 255-285 in M.H. Moore and D. Gerstein, eds., *Alcohol and Public Policy: Beyond the Shadow of Prohibition.* Washington, D.C.: National Academy Press.

Crawford, A.

1984 Alcohol and expectancy—II. Perceived sex differences in the role of alcohol as a source of aggression. *Alcohol and Alcoholism* 19:71-75.

DeBold, J.F., and K.A. Miczek

1985 Testosterone modulates the effects of ethanol on male mouse aggression. *Psychopharmacology* 86:286-290.

DeJong, William

1986 Project DARE: Teaching kids to say "no" to drugs and alcohol. *NIJ Reports* SNI 196(March).

Elliott, D.S., and D. Huizinga

1984 The Relationship Between Delinquent Behavior and ADM Problems. National Youth Survey Report no. 26. Boulder, Colo.: Behavioral Research Institute.

Fagan, Jeffrey

1989 The social organization of drug use and drug dealing among urban gangs. *Criminology* 27(4):633-669.

1990 Intoxication and aggression. Pp. 241-320 in M. Tonry and J.Q. Wilson, eds., *Drugs and Crime (Crime and Justice: A Review of Research, Vol 13).* Chicago: The University of Chicago Press.

Fagan, J., and K. Chin

1989a Violence as regulation and social control in the distribution of crack. In M. de la Rosa, B. Gropper, and E. Lambert, eds., *Drugs and Violence, Research Monograph of the National Institute on*

Drug Abuse. Rockville, Md.: Alcohol, Drug Abuse and Mental Health Administration.

1989b Initiation into crack and cocaine: A tale of two epidemics. *Contemporary Drug Problems* 16(Winter):579-617.

1991 Social processes of initiation into crack. *Journal of Drug Issues* 21(Spring):313-343.

Feldman, H.W., J. Mandel, and A. Fields

1985 In the neighborhood: A strategy for delivering early intervention services to young drug users in their natural environments. In A.S. Friedman and G.M. Beschner, eds., *Treatment Services for Adolescent Substance Abusers*. Rockville, Md.: National Institute on Drug Abuse.

Gandossy, R.P., J. Williams, J. Cohen, and H. Hardwood

1980 *Drugs and Crime: A Survey and Analysis of the Literature*. Washington, D.C.: National Institute of Justice.

Gerstein, D.R., and H.J. Harwood, eds.

1990 *Treating Drug Problems*. Vol. 1. Washington, D.C.: National Academy Press.

Gerstein, D.R., and L.W. Green, eds.

1992 *Preventing Drug Abuse: What Do We Know?* Committee on Drug Abuse Prevention Research, Commission on Behavioral and Social Sciences and Education. Washington, D.C.: National Academy Press.

Goldstein, P.J.

1989 Drugs and violent crime. Pp. 16-48 in N.A. Weiner and M.E. Wolfgang, eds., *Pathways to Criminal Violence*. Newbury Park, Calif.: Sage Publications.

Goldstein, P.J., and D. Hunt

1984 The Impact of Drugs on the Health of the Nation: Final Report. Atlanta, Ga.: Emory University, Carter Center.

Goldstein, P.J., D.S. Lipton, B.J. Spunt, P.A. Belluci, T. Miller, N. Cortez, M. Khan, and A. Kale

1987 Drug Related Involvement in Violent Episodes. Final report. Grants DA-03182 and DA-04017, National Institute on Drug Abuse. New York: Narcotic and Drug Research, Inc.

Goldstein, P.J., H.H. Brownstein, P.J. Ryan, and P.A. Bellucci

1989 Crack and homicide in New York City, 1988: A conceptually based event analysis. *Contemporary Drug Problems* 16(Winter):651-687.

Goodwin, D.W.

1973 Alcohol in suicide and homicide. *Quarterly Journal of Studies on Alcohol* 34:144-156.

Gordon, A.J.

1978 Hispanic drinking after migration: The case of Dominicans. *Medical Anthropology* 2:61-84.

1982 The cultural context of drinking and indigenous therapy for alcohol problems in three migrant Hispanic cultures. *Journal of Studies on Alcohol* 42:217-240.

Greenberg, D.F.
1981 Methodological issues in survey research on the inhibition of crime. *Journal of Criminal Law and Criminology* 72:1094-1108.

Grove, W.M., E.D. Eckert, L. Heston, T.J. Bouchard, N. Segal, and D.T. Lykken
1990 Heritability of substance abuse and antisocial behavior: A study of monozygotic twins reared apart. *Biological Psychiatry* 27:1293-1304.

Gustafson, R.
1986a A possible confounding variable in different versions of the "aggression machine" when used in research on alcohol. *Psychological Reports* 58:303-308.
1986b Alcohol, aggression and the validity of experimental paradigms with women. *Psychological Reports* 59:51-56.

Hamid, A.
1990 The political economy of crack-related violence. *Contemporary Drug Problems* 17(Spring):31-78.

Harwood, H., D. Napolitano, P. Kristiansen, and J. Collins
1984 Economic Costs to Society of Alcohol and Drug Abuse and Mental Illness. Final report. Alcohol, Drug Abuse, and Mental Health Administration. Unpublished.

Heath, D.B.
1983 Alcohol and aggression: A "missing link" in worldwide perspective. In E. Gottheil, K.A. Druley, T.E. Skoloda, and H.M. Waxman, eds., *Alcohol, Drug Abuse and Aggression.* Springfield, Ill.: Thomas.

Inciardi, J.A.
1980 Youth, drugs, and street crime. Pp. 175-204 in F. Scarpitti and S.K. Datesman, eds., *Drugs and the Youth Culture.* Beverly Hills, Calif.: Sage Publications.
1989 The crack/violence connection within a population of hard-core adolescent offenders. Paper presented at the National Institute on Drug Abuse Technical Review on Drugs and Violence, September 25-26, 1989, Rockville, Md.

Isikoff, M., and K. Sawyer
1990 Thornburgh says all drug abusers fuel nation's crisis. *Washington Post*, August 17, p. A25.

Johnson, B., P. Goldstein, E. Preble, J. Schmeidler, D. Lipton, B. Spunt, and T. Miller
1985 Taking Care of Business: The Economics of Crime by Heroin Users. Lexington, Mass.: Lexington Books.

Johnson, Bruce D., T. Williams, K. Dei, and H. Sanabria
1990 Drug abuse in the inner city: Impact on hard-drug users and

the community. In Michael Tonry and J. Q. Wilson, eds., *Drugs and Crime*. Chicago: University of Chicago Press.

Kleiman, M.A.R.
1986 Bringing back street-level heroin enforcement. In J.A. Roth, M.H. Tonry, and N. Morris, eds., *Drugs and Crime: Workshop Proceedings*. Washington, D.C.: National Research Council, Committee on Law and Justice.

Klein, M., C. Maxson, and L. Cunningham
1988 Gang Involvement in Cocaine "Rock" Trafficking. Final report for the National Institute of Justice. Los Angeles, Calif.: University of Southern California.

Levinson, D.
1983 Alcohol use and aggression in American subcultures. In R. Room and G. Collins, eds., *Alcohol and Disinhibition: Nature and Meaning of the Link*. Research Monograph no. 12. National Institute on Alcohol Abuse and Alcoholism. Washington, D.C.: U.S. Department of Health and Human Services, U.S. Public Health Service.

Linnoila, M., M. Virkkunen, M. Scheinin, A. Nuutila, R. Rimon, and F.K. Goodwin
1983 Low cerebrospinal fluid 5-hydroxyindoleacetic acid concentration differentiates impulsive from nonimpulsive violent behavior. *Life Sciences* 33:2609-2614.

MacAndrew, C., and R.B. Edgerton
1969 *Drunken Comportment: A Social Explanation*. Chicago: Aldine.

Marinacci, A.A., and K.O. von Hagen
1972 Alcohol and temporal lobe dysfunction: Some of its psychomotor equivalents. *Behavioral Neuropsychiatry* 3:2-11.

McCord, Joan
1983 Alcohol in the service of aggression. In E. Gottheil, K.A. Druley, T.E. Skoloda, and H.M. Waxman, eds., *Alcohol, Drug Abuse and Aggression*. Springfield, Ill.: Thomas.
1988 Parental aggressiveness and physical punishment in long-term perspective. In G.T. Hotaling, D. Finkelhor, J.T. Kirkpatrick, and M. A. Straus, eds., *Family Abuse and Its Consequences: New Directions in Research*. Newbury Park, Calif.: Sage Publications.

Miczek, K.A., and H. Barry III
1977 Effects of alcohol on attack and defensive-submissive reactions in rats. *Psychopharmacology* 52:231-237.

Mieczkowski, T.
1989 The Operational Styles of Crackhouses in Detroit. Paper prepared for the Technical Review Panel on Drugs and Violence, National Institute on Drug Abuse, September 25 and 26, 1989, Rockville, Md.

Moore, M.H., and D. Gerstein, eds.
1981 *Alcohol and Public Policy: Beyond the Shadow of Prohibition.* Washington, D.C.: National Academy Press.

Murphy, S., D. Waldorf, and C. Reinarman
1989 Drifting into dealing: Becoming a cocaine seller. Unpublished manuscript. San Francisco, Calif.: Institute for Scientific Analysis.

Musto, D.
1973 *An American Disease: Origins of Narcotic Control.* New Haven, Conn.: Yale University Press.

O'Leary, M.R., E.F. Chaney, L.S. Brown, and M.A. Shuckit
1978 The use of the Goldberg indices with alcoholics: A cautionary note. *Journal of Clinical Psychology* 34:988-990.

Pettijohn, T.F.
1979 The effects of alcohol on agonistic behavior in the Telomian dog. *Psychopharmacology* 60:295-301.

Pulkkinen, L.
1983 Youthful smoking and drinking in a longitudinal perspective. *Journal of Youth and Adolescence* 12:253-283.

Reuter, P., R. MacCoun, and P. Murphy
1990 *Money From Crime: A Study of the Economics of Drug Dealing in Washington, D.C.* Santa Monica, Calif.: The RAND Corporation.

Robbins, R.H.
1979 Alcohol and the identity struggle: Some effects of economic changes on interpersonal relations. In M. Marshall, ed., *Beliefs, Behaviors and Alcoholic Beverages: A Cross-Cultural Survey.* Ann Arbor, Mich.: University of Michigan.

Ryan, P.J., P.J. Goldstein, H.H. Brownstein, and P.A. Bellucci
No date Who's right: Different outcomes when police and scientists view the same set of homicide events, New York City, 1988. Research paper provided for Grant 87-IJ-CX-0046 from the National Institute of Justice.

Rydelius, P.A.
1988 The development of antisocial behaviour and sudden violent death. *Acta Psychiatria Scandanavia* 77:398-403.

Sampson, Robert J.
1987 Urban black violence: The effect of male joblessness and family disruption, *American Journal of Sociology* 93(2):348-382.

Schaefer, J.M.
1973 A Hologeistic Study of Family Structure and Sentiment, Supernatural Beliefs, and Drunkenness. Ph.D. dissertation, State University of New York at Buffalo, Department of Anthropology.

Schubert, D.S.P., A.W. Wolf, M.B. Patterson, T.P. Grande, and L. Pendleton
1988 A statistical evaluation of the literature regarding the associations among alcoholism, drug abuse, and antisocial personality disorder. *International Journal of the Addictions* 23:797-808.

Seltzer, A.
1980 Acculturation and mental disorder in the Inuit. *Canadian Journal of Psychiatry* 25:173-181.

Sherman, L.W., L. Steele, D. Laufersweiler, N. Hoffer, and S.A. Julian
1989 Stray bullets and "mushrooms": Random shootings of bystanders in four cities, 1977-1988. *Journal of Quantitative Criminology* 5(4):297-316.

Shuckit, M.A., and J.W. Russell
1984 An evaluation of primary alcoholics with histories of violence. *Journal of Clinical Psychiatry* 45:3-6.

Toborg, M., J.P. Bellassai, and A.M. Yezer
1986 The Washington D.C. Urine Testing Program for Arrestees and Defendants Awaiting Trial: A Summary of Interim Findings. Washington, D.C.: U.S. Department of Justice, National Institute of Justice.

Uchida, C.D., B. Forst, and S.O. Annan
1990 Modern Policing and the Control of Illegal Drugs: Testing New Strategies in Two American Cities. Executive summary of report for National Institute of Justice awards 87-IJ-CX-0058 and 88-IJ-CX-0015.

Van Thiel, D.H., J.S. Gavaler, and R.E. Tarter
1988 The effects of alcohol on sexual behavior and function. Pp. 478-498 in J.M.A. Sitsen, ed., *Handbook of Sexology*. Vol. 6: *The Pharmacology of Endocrinology and Sexual Function*. Amsterdam: Elsevier Science Publishers.

Vigil, James Diego
1987 Street socialization, locura behavior, and violence among Chicano gang members. Pp. 231-41 in Jess F. Kraus, Susan B. Sorenson, and Paul D. Juarez, eds., *Research Conference on Violence and Homicide in Hispanic Communities*. University of California, Los Angeles.
1988 *Barrio Gangs*. Austin: University of Texas Press.

Virkkunen, M.
1974 Alcohol as a factor precipitating aggression and conflict of behaviour leading to homicide. *British Journal of Addiction* 69:149-154.

Virkkunen, M., J. DeJong, J. Barko, F.K. Goodwin, and M. Linnoila
1989a Relationship of psychobiological variables to recidivism in violent offenders and impulsive fire setters. *Archives of General Psychiatry* 46:600-603.

Virkkunen, M., J. DeJong, J. Bartko, and M. Linnoila
1989b Psychobiological concomitants of history of suicide attempts among violent offenders and impulsive fire setters. *Archives of General Psychiatry* 46: 604-606.

Weerts, E.M., W. Tornatzky, and K.A. Miczek
In press Prevention of the proaggressive effects of alcohol by benzodiazepine receptor antagonists in rats and in squirrel monkeys. *Psychopharmacology*.

Westermeyer, J., and J. Brantner
1972 Violent death and alcohol use among the Chippewa in Minnesota. *Minnesota Medicine* 55:749-752.

White House
1990 *National Drug Control Strategy.* Washington, D.C.: U.S. Government Printing Office.

Winslow, J.T., and K.A. Miczek
1985 Social status as determinant of alcohol effects on aggressive behavior in squirrel monkeys (*Saimiri sciureus*). *Psychopharmacology* 85:167-172.

Wish, E., E. Brady, and M. Cuadrado
1986 Urine Testing of Arrestees: Findings from Manhattan. Washington, D.C.: U.S. Department of Justice, National Institute of Justice.

Wish, E.D., and B.D. Johnson
1986 The impact of substance abuse on criminal careers. In A. Blumstein, J. Cohen, J.A. Roth, and C.A. Visher, eds., *Criminal Careers and "Career Criminals."* Washington, D.C.: National Academy Press.

Wurmser, L., and C. Lebling
1983 Substance abuse and aggression: A psychoanalytic view. In E. Gottheil, K.A. Druley, T.E. Skoloda, and H.M. Waxman, eds., *Alcohol, Drug Abuse and Aggression.* Springfield, Ill.: Thomas.

Yates, W.R., W. Meller, and E.P. Troughton
1987 Behavioral complications of alcoholism. *A.F.P.* 35:171-175.

5

Violence in Families

Recently, we have come to realize realize that our homes may be as dangerous as our streets. Family violence in its various forms—spouse assault, elder abuse, sibling violence, child abuse—is more prevalent than the public or officials ever suspected. The National Commission on the Causes and Prevention of Violence report issued 23 years ago does not mention spouse assault in its discussion on violent crime (Winslow, 1972). And although incest has long been considered a crime (more against the natural order than against the law), it has only recently been labeled a violent crime justifying the intervention of the courts. On the terrain of family violence, elder abuse is just being recognized as a phenomenon and sibling violence remains largely invisible. Child abuse has received the most attention, having been documented since the 1950s. However, in common with other forms of family violence, we know more about the barriers to accurately counting it than we do about its rate and prevalence. Long considered family matters rather than criminal matters, we are just beginning to probe the causes and consequences of family violence and to test the effectiveness of interventions designed to reduce its severity, frequency, and impact.

CONCEPTIONS OF FAMILY AND FAMILY VIOLENCE

In Chapter 2 we draw attention to the ways that changes in the social construction of violent behaviors pose difficulties for classifying and counting violent crime. Nowhere in the criminal law and in its administration is the social construction of violent crime changing more rapidly than in what constitutes family violence and society's responses to it.

Because family law is legislated and administered under different statutes and regulations in each state as well as by the federal government, there is no national legal definition of a *family*. Similarly, there is no standardized and generally accepted scholarly definition of what constitutes a family. Information on family violence is usually based on identifications of people by their current marital status (married, separated, divorced, or single), by their spouse status (spouse/ex-spouse; husband/wife), or by relationships among members of a household (e.g., cohabitants; child/parent; brother/sister; father/mother). Statistics about families are not collected according to theoretical constructs; rather researchers sample address locations and identify households; families are then designated within households either by respondents themselves or by interviewers. By this procedure, two or more families of several generations may reside within a household with a single head.[1]

Substantial recent changes in family structure in the United States, which may affect counts of violent behavior by "family" members, are disclosed by some contemporary statistics on marital status and living arrangements (Bureau of the Census, 1990, 1991):[2]

- The proportion of all households accounted for by two-parent families declined from 40 percent in 1970 to 26 percent in 1990.
- The number of unmarried-couple households almost tripled between 1970 and 1980 and grew by 80 percent between 1980 and 1990, from 1.6 to 2.9 million.
- The proportion of children under 18 years of age living with two parents declined from 85 percent in 1970 to 73 percent in 1990, an estimated 15 percent of whom are stepchildren.
- In 1990, 19 percent of white, 62 percent of black, and 30 percent of Hispanic children under age 18 lived with only one parent.

Trends in family violence must be interpreted against a decline in the fraction of households containing exclusively married couples and their natural children. Violence between growing numbers of same-sex and opposite-sex cohabiting partners is increasingly regarded as family violence regardless of legal marital status. Those who record statistics may or may not classify violence between increasing numbers of divorced or separated ex-couples as family violence.

Proportionally more of today's children live in households with a cohabiting couple or at least one stepparent. Legally, a cohabitant unrelated by blood or marriage who physically or sexually abuses children in the household is an unrelated person, although programmatically the abuser may be treated as a family member.

Children today are far more likely to grow up in a female-headed household than heretofore, especially in black households. Parents today are more likely to have never married or divorced. In a purely statistical sense, a child growing up with only one parent has only half the risk of violent victimization by an adult family member; however, the tensions surrounding family breakup may increase the chance that an adult family member or cohabitant will act violently toward a child. Moreover, patterns of divorce, separation, remarriage, and cohabitation expose a fairly sizable proportion of children to several parents.

Although there is no common agreement on when violent behaviors that occur within a household are to be regarded as *family* violence, the panel considered all violent behaviors within households made up of married or cohabiting persons and their relatives and minor children as domestic or family violence. Specifically, *domestic (family) violence* includes *spouse assault* (often referred to as marital violence), *physical and sexual assaults of children*, *sibling assaults*, and *physical and sexual assaults of other relatives* who reside in the household.

These violent behaviors do not include all violent behavior that occurs within families. Among those excluded are nonconsenting sexual behavior among adult family members—especially incest and marital rape—and consensual sexual behavior among spouses or family members that at law is regarded as violent behavior. Attempts have also been made to construct parental physical punishment of children as child abuse. Because so little is as yet known about the nature and extent of these behaviors in families, they are not discussed further in this chapter.

DYNAMIC NATURE OF FAMILY VIOLENCE

Family violence has a number of distinguishing features. Unlike victims and offenders who are strangers, victims and offenders in family violence cases have some form of *continuing* relationship such as spouse or partner, parent and child, or siblings.[3] Interacting almost daily and sharing a common domicile increase the opportunities for violent encounters.[4] Because they are bound together in a continuing relationship, it is quite likely that the victim will be violated repeatedly by the offender. Usually one person in the continuing relationship is relatively powerless and more vulnerable to the aggression and violence of the more powerful one. The more powerful victimizer often threatens the victim with additional violence if the incidents of violence are disclosed to others, or the victim may refrain from disclosure anticipating stigmatization and denigration. Moreover, because many of these episodes occur in private places where they are invisible to others, they are less likely to be detected or reported to the police. For these reasons, family victimization continues for want of intervention by others.

INSTITUTIONAL BARRIERS TO OBSERVING FAMILY VIOLENCE

Major institutional barriers to understanding family violence are limited access to observe violent behavior in the private places where it occurs and the need to obtain consent to gather information on family matters, including violence. The problems of securing access and obtaining consent are especially acute for children and dependent family members who lack the competence to give consent or to report physical and sexual violence by members of their household. Data collectors are limited by the necessity to obtain consent from adults before collecting information about their own, another adult's, or their dependents' victimization. Law enforcement officers likewise must obtain consent for intrusion into private matters or have legal grounds for intervention or investigation in criminal matters—grounds that derive primarily from complaints by persons who have private knowledge of intrafamily violence.

Institutions of privacy are not the only barriers to obtaining information about physical and sexual assaults of minors in the household. There are substantial social and psychological processes that lead family members to conceal intrafamily violence, especially sexual violence. Victims of spouse assault and of sexual violence are often threatened with additional violence if they disclose occurrences to the police. Threats based on financial dependency, uncertainty about their proper role, and family loyalty may all make it difficult to verify the victimization of minors by members of their own household—especially for sexual assault.

The cognitive difficulties people have in separating occurrences of the same event create problems in counting repeated victimization, especially of the same kind of violence. In addition, self-blame and fear of the stigma associated with battering among intimates create a climate for even greater underreporting. Frieze and Browne (1989:182), summarizing what is known about self-reports of those involved in spouse assault, conclude that women who have been victimized over a long period of time tend to underestimate the frequency and severity of the violence they experience when their reports are compared with hospital and other records or the reports of witnesses. Male batterers also underreport their violent actions and minimize their own responsibility for battering, projecting blame onto the battered spouse.

Research is needed on whether and how self-reports of victims and offenders could be used to measure the *prevalence* of family violence (i.e., the proportion of the population that experienced at least one event during some period of time) and its *incidence* (i.e., estimates of the number or rate of events that occur within a given period, usually a year). Research is also needed on the extent to which valid information on physical and sexual violence can be obtained from family members, especially from self-reports of minors and from their adult victimizers.[5]

In episodes of intrafamily violence, it is sometimes difficult to determine the respective roles of victim and offender, since participants often appear to engage in mutual combat. Though the reports were not verified, Straus et al. (1980) found that half of their male and female respondents who reported violence said that both partners had been assaultive. The determination of victim and offender roles is therefore generally judged in terms of consequences of the combat, such as the severity of injuries or the dangerousness of the violent means used by each participant. Although comparable data are lacking for the severity of injury for men and women in domestic assault, the consequences of injury appear more severe for women. Stark and Flitcraft (1991) conclude that a battering may be the most common cause of injury among women seeking emergency department treatment. And men use more dangerous means in domestic assaults. Straus and Gelles (1986) found that men more often used the most injurious and dangerous forms of violence, such as using a gun or knife or physically assaulting the partner.

PATTERNS AND TRENDS IN FAMILY VIOLENCE

Because of the institutional barriers described above, as well as problems stemming from the design of our major national systems that collect and record information on violent behavior, it is not possible to estimate reliably the prevalence and incidence of domestic violence in the United States. Below we present some crude estimates from currently available information, but there is good reason to conclude that intrafamily violence is substantially underreported.

Beginning in 1988, the National Crime Survey (NCS) (Bureau of Justice Statistics, 1990) reports annual estimates of the extent of family violence for persons age 12 and older. Of the violent victimizations reported in 1989 in which the offender was a relative of the victim, 59 percent of the assaults were by a spouse (41%) or ex-spouse (18%). Other relatives accounted for another 29 percent and parents (7%) and children (5%) for the remaining offenders. The NCS lacks the necessary information, however, to reliably determine how much of the reported violence is classifiable as family violence. For example, in considering violence only among married spouses, it excludes violence among cohabitants. Likewise, the NCS does not collect information on children under age 12.

The Uniform Crime Reports (UCR) system does not currently report family violence separately, except for information on the relationship of victim and offender in homicides and for some arrests. The new incident-based reporting system of UCR will have the capability of tabulating information on felony and misdemeanor domestic violence and on other assaults involving family members.[6] The panel urges UCR to utilize the new system to provide information on the status of victims and offenders in all violent offenses so that we may better understand violence in terms of social relationships among victims and their victimizers.[7]

Information on other forms of intrafamily violence is even more problematic. National estimates of violence toward children are based largely on reports of cases of maltreatment known to investigatory bodies such as juvenile probation, coroners, and law enforcement agencies; to major health, education, and welfare organizations whose professional and semiprofessional workers have contacts with children—physicians, nurses, teachers, mental health, public health, and social service workers—and who observe visible injuries;[8] and to child protective service agencies that process referrals from these agencies and from citizen complaints.[9]

Most of the prevalence and incidence estimates for specific types of intrafamily violence come, however, either from special surveys or from samples of victims or offenders known to some agency. In this discussion we rely not only on these special studies and official reports but also on a commissioned review of research on spouse abuse (Fagan and Browne, Volume 3) and previously published reviews by Frieze and Browne (1989) on violence in marriage, by Garbarino (1989) on child maltreatment, and by Pagelow (1989) on violence toward and among other family members.

Marital Violence

The main measure of domestic violence used in surveys, the Conflict Tactics Scale developed by Straus (1979), includes verbal and physically aggressive acts, including violent acts, ranging in severity from hurling objects to the use of a deadly weapon such as a gun or a knife. Using it in an initial national telephone survey of couples in 1975, and in a repeat of the survey in 1985 (Straus and Gelles, 1986), Straus et al. (1980) reported that 16 of every 100 couples reported at least one incident of physical aggression during the year before the survey. The prevalence of severe violence in both surveys was about a third of that; about 4 in 100 females and 5 in 100 males reported experiencing severe violence during the year. There is reason to conclude that these estimates may be somewhat low since the sample excludes unmarried couples and misses segments of the population that do not have phones.

The national rate reported by Straus et al. is well below that found in local surveys of selected segments of the population. Our commissioned review indicates that there is considerable variation in the prevalence rate from local sample surveys (Fagan and Browne, Volume 3). However, almost all of the high estimates were obtained from select populations such as divorce filings, students, or batterers or from small samples. The larger samples—over 1,000 women or couples—have rates around 10 in 100 reporting some form of family violence as measured by the Straus and Gelles scale.

Assaults on Children

National estimates of assaults on children, including physical and sexual abuse and physical neglect, are derived from a series of studies commissioned by governmental sponsors. The U.S. Advisory Board on Child Abuse and Neglect, a governmental advisory board created by the 1988 amendments to the Child Abuse and Prevention and Treatment Act, estimates that in 1989, at least 1,200 and perhaps as many as 5,000 children died as a result of maltreatment, and over 160,000 children were seriously harmed (U.S. Department of Health and Human Services, 1990:15).[10]

Another indicator of the severity of the problem of child maltreatment is the rapid escalation of reports of child maltreatment that are received by municipal, county, or state social service or child protection agencies. The advisory board has stated that in 1974 there were about 60,000 cases of child maltreatment reported. This figure rose to 1.1 million in 1980 and more than doubled to 2.4 million in 1988 (U.S. Department of Health and Human Services, 1988:x). Part of this increase can be attributed to more inclusive definitions of abuse and neglect resulting from broader public awareness of different forms of child maltreatment, and an increase in the likelihood that professionals will recognize maltreatment, rather than an increase in incidence per se (U.S. Department of Health and Human Services, 1988:xxv). However, it is also likely that many cases of child maltreatment are reported to public health or educational agencies that are not known to social service personnel who often supply the "countable" case figures. There are also many cases of interfamilial or third-party assaults on children that are never reported to any professionals concerned with the health or welfare of children.

Under the expanded definitions of child abuse and neglect, the National Incidence Survey published in 1988 (NIS-2) and commissioned by the National Center for Child Abuse and Neglect estimated that the majority of countable cases involved neglect (63%, involving 15.9 per thousand, or 1,003,600 children). Less than half (43%) of these cases involved abuse (10.7 per 1,000, or 675,000 children) (U.S. Department of Health and Human Services, 1988:3-4). Under the revised definitions, reports can be made on behalf of children who may be subject to demonstrable harm but who have not (yet) experienced any demonstrated injury or impairment.

Using the revised definitions, NIS-2 estimated that physical neglect represented the "largest subcategory of countable neglect, representing 57% of all neglected children within these standards (or 571,600 children)" (U.S. Department of Health and Human Services, 1988:3-9). Educational neglect was the second most frequent subcategory (29% of the total neglect cases, or 292,100 children) and emotional neglect was the least frequent subcategory (22% of the total neglect cases, or 223,100 children) (U.S. Department of Health and Human Services, 1988:3-8).

Within the category of abuse, physical abuse is the most frequent subcategory, accounting for 358,300 children reported in the NIS-2 study (5.7 children per 1,000). Emotional abuse was the next most frequently occurring subcategory of abuse (211,100 children, or 3.4 children per 1,000) and sexual abuse was the least frequent of all three major subcategories of abuse in the NIS-2 study (155,900 cases, involving 2.5 children per 1,000) (U.S. Department of Health and Human Services, 1988:3-8).

In comparing changes between the NIS-1 study (conducted in 1980) and the NIS-2 study conducted in 1986, there are significant increases in the incidence of both physical and sexual abuse. In particular, the incidence of countable sexual abuse more than tripled since 1980, an increase of high statistical significance (U.S. Department of Health and Human Services, 1988:3-8).

In contrast, however, one other national incidence survey conducted by Richard J. Gelles and Murray A. Straus, funded by the National Institute of Mental Health, reported a decrease in the self-reported incidence of physical abuse by parents between 1975 and 1985 (U.S. Department of Health and Human Services, 1988:xi). Their study involves information about patterns of violence reported by persons contacted through a telephone survey of two-parent families with children over 3 years of age. To what extent the reports reflect an actual decline as opposed to less candid responses by the parents is simply not known.

Assaults Against the Elderly

Surprisingly little is known about violence toward the elderly in families. A main reason for knowing so little is that previous research has not distinguished between elder abuse and elder neglect, terms that include different types of mistreatment of the elderly (Pedrick-Cornell and Gelles, 1982). Another is the small and selective data base. National victim surveys in the United States do not report the prevalence and incidence of domestic violence toward the elderly. Conclusions consequently are based either on surveys of local communities or assessments by professional caregivers.

The more reliable of the surveys conducted in recent years conclude that domestic violence toward the elderly may be less than presumed from surveys of professionals. A stratified random sample of all persons 65 and older resident in households in the Boston metropolitan area (Pillemer and Finkelhor, 1988) estimated that between 2.5 and 3.9 percent of Boston elderly persons had experienced physical violence, verbal aggression, or neglect. Similar results, with some differences in definitions of abuse, were found for a national survey of elder abuse in Canada (Podnieks and Pillemer, 1989).

A recent review of domestic violence against the elderly (Pillemer and Frankel, 1988) concludes that only a few findings consistently emerge from these studies of the abused elderly population. Elderly victims are disproportionately over age 75. They are more vulnerable to victimization because of illness or impairment and usually reside with the perpetrator of abuse. Although most studies report that women are more at risk of elder abuse than men, they do not take into account women's greater risk exposure because of their longer life expectancy. Because of the broad definitions of elder abuse and the absence of information on its prevalence in family settings, little is known about the prevalence of different forms of violence toward the elderly or its consequences.

Given this current state of knowledge, priority should be given to the collection of more precise information about the prevalence and incidence of violence toward the elderly and its consequences. Moreover, studies of the perpetrators of violence toward the elderly and a better understanding of the situations that give rise to their behavior are essential to develop and implement programs of violence prevention and intervention.

Violence Among Related Family Members

Although the available data are severely limited, the view is firmly held that a considerable amount of violence goes on amongst other members in a household (Pagelow, 1989). Of particular concern is violence of children toward parents and of siblings toward one another. Available estimates for these forms of violence vary substantially and are subject to considerable error. It is generally concluded that physical violence of children toward parents is less severe than is violence of parents toward children (Pagelow, 1989), but there are no precise estimates of its magnitude.

Violence between children is regarded as the most common form of family violence. In the national survey by Straus et al. (1980), 82 percent of the parents of more than one child aged 3 to 17 reported sibling violence, the highest rate for all types of intrafamily violence. There are few studies of either physical or sexual violence among siblings, however.

Risks of Intrafamily Violence

Current reporting systems are not designed to estimate the magnitude of the risks of different types of family violence or to isolate the principal risk groups. The highly aggregated nature of current classifications of violent offenses masks much of the variation important for understanding the risks involved.

For example, the national reporting systems rarely use the available classifications of sexual abuse and sex crimes. When the sole classification is "sexual abuse," it is impossible to understand the nature of the sexual abuse of children—nor, with such gross categorization, can one understand the differences in risk for male and female children.

The classification of intrafamily violence is similarly crude. Classifications of homicide and of assault cloak considerable variation in types of family violence. Moreover, the failure to distinguish the relationships among persons involved in family violence—such as cohabitants of the same or opposite sex, married, separated—limits understanding.

Recognizing these limitations, the panel recommends that efforts should be made to develop classifications of intrafamily violence that lend themselves to understanding risks of victimization and offending and provide a basis for intervention and control.

Assault

According to the National Crime Survey, 9 of every 10 violent victimizations by family members or relatives of the victim are assaults (Bureau of Justice Statistics, 1990). Women, however, experience a higher rate of both simple and aggravated assault by relatives than do men. It is generally assumed that this greater vulnerability of women to assault by relatives is due to their greater vulnerability to assault by a spouse—men are victims in only about 1 in 10 misdemeanor spouse assaults. Yet it may also be a function of women's greater vulnerability to violence by male partners or cohabitants. Unfortunately, the data available to the panel did not permit exploration of the general vulnerability of women to all forms of male family violence, although they are consistent with an explanation of general vulnerability.

Although women are more vulnerable to simple and aggravated assault by relatives than are men, women and men are both more vulnerable to assaults by nonrelatives well known to them and by strangers (Table 5-1). Men are not only more vulnerable to assault by strangers than are women—they are also more vulnerable to assault by strangers than by nonrelatives well known to them. These comparisons do not take into account presumed differences in reporting of assaults by relationship to the victim.

TABLE 5-1 Family Violence, 1989: Victimization Rates by Victim-Offender Relationship and Type of Assault

		Rate per 1,000 Persons Age 12 and Over							
		Aggravated Assault				Simple Assault			
Characteristic	Population	Relatives	Well Known	Casual Acquaintances	Strangers	Relatives	Well Known	Casual Acquaintances	Strangers
Sex									
Male	96,875,920	0.3	2.2	1.2	7.4	0.5	3.1	3.0	10.3
Female	104,499,700	0.7	1.2	0.6	2.0	2.6	3.6	1.7	4.1
Race									
White	172,071,010	0.5	1.6	0.9	4.5	1.7	3.4	2.3	7.3
Black	23,378,200	0.4[a]	2.5	1.3	4.9	1.0	3.4	2.5	5.1
Other	5,926,410	0.4[a]	1.6[a]	0[a]	5.0	2.0[a]	2.9	0.7[a]	9.3
Age									
12-15	13,256,460	0.5[a]	4.4	1.6	6.5	1.7	11.2	9.7	14.4
16-19	14,235,270	0.6[a]	4.9	2.6	13.3	1.8	10.7	7.0	17.2
20-24	18,084,190	1.1	3.1	1.8	9.9	3.9	5.6	4.1	15.7
25-34	43,335,460	0.7	1.7	1.2	5.6	2.6	3.4	2.1	9.1
35-49	50,293,180	0.6	1.2	0.5	3.5	1.5	1.9	1.1	4.6
50-64	32,774,300	0.1[a]	0.4[a]	0.2[a]	1.2	0.4[a]	0.7	0.3[a]	2.1
65 and over	29,396,730	0[a]	0.2[a]	0.2[a]	0.6	0.2[a]	0.2[a]	0.1[a]	0.4[a]

Marital status[b]									
Married	110,124,950	0.3	0.8	0.5	2.7	0.8	1.1	1.0	3.5
Widowed	13,407,180	0[a]	0.1[a]	0.6[a]	0.4[a]	0.1[a]	0.4[a]	0.3[a]	0.4[a]
Divorced or separated	18,786,270	2.3	2.5	2.0	5.7	8.6	5.0	1.4	10.4
Never married	58,618,550	0.3	3.5	1.4	8.8	1.2	7.7	5.5	14.2
Family income[c]									
Less than $7,500	20,425,690	0.7[a]	3.8	1.6	5.5	3.8	6.7	3.1	9.0
$7,500-$9,999	8,374,160	1.0[a]	2.7	0.8[a]	4.0	1.7[a]	6.2	2.5	5.3
$10,000-14,999	19,790,200	0.6[a]	1.8	1.0	4.8	3.2	3.7	2.5	8.0
$15,000-$24,999	35,690,810	0.5	2.1	1.0	5.1	1.6	4.2	2.7	6.8
$25,000-$29,999	15,302,260	0.4[a]	1.4	1.1	4.5	1.3	3.8	2.2	7.3
$30,000-$49,999	45,673,340	0.4	0.7	0.6	4.2	1.0	2.2	2.0	7.4
$50,000 or more	28,905,330	0.3[a]	1.1	0.6	3.9	0.6	1.3	2.1	5.9

[a]Estimate is based on about 10 or fewer sample cases.
[b]Excludes data on persons whose marital status was not ascertained.
[c]Excludes data on persons whose family income was not ascertained.

A number of studies conclude that women who are separated from a spouse or divorced are most at risk of violence and that women who cohabit are more at risk than are those who are married. Available NCS data provide indirect support for this conclusion (Table 5-1). The rate of simple and aggravated assault by relatives is more than 10 times greater for divorced and separated people than it is for the married and widowed ones.[11] Unfortunately, marital status risks are not reported separately for women and men, nor are they related to other statuses in the table, such as their age and income. Information is likewise lacking on assaults among cohabitants of both the same and the opposite sex. Such reporting would make more refined risk assessment possible.

Homicide

Assessments of the risks of intrafamily homicide are more accurate than for other forms of assault, and several patterns are noteworthy:

- Newborns, infants, and children ages 1 to 4 are more vulnerable to homicide than are children ages 5 to 9 years (Federal Bureau of Investigation, 1990:11).[12]
- Infants and small children are more likely to be killed by their mothers than their fathers, perhaps in part as a result of differential risk exposure.
- The risk of homicide for children under age 5 is greater for male than female children, according to a recent case control study (Winpisinger et al., 1991:1053-1054).
- Although men's overall homicide risk is three times that for women, women face a greater risk of homicide by their spouse than do men (Federal Bureau of Investigation, 1990:8).
- At a minimum, intrafamily violence accounted for 15 percent of all homicides in 1989. Violence between husbands and wives accounted for less than half (44%) of the family homicides; family members in male roles—fathers, sons, and brothers—were more likely victims of family homicides than were female members—mothers, daughters, and sisters. Brothers were five times more likely to be killed than sisters (Federal Bureau of Investigation, 1990:12).

Because the data are either unavailable or subject to considerable error, calculation of lethality for types of intrafamily assaults seems unwarranted. The higher homicide death rate for the female partner in spouse assault is consistent, however, with the higher rates of aggravated assault and serious injury for female victims of assault.

Child Abuse

Although there is a paucity of information on the prevalence and incidence of child abuse, a national profile of risk factors can be derived from the National Incidence Surveys.

Female children are three times as likely as males to be sexually abused: 2.9 females per 1,000 compared with 0.9 for males (Sedlak, 1991a,b). Physical abuse is more prevalent than sexual abuse for both sexes. Among males, their less frequent experience of sexual abuse is offset by the greater prevalence of serious injuries among them (Sedlak, 1991a,b).

Although female children are at greater risk of sexual abuse, one-fourth of all sexually abused children reported in NIS-2 were male (Sedlak, 1991a,b). Others report a somewhat higher proportion of sexual abuse of male children—about 29 percent—and an even higher rate of abuse for cases in day care centers—38 percent (Finkelhor and Associates, 1986; Finkelhor et al., 1988). They suggest that the higher rate for male children in day care may result from fewer pressures on younger boys against reporting assault by day care providers.

Black children were one and one-half times more likely to be physically abused than white children and five times more likely to die of physical abuse or neglect (Sedlak, 1991a,b). There is disagreement about how the severity of the physical assault of children varies with their age. The national survey of Straus et al. (1980) found a curvilinear relationship with age but that parents use more severe and potentially lethal violence against their older than younger children. NIS-2 found however that both fatal and more serious injuries were more numerous among young children (Sedlak, 1991a,b) perhaps because of their greater fragility (Sedlak, 1991a,b).

Social status (measured by family income) is substantially related to children's risk of injury from abuse and neglect. For children from families with incomes less than $15,000, the rate of physical abuse was three and one-half times greater and the rate of sexual abuse six times greater than for other children. The general pattern that physical abuse was more frequent than sexual abuse held for both high-income and low-income families (Sedlak, 1991a,b). Moreover, the seriousness of injury or impairment was substantially related to family income: the rate of serious injury was almost seven times greater, of moderate harm nearly five times greater, and of probable injury seven times greater for children from lower-income than from higher-income families (Sedlak, 1991a,b).

There is relatively little information on the consequences of child sexual abuse apart from that provided by clinicians for small numbers of cases (Wolfe et al., 1988:163-166; Bolton et al., 1989:Tables 3.3 and 3.4). In general, that literature concludes that a major consequence is sexual dysfunction when abused children reach adulthood, but that result is not unexpected, given the limitation of the samples to treatment cases. Also, clinicians report that victims of child sexual abuse display fear, immaturity, and neurotic behavior as well as high levels of aggression and antisocial behavior (Finkelhor, 1991:87).

Given the general lack of information on child sexual abuse and its consequences, the panel recommends that research be funded to secure information for cross-sectional samples of families and of children in different settings. Although such studies preferably should be part of prospective longitudinal designs, the cost may be prohibitive. Efforts should be made both to improve the reporting of information on victims and offenders and to determine how to improve the quality of retrospective and surrogate reporting of child sexual abuse. Particular attention should be given to ways of securing self-reports from children who are sexually abused in families.

Repeat Family Violence

A distinguishing feature of family violence is that it occurs among intimates who are bound in recurring, often dependent, relationships that are not easily broken and who share a private space where much behavior is treated as private. Using aggregated data from NCS surveys for the years 1978 to 1982, Langan and Innes (1986) concluded that 32 percent of those assaulted at least once by a domestic partner in the previous six months were victimized again within six months of the incident.[13] By contrast, only 13 percent of the victims of violence by strangers were victimized again within six months.

To the extent that intrafamily violent acts are more repetitive than other violent acts and tend to be omitted from arrest records and self-reports of violent offending, the extent of repeated violent behavior may be understated. Recent research on intrafamily violence provides evidence that there is substantial repeat offending among perpetrators of spouse assault (Dunford et al., 1990; Hirschel et al., 1991). The national survey of child abuse (Straus and Gelles, 1990) found that in 94 percent of the child abuse cases more than a single assault was reported. Evidence also suggests that assaults on children in day care centers and nursery schools frequently involve repeated victimization by the same offender (Finkelhor et al., 1988:91-92).

Perpetrators of Family Violence

Surprisingly little is known about perpetrators of family violence. The panel recommends that more research be undertaken on spouse assaulters' characteristics.

Both clinical and case studies and police reports draw attention to the seemingly high rate of drug and alcohol use by both victims and offenders in incidents of family violence. In a recent Milwaukee, Wisconsin, replication of an experiment to test the effect of arrest in preventing recurrences of spouse assault, one-fifth of the female victims and almost two-fifths of the accused males were judged by the officers to be intoxicated at the time of the arrest (Sherman, 1992). Unfortunately, there is no baseline for drug and alcohol use in the general population or in the geographic areas in which the experimental cases occurred. Consequently, how this level of use compares with that among nonabusive husbands cannot be ascertained.

Both victims and their batterers may substantially underreport the use of drugs. Urinalyses of randomly selected accused batterers indicate alcohol use by three-fourths and some kind of drug use by at least half of those accused (Sherman, 1992); almost 3 in 10 showed some evidence of cocaine use. The drug use was not necessarily immediately prior to the incident; marijuana in particular leaves substantial traces that can be detected over a period of time. Also, it is not clear that cocaine use precipitated any violent events, since its effects depend on the time since ingestion and are confounded by the concurrent use of alcohol.

Consequences of Family Violence

A common immediate consequence of family violence is physical harm of the victim requiring emergency department treatment or outpatient medical attention. In a recent review of spouse abuse, Stark and Flitcraft (1991:139) conclude that spouse assault may be the single most common cause of injury for which women seek emergency medical attention. From their investigation of emergency treatment of women in a metropolitan hospital, they report that battered women were 13 times more likely than other women receiving emergency treatment to be injured in the breast, chest, and abdomen and three times as likely to be injured while pregnant (Stark and Flitcraft, 1991:140; Stark and Flitcraft, 1982). No estimates of the health consequences of other types of family violence are available, nor are there estimates of health and treatment costs for any type of family violence, although the need for such information to guide policy and interventions seems apparent.

Suicide and attempted suicide have been linked to domestic violence. Although there appear to be no differences between battered and nonbattered women in the risk of attempted suicide, the risk increases substantially with repeated victimization (Stark and Flitcraft, 1982). The risk of suicide and attempted suicide has not been estimated following other types of family violence. Given the high rates of suicide in the United States, their relationship to types of family violence would appear worthy of investigation.

The different forms of family violence have also been linked to mental illness and personality disorders, although these links have been established for clinical populations rather than by using case control methods or general population samples. Studies of psychiatric (Stark, 1984) and women's shelter (Frieze and Browne, 1989:197) populations report that depression is quite common among women who are repeat victims of domestic violence. Battered women are also reported to require significantly higher levels of psychiatric care than nonbattered women (Stark, 1984).

It is difficult to determine what role depression has in abusive behavior since there are reported biological correlates of affective disorders such as depression. Because there appear to be generational links in depression, the question of social versus genetic transmission of depression and concomitant violence is also at issue.

Some evidence suggests that depressed persons may be more prone to violence, especially toward family members. A number of studies report that abusive mothers often suffer from depression (Zuravin, 1989). Studies report that males who physically abuse their partners show signs of depression. Yet the causal direction is not clear. While some sources of depression (e.g., repressed anger toward others) may cause the abuse, the depression may result from becoming labeled as abusive, or other consequences of the violent act.

In a study of 50 mothers and fathers who had abused and neglected their children and lost custody of them by court order, 30 percent of the mothers and 25 percent of the fathers were diagnosed as suffering from major depression. An additional 17 percent of the mothers and 15 percent of the fathers showed clinical signs of a minor depression. Despite many social service contacts with almost all of the abusing families, only one parent had received any pharmacological treatment and most of the parents had no previous diagnosis of a specific affective disorder. By contrast, the comparison group appeared to have no signs of depression.

Depression may affect the severity of maltreatment of children as well as lead to their neglect. If a significant subgroup of abusing parents or partners suffers from affective disorders, especially major depression, then chemical and other forms of treating depression may be a means of controlling some family violence. This assumes that reasonably effective means are available for controlling affective disorders, particularly any volatile mood swings associated with them.

A significant consequence of family violence is its transmission from one generation to the next. A substantial body of studies concludes that the experience of violence passes from generation to generation. For example, one study concludes that, among adults who were abused as children, more than one-fifth later abuse their own children (Straus et al., 1980). Unfortunately, methodological limitations in these studies, especially their retrospective designs, restrict the validity of conclusions about the long-term consequences of abuse in childhood (Widom, 1989:161).

Widom concluded from a prospective longitudinal design controlling for age, sex, and race, that people who were physically abused or neglected as children had a significantly greater likelihood of arrest for a violent offense than did persons in a control group: 15.8 percent for the physically abused compared with 7.9 percent for the controls (Widom, 1989:163). She also found that the rate was significantly higher for neglected children at 12.5 percent, raising questions about whether the correlation reflected intergenerational transmission of violence or some more complex causal chain that involves both abuse and neglect.

EXPLANATIONS OF FAMILY VIOLENCE

No explanation, to our knowledge, attempts to explain all the forms of violence within families that we have discussed. Most explanations are partial in one of two senses: either they attempt to explain a single type or a few types of family violence, such as partner assault, or they seek to identify a particular factor or set of variables that account for some of the observed variation in behavior between violent and nonviolent persons or acts. Gelles (1983) is one of the few to have attempted an integrated theory of violence. We review below some of the explanations that might lead to the development of a more integrated theory or explanation or that seem especially useful in considering forms of intervention to prevent or control family violence.

Cultural and Structural Determinants and Social Learning

A major assumption of feminist theory is the unequal distribution of power between men and women in most societies. In this view, women are subject to male dominance, which keeps them in subordinate positions in all spheres of family, work, and community life. The many ways in which coercion is exercised in relationships between men and women depend primarily on men's use of both their physical power and their social power to maintain a dominant position (Finkelhor, 1983). Power extends to the sexual relationship between men and women as well as to their ordinary work and social relationships. Feminists argue that marital rape occurs when male coercion rather than consent is the basis of the sexual union (Russell, 1982).

The unequal distribution of power is also the basis for explaining parental physical and sexual maltreatment of children. The exercise of parental power over the child victim leads to disempowerment of the child, rendering the child helpless (Finkelhor and Browne, 1986:183). Children as dependents are particularly vulnerable to the exercise of power by women as well as men. Similarly, violence toward the elderly family members is seen as an exercise of youthful power over the weak. The theory does not explain why some men exercise this power and others do not, or why some women do so toward children and the incapacitated.

In this framework, growing up in a patriarchal society that emphasizes male dominance and aggression and female victimization, children are socialized into their respective sex roles (Dobash and Dobash, 1979). Moreover, they are said to learn through the intimate experiences of the family. These are reinforced in the larger community when male and female roles similarly rest on elements of macho culture. In this sense, male dominance and aggression and female acquiescence are said to be learned most critically in family and peer relationships.

Major recent changes in family organization and structure may account for some family violence as well. Among those believed to be of significance are changes that affect the social and moral bonding among family members. One such change is deinstitutionalization, in the past 15 to 20 years, of children in foster care, the mentally ill, and the disabled. Distinct subpopulations of the deinstitutionalized are at risk of violent victimization—the homeless and those cared for in homes. The temporary placement of children in foster homes, adoption, and the informal placement of children with relatives exposes some of them to the risk of violence from caretakers for whom the constraints on parenting are less controlling. Social service agencies responsible for such placement attempt to screen out potentially abusive and neglectful surrogate parents, but the means for doing so are quite crude and unreliable.

A second major change is the increase in the number of children who are not living with their natural parents. Their numbers are substantial owing to serial cohabitation, divorce, and desertion. Lacking the bonds of natural parenthood increases the risk of violence to minors in the family, especially of female adolescents to sexual violence. There is some conjecture also that younger children in these households are more often left without adult supervision and hence subject to more physical violence from older siblings.

Social Isolation

Although there is some evidence that social isolation is an indicator of family violence, it is unclear whether it is largely an antecedent of family violence or a consequence of it. There are no models of how social isolation develops prior to family violence or of how it contributes to particular violent incidents. Moreover, there are no empirical studies of the extent to which social isolation is generally present for all forms of family violence.

Social isolation is a characteristic of some families that are at high risk of physical and sexual abuse of a spouse or children (Garbarino and Crouter, 1978; Pike, 1990). Some batterers enforce social isolation on their partners, and shame may lead the visibly battered spouse to further withdrawal and further social isolation. Members of such families lack the basic social support systems for family life, integration or embeddedness in a network of support systems. They are isolated from friends, acquaintances, or anyone acquainted with what goes on within the family. Such families isolate themselves from others in many different and often subtle ways. They have an unlisted telephone number or no phone, they lack any means of transportation, and their homes or apartments may be physically shuttered from the gaze of outsiders. They are socially isolated from normal social interactions in their neighborhood and lack organizational ties of any kind (Garbarino and Sherman, 1980). Resick and Reese (1986) suggest that violent families rarely invite others to their home, do not engage in social and recreational activities of any kind, and place less emphasis on personal growth and development.

INTERVENTIONS

In recent years, a large number of interventions has been developed to prevent intrafamily violence, to reduce the likelihood of its recurrence, and to repair its consequences. We discuss the prospects for detecting and preventing child abuse. We then discuss two responses to spouse assault and conclude with a proposed comprehensive strategy to reduce it.

Child Abuse

For the same reasons that accurate measurement is so difficult, the problem of detection for intervention purposes is especially acute for physical and sexual violence toward children. The NIS, for example, limited its inquiry into child abuse and neglect to three major sources: (1) cases reported to state and/or local child protective service agencies; (2) cases known to other investigatory agencies such as police, courts, and public health departments; and (3) cases known to professionals in other major community agencies such as schools, hospitals, day care centers, and social services and mental health agencies (Sedlak, 1991a,b). The NIS survey developers recognized that it would be possible to develop a fourth source of cases: survey interviews of the general population to secure reports from persons who know others who are abusing their children, from other family members, or from self-reports of the abusers and the abused. However, acknowledging the difficulties in securing reliable information on uniquely identified persons who are abusing and being abused, the NIS opted not to attempt such surveys (Sedlak, 1991a,b).

How to identify the victims of intrafamily violence and their assailants remains an important issue for the design, implementation, and testing of programs to prevent the occurrence or recurrence of intrafamily violence. Attention should be given to ways to detect victims of intrafamily violence and their assailants.

Foster Care Placement

A major intervention in child abuse cases is to remove the child from the home and arrange for foster placement. An estimated 15 percent of victims of child maltreatment are placed in an unrelated foster home (American Humane Association, 1979; Runyan et al., 1981). One of the recurring findings is that the more changes in placement a child experiences, the greater the likelihood of adult criminality and violent criminal behavior (Hensey et al., 1983; Lynch and Roberts, 1982; Widom, 1990). Large numbers of placement changes, however, may be both an effect and a cause of children's emotional and behavioral problems that precede adult violent crime. Long-term longitudinal studies are necessary to determine how placement experiences mediate the consequences of early childhood victimization, how other behavior problems affect the frequency of changes in foster placement, and how these distinct processes affect the probability of violent adult criminality.

Home Nurse Visitation

A home visiting program for infants and preschoolers is one proactive means of detection that also provides a basis for intervention. National programs of this kind exist in the United Kingdom and some European countries, although most are unevaluated. Only one randomized experiment involving a visiting nurse program has been reported in the United States. Olds (1988) and his collaborators randomly assigned 400 first-time mothers at high risk for child maltreatment to one of four treatment groups that offered different services. Among the highest-risk group—poor, unmarried, teenage mothers having their first child—the most comprehensive treatment was found to decrease the incidence of child abuse in comparison with the groups that did not receive nurse home visits. There were other positive effects as well. At 12 and 24 months, infants of poor, unmarried teenagers assigned to the nurse-visited treatment showed improved intellectual functioning on development tests and there was some evidence of improved family function with less evidence of conflict and scolding and less punishment of infants.

Olds and Henderson (1989) suggest caution in generalizing from these findings. Although the home nurse condition resulted in a lower rate of child abuse than did comparison treatment groups, the rate of child abuse or neglect was nonetheless around 5 percent, suggesting the necessity for additional preventive or ameliorative interventions. They also concluded that although the nurses can link families to community and social services—to meliorate the effects of poverty, violence, and drug use—the lack of employment opportunities in the neighborhoods where these families live poses severe constraints on their improvement efforts.

Spouse Assaults

Common responses to spouse assaults include arrest by police, individual or joint counseling of the perpetrator and the victim, education and training programs for batterers, and relocating the victim to a shelter in a concealed location. Except for police arrests in misdemeanor cases, these interventions have not been systematically evaluated. We review available findings about two of the strategies—police interventions and services in battered women's shelters. We then explain some of the difficulties in evaluating and comparing the effects of interventions and conclude by recommending a comprehensive initiative for improving the understanding and control of spouse assault.

Police Responses

Most research has focused on police interventions in misdemeanor spouse assault, particularly on the effectiveness of arrest in preventing recurrence. The National Institute of Justice (NIJ) sponsored a program of randomized field experiments and replications to test the relative effectiveness of different forms of police intervention in preventing recurrences of spouse assault—the Minneapolis Domestic Violence Experiment. The randomized treatments included arrest of the offending spouse, police counseling of both parties, and temporary separation of the assailant. Sherman and Berk (1984) concluded that arrest was the most effective of these three methods. To further test the validity of that finding, replications were carried out in six areas: Atlanta, Ga.; Charlotte, N.C.; Colorado Springs, Colo.; Metro Dade County, Fla.; Omaha, Neb.; and Milwaukee, Wis. The experiments replicated the arrest treatment but tested other police interventions in each jurisdiction.

On the basis of results available to the panel at this writing, it appears that, as with violence outside the family, arrest is not usually a deterrent to repeat domestic violence. Indeed, it may well increase the incidence of domestic violence of unemployed males with low socioeconomic status (Sherman, 1992). There is some evidence that a particular treatment may be effective for some subgroup of the population. For example, in Omaha, Nebraska, the issuance of a prosecutorial warrant for the appearance of an assailant who left the household before the police arrived appears to have had a modest deterrent effect (Dunford et al., 1989). Yet overall no treatment had a major impact on reducing domestic violence.

The panel was impressed by the relatively small impact that these police responses have on repeat domestic violence. Moreover, it is clear that most other interventions to reduce domestic violence have not been effectively evaluated. Given the substantial amount of violence inflicted in domestic situations, it seems imperative to the panel that agencies allocate resources to comparative tests of existing and new interventions that show promise of reducing domestic violence. Because police are in a strategic position to detect some domestic violence situations, the search for and testing of police-administered treatments should continue. But incidents detected by other authorities should also be studied, and interventions that involve police referrals to social service and substance abuse treatment agencies and to battered women's shelters should also be tested.

Shelters and Other Services

In recent decades, programmatic efforts have focused primarily on providing shelters for battered women, residences where abused women and their children can reside safely and receive emotional support. Starting in the early 1970s, shelters were established in the United States, following a model developed in England. There are now approximately 1,200 shelters offering temporary, emergency housing (typically families stay from two days to three months) to more than 300,000 women and their children each year. And, in response to housing shortages and the desire of many women to establish independent households, transitional housing (where families can stay for up to 18 months) has been developed. The New York City Victim Services Agency opened the first permanent housing for battered women in 1990.

A safe harbor is the first goal of shelters. Other services, provided to help women become self-sufficient, include relocation assistance, day care for children, and welfare advocacy. Services directed at increasing self-esteem include support groups and courses in parenting, job readiness, and budgeting. Increasingly, therapeutic services for children who have witnessed violence are incorporated into shelter programs.

Many battered women have reported that the most effective

strategy preparing them for self-sufficiency and counteracting the isolation and powerlessness that resulted from being abused was the support they got from other women. Formal and informal groups reinforce for an abused woman that she is not to blame, that she can be a nurturing mother, and that she can develop healthy relationships. Although services for battered women are not limited to shelter, nonresidential programs offering counseling and practical help have been slower to develop and have had even more difficulty than shelters in securing stable funding.

Law enforcement offers one possibility for early intervention; health institutions offer another. Studies have shown that abused women are routinely underidentified in hospital emergency departments (Stark and Flitcraft, 1991). Whether early more complete detection would be effective in reducing the risk of further violence or in encouraging women to seek services is unknown.

A Comprehensive Initiative to Reduce Partner Assault

A wide array of interventions is available to prevent family violence or reduce its escalation. Strategies include public education and awareness campaigns and programs for batterers. Education targets youngsters to develop nonviolent ways of coping with anger and frustration; public awareness speaks to men and women with the message that family violence is a crime and that help is available. Programs for abusive men seek to teach batterers, often coerced to attend by a court mandate, alternative ways to behave. Psychotherapy may have preventive value. Alcohol or drug abuse treatment may reduce violent attacks by some batterers. Where other interventions fail, isolation—by arresting and incarcerating the perpetrator or by relocating the victim to a shelter—at least reduces the opportunity for recurrences.

With the exceptions of arrest in misdemeanor cases and programs for batterers (both of which have generated mixed favorable effects), few of these interventions have been systematically evaluated. Perhaps more important, there has been no systematic investigation of their comparative effectiveness or of how they might be used together—in part because these interventions are offered by different public authorities and/or community-based organizations. This leads us to recommend a comprehensive initiative against spouse assault, with the following components:

1. risk assessment: better estimates in local surveys and the NCS of the incidence and prevalence of all types of family violence, including attention to cohabiting families; special atten-

tion to the incidence of spouse abuse, especially to repeat victimization; tabulations of more information on types of family violence within legal/statistical categories (e.g., disaggregating specific family relationships, capturing sexual assaults on minors);

2. case control or randomized experimental studies that follow two groups of families over several years: one group would be exposed to a public awareness and education campaign; another offered an infusion of services including shelter, parenting, vocational assistance, assertiveness training, and day care; these treatments could be provided in communities with different law enforcement policies;

3. a jurisdictional comparative analysis of shelter availability with assault and homicide rates;

4. evaluation of batterers' programs through experiments using randomized assignment; and

5. evaluation of law enforcement and criminal justice interventions including arrest as well as less expensive interventions: (a) restraining orders, (b) police warnings in cases without probable cause, (c) police training coupled with intense public education campaigns, and (d) sanctions varying from mandated courses to work programs.

Extensive collaboration will be required, involving all the agencies concerned with spouse assault. And considerable care will be needed to overcome the methodological barriers discussed below.

Barriers to Evaluation

A number of difficulties arise in evaluating strategies to prevent family violence, to deter its recurrence, or to meliorate its consequences. We illustrate these difficulties with reference to the NIJ-sponsored domestic violence experiments (Sherman and Berk, 1984).

First, local eligibility criteria for inclusion in the experiment eliminated a substantial proportion of cases and introduced selection biases. Among the exclusions from eligibility for a randomized treatment were the following:

- Arrest was mandated for all felony assaults in all experimental sites, so eligibility was limited to misdemeanor domestic assault.
- State laws vary considerably in what qualifies as misdemeanor domestic violence; some jurisdictions, for example, excluded same-sex couples and others excluded cohabiting couples.

- Some jurisdictions consider minors ineligible, even though they may be in a cohabiting or marital relationship that would otherwise qualify.
- Most jurisdictions require that an arrest be made if the victim requests it or if the officer regards it as necessary to ensure the victim's safety, thereby excluding those cases from any randomized treatment evaluation.

Second, treatments were limited for a variety of reasons, among them the fact that no treatment not provided at law can be mandatory unless it is ordered by a court of law. Consequently the police had to rely on voluntary compliance with some counseling treatments; voluntary compliance with repeat counseling sessions is generally so low as to preclude effective evaluation. Moreover, the police cannot effectively administer most treatments (other than arrest) when the subject is intoxicated with alcohol or other drugs. Some treatments are limited by the presence of children if the parent has responsibility for the care of those children. What constitutes a realistic treatment then depends very much on whether it is voluntary or mandatory and in what circumstances it can be administered.

Third, intrafamily violence cases may be detected or reported by a large number of different agencies that appear to have different case populations. There can be considerable selection bias, then, when cases are drawn for intervention from just a single source. Therefore, findings from the experiment and its replications may not apply to different populations, such as events that come to the attention of emergency departments, women's outreach groups, or other programs rather than police. Victims in new immigrant families may be especially difficult to account for.

Fourth, determining the outcome of treatment is difficult. Changes in family structure, for example when the cohabiting assailant moves out of the household, affect the extent to which one can evaluate the effect of assailant treatments. Moreover, while it is difficult enough to locate victims and secure their self-reports, it is far more difficult to do so for their assailants. We know relatively little, therefore, of the effect of the treatment on the assailant.

NOTES

1 Current procedures are based primarily on U.S. Bureau of the Census rules (1988). Its definition is "a family or household requires the

presence of at least two persons: the householder and one or more additional family members related to the householder by birth, adoption, or marriage." Any householder living alone or exclusively with persons who are not related are defined as living in a "non-family household." By this definition, all cohabiting couples are excluded from family statistics. Under these rules, to avoid a sex bias, any adult member of the household who responds may be designated as the householder.

2 The Census Bureau currently identifies families, family households, family groups, married couples, and unmarried couples, among other living arrangements (U.S. Bureau of the Census, 1991:Appendix A).

3 These characteristics are shared by a number of other continuing relationships, such as teacher and pupil; child and caretaker; custodian and inmate in institutions such as jails, prisons, and mental hospitals; and employer and employee (Finkelhor and Associates, 1986; Finkelhor et al., 1988).

4 Although most intrafamily violent incidents occur within the home, each type of intrafamily violence occurs elsewhere as well—for example, in bars and on streets, in the workplace, and in school and playground settings.

5 The panel made no effort to deal with the many measurement and consent issues that arise in self-reporting of family violence, especially for physical and sexual offenses against children. The fact that many households have a substantial turnover in membership, especially of the male members in cohabiting relationships, poses substantial sampling and response problems, in addition to the measurement problems associated with self-reporting.

6 Because the information is based on incident reports for offenses known to local police, assaults, especially misdemeanor assaults, will be substantially underreported in comparison with the assaults reported in self-reports for the NCS.

7 As of 1991, UCR provided no information on intrafamily violence for any violent crime either for offenses known to the police or for arrests. The combined arrest classification of "offenses against family and children" includes "abuse of family and children" but that category also includes nonviolent misdemeanors such as arrest for nonsupport, neglect, and desertion. (See the definition of "offenses against the family and children" in Federal Bureau of Investigation, 1991:Appendix II.) The number of these arrests grew by 18 percent between 1980 and 1990 to a rate of 29.2 arrests for every 100,000 inhabitants in 1989 (Federal Bureau of Investigation, 1991:Tables 26 & 27).

8 Parenthetically we note that countries such as the United Kingdom that provide for a health care worker to routinely make home visits to preschoolers detect considerably more physical child abuse because they regularly conduct a physical examination of the child.

9 The reporting rates of child protective services increased between 1980 and 1986. Despite the increase, the majority of children reported still are screened out of consideration. Sedlak (1991a,b) concludes that

this failure is due to the use of more stringent screening standards when accepting cases for investigation—standards that have become more restrictive in the face of an increase in cases reported and a decrease in resources to deal with them. Research is needed to determine what effects this change in eligibility for allocation resources for child protective services may have on the recent gains in the detection and reporting of physical and sexual abuse of children.

10 The sources cited by the U.S. Advisory Board on Child Abuse and Neglect include the following: Daro et al. (1990), Christoffel and Samler (1981), and U.S. Department of Health and Human Services (1988:3-11).

11 Unfortunately, cohabitants and cross-sex friendships are included in the "well-known" relationship in Table 5-1, as are persons of the same sex who are well known to one another. Consequently, we cannot determine the rate for cohabiting and former cohabiting spouses, although presumably it is also very high.

12 There is some error in attributing all of these deaths to family violence since UCR does not tabulate the relationship between victim and offender by age of victim.

13 The design of the NCS does not control for prior victimization by any type of crime, so that repeat victimization can be measured only in the context of the "first" report of a sample respondent during the period he or she is in the sample; an unknown proportion of these first reports are not an initial victimization by the offender. Moreover, because the NCS does not take the unique identity of the offender into account, it is not always possible to determine if it is the same offender for a given victim. As for all forms of violence, different offenders can victimize the same family member.

REFERENCES

American Humane Association

1979 *National Analysis of Official Neglect and Abuse Reporting.* Denver: American Humane Association.

Bolton, Frank, L. Morris, and A. MacEachron

1989 *Males at Risk: The Other Side of Child Sexual Abuse.* Newbury Park, Calif.: Sage Publications.

Bureau of Justice Statistics, U.S. Department of Justice

1990 *Criminal Victimization in the United States, 1988.* A national crime survey report, December, NCJ-122024. Washington, D.C.: U.S. Government Printing Office.

Christoffel, Liv, and Samler

1981 Epidemiology of fatal child abuse: International mortality data. *Journal of Chronic Diseases* 34:57-64.

Daro, Deborah, Kathleen Casey, and Nadine Abrahams

1990 Reducing Child Abuse 20% by 1990: Preliminary Assessment. National Center for Prevention of Child Abuse. Working Paper No. 843.

Dobash, R.E., and R.P. Dobash
1979 *Violence Against Wives: A Case Against Patriarchy.* Glencoe, Ill.: Free Press.

Dunford, F.W., D. Huizinga, and D.S. Elliot
1989 *The Omaha Domestic Violence Experiment.* Final Report to the National Institute of Justice and the City of Omaha. Institute of Behavioral Science, University of Colorado, Boulder (June).
1990 The role of arrest in domestic assault: The Omaha police experiment. *Criminology* 28:183-206.

Federal Bureau of Investigation
1991 *Uniform Crime Reports for the United States: 1990.* Washington, D.C.: U.S. Government Printing Office.

Finkelhor, David
1983 Common features of family abuse. In D. Finkelhor, ed., *The Dark Side of Families: Current Family Violence Research.* Newbury Park, Calif.: Sage Publications.
1991 Child sexual abuse. Pp. 79-94 in Mark L. Rosenberg and Mary Ann Fenley, eds., *Violence in America: A Public Health Approach.* Oxford University Press.

Finkelhor, David, and Angela Browne
1986 Initial and long-term effects: A conceptual framework. Pp. 180-198 in David Finkelhor et al., eds., *A Sourcebook on Child Sexual Abuse.* Newbury Park, Calif.: Sage Publications.

Finkelhor, D., and Associates
1986 *A Sourcebook on Child Sexual Abuse.* Newbury Park, Calif.: Sage Publications.

Finkelhor, D., L.M. Williams, and N. Burns
1988 *Nursery Crimes: Sexual Abuse in Day Care.* Newbury Park, Calif.: Sage Publications.

Frieze, Irene Hanson, and Angela Browne
1989 Violence in marriage. Pp. 163-218 in Lloyd Ohlin and Michael Tonry, eds., *Family Violence.* Chicago: University of Chicago Press.

Garbarino, James
1989 The incidence and prevalence of child maltreatment. Pp. 219-261 in Lloyd Ohlin and Michael Tonry, eds., *Family Violence.* Chicago: University of Chicago Press.

Garbarino, J., and Crouter, K.
1978 Defining the community context of parent-child relations: The correlates of child maltreatment. *Child Development* 43:604-616.

Garbarino, J., and D. Sherman
1980 High-risk families and high-risk neighborhoods. *Child Development* 51:188-198.

Gelles, Richard J.
1983 An exchange social control theory. In David Finkelhor, Richard

J. Gelles, Gerald T. Hotaling, and Murray A. Straus, eds., *The Dark Side of Families*. Beverly Hills, Calif.: Sage Publications.

Hensey, O.J., J.K. Williams, and L. Rosenbloom
1983 Intervention in child abuse: Experiences in Liverpool. *Developmental Medicine and Child Neurology* 25:606-611.

Hirschel, J.D., I.W. Hutchison III, C.W. Dean, J.J. Kelly, and C.E. Pesackis
1991 *Charlotte Spouse Assault Replication Project: Final Report.* University of North Carolina at Charlotte.

Langan, P.A., and C.A. Innes
1986 *Preventing Domestic Violence Against Women.* Bureau of Justice Statistics Special Report NCJ-102937. Washington, D.C.: U.S. Department of Justice.

Lynch, M.A., and J. Roberts
1982 *Consequences of Child Abuse.* London: Academic Press.

Olds, David L.
1988 The prenatal/early infancy project. Pp. 9-32 in R.H. Price, E.I. Cowen, R.P. Lorion, and Ramos-McKay, eds., *Fourteen Ounces of Prevention: A Casebook for Practitioners.* Washington, D.C.: American Psychological Association.

Olds, David L., and C.R. Henderson
1989 The prevention of maltreatment. Pp. 722-763 in D. Cicchetti and V. Carlson, eds., *Child Maltreatment: Theory and Research on the Causes and Consequences of Child Abuse and Neglect.* New York: Cambridge University Press.

Pagelow, Mildred Daley
1989 The incidence and prevalence of criminal abuse of other family members. Pp. 263-313 in Lloyd Ohlin and Michael Tonry, eds., *Family Violence.* Chicago: University of Chicago Press.

Pedrick-Cornell, C., and R.J. Gelles
1982 Elder abuse: The status of current knowledge. *Family Relations* 31:457-465.

Pike, K.M.
1990 Intrafamilial sexual abuse of children. Paper prepared for the National Research Council Panel on the Understanding and Control of Violent Behavior.

Pillemer, Karl, and David Finkelhor
1988 Prevalence of elder abuse: A random sample survey. *Gerontologist* 28:51-57.

Pillemer, Karl, and Susan Frankel
1988 Domestic violence against the elderly. Pp. 158-183 in Mark L. Rosenberg and James A. Mercy, eds., *Violence in America: A Public Health Approach.* New York: Oxford University Press.

Podnieks, E., and K. Pillemer
1989 *Final Report on Survey of Elder Abuse in Canada.* Ottawa: Health and Welfare.

Resick, P.A., and D. Reese
1986 Perception of family social climate and physical aggression in the home. *Journal of Family Violence* 1:71-83.

Runyan, D.K., C.L. Gould, D.C. Trost, and F.A. Loda
1981 Determinants of foster care placement for the maltreated child. *Child Abuse and Neglect* 6:343-350.

Russell, D.H.
1982 *Rape in Marriage.* London and New York: MacMillan.

Sedlak, Andrea J.
1991a *National Incidence and Prevalence of Child Abuse and Neglect: 1988.* Washington, D.C.: Westat, Inc. (Revised September 5, 1991).
1991b *Supplementary Analyses of Data on the National Incidence of Child Abuse and Neglect.* Washington, D.C.: Westat, Inc. (Revised August 30).

Sherman, Lawrence W.
1992 *Policing Domestic Violence: Experiments and Dilemmas.* New York: Free Press.

Sherman, Lawrence W., and Richard A. Berk
1984 The specific deterrent effects of arrest for domestic assault. *American Sociological Review* 49:261-272.

Stark, Evan
1984 The battering syndrome: Social knowledge, social therapy, and the abuse of women. Ph.D. dissertation, State University of New York-Binghamton.

Stark, E., and A. Flitcraft
1982 Medical therapy as repression: The case of the battered woman. *Health and Medicine* 1:29-32.
1991 Spouse abuse. Pp. 123-154 in Mark Rosenberg and Mary Ann Fenley, eds., *Violence in America: A Public Health Approach.* New York: Oxford University Press.

Straus, M.A.
1979 Measuring family conflict and violence: The conflict tactics scale. *Journal of Marriage and Family Living* 36:13-19.

Straus, M.A., and R.J. Gelles
1986 Societal change and change in family violence from 1975 to 1985 as revealed by two national surveys. *Journal of Marriage and the Family* 48:465-479.

Straus, M.A., R.J. Gelles, and S.K. Steinmetz
1980 *Behind Closed Doors: Violence in the American Family.* Garden City, N.Y.: Doubleday.

U.S. Bureau of the Census
1988 *Households, Marital Status, and Living: March, 1988.* Advance Report. Washington, D.C.: U.S. Department of Commerce.
1990 Household and family characteristics: March 1990 and 1989. *Current Population Reports, Population Characteristics.* Series P-20, No. 447. Washington, D.C.: U.S. Government Printing Office.

1991 Marital status and living arrangements: March 1990. *Current Population Reports.* Series P-20, No., 450. Washington, D.C.: U.S. Government Printing Office.

U.S. Department of Health and Human Services

1988 Study Findings: Study of National Incidence and Prevalence of Child Abuse and Neglect. National Center on Child Abuse and Neglect, Washington, D.C.

1990 Child Abuse and Neglect: Critical First Steps in Response to a National Emergency. Washington, D.C.: U.S. Government Printing Office.

Widom, Cathy Spatz

1989 The cycle of violence. *Science* 244:160-166.

1990 Research, clinical, and policy issues: Childhood victimization, parent alcohol problems, and long term consequences. National Forum on the Future of Children, Workshop on Children and Parental Illegal Drug Abuse, National Research Council: Institute of Medicine, March 8.

Winpisinger, Kim A., Richard S. Hopkins, Robert W. Indian, and Jeptha R. Hostetler

1991 Risk factors for childhood homicides in Ohio: A birth certificate-based case-control study. *American Journal of Public Health* 81 (August):1052-1054.

Winslow, Robert W.

1972 *Crime in a Free Society. Selections From the President's Commission on Law Enforcement and Administration of Justice, the National Advisory Commission on Civil Disorder, the National Commission on the Causes and Prevention of Violence, and the Commission on Obscenity and Pornography.* Encino, Calif.: Dickenson Publishing Company.

Wolfe, David A., Vicky V. Wolfe, and Connie L. Best

1988 Child victims of sexual abuse. Pp. 157-185 in Vincent B. Van Hesselt et al., eds., *Handbook of Family Violence.* New York: Plenum Press.

Zuravin, S.J.

1989 The ecology of child abuse and neglect: Review of the literature and presentation of data. *Violence and Victims* 4(2):101-120.

6

Firearms and Violence

An analysis of violence in the United States would be incomplete without a discussion of firearms, which are involved in about 60 percent of all homicides. The most widely debated methods of preventing gun violence involve legal restrictions on firearm owners or licensed dealers. While evaluations have found several regulations that have reduced gun homicides when they are enforced, regulations arouse controversy among law-abiding dealers and owners—some of whom acquired guns precisely because they feared gun violence. Our review of available evidence revealed several promising preventive strategies, none requiring new laws, which are ripe for rigorous evaluation. We also concluded that like "drug-related violence," "gun violence" may be best understood in terms of illegal markets and reduced through tactics that police already apply in illegal drug markets.

We begin by discussing overall patterns and trends in firearms ownership and use in violent crimes. Then, proceeding from best understood to least understood, we examine how firearms alter a series of conditional probabilities in violent events: the chance that an injury causes death, the chance that an encounter (e.g., robbery, assault) produces an injury, and the relationship of firearms availability to the frequencies of such encounters. We then discuss what little is known about the channels through which firearms reach violent crime scenes and conclude by examining the empirical basis for alternative strategies for reducing the incidence and consequences of violent firearm use.

PATTERNS AND TRENDS IN FIREARM OWNERSHIP AND VIOLENT USE

Firearms are widely owned and widely available in the United States. No precise count is available since no enumeration system exists, but the best estimates are that the national gun population was in the range of 60-100 million in 1968 (Newton and Zimring, 1969), 100-140 million in 1978 (Wright et al., 1983), 130-170 million in 1988 (Cook, 1991), and 200 million in 1990 (Bureau of Alcohol, Tobacco, and Firearms, 1991). For at least three decades, the fraction of all households owning any type of gun has remained stable at about 50 percent; however, the fraction owning a handgun rose from 13 percent in 1959 to 24 percent in 1978, where it has remained, more or less, since then (Bureau of Justice Statistics, 1989, cited in Cook, 1991). Surveys generally conclude that the fraction of households owning firearms is greatest in rural areas and small towns, higher for whites than for blacks, highest in the South, lowest in the Northeast, and higher for high-income households than for low-income households (Cook, 1991; Wright et al., 1983).

Violent uses of guns impose both human and monetary costs. In 1989 gun attacks resulted in about 12,000 homicides—about 60 percent of all homicides (Federal Bureau of Investigation, 1989). In addition, Cook (1991) estimates that 5.7 nonfatal gunshot injuries occur for every homicide—a projection on the order of 70,000 for 1989. For 1985, Rice and associates (1989) estimate the total cost of intentional and unintentional gun injuries at over $14 billion, including both the direct costs of hospital and other medical care and the indirect costs of long-term disability and premature death.

The risk of death from homicide by a gun is not uniformly distributed throughout the population; rather, it is highly elevated for adolescents, particularly black males. In 1988 the gun homicide rate per 100,000 people was 8 for teenagers ages 15-19, but less than 6 for the population as a whole. Among teenagers ages 15-19, the 1989 rate was 83.4 for black males compared with 7.5 for white males (unpublished data from the National Vital Statistics system, 1992)—a ratio of more than 11:1.

The elevated risk for teenagers reflects both a concentration of homicides in ages 15-34 and a peak in gun use by killers of young

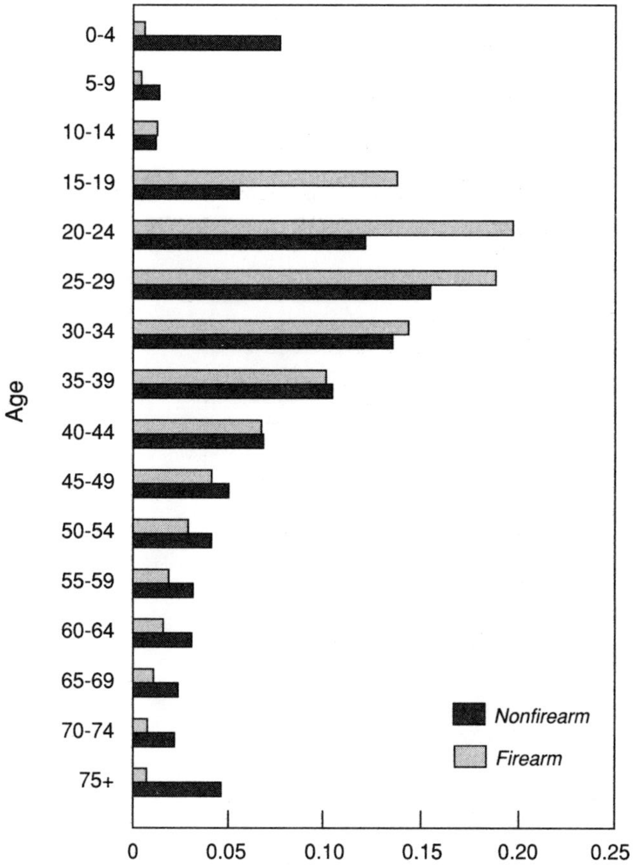

FIGURE 6-1 Age distribution for homicide victims at five-year intervals. SOURCE: Adapted from Federal Bureau of Investigation (1989:11).

people. Figure 6-1, which displays 1989 age distributions for homicide victims in five-year intervals, shows that the largest fraction of nonfirearm homicide victims was in the 25-29 age range; the largest fraction of firearm homicide victims was slightly younger, in the 20-24 age range. The fraction of homicides committed with guns peaks even earlier, at 81 percent for victims ages 15 to 19, then declines gradually but monotonically for victims age 20 and older (Figure 6-2).

Although the 1989 risk of gun homicide for black teenage males ages 15-19 was 11 times the risk for their white counterparts, black victims outnumbered white victims in that age range by

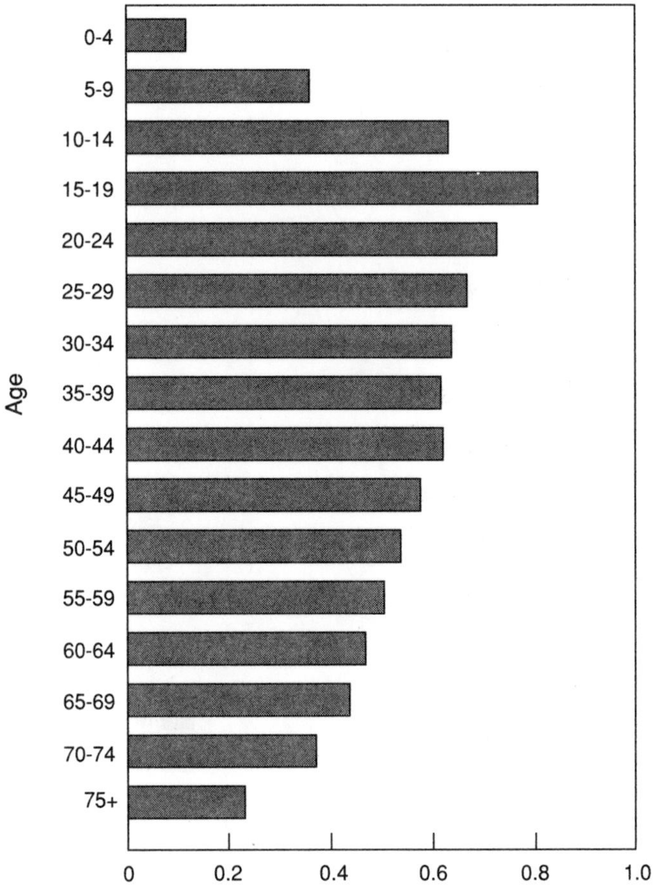

FIGURE 6-2 Fraction of homicides committed with firearm by age of victim. SOURCE: Adapted from Federal Bureau of Investigation (1989:11).

only 1,163 to 547, because whites are so much more numerous in the population (unpublished data from the National Vital Statistics system, 1992). Despite the small numbers involved, the firearm homicide risk for young black males warrants special attention. Not only is the recent increase in this risk a significant social inequity, but also such a huge increase is unique to this particular intersection of sex, race, age, weapon type, intent, and time period.

Trends between 1979 and 1988 in teenage deaths were reported by Fingerhut et al. (1991). During that period, no increases of similar proportions occurred in firearm homicides of black fe-

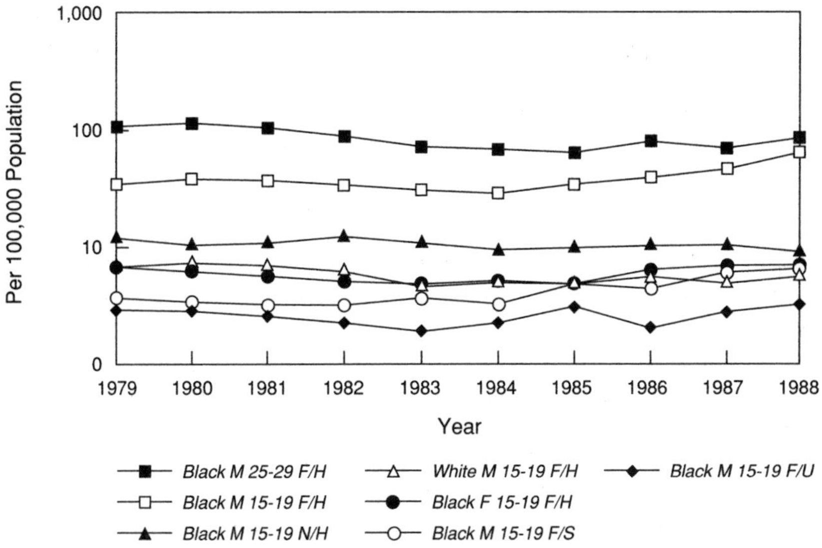

FIGURE 6-3 Death rates for selected demographic groups and manners of death: United States, 1979-1988. F/H = firearm homicide; N/H = nonfirearm homicide; F/S = firearm suicide; F/U = unintentional firearm death. SOURCE: Fingerhut et al. (1991:Table 1).

males or white males of the same age, or among older black males ages 25-29 (Figure 6-3).[1] And between 1987 and 1988 nonfirearm homicides actually declined for black male teenagers, from 10.8 per 100,000 to 9.5, essentially the 1984 level. The rate for unintentional firearm death, a measure more closely related to firearm availability, rose only about 50 percent (from 2.3 to 3.4 per 100,000) among black male teenagers between 1984 and 1988. And every rate displayed in the figure declined during the immediately preceding period, 1979-1984. The most comparable trend during the period 1984-1988 is in the other form of intentional injury: a 100 percent increase (from 3.4 to 6.8 per 100,000) in the firearm suicide rate for black male teenagers—a higher relative increase than for other race and sex categories in this age group or for older black males.

In short, the increase during the period 1984-1988 in firearm homicides cannot be explained solely in terms of either demographics or firearm availability; rather, one must look at these factors in conjunction with other events that affected young black males during those specific years.

The risks of violent gun use are not evenly distributed across type of gun. Of all guns in the United States, approximately one-third are handguns and two-thirds are long guns—a heterogeneous category that includes, for example, both small-caliber and large-caliber rifles, shotguns, and semiautomatic and automatic rifles. Handguns are disproportionately likely to be used in homicides, by a factor of more than 3 to 1. In gun homicides for which the type of weapon was known, handguns accounted for nearly 80 percent in 1989, compared with 8 percent for rifles and 12 percent for shotguns (Federal Bureau of Investigation, 1989). Despite substantial recent public attention to what are called assault weapons, we were unable to find national statistics on the availability, use, or lethality of this rather ill-defined category of firearm (Zimring, 1989; Kleck, 1991).

Even for handguns, the weapon of choice in violent crimes in the United States, the risk of violent use is not evenly distributed. Based on estimates by Cook (1981), it appears that, of each cohort of new handguns sold, about one-third are involved in crime (i.e., displayed or fired) at least once during their usable lifetimes.[2] New handguns, those acquired most recently, are especially likely to be involved in violent crimes (Zimring and Hawkins, 1987). But there is little information available about the kinds of places, encounters, handgun attributes, ownership patterns, and distribution channels that heighten the risk that a given handgun will be used in a violent manner. Research on this question is complicated by the lack of data systems to track unique identifiers of firearms and by their frequent movement, through burglary, unregulated sales, and simple carrying, from one situation to another. (On request from a law enforcement agency, the Bureau of Alcohol, Tobacco, and Firearms attempts to trace the ownership paths of guns used in crime, but these do not provide a basis for comparing their ownership histories to those of other guns.) There are no accurate profiles for distinguishing "dangerous" handguns or locations from "safe" ones.

THE LETHALITY OF FIREARM INJURIES

A focus on violent injuries produces one clear correlation. The case fatality rate—the fraction of injuries that lead to death—is much greater for guns than for knives, the next most lethal weapon. Zimring (1968) reports fatality rates of 12.2 percent for gun attacks and 2.4 percent for knife attacks, a lethality ratio of about 5 to 1. Others report somewhat smaller lethality ratios, but no estimate is less than 2 to 1 (Curtis, 1974, reported in Wright et al., 1983; Vinson, 1974).

From scientific and policy perspectives, the difficulty lies in determining how much of the difference in lethality among weapons is due to instrumental effects (i.e., properties of the weapon or ammunition) and how much to the perpetrator's intent. For more than 30 years, people have argued that the perpetrators most intent on killing not only select firearms more frequently but also aim more carefully, fire more bullets, and take other steps that further increase the lethal effects (Wolfgang, 1958). In this view, intent contributes most of the lethality and, if guns became unavailable, such intent killers would succeed in killing with knives, blunt instruments, fists, or feet.

This argument is plausible for some shootings, but there is no basis for estimating how often it applies. Firearms are rarely used by serial killers, for example, who are considered among the most intent of all killers. Often guns are used to achieve some objective other than killing, such as to threaten. The use of guns to threaten that has been the best measured is robbery, in which the purpose is to get persons, usually strangers, to hand over property. Guns are also used to threaten or to inflict harm against family members or casual acquaintances in many different situations—disputes, revenge for some perceived slight or chronic harassment, and the like. Another use of threat is self-defense, in which, for example, a surprised homeowner may brandish or fire a gun primarily to frighten a burglar away.

The choice of a firearm to communicate threats has two potentially offsetting effects on lethality. If use of a gun instead enables the initiator to achieve his or her goals without firing, physical harm is prevented (Kleck, 1991). But having a gun may encourage some people to initiate robberies or altercations against others who would otherwise appear too invulnerable to challenge; occasionally the gun will be discharged in those encounters, causing physical harm.

Guns may also be fired in circumstances that involve no strategy. Such incidents include gratuitous murders at the successful conclusion of a robbery—perhaps as a manifestation of hate or of what has been termed recreational violence. Also, guns may be fired in conflicts between intimates or more casual acquaintances involving intense anger, fear, or both. Between 1976 and 1987, more than twice as many women were shot and killed by their husband or intimate partner as were killed by strangers using any means. In violent domestic disputes, the choice of a weapon may well be the nearest available object that can project force, and it seems likely that instrumentality rather than intent contributes most of the firearm's lethal effect.

Police and court records make clear that neither these scenarios nor countless others should be ignored in debates over firearms policy. The difficulty, as any trial judge knows, is that establishing the motive for an instance of gun use is a formidable, time-consuming, judgmental task, often with an uncertain outcome.

Available information is therefore indirect and imprecise. In an analysis of gun assaults in Chicago (Zimring, 1968), the victim received a single wound in over 80 percent of both fatal and nonfatal gun assaults. Since most guns have the capability to inflict multiple wounds, this suggests that at least some assaulters with guns lacked sufficient intent to exhaust all options for killing the persons they attacked.[3] An analysis of survey data for victims of 12,000 robberies (Cook, 1980) is consistent with Kleck's conclusion that guns are sometimes used to threaten victims who would otherwise be relatively invulnerable: 55 percent of commercial robberies but only 13 percent of other robberies involve guns; the few gun robberies of persons tend to target relatively invulnerable groups and young adult males; and nongun street robberies are most likely to target women, children, and elderly victims. Similarly, Sampson and Lauritsen (Volume 3) report that, between 1973 and 1982, approximately 41 percent of male victims of violent crimes other than homicide, but only 29 percent of female victims, were attacked by persons with weapons—a pattern consistent with the use of weapons to overcome victim invulnerability rather than necessarily to kill.

A survey of 1,874 incarcerated convicted felons interviewed during 1982 provides a more precise but perhaps unrepresentative distribution of the motivations of criminal gun users (Wright and Rossi, 1985). Of the 184 who fired a gun while committing the offense for which they were incarcerated, only 36 percent reported doing so "to kill the victim." More commonly reported motivations were "to protect myself" (48%) and "to scare the victim" (45%). Incarcerated offenders are not representative of all offenders and may be reluctant to report an intent to kill. Nevertheless, the data suggest strongly that many criminals who fire guns do so for reasons other than a single-minded attempt to kill. In fact, as the authors conclude, "*most of the men [76%] who actually fired guns in criminal situations claimed to have had no prior intention of so doing*" (Wright and Rossi, 1985:15; emphasis in original).

These findings indicate that, even in violent felonies, firearms are sometimes fired without a premeditated intent to kill. Consequently, a problem for future research is to measure what fraction of the difference in lethality between firearms and other weapons is due to instrumentality rather than intent. Since this fraction of lethality would be reduced if guns became less available, the research findings should be integral to debates over firearms policy.

FIREARMS, ENCOUNTERS, AND INJURY RATES

To this point, our discussion has treated the gun victim as a passive target. Usually, of course, violent gun use occurs during an encounter between two or more people and depends on the nature of their interaction. As we indicate in Chapter 3, far too little is known about these interactions generally, in part because records of representative samples of assaults are difficult to construct, compile, and analyze. However, the choice of weapon for attacks and for self-defense is important in determining the probability and severity of injury when a gun is involved.

Weapon Choice by Perpetrators

Most of the evidence about perpetrators' weapon choice and lethality comes from studies of robberies and assaults. Studies of robbery reviewed by Cook (1991) indicate that, compared with other robbers, those who carry a gun are more likely to complete their robberies without experiencing victim resistance and without injuring the victims. However, because gun injuries are so much more likely to be lethal, the fatality rate for gun robberies, 4 per 1,000, is about triple the rate in knife robberies and 10 times the rate in robberies with other weapons (Cook, 1980). Zimring and Zuehl (1986) report a similar differential for nonresidential robberies known to the police. But because nonlethal residential robberies are more likely to be reported if a gun was used, including residential robberies in the analysis attenuates the lethality differential.

Kleck and McElrath (1989) report a somewhat different pattern for assaults. The presence of a lethal weapon decreases the chance of actual physical attack. If an attack occurs, injury is less likely with a gun than with a knife. When an injury occurs, the fatality rate is higher in gun incidents than in knife incidents. The latter effect approximately offsets the first two, so that fatalities are about equally likely in gun assaults and knife assaults.

The Bureau of Justice Statistics (1986:Table 12) reported, by weapon type, the distribution of injury outcomes for violent victimizations of all types, based on National Crime Survey data for the period 1973-1982. Escalation from threat to attack, and especially to an attack causing injury, was far less probable when the offender was armed with a gun (probability = .14) than when he or she was unarmed (.30), armed with a knife (.25), or armed with any other weapon (.45). Given that they were injured, just over half of both gun victims and knife victims required medical attention, but gun victims were somewhat more likely to be hospitalized (.83) than were knife victims (.74) if they required medical help. Nevertheless, because of the low probabilities of attack and injury when the offender displayed a gun, the overall probability of being hospitalized following victimization by a gun-wielding offender was only .06—the same as when the offender was unarmed, and less than when the offender was armed with a knife (.10) or with another weapon (.16).[4]

The data do not of course explain the low probabilities of attack and injury in events in which guns are involved. The attacker's display of the gun may intimidate the victims into submission rather than resistance; the attacker may fire the gun but miss (an event that has no analog in statistics on attacks by unarmed offenders); or the intended victims of gun wielders may themselves be more likely to be carrying guns, which they display or use in self-defense.

Firearm Use in Self-Defense

The use of guns for self-defense is one of the most controversial topics in firearms policy, and it promises to become more so if residents of high-crime areas grow more skeptical that police can or will effectively protect them and their property. In a 1979 survey, 20 percent of all gun owners and 40 percent of all handgun owners cited self-defense at home as the most important reason for their gun ownership; for handgun owners, self-defense was the most commonly cited reason (Decision-Making Information, Inc., 1979, cited in Wright et al., 1983:96). But self-described "self-defense" is ambiguous; it may refer, for example, to homeowners with a generalized fear of burglary, to single women who have received specific threats of rape, to belligerent regular patrons of "fighting bars" who anticipate confrontations, to gang members preparing for neighborhood intrusions by violent rival gangs, to criminals fearing retaliation for their previous crimes, and even to criminals in the course of their crimes—recall that in Wright and Rossi's sample of incarcerated felons, 48 percent of those who fired guns cited self-defense as a motive. Police report anecdotally hearing "It was him or me" as an increasingly common excuse offered by alleged youthful killers with guns.

Counts of Gun Use for Self-Defense

Because self-defense is such an ambiguous term, it is not surprising that there is great dispute over how often firearms are actually used for self-defense. Using National Crime Survey data, Cook (1991) estimates incidents of self-defense firearm use at 78,000 per year, just below the number of people killed and wounded by firearms. Drawing on a number of surveys that ask about self-defense uses of guns without tying them to specific incidents, Kleck puts the annual number of self-defense uses about 10 times higher—between 700,000 (G. Kleck, personal communication to Jeffrey A. Roth, National Research Council, 1990; Kleck, 1991) and 1 million (Kleck, 1988) per year, about equal to the number of violent crimes involving guns.

Part of the discrepancy is no doubt accounted for by methodology. The National Crime Survey excludes commercial robberies, and it undercounts attempted and completed rapes and sexual assaults, particularly by family members; self-defense gun uses in those incidents would be missed as well. The surveys reviewed by Kleck (1988, 1991) have smaller sample sizes and longer reference periods, and they leave definitions of *self-defense* and *use* to respondents. Besides the ambiguity in defining self-defense, the counts may be inflated by respondents' inadvertent telescoping of incidents of self-defense into the reference period from previous periods. Also, some reported instances of self-protection are not comparable to specific criminal victimizations: respondents in some surveys could well have been concerned about animal rather than human attackers; others may have simply brought the gun nearby in anticipation of an encounter that never occurred.[5] To correct for these and various other methodological artifacts, Kleck uses a number of adjustment factors, some of which rely on untested assumptions. He presents no sensitivity analyses of alternative adjustment procedures, and some of them are incompletely documented. Our calculations indicate that making alternative plausible assumptions would substantially decrease Kleck's estimates of annual self-defense uses.[6]

Because of the likely undercounts in the National Crime Survey and the uncertainties surrounding Kleck's sources and adjustments, the discrepancy about how and how often guns are used for self-defense remains approximately 80,000 to 700,000. Some of it can be accounted for by Kleck's adjustment factors. But an additional cause is almost certainly that some of what respondents designate as their own self-defense would be construed as aggression by others. As recommended by Cook (1991), there is a need for estimates that are free of the threshold and reporting problems associated with the National Crime Survey and the FBI's Supplementary Homicide Reports but that differentiate among self-defense uses and that rest on surveys of sufficiently high quality to eliminate the need for dubious adjustment procedures.

The Probability of Gun Use for Self-Defense

In making the decision whether to purchase a gun for protection, it is less relevant to know how often guns are used for self-defense than to know either the probability of using the gun if victimized or the consequences of using it. According to National Crime Survey tabulations, victims rarely defend themselves with firearms—1.2 percent of robberies, 1.4 percent of assaults, 3.1 percent of all residential burglaries, and 4.6 percent of residential burglaries by strangers.[7] Self-defense gun use, however, is associated with a reduced risk of physical attack and injury. Of intended robbery victims who defended themselves with guns, only 17 percent reported being injured, compared with 33 percent overall and 25 percent of those who made no self-protection effort. For assaults, the injury rates were 12 percent for targets who used guns, compared with 30 percent overall and 27 percent who took no self-protective action (Kleck, 1988:Table 4).

Statistical associations such as these have been interpreted as demonstrations of the self-defense value of guns. However, since such self-defense uses are so rare in victimizations, they may well represent anomalies—scenarios in which, for example, the initiator failed to surprise the intended victim. In losing the advantage of surprise, the initiator may simultaneously become more vulnerable to any form of self-defense and give a gun-owning intended victim time to arm himself. Without detailed comparisons of situational dynamics in events in which gun-owning victims did and did not use their guns in self-defense, claims that average victims can successfully defend themselves with guns against robbery, burglary, and assault remain unproven.

Firearm ownership can carry substantial risks. In confrontations with assailants, even experienced owners of firearms can find their weapons turned against them. Between 1984 and 1988, 93 percent of all law enforcement officers killed in the line of duty died of gunshot wounds. Sixty-four of these officers (19%) lost their lives when their service weapons were turned against them (unpublished data, Federal Bureau of Investigation).

Guns in the home may also increase a family's risk of serious injury or death through mishandling, family violence, or suicide. Kellermann and Reay (1988) studied all gunshot deaths occurring in King County, Washington, between 1978 and 1983 and found that 52 percent occurred in the home where the firearm involved was kept. For every time a gun in the home was involved in a self-protection homicide, they noted 1.3 unintentional deaths, 4.5 criminal homicides, and 37 firearm suicides. Wintemute et al. (1987) studied 88 incidents in which young California children fatally shot a playmate or themselves and noted that 75 percent occurred while children were playing with a gun or demonstrating its use. In at least 48 percent of fatal residential shootings, children gained access to unlocked firearms that were stored loaded. Below the age of 8, few children can reliably distinguish a toy gun from a real one.

Firearm Availability and Violence

How is the availability of guns related to overall levels of violence? The discussion above has established that greater gun availability is associated with more robberies, home burglaries, assaults, and homicides using guns—but this is only one of several countervailing relationships to be considered. By reducing robbery and home burglary completion rates, self-defense gun use theoretically decreases the rewards for these crimes and increases the perceived risks to offenders. Yet guns in the homes of law-abiding citizens are themselves tempting targets for burglars. Moreover, by analogy from theoretical models of international arms races (Downs, 1991), the fear that potential victims or adversaries may be armed may simply encourage someone planning an attack to acquire superior firepower and carry out the attack regardless. Because of these conflicting potential incentives, it is not clear a priori whether greater firearms availability should be expected to increase or decrease aggregate violence levels.

Indirect empirical evidence on this question is available from four kinds of studies: multivariate statistical analyses of nonfatal violent crime levels, using the prevalence of gun use in homicides and suicides as a proxy measure for gun availability (Cook, 1979, 1985); cross-national comparisons of gun availability measures and gun crimes (van Dijk et al., 1990); time-series analyses of gun availability measures and homicide rates (Phillips et al., 1976; Kleck, 1984; McDowall, 1991); and comparisons between jurisdictions in which substantial availability differences are generally acknowledged without being precisely measured (Sloane et al., 1988).

Studies of all these types are discussed by Cook (1991). They find no relationship between gun availability and the number of nonfatal violent crimes. For crimes that end in death, they generally find that greater gun availability is associated with somewhat greater use of firearms and somewhat greater rates of felony murder, but do not account for a large fraction of the variation.[8] Cook (1979) finds no discernible effect of gun ownership prevalence on robbery rates. Comparing experience in Seattle and Vancouver, two neighboring jurisdictions that are demographically and socioeconomically similar but have different gun laws, Sloane et al. (1988) found no differences in event measures—burglary and simple and aggravated assault rates—but Seattle, which has more permissive gun laws, had an overall homicide rate more than 60 percent higher and a firearm homicide rate 400 percent higher.

Even where positive correlations are found between measures of gun availability and nonfatal violent crime, the direction of the causal chain is unclear. Some households may be arming themselves in response to increases in violent crime rates (G. Kleck, personal communication to Jeffrey A. Roth, National Research Council, 1990). Differences across nations, states, and communities may reflect separate local traditions about guns and about violence, rather than any direct connection between guns and violence (Cook, 1991). To the extent that alienation from public institutions exists in black communities (discussed in Chapter 3), it could account for higher levels of gun ownership and of violent crime; mistrust of the police and courts could trigger a "vigilante" mentality in which citizens arm themselves in order to be prepared to settle disputes without recourse to the civil or criminal justice system.

The strongest empirical evidence on how variations in firearms availability affect levels of violent crime and felony homicides can be obtained from carefully controlled evaluations of changes in laws and especially in enforcement efforts, that reduce firearms availability. As background for a such a discussion, we summarize what little is known about the sources of firearms used in violent events.

Sources of Firearms

According to recent estimates, only about one firearm of every six used in crimes was legally obtained. The high rate of handgun murders in cities such as New York and Washington, which have highly restricted legal access to handguns, is further evidence that guns are often obtained illegally, as is the recent increase in firearm homicides among black males ages 15-19, since minors are legally prohibited nearly everywhere from owning handguns.

Most published research on illegal and unregulated sources of firearms is several years old and is, as one might expect, sketchy and unrepresentative. But at least during the 1970s and early 1980s, the path from manufacturer to gun felon involved theft and unregulated private transfers far more often than licensed dealers. The small volume of illegal sales by dealers is usually a small-scale, decentralized, off-the-books activity involving used guns rather than a trade in new guns dominated by large organizations.

Theft—from licensed dealers, from residences, and from other criminals—is an important source of firearms used in felonies. Moore (1981) reports the results of manufacturer-to-user traces by the Bureau of Alcohol, Tobacco and Firearms of 113 handguns used in Boston felonies during 1975-1976. Of the guns whose histories could be traced, 40 percent were stolen at some point: 12 percent of those used in assaults, and 56 percent of those used in other crimes, which presumably were more likely to involve advance planning. Another 29 percent were purchased directly from licensed retailers (27% by legally eligible purchasers, and 2% by proscribed persons), and 20 percent involved a chain of private transfers, which are not federally regulated.

In a survey of 1,874 incarcerated felons, 32 percent of those who used guns in the instant offense reported stealing them, 16 percent purchasing them from dealers, and 52 percent buying or borrowing them from private sources (Wright and Rossi, 1985). Of special interest are the 52 percent of respondents who rated "need gun to do crime" as a "somewhat" or "very" important motive for obtaining their guns. Of these, 45 percent reported stealing them and 30 percent reported buying them on black markets—compared with only 24 percent and 22 percent, respectively, among respondents for whom use in crime was rated "not important" as a motive for obtaining their guns (calculated from Wright and Rossi, 1985:Table 21).

To explore the nature of the illegal market in firearms, Moore (1981) tabulated the investigative files for 131 cases of "dealing without a license" that were closed by the Bureau of Alcohol, Tobacco, and Firearms during 1974-1976; these were virtually all the cases closed in seven regional offices. According to these files, the trade is of small scale: the majority of traders had no inventories at the time of arrest, only 10 percent had more than 20 guns on hand, and the majority sold fewer than 5 guns per month. Despite the small scale of operations, the sources of illegally sold guns were diverse: thefts from residences and other dealers, legal purchases from other dealers, and unregulated purchases from private owners were all represented in substantial numbers.

While this information must be considered dated and imprecise, it establishes four points about the acquisition of guns used in crimes during the 1970s and early 1980s. First, all distribution channels—legal and illegal purchases from licensed dealers, unregulated private transactions, and theft—are potentially important sources of guns used in violent crime. Second, illegal sources were most important for those acquiring guns in explicit preparation for later crimes. Third, illegal sellers of firearms tend to be small-scale independent operators rather than members of large organizations. Fourth, most people who buy guns from licensed dealers that they later use in crimes were legally entitled to make their purchases.

If these findings still hold today, they suggest that illegal firearms transactions more closely resemble today's decentralized crack trade than the earlier highly organized distribution of heroin and powdered cocaine (see Chapter 4). In turn, this suggests that local-level interdiction efforts in illegal firearms traffic may reduce firearm violence more effectively than expanded federal regulation of licensed dealers and interstate commerce. This inference was drawn by Moore more than a decade ago, and it is echoed (for different reasons) in the call by participants in the December 1990 Forum on Youth Violence in Minority Communities for greater community involvement in the formulation of local firearm policy (Centers for Disease Control, 1991). However, there is as yet no strong evidence bearing on which centralized or decentralized approaches, if any, are most effective in enforcing existing firearms regulations, and on the importance of community involvement in increasing the effectiveness of enforcement.

INTERVENTIONS TO REDUCE FIREARM VIOLENCE

The strongest evidence on how firearms availability affects levels of violent crime and felony homicides can be obtained from carefully controlled evaluations of interventions that reduce firearms availability. This principle is true not only of interventions to modify the *availability* of firearms, but also of interventions to modify their *uses*, their *allocation* across owner categories, and their *lethality*. (This classification of interventions appears in Moore, no date; other useful classifications appear in Zimring, 1991; and Kellermann et al., 1991). The need for evaluations encompasses legal interventions; technological interventions that modify firearms, ammunition, and shields; and interventions involving public education about uses and misuses of firearms. Although substantial experience has been gained with several of these intervention strategies, there is a dearth of evaluations sound enough to permit us to learn from that experience.

Table 6-1 lists legal, technological, and public education interventions classified by their objective: to alter the uses, allocation, lethality, or availability of firearms. These objectives are not mutually exclusive, and some interventions are intended to achieve several of them simultaneously. For example, the Federal Gun Control Act of 1968 contained provisions to reduce gun availability (by restricting imports) and allocation (by prohibiting sales to convicted felons, minors, and certain others). Statutory waiting periods for purchases from licensed gun dealers, which are intended primarily to affect firearms allocation (by improving enforcement of the 1968 act), may affect uses (e.g., if a prospective purchaser's passionate anger subsides during the waiting period).

Theoretically, some of these intervention strategies may reinforce each other if introduced as a package. For example, mandatory waiting periods may be more effective if accompanied by interventions to disrupt illegal gun distribution channels. Or public education on safe use and storage of guns may be a useful requirement as part of an owner licensing program; however, experience with driver's education in reducing automobile deaths is not encouraging (Robertson, 1983). Registration of guns to particular owners, like automobile registration, might facilitate other interventions intended to achieve one of the listed objectives (Moore, no date).

Unfortunately, there is little evidence that bears on these speculations about control strategies. The technological strategies—many of which arise from the public health approach to injury control—are relatively untested. And there are few evaluations of the effects of legal strategies embodied in existing federal, state, and local laws (Wright et al., 1983:244). The opportunities to learn from enactment and enforcement of restrictions are some-

TABLE 6-1 Evaluation Status of Strategies and Interventions for Reducing Gun Violence

Strategy and Intervention	Evaluated?	Effective?
Strategy 1: Alter gun uses or storage		
Place and manner laws		
Restrict carrying		
Bartley-Fox Amendment	Yes	Yes
Enhance sentences for felony gun use		
Michigan	Yes	Partial[a]
Pennsylvania	Yes	Partial[a]
Increase probability of sentences for felony gun use		
Operation Triggerlock	No	?
Civil/administrative laws		
Owner liability for damage by gun	No	?
Technological		
Enhance/maintain firearm detectability	No	?
Metal detectors in dangerous places	No	?
Enhance visibility of dangerous illegal uses	No	?
Shields for vulnerable employees	No	?
Public education		
Safe use and storage	No	?
Role in self-defense	Yes	?
Strategy 2: Change gun allocation		
Civil/administrative laws		
Permissive licensing of owners (e.g., all but felons, drug users, minors, etc.)	No	?
Waiting periods for gun purchases	No	?
Restrict sales to high-risk purchasers		
Gun Control Act of 1968	Yes	No
Law enforcement		
Disrupt illegal gun markets	No	?
Mandatory minimum sentences for gun theft	No	?
Technological		
Combination locks on guns	No	?
Strategy 3: Reduce lethality of guns		
Protective clothing in dangerous encounter	No	?
Reduce barrel length and bore	No	?
Reduce magazine size	No	?
Ban dangerous ammunition	No	?

TABLE 6-1 (cont.)

Strategy and Intervention	Evaluated?	Effective?
Strategy 4: Reduce number of guns		
Restrictive licensing systems		
D.C. Firearms Control Act of 1968	Yes	Yes
Restrict imports	No	?
Prohibit ownership	No	?

[a]Reduced gun homicides, no consistent effect on robberies, assaults, or non-gun homicides.

times overlooked by both their advocates and their opponents in public debates.

The Legal Environment

As background, a brief overview follows of laws that attempt to implement the strategies in Table 6-1. The reader is referred to Wright et al. (1983) for a comprehensive overview as of a decade ago, and to Bureau of Alcohol, Tobacco and Firearms (1988, 1989) for more detailed compilations of federal, state, and local laws.

Briefly, the Federal Gun Control Act of 1968 attempts to restrict imports of military weapons and to interdict interstate retail trade in all firearms by limiting legal firearms shipments to federally licensed dealers. Licensed dealers are prohibited from selling guns through the mail or across state lines except to other licensed dealers. The law also prohibits gun sales to certain categories of persons: minors, illegal aliens, felons convicted or under indictment, drug users, and former involuntarily committed mental patients. The 1968 act is enforced by the Bureau of Alcohol, Tobacco and Firearms. Bureau staffing decreased by about 24 percent between 1981 and 1983 and did not return to 1981 levels until 1989, despite its assumption of new responsibilities in arson and drug law enforcement (General Accounting Office, 1991:13-15). There have been no rigorous evaluations of the effects of these changes in enforcement resource levels. However, the General Accounting Office (1991:39) noted a recent doubling of the police waiting time for routine traces of firearms used in crimes. Also, newspaper accounts provide anecdotal reports of convicted felons and active drug dealers obtaining licenses as federal firearms dealers; the licenses enable them to obtain large numbers of firearms for personal use or for off-the-books sales to others (Isikoff, 1991).

Federally licensed dealers are also required to comply with state and local requirements, most of which are intended to keep guns away from designated high-risk categories of persons. The most common such restriction is a requirement that gun purchasers obtain a permit or license before taking possession. In most of the 21 states with license requirements as of 1989, eligibility for a license was "permissive" (i.e., open to most categories of persons), but a few jurisdictions have adopted "restrictive" licensing requirements, with eligibility limited to a few select groups. Among the nation's most restrictive laws is the District of Columbia's 1977 Firearms Control Act, which prohibits handgun possession by virtually anyone except police officers, security guards, and those who owned their handguns before the law went into effect. Nevertheless, Isikoff (1991) reported that there were 41 federally licensed dealers in Washington, D.C.

A fundamental political and ethical issue in firearms regulation is the trade-off between the effects on deaths and injuries and the costs imposed on members of law-abiding society who use guns for recreation or other legal purposes—a policy evaluation criterion noted by Zimring (1991), Wright et al. (1983), and others. Consequently, some firearm regulations apply a strategy to a limited domain: only "high-risk" firearms, firearm users, or firearm uses. Examples include bans on Saturday night specials or assault weapons (considered high-risk weapons, respectively, because of concealability and rapid-fire capability), computer systems to verify that prospective gun buyers are not members of a prohibited category, and "place and manner" laws that prohibit designated high-risk firearm uses such as carrying concealed weapons or firing them in densely populated areas.

In short, there is a variety of legal, public education, and technological strategies for interventions with licensed firearm dealers, firearm owners, and the firearms themselves. For several reasons, it is impossible to predict a priori their effects on frequencies of violent events and violent deaths. The effects of strategies to alter firearm uses depend on individuals' behavioral responses to public education and to the disincentives of legal penalties; these cannot be known in advance. Interventions intended to reduce the lethality of firearms, or to reduce the availability of firearms in certain categories, may be thwarted by the substitution of other, more lethal categories; one cannot know the extent of substitution in advance. And interventions to alter the allocation or availability of firearms may be circumvented by illegal markets, to an extent that cannot be known in advance. Therefore, carefully controlled evaluations represent the only way of ascertaining intervention effects.

Findings From Previous Evaluations

As previously mentioned, there have been few evaluations of the legal, technological, and public education intervention strategies displayed in Table 6-1. We summarize findings from those that are available.

Strategy 1: Alter Gun Uses or Storage

Of the tactics listed in the table to alter gun uses or storage, three have been more or less rigorously evaluated: restrictions on carrying firearms, sentence enhancements for using guns to commit felonies, and public education concerning gun use for self-defense. Evaluations provide strong evidence that carrying restrictions and sentence enhancements reduced the harm from gun violence in the urban jurisdictions in which they were evaluated. The evaluations of gun use promotion for self-defense were of poorer quality, and so their violence control effectiveness remains to be demonstrated. Although we could find no evaluations of actual experience with technological protections against dangerous uses of firearms or with owner liability laws for gun injuries or damage, their logic seems sufficiently persuasive to warrant systematic evaluation programs.

The most thoroughly evaluated restriction on gun uses is the 1974 Bartley-Fox Amendment, which expanded Massachusetts licensing procedures and mandated a one-year sentence for unlicensed carrying of firearms in public. Process evaluations suggest that the law was vigorously enforced immediately following passage, but that over the following two years police confusion about the law and growing judicial discretion in its application partially undercut its intent (Beha, 1977; Rossman et al., 1979). Early evaluations of the law's effects in Boston produced conflicting findings, but a more extensive evaluation that compared statewide trends with trends in neighboring states demonstrated rather clearly that the law decreased gun use in assaults and robberies and also decreased gun homicides during the two-year evaluation period (Pierce and Bowers, 1979).

Another approach to restricting high-risk gun use is a mandatory sentence increase for felonies in which a gun is used. This approach has been evaluated in six jurisdictions, and a meta-analysis of the findings concludes that the sentence enhancements decreased gun homicides, left nongun homicide levels unchanged, and produced no consistent effect on gun robberies or assaults (McDowall et al., 1992a, b). The homicide effects are consistent with a strong instrumental effect for guns and very little substitution of other weapons in homicides. The mixed results for robberies and assaults are puzzling because the one-year sentence enhancement is a smaller relative increment to the average homicide sentence than to the average assault or robbery sentence. It may well be that a clearer picture would have emerged if the available data had permitted a separate evaluation for commercial robberies (in which guns are most likely to be used) and provided more systematic recording and classification of assaults.

Currently, under Operation Triggerlock, special investigation and prosecution efforts are being employed to increase the *probability* of punishment for felony firearm use. Evaluation results are not available at this writing.

There have been at least two evaluations of interventions to promote the use of firearms for self-defense. Both involved simple comparisons of violent crime levels before and after the interventions, with no measures taken of gunshot injuries, fatal homicides, or firearm accidents. A highly publicized antirape police initiative that trained some 2,500 women residents of Orlando, Florida, in the safe use of firearms was followed by an 88 percent decrease in the recorded rape rate the following year (Kleck and Bordua, 1983). But the recorded rape rate in one year not long before the intervention had actually dropped to zero, suggesting problems with recording accuracy. Green (1987, cited in Cook, 1991) questioned the reliability of the police department's records in evaluating its own antirape program, and McDowall et al. (1991) found the decrease well within the bounds of normal year-to-year variation at that time. Similarly, a local ordinance requiring each household to own a firearm was passed in Kenesaw, Georgia, in 1982 and was followed by a drop in burglary rates (Kleck, 1988). However, a subsequent analysis of long-term trends by McDowall et al. (1991) demonstrated that the drop was well within the bounds of year-to-year variation in Kenesaw's burglary rates. Further evaluations, preferably involving randomized experiments and multiple outcome measures, are needed to yield a strong conclusion on the effectiveness of this approach.

Strategy 2: Change the Allocation of Firearms

Of the tactics for changing the allocation of firearms, we could find a rigorous evaluation of only one: the provision of the Federal Gun Control Act of 1968 that prohibits gun dealers from selling to certain categories of persons designated "dangerous." This provision seems to have had no significant effect on firearms injuries or deaths.

Because this law focused on interstate transactions, its effects on handgun use in assaults and homicides should have been evident in New York and Boston, where the incentives for out-of-state purchases were high because of unusually restrictive local license requirements. In fact, Zimring (1975) found that, before and after the law was enacted, trends in those jurisdictions were not significantly different from trends in other large cities.

The lack of effect may have been due to a lack of enforcement effort. A 1970 crackdown to enforce the federal gun law in the District of Columbia, involving a seven- to tenfold increase in enforcement agents on the street, did accompany a six-month decrease in gun homicides, while other homicides remained constant. But evaluation results for the 1968 act may also reflect the fact that purchases by ineligible persons from licensed dealers make only a small contribution to gun use in violent crimes. We consider interventions in gun markets involving unlicensed dealers in the conclusion to this chapter.

Strategy 3: Reduce the Lethality of Available Firearms

The third strategy is to designate certain firearms dangerous because of their concealability, firepower, or other characteristic, then either to restrict access to them by law or to make them less dangerous through technological means.

Recently, the most conspicuous proposals to implement this strategy have focused on assault weapons. The term has no generally accepted precise definition but seems to apply to rifles and pistols capable of automatic or semiautomatic fire and having a military appearance (Kleck, 1991). Except for military cosmetics (e.g., plastic rather than wood stocks, nonreflective rather than reflective surfaces) and a shift from American to foreign brands, the semiautomatic rifles that have recently become more visibly associated with urban homicides differ little from semiautomatic weapons that have been available for decades. This fact, which receives little attention from either advocates or opponents of special restrictions on these weapons, has complicated the problem of drafting legislation.

There is controversy over how much more lethal assault weapons are than other rifles and pistols (Kleck, 1991). But this controversy has been carried out entirely in terms of laboratory observations of the firepower of particular weapons. Resolution of that controversy in laboratory settings would provide little useful information about actual use of such weapons in violent crimes.

Given the imprecision of the term *assault weapon*, it should not be surprising that there are no generally accepted estimates of the number of such weapons in the United States, of ownership patterns, of their lethality compared with other weapons, or of their uses in crimes (Zimring, 1991). Therefore, legislative efforts to restrict their availability are proceeding with very little basis in knowledge.

Even if workable restrictions on assault weapons can be specified and implemented, past experience suggests that continuing enforcement efforts would be required to avoid circumvention through illegal markets. Therefore, the needs for evaluation cited in connection with Strategy 2 apply here as well.

Strategy 4: Reduce the Availability of Firearms

Perhaps the most ambitious effort to reduce the number of firearms in a community was the 1977 District of Columbia Firearms Control Act, which prohibited handgun ownership by virtually everyone except police officers, security guards, and previous gun owners. Three evaluations of this intervention are available: U.S. Conference of Mayors (1980), Jones (1981), and Loftin et al. (1991). As discussed by Cook (1991), the first two evaluations indicate that, during periods of vigorous enforcement, the District of Columbia law did reduce the rates of gun robbery, assault, and homicide during the three years following implementation. The effect was especially strong for homicides arising from disputes among family members and acquaintances. The Loftin et al. (1991) evaluation found decreases of about one-fourth in D.C. gun homicides and suicides immediately after passage of the law. The effect persisted until 1988, when gun homicides associated with crack markets increased, and it was not mirrored by trends in D.C. nongun homicides or suicides, or in gun homicides or suicides in nearby suburban areas that were not subject to the law. While none of these findings should be considered conclusive or universally applicable, their convergence—despite different approaches—

suggests that local restrictive licensing laws, when enforced, may reduce firearm homicides and warrant evaluations in other communities.

RESEARCH AND EVALUATION NEEDS

Violence involving firearms exacts a large toll in terms of deaths, injuries, and monetary costs. The risk of firearm violence is high and rising, especially among young black males.

Research is needed to determine answers to a number of questions about the multiple complex relationships between firearms and violence. Ignorance is especially profound concerning so-called assault weapons, a poorly defined category.

One or more surveys are needed to develop accurate estimates of ownership by gun type, of motives and sources for obtaining guns, and especially of gun acquisition patterns among juveniles and criminals. Case control, ethnographic survey, and other studies are needed of robberies and assaults involving guns to discover the risk factors associated with actual shootings and the role of guns in self-defense.

Existing data are inadequate for measuring the annual incidence of self-defense gun use. The National Crime Survey is subject to event threshold and recall problems, and other estimates are subject to definitional ambiguities and other methodological problems that cannot be solved without resorting to dubious adjustment factors. For informing individuals' choices about gun ownership, however, the more important questions are how often and under what circumstances intended victims deploy their guns in self-defense and how the deployment affects the outcome of the event. These questions bear further analysis not only through victimization surveys but also through analyses of event records.

Analyses of natural variation have established that increased firearm availability is associated with increased firearm use in violent crime. But the methods used to date have been insufficient to answer a more basic question: Do changes in gun availability cause changes in violence levels overall? To answer this question, evaluations are needed of the effects of gun supply reduction initiatives on violence levels in particular geographic areas.

Educational, technological, and legal strategies can be devised with the objectives of changing how handguns are used and stored, changing their allocation from higher-risk to lower-risk segments of the population, reducing their lethality, or reducing their numbers. For any of these policies to reduce homicides, they must reduce violent uses of at least some types of guns to an extent that is not offset by substitution of other more lethal weapons.

It is not clear in advance whether this condition would be met for any policy focused on handguns. While intentional firearm injuries are two to five times as lethal as injuries from knives, the next most lethal weapon, it is not known how much of this difference in lethality is due to weapon characteristics and how much to more lethal intentions by those who attack with guns. We also do not know the extent to which long guns or assault weapons would be substituted if handguns became less available, or indeed whether those weapons are more lethal than handguns when used in violent crimes.

Without a priori knowledge, an assessment must depend on evaluations of experience, which are conditionally encouraging. Examples exist of reductions in violent gun uses caused by legal restrictions on carrying guns, by enhanced sentences for felony gun use, and by restrictive licensing of firearms in particular jurisdictions. However, the success of legal strategies depends critically on the nature and intensity of enforcement efforts, since illegal or unregulated gun transfers supply most of the guns used in crimes.

Enforcement efforts directed against illegal gun markets combine elements of the first three strategies shown in Table 6-1. Also, unlike interventions involving licensed dealers and gun owners, most of whom are law abiding, disruption of illegal markets focuses on persons who are violating laws. Interventions against illegal drug markets should be more effective if they are informed by more specific research on the nature of those markets—their size, their distribution channels, and their retail-level marketing techniques. As a starting point, however, efforts to disrupt local illegal gun markets might reasonably borrow tactics that are currently being used against illegal drug markets. These could include buy-bust operations,[9] high-priority investigation and prosecution of alleged unregulated gun dealers, the development of minors arrested in possession of guns as informants against gun sources, phony fencing operations for stolen guns, high-priority investigations and prosecutions of burglaries and robberies in which guns are stolen, and high mandatory minimum sentences for those who steal or illegally sell guns.

In Chapter 4 we suggest that the success of street-level disruption of drug markets may depend on the extent of local community support. Community support was also cited as a necessary ingredient of firearm policy development at the December 1990

Forum on Youth Violence in Minority Communities (Centers for Disease Control, 1991). This suggests that community-oriented or neighborhood-oriented police work involving close coordination with community-based organizations may be useful in reducing residents' motivations to acquire guns for self-defense, in encouraging community members to notify police anonymously about illegal gun transactions and persons illegally carrying guns, and in supporting market disruption tactics when necessary.

In view of the lack of available evidence, a high priority should be placed on evaluations of the violence-reduction effects—on gun and nongun violence and on illegal and unregulated gun transfers—of interventions to reduce illegal sales of firearms.

Specifically, high priority should be placed on evaluating the effects of three intervention strategies:

- disrupting illegal gun markets using the centralized and street-level tactics currently in use for disrupting illegal drug markets;
- enforcing existing bans on juvenile possession of handguns; and
- community-oriented or neighborhood-oriented police work involving close coordination with residents and community-based organizations.

At this writing, the Department of Justice is expanding its pilot testing of "Operation Weed and Seed"—a program under which these and other initiatives involving police-community cooperation could be systematically evaluated.

Rigorous evaluations should also be made of the effects of strategies other than law enforcement interventions: public education interventions to change how guns are stored and used and technological interventions to reduce the lethality of firearms. To the extent that consideration is given to reducing the availability of assault weapons through new statutes, there is a need to reach consensus on a definition of that term, and then to ascertain their level of violent use, their lethality in actual use, and the effects of alternative enforcement strategies in reducing the violence associated with them.

NOTES

1 For legibility, trends in the 1984-1988 firearm homicide rate for black males are not displayed in Figure 6-3 for all available age groups. The rate for ages 15-19 increased from 30 to 68 per 100,000, a 126 percent increase. The corresponding increases were from 2.1 to 4.5 (114%) for

ages 10-14; from 63 to 104 (65%) for ages 20-24; from 70 to 90 (29%) for ages 25-29; and from 62 to 69 (11%) for ages 30-34 (Fingerhut et al., 1991).

2 Cook has estimated that for each new cohort of 100 guns, 33 uses in crime are reported. But because the frequency of repeat uses is unknown, the fraction that is ever used in this way is unknown.

3 Wright et al. (1983) point out that in some of the 80 percent, the shooter may have shot a second time but missed, and in others the killer may have failed to shoot a second time because the victim appeared to be dead already. It seems likely that both explanations apply to some incidents but that even together they are insufficient to account for all one-shot incidents.

4 Because National Crime Survey data include only nonfatal victimizations, the publication does not report conditional probabilities of being hospitalized or killed. Because deaths are so rare, however, those probabilities would not be substantially altered.

5 Respondents to one of the surveys of the uses of self-defense (Decision-Making Information, Inc., 1979) stated that only 31 percent of the incidents involving gun use for self-defense were "important enough to report to the police."

6 As one example, in a survey by Decision-Making Information (1979, cited in Wright et al., 1983:96), 15 percent of respondents reported "ever" using a gun for self-protection. To convert this lifetime prevalence to an annual prevalence, Kleck multiplies it by the ratio 1.4/8.6, the ratio of annual to lifetime prevalence rates for self-defense uses obtained in another survey and obtains an estimate of 897,000 annual self-defense uses. Yet elsewhere in the same publication, he reports that the mean duration of gun ownership in a representative sample of gun owners is 23.4 years. If one accepted the 1.4 percent rate as accurate but assumed that self-defense uses were distributed uniformly over the life of each gun, the implied adjustment ratio would be 1.4/23.4, which would reduce Kleck's annualized estimate to 329,000.

As another example, Kleck (1988:5 and Table 2) adjusts justifiable civilian homicides with guns for assumed underreporting in the Uniform Crime Reports Supplementary Homicide Report. The adjustment involves 57 "other civilian legal defensive homicides" (OCLDHs) in Detroit and leads to a national estimate of 2,819 total firearm OCLDHs for 1980. Yet the estimation method for the Detroit OCLDHs is not explained, their cited source does not appear in the reference list, and no more than one OCLDH was estimated for any of the other five large jurisdictions included in Kleck's Table 2. Omitting the Detroit OCLDHs from the adjustment would reduce the national estimate from 2,819 to 1,711.

7 Because some incidents of self-defense with a firearm in events outside the home entail illegal firearms carrying, the rates for assaults and robberies may be underreported to interviewers. However, given the difficulty of gun deployment during a surprise robbery or assault, it seems

unlikely that the rates for assaults and robberies are as high as those for residential burglaries, in which self-defense with a gun is generally legal.

8 Based on a multivariate analysis, Cook (1979) finds that a 10 percent reduction in the prevalence of gun ownership in a city is associated with about a 5 percent reduction in the gun robbery rate and a 4 percent reduction in the robbery murder rate. Killias (1990, cited in Cook, 1991) reports a correlation of .72 between the gun fraction in homicide and the prevalence of gun ownership for 11 countries.

9 In a buy-bust operation, a dealer is arrested following one or more illegal sales to undercover officers, which are usually recorded on videotape for use as evidence.

REFERENCES

Beha, J.A., III

1977 "And nobody can get you out": The impact of a mandatory prison sentence for the illegal carrying of a firearm on the use of firearms and the administration of criminal justice in Boston. *Boston University Law Review* 57:96-146, 289-233.

Bureau of Alcohol, Tobacco and Firearms

1988 *(Your Guide to) Federal Firearms Regulation, 1988-89.* Bureau of Alcohol, Tobacco and Firearms publication No. 5300.4. Washington, D.C.: U.S. Government Printing Office.

1989 *State Laws and Published Ordinances—Firearms.* Washington, D.C.: U.S. Government Printing Office.

1991 How many guns? ATF News (Press release). May 22.

Bureau of Justice Statistics

1986 *The Use of Weapons in Committing Crimes.* Washington, D.C.: U.S. Government Printing Office.

1989 *Criminal Victimization in the United States, 1987.* Washington, D.C.: U.S. Bureau of Justice Statistics.

Centers for Disease Control

1991 Forum on Youth Violence in Minority Communities: Setting the Agenda for Prevention, December 10-12, 1990. Summary of the proceedings. *Public Health Reports* 106(3):225-277.

Cook, P.J.

1979 The effect of gun availability on robbery and robbery murder: A cross section study of fifty cities. *Policy Studies Review Annual* 3.

1980 Reducing injury and death rates in robbery. *Policy Analysis* 6(1):21-45.

1981 Guns and crime: The perils of long division. *Journal of Policy Analysis and Management* 1:120-125.

1985 Report on a City-Specific Gun Prevalence Index. Mimeographed. Durham, N.C.: Duke University, Institute of Policy Sciences.

1991 The technology of personal violence. Pp. 1-72 in M. Tonry, ed.,

Crime and Justice: A Review of Research. Vol. 14. Chicago: University of Chicago Press.

Curtis, L.A.
1974 *Criminal Violence: National Patterns and Behavior.* Lexington, Mass.: D.C. Heath.

Decision-Making Information, Inc.
1979 *Attitudes of the American Electorate Toward Gun Control.* Santa Ana, Calif.: Decision-Making Information, Inc.

Downs, G.W.
1991 Arms race and war. Pp. 73-109 in P.E. Tetlock, J.L. Husbands, R. Jervis, P.C. Stern, and C. Tilly, eds. *Behavior, Society and Nuclear War.* New York: Oxford University Press.

Federal Bureau of Investigation
1989 *Crime in the United States, 1988: Uniform Crime Reports.* Washington, D.C.: U.S. Government Printing Office.

Fingerhut, L.A., J.C. Kleinman, E. Godfrey, and H. Rosenberg
1991 Firearm mortality among children, youth, and young adults 1-34 years of age, trends and current status: United States, 1979-88. *Monthly Vital Statistics Report* 39(11, Supplement). Hyattsville, Md.: National Center for Health Statistics.

General Accounting Office
1991 *BATF: Management Improvements Needed to Handle Increasing Responsibilities.* Report to the Chairman, Subcommittee on Oversight, Committee on Ways and Means, House of Representatives. GAO publication No. GGD-91-67. Washington, D.C.: U.S. General Accounting Office.

Green, G.S.
1987 Citizen gun ownership and criminal deterrence: Theory, research, and policy. *Criminology* 25:63-82.

Isikoff, Michael
1991 Gun dealers' "great scam": U.S. licenses grow popular with criminals. *Washington Post* May 8, pp. A1,A8.

Jones, E.D., III
1981 The District of Columbia's Firearms Control Regulations Act of 1975: The toughest handgun control law in the United States—or is it? *Annals of the American Academy of Political and Social Science* 455:138-149.

Kellermann, A.L., and D.T. Reay
1988 Protection or peril? An analysis of firearm related deaths in the home. *New England Journal of Medicine* 319:1256-1262.

Kellermann, A.L., R.K. Lee, J.A. Mercy, and J. Banton
1991 The epidemiologic basis for the prevention of firearm injuries. *Annual Review of Public Health* 12:17-40.

Killias, Martin
1990 Gun ownership and violent crime: The Swiss experience in international perspective. *Security Journal* 1(3):169-174.

Kleck, G.
1984 The relationship between gun ownership levels and rates of violence in the United States. In D.B. Kates, Jr., ed., *Firearms and Violence: Issues of Public Policy*. Cambridge, Mass.: Ballinger.
1988 Crime control through the private use of armed force. *Social Problems* 35:1-22.
1991 *Point Blank: Guns and Violence in America*. New York: Aldine de Gruyter.

Kleck, G., and D.J. Bordua
1983 The factual foundation for certain key assumptions of gun control. *Law and Policy Quarterly* 5:271-298.

Kleck, G., and K. McElrath
1989 The Effects of Weaponry on Human Violence. Mimeographed. Tallahassee, Fla.: Florida State University, School of Criminology.

Loftin, C., D. McDowall, B. Wiersema, and T.J. Cottey
1991 Effects of restrictive licensing of handguns on homicide and suicide in the District of Columbia. *New England Journal of Medicine* 325(December 5):1615-1620.

McDowall, D.
1991 Firearm availability and homicide rates in Detroit, 1951-1986. *Social Forces* 69(4):1085-1101.

McDowall, D., A.J. Lizotte, and B. Wiersema
1991 General deterrence through civilian gun ownership: An evaluation of the quasi-experimental evidence. *Criminology* 29(4):541-559.

McDowall, David, Colin Loftin, and Brian Wiersema
1992a A comparative study of the preventive effects of mandatory sentencing laws for gun crimes. *Journal of Criminal Law and Criminology*, forthcoming.
1992b Preventive effects of mandatory sentencing laws for gun crimes. Pp. 87-94 in *Proceedings of the Social Statistics Section*. Annual meeting of the American Statistical Association, Atlanta, Ga., August 18-22, 1991. Alexandria, Va.: American Statistical Association.

Moore, M.H.
1981 Keeping handguns from criminal offenders. *The Annals of the American Academy of Political and Social Science* 455:92-109.
No date Alternative Policy Approaches to the Control of Handgun Abuse. Unpublished manuscript available from the Kennedy School of Government, Harvard University.

Newton, G.D., Jr., and F.E. Zimring
1969 *Firearms and Violence in American Life*. Washington, D.C.: U.S. Government Printing Office.

Phillips, L., H.L. Votey, Jr., and J. Howell
1976 Handguns and homicide: Minimizing losses and the costs of control. *Journal of Legal Studies* 5:463-478.

Pierce, G.L., and W.J. Bowers
1979 The Impact of the Bartley-Fox Gun Law on Crime in Massachusetts. Unpublished manuscript. Boston: Northeastern University, Center for Applied Social Research.

Rice, Dorothy P., Ellen J. MacKenzie, and Associates
1989 *Cost of Injury in the United States: A Report to Congress.* San Francisco, Calif.: Institute for Health and Aging, University of California and Injury Prevention Center, The Johns Hopkins University.

Robertson, L.S.
1983 *Injuries: Causes, Control Strategies, and Public Policy.* Lexington, Mass.: Lexington Books.

Rossman, D., P. Froyd, G.L. Pierce, J. McDevitt, and W. Bowers
1979 *The Impact of the Mandatory Gun Law in Massachusetts.* Boston University School of Law: Center for Criminal Justice.

Sloane, J.H., A.L. Kellermann, D.T. Rey, J.A. Ferris, T. Koepsell, F.P. Rivara, C. Rice, L. Gray, and J. LoGerfo
1988 Handgun regulations, crimes, assaults, and homicide: A tale of two cities. *New England Journal of Medicine* 319:1256-1262.

U.S. Conference of Mayors
1980 The Analysis of the Firearms Control Act of 1975: Handgun Control in the District of Columbia. Mimeographed. Washington, D.C.

van Dijk, Jan J.M., Pat Mayhew, and Martin Killias
1990 *Experiences of Crime Across the World: Key Findings From the 1989 International Crime Survey.* Deventer, The Netherlands: Kluwer Law and Taxation Publishers.

Vinson, T.
1974 Gun and knife attacks. *Australian Journal of Forensic Science* 7(2):76-83.

Wintemute, G.J., S.P. Teret, J.F. Kraus, and M.A. Wright
1987 When children shoot children. 88 unintentional deaths in California. *Journal of the American Medical Association* 257:3107-3109.

Wolfgang, M.
1958 *Patterns in Criminal Homicide.* New York: Wiley.

Wright, J.D., and P.H. Rossi
1985 *The Armed Criminal in America: A Survey of Incarcerated Felons.* National Institute of Justice Research Report (July).

Wright, J.D., P.H. Rossi, and K. Daly
1983 *Under the Gun: Weapons, Crime and Violence in America.* Hawthorne, N.Y.: Aldine Publishing Company.

Zimring, F.E.
1968 Is gun control likely to reduce violent killings? *The University of Chicago Law Review* 35:721-737.

1975 Firearms and federal law: The gun control act of 1968. *Journal of Legal Studies* 4:133-198.

1989 The problem of assault firearms. *Crime & Delinquency* 35(4):538-545.

1991 Firearms, violence, and public policy. *Scientific American* (November):48-54.

Zimring, F.E., and G. Hawkins

1987 *The Citizen's Guide to Gun Control.* New York: Macmillan Publishing Company.

Zimring, F.E., and J. Zuehl

1986 Victim injury and death in urban robbery: A Chicago study. *Journal of Legal Studies* XV(1):1-40.

Part III
Harnessing Understanding to Improve Control

In Part II we describe what is currently known about certain types of violence. As those chapters show, some useful advances have been made in identifying risk factors—but causal understanding is limited, and there is a shortage of preventive interventions whose effectiveness has been documented through rigorous long-term evaluations.

Lacking clear-cut evidence of successful preventive interventions in social and family problems—poverty, unemployment, unstable family life, poor parenting skills, etc.—some people favor greater use of incarceration to reduce violence through the effects of incapacitation and deterrence. In Chapter 7 we examine recent experience with violent crime levels during an unprecedented increase in the prison population. Based on official statistics, a near-tripling of average prison time served per violent crime during the past 15 years appears not to have produced a concomitant decrease in levels of violent crime. Although the results are not definitive, this suggests that the increased use of prison had a limited violence reduction effect, that other criminogenic processes were at work, or both.

If that is so, then a broader perspective will help to expand thinking about possibilities for preventive interventions in the processes that culminate in violent events, and a more systematic development strategy for such interventions may, over time, expand the array of useful violence prevention tools.

To help organize our thinking about potential interventions, Chapter 7 presents a matrix that oversimplifies the complexities explored in Part II but that organizes the factors and processes discussed there in a way that highlights promising points for preventive interventions. Because not much is known yet about the interactions between the cells of the matrix, they do not lead immediately to specific policy prescriptions, but do suggest a number of ideas worth testing. Therefore, the chapter concludes with a discussion of the kinds of rigorous evaluations that, by testing promising ideas, can simultaneously improve the capacity to control violence and advance its understanding.

In Chapter 8 the panel presents recommendations that, taken together, are designed to fill gaps in knowledge and improve the capacity to diagnose and remedy specific problems. They cover four areas:

- initiatives to solve specific violence problems through systematic testing of interventions,
- improvements in statistical systems to measure overall violence more completely and specific violence problems more accurately,
- neglected areas of violence research, and
- a multicommunity longitudinal study of violence and aggression.

Chapter 8 concludes by examining the capacity of the current structure of the federal system to support the necessary research. Other important basic research questions have been raised throughout the chapters of Part II.

7

Expanding the Limits of Understanding and Control

We begin this section by considering the effectiveness of one *response* to violent crime—incarceration of convicted violent offenders. We then present a framework for broadening perspectives on approaches to *prevention*.

APPROACHES TO CONTROLLING VIOLENCE

THE ROLE OF INCARCERATION

Incarceration may reduce violent crime through two mechanisms, deterrence and incapacitation. Deterrence operates because incarceration provides a disincentive intended to discourage violent crime.[1] In theory, the threat of incarceration deters violent crime by reducing the number of violent offenders or the frequency or seriousness of their violent crimes. In contrast to deterrence, which theoretically alters behavior, incapacitation reduces violent crimes simply by physically isolating persons who engage in violence from the general community.

The existence of deterrence and incapacitation effects is not at issue. If incarceration were eliminated entirely, we have no doubt that violent crime would increase (Blumstein et al., 1978). But there is substantial uncertainty about the relevant policy question: What are the *marginal* effects of *changes* in either the chance of incarceration per violent crime or the average time served by those incarcerated? These effects cannot be observed directly, because they are measured in terms of potential crimes that did not occur. Rather, their magnitudes must be estimated from data on trends in violent crime and in incarceration levels.

Recent Experience

The unprecedented increase in prison population since 1975 offers a case study for analyzing the effects of changes in the prison population on levels of violent crime. However, the results remain tentative because the accuracy of the estimates depends on both the accuracy of the data and the validity of assumptions that underlie the analyses.

Between 1975 and 1989, the inmate population nearly tripled, while reported annual violent crime levels varied around the level of about 2.9 million. This experience raises an important set of policy issues about how prison population and violent crime levels are related. To examine them the panel commissioned an analysis by Cohen and Canela-Cacho (Volume 4) and also benefited from an analysis by Langan (1991).[2] Some pieces of the puzzle can be understood more precisely than others, but one implication of the 15-year experience seems inescapable: if tripling the average length of incarceration per crime had a strong deterrent effect, then violent crime rates should have declined in the absence of other relevant changes. While rates declined during the early 1980s, they generally rose after 1985, suggesting that changes in other factors, including some of those discussed in Part II, may have been causing an increase in potential crimes.

Two potential influences on prison population can be discounted. The increases cannot have been due to increases in the *probability of arrest per violent crime*, because that probability remained essentially constant throughout the period. Similarly, growth in the number of young adults in the aftermath of the baby boom could not by itself have increased prison population (or violent crime) levels by much more than 24 percent, the increase in the U.S. adult population.

One relevant factor clearly did change: *average prison time served per violent crime* approximately tripled between 1975 and 1989, returning to the levels of the 1950s. How did this increase occur? Experience varied somewhat by crime type and state, but the data point to general increases in both the average time served if incarcerated and the chance of imprisonment if arrested. This is consistent with the proliferation of statutes mandating minimum sentences, especially for offenses involving violence or firearms.

An increase in average prison time served per crime may prevent crimes either through incapacitation or deterrence. Estimates of incapacitation effects are necessarily imprecise and uncertain because they depend on many specific assumptions. However, under a variety of alternative scenarios (Cohen and Canela-Cacho, Volume 4), the estimated incapacitative effect of tripling the average time served per violent crime was fairly small—preventing on the order of 10 to 15 percent of the crimes that potentially would have been committed otherwise.

Two facts seem to explain the limited incapacitative effect of the increase in prison time. First, while the average annual frequency of violent crimes per offender is fairly small (e.g., 5 to 10 robberies per year), a small fraction of offenders commits hundreds of crimes per year. But even before the increase in average prison time per crime, these high-frequency offenders were spending much of their criminal careers in prison—both because their high crime rates presented more opportunities to be arrested and incarcerated and because, under otherwise comparable circumstances, convicted offenders with extensive prior records tend to receive longer prison sentences. Second, incapacitation is subject to diminishing marginal returns, because most criminal careers are fairly short. Successive increases in the per-crime chance of incarceration bring into prison less serious offenders, thus preventing fewer crimes per inmate-year. Successive increases in average time served by those incarcerated allocate larger shares of prison space to offenders who would have stopped committing crimes even if they had been free in the community.

The tripling of average prison time served per crime also produces a potential marginal deterrence effect: the additional threat of incarceration presumably deters more people from becoming violent offenders and deters some violent offenders from committing more crimes. Methodological problems prevent sound estimates of deterrence effects from being made (Blumstein et al., 1978); however, the flat trend in violent crimes between 1975 and 1989 in the face of a tripling in the average prison time served per crime is not compatible with any substantial deterrence effect—*unless*, for reasons unrelated to incarceration, the potential violent crime rate would have substantially increased during the period. Otherwise, the tripling of time served per crime would have been followed by decreases in violent crime levels, which did not occur according to official statistics. (These conclusions are explained in more detail in Cohen and Canela-Cacho, Volume 4.)

Alternative Incarceration Policies

On the heels of this unprecedented increase in prison population, there is active discussion of pursuing crime control through further increases in the certainty of incarceration following a violent crime, in the term of incarceration, or both (Methvin, 1991).

Through incapacitation, increasing the chance of incarceration reduces crime levels more efficiently than does increasing the average time served.[3] The different incapacitative effects occur because, when the probability of incarceration following each crime is higher, offenders tend to be incapacitated earlier in their careers. But the longer that time served becomes in relation to career length, the more likely it is that offenders will end their careers while they are still incarcerated and would therefore commit no more crimes in the community even if they were released. For example, projecting the incapacitation effects of 50 percent increases in certainty and in average time served from their base levels for robbery in the late 1970s, Cohen and Canela-Cacho (Volume 4) estimate that a 50 percent increase in the chance of incarceration prevents twice as much crime as a 50 percent increase in the average time served by those incarcerated.

Deterrence theory also suggests that increasing certainty reduces crime more efficiently than increasing severity, but for different reasons. Theoretically, the disincentive effect of increasing the probability of incarceration begins at the time the offender enters prison. The disincentive effect of adding additional expected time served begins later, after the preexisting average time served is reached, and is therefore theoretically reduced because of "time discounting"—events farther in the future receive less weight in the offender's decision making.

One might expect that weakening restrictions on the use of improperly obtained evidence would increase the certainty of incarceration for each crime. The effect on the probability of arrest per violent crime is unclear, since it is not known how frequently such arrests are not made solely because of officers' concerns over dismissal because evidence was obtained improperly. But because problems of due process virtually never arise as a reason for declinations or dismissals in violent offense cases in large urban prosecutors' offices (Boland et al., 1992), loosening restrictions on evidence should not be expected to perceptibly increase the certainty of incarceration given arrest for a violent crime.

A Broader Perspective

We have noted an important finding: recent trends in crime and criminal justice policy responses have resulted in the near-tripling of prison populations between 1975 and 1989—with no apparent decrease in levels of violent crime. This strongly suggests that other factors that tend to increase violent crime levels—some of which can be changed by governments or individuals—are at work.

Taking a broader perspective shifts attention in several directions. One is to understand and ultimately modify the psychosocial and biomedical processes through which individuals develop potentials for violent behavior. Others are to consider the settings—communities, markets, gangs, families, places, and encounters—in which violent events occur, looking for ways to intervene. In this report we have looked at violent events from all these perspectives.

Too often, theories or interventions grounded in different perspectives are treated as if they were mutually exclusive. This is unfortunate, because each one contributes significant facets to the understanding and control of violence. In part this is because the concept of violence lumps together many different types of behavior and a great diversity of events. As this volume demonstrates, for every type of violent event, there are many risk factors; consequently, there are opportunities for intervention at many different points. Situations differ in terms of triggering elements for violent events; settings differ in terms of the situations that occur in them and the violence potentials of the people who congregate in them. Exploring all these relationships expands the range of promising but untested preventive opportunities—particularly because of the diversity of violent behaviors and events that has been documented in previous chapters.

Except perhaps when self-preservation requires it, no situation—no dispute, no opportunity for gain or power, no degree of anger or sexual arousal—provokes violent behavior in a majority of people. Some predisposing individual characteristic must be present in most events. Nevertheless, some situations and encounters provoke violent behavior from more people than do others, and identifying such situational hazards for violence is a first step in eliminating them. Similarly, very few predisposing individual characteristics provoke violent outbursts regardless of the situation. Nevertheless, identifying and modifying predisposing individual characteristics for some violent behavior are a step toward preventing some violent events.

Predisposing factors for violence vary in terms of their proximity to the violent event. The development of some relevant individual characteristics, such as a temperamental disposition that favors high thresholds for anxiety or fear, begins before birth or in early childhood. But some individuals' potentials for violence are raised by experiences in adulthood, such as the accumulation of frustration or anger. Similarly, some societal conditions, such as widespread acceptance of violence as an appropriate dispute resolution technique, may take centuries to develop; these are sometimes dismissed as immutable root causes. Other societal risk factors, such as the concentration of poverty in a particular geographic area, may develop over only a few years.

A MATRIX FOR UNDERSTANDING AND CONTROL

To give ourselves a system for thinking about potential interventions to control violence, we found it useful to classify risk factors for violent events using the matrix in Table 7-1. The columns in the matrix classify risk factors by their proximity to a violent act: from left to right, as *predisposing factors and processes*, *situational elements*, or *triggering events*. These categories span four levels of social and individual description that are commonly used in studies of violence. Studies of social factors are concerned with *macrosocial institutions*, such as societies and communities, as well as with *microsocial encounters* among pairs or small groups either as individuals or as members of gangs or families. At the individual level, studies are concerned with both *psychosocial* and *biological* components of behavior. Of course, the factors in each cell of Table 7-1 are only illustrative examples. Far more are discussed in Chapter 3.

We do not assume that any single level is more fundamental than the others in explaining a particular type of violence. Rather, as Chapter 3 explains, violent events and community violence levels arise out of interactions across the levels, and these interactive processes differ from one type of violence to another. Because these interactions are so poorly understood, modifying risk factors and observing responses is the most promising method of simultaneously accumulating understanding while building a capacity for violence prevention.

Research into causes of violence and evaluations of preventive interventions are usually compartmentalized. Academic disciplines concerned with violent behavior tend to focus on one level of description at a time. Public agencies tend to modify only one

TABLE 7-1 Matrix for Organizing Risk Factors for Violent Behavior

Units of Observation and Explanation	Proximity to Violent Events and Their Consequences		
	Predisposing	Situational	Activating
Social			
Macrosocial	Concentration of poverty Opportunity structures Decline of social capital Oppositional cultures Sex-role socialization	Physical structure Routine activities Access: Weapons, emergency medical services	Catalytic social event
Microsocial	Community organizations Illegal markets Gangs Family disorganization Preexisting structures	Proximity of responsible monitors Participants' social relationships Bystanders' activities Temporary communication impairments Weapons: carrying, displaying	Participants' communication exchange
Individual			
Psychosocial	Temperament Learned social responses Perceptions of rewards/penalties for violence Violent deviant sexual preferences Cognitive ability Social, communication skills Self-identification in social hierarchy	Accumulated emotion Alcohol/drug consumption Sexual arousal Premeditation	Impulse Opportunity recognition
Biological	Neurobiologic[a] "traits" Genetically mediated traits Chronic use of psychoactive substances or exposure to neurotoxins	Transient neurobiologic[a] "states" Acute effects of psychoactive substances	Sensory signal-processing errors Interictal events

[a]Includes neuroanatomical, neurophysiological, neurochemical, and neuroendocrine. "Traits" describes capacity as determined by status at birth, trauma, and aging processes such as puberty. "States" describes temporary conditions associated with emotions, external stressors, etc.

cluster of risk factors at a time—police agencies rarely offer professional psychological counseling; juvenile courts rarely offer preventive interventions in early childhood.

Although some specialization is essential, it creates a fundamental difficulty for understanding and controlling violence. We believe that interactions and feedback loops across the cells of the matrix have important effects on violence levels, but with existing research we cannot be sure. Do drug markets attract people with high potentials for violence, do characteristics of drug markets raise the violence potentials of buyers and sellers, or both? Did a theoretically promising cognitive-behavioral preventive intervention fail to change some children's behavior because of neurological deficits that kept them from comprehending the intervention, or because the proffered rewards had no status in the local neighborhood culture?

Because of specialization, when effects such as these are recognized at all, they usually show up in research reports as "untested rival hypotheses" and in evaluations as "unexpected consequences." Better understanding requires more research that follows up such hypotheses even when they cross academic disciplinary boundaries, and unexpected consequences even when they lead beyond an agency's traditional array of interventions. Better understanding and better violence control both require more evaluations that compare different agencies' intervention techniques, using outcome measures at multiple levels of description. We take up this matter later in the chapter.

The following pages illustrate the processes and risk factors arrayed in the matrix. A violent event requires the conjunction of a person with some (high or low) predisposing potential for violent behavior, a situation with elements that create some risk of violent events, and usually a triggering event. Development of an individual's potential for violence may have begun before birth: perhaps with conception involving an alcoholic father, or through abnormal prenatal neural development. It may have begun during early childhood in a violent household, or through school failure, or through frequent exposure to violence in the neighborhood or from the media.

A hazardous situation for violence could involve a dispute, perhaps aggravated by a miscommunication in a bar because of loud background noise, which was misinterpreted as an insult because of intoxication and escalated because participants were afraid of losing face in bystanders' eyes. The surrounding community could be gang turf, the site of illegal drug or gun markets, or a neighborhood where large numbers of unsupervised teenagers reside. It may be the scene of recent aggravating events such as police brutality, or of frequent brawls between members of different ethnic groups. The neighborhood may be experiencing social disruption as stable families move to the suburbs, as businesses close, and as public services decline.

Risk factors such as these make differential contributions to different categories of violent events and suggest different interventions for control. Obviously, not all of them contribute to any single event. A major problem in *understanding* violence is to describe the probability distributions of predisposing factors, situational elements, and triggering events at the biological, psychosocial, microsocial, and macrosocial levels. The problem in *controlling* violence is to choose among possible interventions. This choice, indeed the decision whether to intervene at all in a triggering event, a hazardous situation, or a predisposing process, properly depends on both understanding and values. The knowledge requirements include predictive accuracy in assessing the risk of violence, evidence that the intervention prevents violence, and evidence about side effects.

One barrier to achieving predictive accuracy is that many risk factors have been identified in relation to aggressive behavior, not violent behavior, and the relationships between the two are not well understood. Another barrier is the aforementioned feedback loops and interactions, which are poorly understood and may cross the boundaries of the cells in the matrix—risk factors such as family size and maternal drug abuse during pregnancy may be stronger predictors in poor neighborhoods than in wealthy neighborhoods, for example. Consequently, the panel found scientific bases for very few unambiguous policy recommendations. However, we found a number of promising candidate strategies. The ones that we believe would also satisfy public criteria of fairness are recommended in Chapter 8 for development, evaluation, and refinement in violence problem-solving initiatives.

Because investigations of violent events commonly discover triggering events first, then contributing situational elements, then (if at all) predisposing processes, we discuss them below in that order.

TRIGGERING EVENTS

Describing an event that triggers violence does not provide a basis for inferring motivation for the violent behavior. But in the

American legal system, elements of the triggering event determine which authorities, if any, are empowered to intervene in the event or punish those involved. Analyses of events may also suggest useful clues to how high-risk events might be prevented in the future. Triggering events associated with violence between spouses and between competing crack dealers are very different, and many interventions intended to prevent one type of violence have little relevance for the other.

As shown in Table 7-1, events that trigger violent behavior can be observed at all four levels of description. At the biological level, for example, an error in processing social signals can trigger a violent reaction that would not have occurred had the signal been correctly processed. Brain activity during the aura that precedes a seizure or during the interictal period between seizures can trigger violent behavior. At the psychosocial level, a violent act may arise out of heightened impulsivity or, in the case of premeditation, from the recognition of an opportunity.

Most events that trigger violence, however, reflect none of those, but rather a sequence of information processing operations, described by Dodge (1986) as encoding, interpretation, response search, response decision, and enactment. At the microsocial level, triggering events occur in the dynamic communications with others that generate a continuing flow of information to be processed. At the macrosocial level, political assassinations, killings by police officers, and controversial jury verdicts are examples of catalytic social events that have triggered major episodes of violence.

Awareness of all four levels of triggering events suggests a range of preventive strategies. Examples include pharmacological interventions, teaching children to process information in ways that lead them to choose nonviolent responses, and preventive responses immediately following catalytic social events—the difficulty lies in developing tactics and demonstrating their effectiveness.

Situational Elements

In most violent events, contributing situational elements are most visible in the microsocial encounter that precedes the event. These elements include the dynamics of communications among participants, such as disputes, threats and counterthreats, exchanges of insults, robbery and resistance, and the urgings of bystanders. Both the nature and the interpretation of these exchanges may be conditioned by preexisting social relationships among participants: an intimate relationship, a power or status hierarchy (e.g., guard/

inmate, weaker/stronger, armed/unarmed, shielded/vulnerable), or a culturally defined relationship (e.g., membership in rival gangs, or in different ethnic groups, or in a "hate group" and the category against which it is prejudiced). The risk of violence in an exchange may be increased by communication impairments that are due, for example, to language barriers, to culturally defined connotations of words, to different definitions of insults, or to the influence of alcohol or other drugs.

But the outcome of the microsocial encounter is not independent of participants' psychological and biological state at the time. Accumulated or "flash" emotions—anger, frustration, stress, fear, for example—all contribute. Premeditation, sexual arousal, or urges to "prove one's manhood" sometimes play roles. Though these psychological states must usually be inferred by observing external behavior, each of them has an associated neurological profile, which could in principle be measured in terms of electrical, hormonal, and neurochemical activity in different regions in the brain. If these processes are altered by consumption of alcohol, other drugs, toxic substances, or injury, the resulting behavioral changes may alter the risk of violence.

At the macrosocial level, interactions between characteristics of places and people create situations, elements of which influence the probability and consequences of violence. The routine activities of the people involved—whether drug dealers and customers, or cab drivers and convenience store clerks working alone at night—may create occasions for violence. But whether violence actually occurs depends also on physical characteristics of the place (e.g., lighting, alarms, shields), and on the proximity of responsible monitors (e.g., police, respected "old heads" in the neighborhood, passersby, guard dogs). If violence does occur, its consequences will depend on the nature of accessible weapons. The prospects for limiting damage often depend on the promptness and quality of emergency medical services that respond.

Because situational elements from all levels contribute to the outcome, the possibility exists that even without full causal understanding, altering one link in a chain of events might have prevented a violent event or prevented an assault from becoming a homicide.

Predisposing Factors

Beyond the immediate situation, factors and processes at all four levels create predisposing conditions for violence. We discuss first the psychological and biological processes that interact to determine an individual's potentials for different violent behaviors, and second the social processes that make some environments more likely than others to become locations of violence.

Biological and Psychosocial Processes

Modern perspectives see some violent behavior in part as the result of complex, long-term developmental processes that shape the personality and character of the violent actor. Basic descriptions of these processes often emphasize childhood learning of individual behavior: children are assumed to learn "scripts" of what events are about to occur, how one should react, and what the outcome will be. These scripts guide behavior and are more likely to elicit violent behavior if they include violent acts that are rewarded rather than punished.

More recent refinements have expanded on this basic description in at least three ways. First, not every violent act can be traced back to scripts; certain situations, which are beyond most people's range of experience, would provoke violent behavior in nearly everyone. Second, while the existence of scripts is nearly universal, their content will depend on chance events during childhood and adolescence. The family, peer groups, and the macrosocial environment all influence an individual's range of experience. Examples of potentially relevant developmental events include the amount of violence seen in the home, through the news and entertainment media, or in the neighborhood; the economic and social rewards to those who commit violence, those who seek to prevent it, and those who become its victims; and cultural practices that tend to instill or disable empathy for victims.

Third, the explanation is becoming enriched through attention to biological influences. A person's nervous system is constantly shaping and being shaped by its environs. Each individual's nervous system responds to a given event in a slightly different way. Information processing in the nervous system is based on excitatory and inhibitory neural signals in sensory and motor pathways that interact with arousing, affective, and memory processes that involve chemical neurotransmitters and hormones. For example, alcohol's action on $GABA_A$ or serotonin receptors may differ in violence-prone individuals due to genetic or maturational factors or due to past exposure to environmental or pharmacological stressors.

In short, the processes that develop an individual's potentials for different violent behaviors are not understandable *exclusively* in any of the following terms: learning, the macrosocial environment, or a biologically determined temperament. Yet each is relevant. Of the many people with the capacity for violent behavior, the few who display it are more likely to have grown up in families and neighborhoods in which it was easy to learn that violence was not negatively sanctioned (or was rewarded), or in which opportunities for violent expressions of frustration occurred frequently. Of the many individuals who live in such high-risk environments, those with certain temperaments will be more likely to act on impulses toward violent behavior, and especially to develop patterns of chronic violent behavior. Regardless of the roles played by learning, the environment, or temperament, when such people commit violent acts, they enter a category that is sometimes assigned such labels as dangerous offenders.

Macrosocial and Microsocial Processes

There is tremendous variation in violence rates over short and long time periods and across macrosocial units—nations, cities, communities within cities, and addresses within communities. Variations over time are too large and transient to be explicable simply by genetic processes over time. Variations across areas are too large to be attributable solely to the congregation of individuals with certain temperaments in certain places. Logically, predisposing factors at the social level must be important determinants of violence levels. The difficulty is in determining what the relevant factors are—a search that is made more difficult by the fact that so many candidates tend to occur together in communities that are plagued by high violence rates.

In communities, one such candidate is the structure of nonviolent channels for acquiring money and power, for dealing with anger, and for achieving sexual gratification. A general lack of legitimate economic opportunity; a widespread, persistent feeling of powerlessness; the decline of social capital that would otherwise pass nonviolent norms from one generation to the next; the lack of constructive recreational activities; a high prevalence of disrupted intimate relationships—all these are symptoms of a macrosocial structure that fails to offer legitimate opportunities to achieve the purposes for which violence is used.

Cultural and subcultural norms, such as acceptance of behavior degrading to women or alienation among members of some ethnic categories against social control agencies managed by members of others, may reduce inhibitions against violence. Cultural practices within a subculture (e.g., trading insults, termed "jonin'" or "playing the dozens" by black teen-age males) sometimes create encounters that culminate in violence. Spike Lee's movie *Do the Right Thing* provides a fictional but plausible account of how conflicts between ethnic subcultures may create a backdrop against which a small altercation triggers a violent confrontation.

Recent research discussed in Chapter 3 focuses attention on what has been called the concentration of poverty—and its consequences such as single-parent households, unsupervised unemployed teenagers, and crowded housing—and its relationship to violence. Enhanced exposure to potentially addictive and expensive drugs without a means of earning the money to buy them may be a potential macrosocial risk factor. And, as discussed in Chapter 6, widespread firearm availability may not affect violence rates but clearly increases the lethal effects of violent events.

Interactions and Interventions

As Chapter 3 illustrates, the difficulty—for both understanding and control—is that predisposing processes interact across all four levels to determine violence levels. A family's place in the economic opportunity structure influences both the risk that a child's neural system will be damaged through premature birth or head injury and the family's access to medical care that might fix the damage. A young adult male's position in the economic structure influences his chance of being chosen as a marriage partner—a fact that influences the risk of violent behavior by both the young adult male and the children he fathers. Neurological problems, by limiting a child's cognitive or communications capacity, make early school failure more likely—perhaps setting the stage for frustration, exclusion from upwardly mobile peer groups, and a low position in the adult opportunity structure.

How frequently individuals engage in acts of violence depends not only on their underlying potentials but also on how frequently they encounter occasions for violence, on the social and legal rewards and punishments for violent behavior, and on interactions between occasions for violence and individual potentials. Whether temperament that predisposes a person to violent behavior is actualized at a particular point in time depends not only on physiology but also on recent exposure to stress, on the chronicity and intensity of recent intoxication, and on other conditions that are influenced by the surrounding environment.

This raises the possibility that so-called dangerous offenders emerge from social structures that generate frequent occasions for violence as well as from high individual potentials toward violent behavior. Moreover, it is likely that their experiences—through the media, within the family, in the community—with violence and its rewards and punishments will be incorporated in their development and will influence their future likelihoods of violence.

Effects on the Environment

Even the preceding discussion oversimplifies by implicitly assuming that the environment is fixed as individuals move through life. In reality, of course, the number and concentration of people pursuing different developmental paths—and the violence level itself—have profound effects on the environment. Unpunished violence may increase the probability of future episodes not only by providing examples that get absorbed into children's development, but also by weakening neighborhood and community institutions or by motivating neighborhood residents to arm themselves.

Chapter 4 recounts an example of how crime and violence may have changed the social structure in some communities in ways that contributed to increases in homicide rates that accompanied the crack epidemics in many cities but did not generally decline as the crack epidemics subsided. In brief, the story runs as follows: the ease of turning powdered cocaine into crack allowed small-scale amateurs to decentralize and expand drug markets that had long been monopolized by organized crime. The market expansion, turf battles, and evolution of the "rules of the game" sparked increases in violence. The resulting fear provided a predisposition, and the crack profits a means, to purchase firearms. In the aggregate, the escalation of violence choked out legitimate economic opportunities and encouraged a mass exodus to the suburbs of families with attachments to the legitimate economy and with the means to relocate. In the eyes of teenagers in the families who stayed behind, the social status of the few remaining "old heads" fell beneath that of successful teenage drug entrepreneurs—leaving open-air drug markets, boarded-up vacant houses, and unemployed youth armed with semiautomatic weapons in communities where homes, thriving businesses, orderly schools, and churches once stood.

The evidence that supports this explanation is fragmentary and inconclusive. Nevertheless, as a theory of violence levels, population movement, and economic decline, it illustrates the point that social-level processes are more than the sum of individuals' actions. In the aggregate, the distributions of individuals' potentials for violence and of occasions for violence damage communities' stocks of social capital—the families, markets, churches, social networks, and other organizations and social institutions that individuals build, maintain, or destroy.

IMPROVING UNDERSTANDING AND CONTROL THROUGH EVALUATION

Table 7-1 presents a scheme for classifying risk factors related to violent behavior. What is required to use it to reduce violence are better data and research on how individuals and communities respond to interventions that modify the risk factors. Because of poorly understood processes that cut across cells of the matrix, neither theoretical nor empirical research confined to a single cell or descriptive level is fully adequate for policy prescriptions. Progress in learning what works depends on sound evaluations of specific policy innovations. If an evaluation can answer a simple question—What effect did this particular innovation have on violence in this time and place?—then, if utilized, that answer becomes a building block for *both* a more generic understanding *and* an improved capacity to control violence.

An analogy may be useful. In the pharmaceutical industry, the development of new therapies proceeds by trial and error within general guidelines offered by basic science and experience. Many promising drugs are tested in this process, but only a few of them are ever approved for general therapeutic use. The Food and Drug Administration requires that any new drug be subjected to extensive testing and proven to be both effective and safe. The selection principle there gives systematic evaluation a primary role that is currently lacking in social program innovations. In our view there should be no greater presumption in social programs than in pharmaceuticals that a new intervention is either safe or effective. Yet, as with pharmaceutical development, the absence of that presumption should be a stimulus for problem solving—iterations of diagnosis, intervention design, evaluation, and intervention refinement in light of evaluation results—not an excuse for inaction.

Learning From Interventions

Three categories of interventions can yield basic lessons concerning the causes and control of violence. The first category includes all those interventions for which violence is the central concern—examples could include legal restrictions on carrying guns in public, school curricula intended to teach conflict resolution skills, incarceration, shelters for battered women, and restrictions on the sale of violent pornography. The case examples of evaluations presented later in this chapter are drawn from this category.

Policy interventions in this category may reduce or mitigate violence through mechanisms such as the following: deterrence through the threat of punishment; incapacitation by isolating people who have demonstrated patterns of violent behavior; opportunity reduction whereby potential targets for robbery, rape, and other violent crimes are rendered less vulnerable to victimization; restriction of violence-related commodities such as guns, some psychoactive drugs, and perhaps sadistic pornographic materials; mitigation of the consequences of violent attack through improved emergency medical response, counseling for rape victims, and so forth; and education in techniques for avoiding violent confrontations.

The second category includes programs and policies that have some effect on risk factors for violent behavior—examples are prenatal care, early childhood education, drug treatment, welfare programs, abortion funding, the minimum legal purchase age for alcohol, and the design and control of public housing. Although these are sometimes advocated as part of a general effort to make streets and homes safer, their other effects are more direct and generally come first in any evaluation of these programs.

The third category includes interventions that have pervasive influence on the quality of life—examples are macroeconomic stabilization policy, zoning rules, and minimum wage legislation. While there is an occasional congressional hearing on how the condition of the economy influences the homicide rate, or how international conflict affects domestic violence, those possible connections have negligible influence on policy making in those areas.[4]

Methods

What methods are available to evaluators of specific interventions? Suppose that a state legislature forms a study commission to consider the possibility of amending the criminal sentencing code to institute enhanced sentencing provisions for gun use in violent crime. One important consideration is whether such enhanced sentences would reduce the murder rate in robberies and other felonies. To form a judgment on the matter, there are various possibilities:

- informed speculation,
- extrapolation from interview data,
- study of natural variation,
- evaluation of changes in law or policy, and
- randomized controlled field experiment.

While each of these approaches has been widely used in other contexts, and each may yield persuasive results under some circumstances, they are not equal: arguably the five research designs form a hierarchy of increasing validity. The randomized experiment generally provides a more valid basis for reaching conclusions concerning effects of the intervention.

The use of randomized field experiments in evaluating crime control and public health measures has been endorsed by various groups of experts (Farrington et al., 1986; Reiss and Boruch, 1991; Coyle et al., 1989), and despite the practical difficulties there have been a number of such experiments successfully completed. The methodological superiority of these studies has tended to enhance their influence with researchers and policy makers. One notable example, the Minneapolis domestic violence experiment, is discussed later in this chapter.

The methodological strengths of randomized controlled field experiments may be unattainable in practice. Ethical, constitutional, or legal restrictions properly prevent some experiments from being undertaken. When experiments are undertaken, difficulties are likely to arise in preserving and monitoring the intended treatments for the experimental and control groups, especially since these treatments typically require that the implementing agency relinquish part of its ordinary discretion and accede to the artificial dictates of the experimental design. Furthermore, collecting complete and reliable data on outcomes may prove difficult due to nonrandom attrition of sample members, and the possibility that the measurement process will be influenced by the experimental interventions. These problems are of course also present in nonexperimental evaluations (Berk, 1989).

A more serious problem with field experiments may arise in extrapolating from the experimental setting to full-scale implementation (Manski, 1990). An experiment is conducted under somewhat artificial conditions and usually on a limited scale. In going from experimental trial to policy, the intervention may change in important ways that influence its effects: administrative and funding arrangements change, the scale of the program increases, the interaction between the program and the sociolegal environment may differ in practice from what it was in the experiment. These and other changes associated with operationalizing experiments often change their outcomes. These problems tend to argue in favor of evaluating "real" changes, using quasi-experimental methods (Cook and Campbell, 1979), paying close attention to understanding the process by which the treatment was "assigned" (Heckman and Hotz, 1989). In many cases the option of conducting a true experiment is not available, and even if it is possible to conduct some sort of experiment, it is unlikely to preempt other approaches. Evaluation research using rigorous quasi-experimental designs is an important tool for assessing the effects of violence control interventions.

Organizational Contexts

Two communities of actors and interests are involved in evaluation research. The community of policy makers and program managers includes legislators, police chiefs, school officials, store owners, television producers, and others responsible for formulating and implementing policies that may influence violence. The community of evaluation researchers involves both the discipline and the experts who do this work and promulgate its norms. Productive evaluation research is of course fostered by a cooperative relationship between these two communities—but that is sometimes difficult to achieve.

Evaluation researchers tend to share certain beliefs about what constitutes persuasive evidence, beliefs that are sometimes at odds with those of the policy-making community. In the public forum in which suggestions for innovations are exchanged, an assertion of efficacy is usually evaluated by whether those making the assertion have suitable credentials, whether the basic idea makes sense, and whether the suggested innovation is responsive to pressing needs of the relevant agency. The research community is also influenced by these considerations but is inclined to withhold judgment until efficacy has been demonstrated through systematic evaluation. Thus the norms of researched evaluation require a wait-and-see attitude that often conflicts with the needs of policy makers to commit to some action quickly in response to public concern and to protect past actions from criticism. In the course of innovation, implementers are usually more exposed than evaluators to external pressures to conform to ideological agendas and to minimize exposure to risks of public failure. A productive relationship between the two communities requires that these differences in timing and vulnerabilities be acknowledged.[5]

Agencies have much to gain from successful evaluations, regardless of the findings. The evaluation is a source of information that is of potential value to the agency concerning the efficacy of a new policy to which there is no long-standing organizational commitment. In some cases the evaluation may be part of a political stratagem for reform, or simply a means for garnering public attention for a new program. If funding for the evaluation comes from outside the agency, it may increase the agency's budget and help support activities that are of value to the agency. The chief executive may receive recognition outside the agency for his or her participation.

Cooperation is fostered by a relationship of mutual trust between the agency and the evaluator, by keeping the financial and organizational burden on the agency small, and by providing the relevant actors in the agency something of value in return for their cooperation. Both agency and evaluator must deal with organizational constraints. The burdens and rewards of conducting the experiment may be unequally distributed among the different layers of the agency organization; in such circumstances, agreement in principle between the agency executive and the evaluators may be insufficient to ensure proper implementation. It will be necessary to secure the compliance of those who are immediately responsible for implementation—the cop on the beat, the classroom teacher, the assistant district attorney.

Another important institutional constraint on evaluations is the availability and quality of data from official records. The opportunity to evaluate an intervention is limited by the quality of data available on outcome measures. While in some cases the evaluator can gather some data with interviews and other procedures, it is usually true that data from official records play an important part in the evaluation of violence countermeasures.

EVALUATION CASE STUDIES

The general observations in the preceding discussion are illustrated here with four cases, each of which involves an evaluation of an intervention intended to reduce violence. Table 7-2 summarizes key aspects of these cases. They differ with respect to the mechanism by which the intervention is intended to reduce violence, by the evaluation strategy, and by the nature of the interaction between evaluator and policy makers. In each case the interventions have been considered for adoption in a number of jurisdictions.

These four cases were not selected on the basis of either methodological excellence or findings of success—they illustrate wide variation in these terms. Rather, this group was assembled to illustrate the importance of sound evaluation methodology, the need for long-term commitments, the likelihood of mixed results, the need for replication, the need for cross-disciplinary collaboration, and the mutually reinforcing roles of basic science and evaluation research. These issues are discussed at the conclusion of this chapter.

Controlling Domestic Violence

In the early 1980s Sherman and Berk (1984) designed and implemented an experiment concerning the consequences of each of the three common police actions in domestic assault cases: arrest, mediation, and ordering the offender off the premises.[6] The experiment was conducted in Minneapolis, using police officers who were assigned to target areas in the city and who volunteered to participate. A participating officer investigating a domestic violence call first determined whether it fit the definition of experimental cases (i.e., misdemeanor assault in which the victim did not want to seek an arrest warrant). If so, he followed one of the three responses designated in advance, depending on the outcome of a random drawing. The researchers followed up each of these experimental cases for six months with biweekly interviews of the victim (whenever possible) and by monitoring police records to determine if the suspect had been rearrested for a subsequent offense. As it turned out, the rearrest rate was about 50 percent lower for the arrest group than for the other two groups combined (Sherman and Berk, 1984).

The policy importance of this result persuaded the National Institute of Justice to fund several replications in other cities. The results of these follow-up experiments in Omaha, Charlotte, and Milwaukee have been substantially different from those of the Minneapolis experiment. In particular, the replications offered no evidence that in these three cities an on-scene arrest reduces the average recidivism rate of suspects relative to other

TABLE 7-2 Summary of Four Case Studies

	Sanctions for Domestic Violence	Mandatory Sentences for Gun Crimes	Violence Prevention Curriculum	Two-Clerk Requirement
Intervention	Alternative police responses to misdemeanor domestic assaults	Law mandating longer sentences if felony involving a gun	10-hour curriculum to teach youths about violence	Law mandating two clerks in stores at night
Violence reduction mechanism	Specific deterrence	General deterrence and incapacitation	Enhance skills in avoiding violent encounters	Reduce criminal opportunity
Implementing agency	Police	Courts	Schools	Convenience stores
Evaluation method	Randomized controlled field experiment (multiple sites)	Quasi experiment (multiple sites)	Controlled field experiment	Quasi experiment
Data	Interviews Police records	Vital statistics Police and court records	Questionnaires	Police records

police actions (Dunford et al., 1990; Hirschel et al., 1990; Sherman and Smith, 1991). Analysis of the Milwaukee data suggests that the consequences of arresting a domestic violence suspect may differ depending on his socioeconomic status, with positive effects for some groups canceling negative effects for others (Sherman and Smith, 1991). The results in Colorado Springs and Dade County, Florida, showed a deterrent effect of arrest in victim interview measures but not in official data (Sherman, 1992).

The Minneapolis experiment was originally justified in terms of its potential contribution to basic deterrence research, rather than as an evaluation of specific policy alternatives for domestic violence (Sherman, 1980). The National Institute of Justice funded it as part of its Crime Control Theory Program. As a random assignment experiment in the use of arrest, it is an important methodological innovation in the study of specific deterrence. The results of the Minneapolis experiment and its replications are widely cited by criminologists seeking general principles concerning the effects of sanctions on the subsequent behavior of criminals. As it turned out, however, the Minneapolis results also figured importantly in the policy arena, being frequently cited as justification for the police to adopt a more punitive approach in domestic violence cases (Lempert, 1989).

Minneapolis was chosen as the site of the original experiment because the new police chief there, Anthony Bouza, believed in the importance of field research and was a friend and mentor of the principal investigator, Lawrence Sherman. The Minneapolis City Council members welcomed the project as a federally financed mechanism for training police to be more sensitive to domestic violence victims. And although the midlevel management in the police force actively opposed the experiment, a number of patrol officers were recruited to participate after an intensive "marketing" effort by the evaluator. Maintaining their cooperation proved to be one of the most difficult challenges facing the evaluators. Similar problems were encountered in the replication cities.

Despite these problems of implementation, the experiments were able to preserve the experimental manipulation and generate an adequate number of cases for statistical purposes. From the perspective of science, then, the Minneapolis experiment and its successors have been valuable. They have demonstrated that within the range of sanctions that were studied, the special deterrence mechanism of arrest is only conditionally effective in reducing the average recidivism rate of domestic violence suspects, and the necessary conditions are not yet known.

The strength of the experimental design was in the internal validity of the results—yet there are important questions that could not be addressed within this approach. Police departments that increase the use of arrest in domestic violence cases may produce a general deterrent effect, whether or not there is any effect on recidivism rates. Measuring this general effect requires a different approach than measuring recidivism. The focus shifts from the level of the individual to the level of the jurisdiction, and a true experiment would require implementation of new police procedures in samples of randomly selected *jurisdictions* rather than *cases*—an approach that would raise truly formidable implementation problems in the absence of an agency authorized to impose such procedures on jurisdictions. Fortunately, data are available on jurisdiction-level victimization rates for domestic violence, so it is possible to employ quasi-experimental methods to evaluate the general deterrence effect of changes in police practice and related interventions. This type of evaluation has not been done in the case of domestic violence, but has been widely employed elsewhere. The basic approach is illustrated by the next case.

Mandatory Sentences for Gun Crimes

In 1975 Florida implemented a highly publicized law that required three-year mandatory sentences for carrying a firearm while committing a felony. A number of other states followed suit in subsequent years. These laws, and the means by which they were implemented, were sufficiently alike in Florida, Michigan, and Pennsylvania that they can be viewed as near-identical "treatments" in a natural experiment. Colin Loftin and his associates (Loftin and McDowall, 1981; Loftin et al., 1991) evaluated the impact of these laws in each of six cities, using a quasi-experimental statistical method. They found clear evidence that implementation of these mandatory sentencing provisions tended to reduce the gun homicide rate while having little or no effect on the nongun homicide rate. This result is important evidence on the general deterrent effect of sentence severity.[7] This result is particularly interesting given the near-consensus by criminologists that sentence severity does not matter much in deterring violent crime (Cook, 1980).

In their evaluation of the mandatory sentencing law, Loftin et al. analyzed monthly data on homicides for several years before and after the law's implementation in each of six cities. Their evidence for its effectiveness is that the monthly gun homicide counts tend to be lower following the intervention than would be expected based on an extrapolation (using the ARIMA technique) of the monthly series before the intervention. While it is possible that the change in gun homicide rates was the result of some other change in policy or environment that happened to coincide with the implementation of the gun law, that seems unlikely.[8] First, while such a coincidence could happen once, the results are based on six cities in three different states. Second, *nongun* homicide rates did not shift (either up or down) at the time of the interventions, as they most likely would have if there had been some other change in the factors influencing criminal violence.

The domestic violence experiments required a close working relationship between the evaluator and the agency, with patrol officers agreeing to relinquish their discretion to the dictates of the experiment. In contrast, the quasi-experimental evaluation of mandatory sentencing laws was carried out almost entirely at arm's length. The evaluators made no effort to manipulate the behavior of the front-line agencies. The evaluation was conducted on the basis of data generated by the routine reporting systems of police departments and the medical examiner's office (for homicide data).

Of course, the quality of these data limits the potential of the quasi-experimental approach. The monthly homicide counts were reliable. But in assessing the effect of mandatory sentencing on other types of violent crime, the evaluators faced serious data limitations. First, the Uniform Crime Reports did not distinguish between gun robbery and other armed robbery prior to 1975. Second, it appeared to the investigators that the time series data for both assault and robbery were seriously flawed by variations in reporting and recordkeeping practices. They conclude that their only trustworthy results are for homicide.

Even with that limitation, this quasi-experimental evaluation offers credible evidence concerning some of the effects of this type of intervention, and hence about the basic mechanism of general deterrence.

The Two-Clerk Ordinance

In April 1987, the city of Gainesville, Florida, began requiring convenience stores to employ two clerks during nighttime hours of operation. This ordinance was adopted in response to a detailed analysis by the Gainesville Police Department of convenience store robberies. The department's analysis, which was based on interviews with robbers and other types of information, concluded that having two clerks on the premises was a substantial deterrent to robbers.[9] In the six months following implementation of the rule, the number of convenience store robberies was less than half the number in the corresponding period of the previous year ((Wilson, 1990). The apparent success of the two-clerk rule in Gainesville was touted by the police department and later encouraged the state legislature in Florida to consider making that city's requirement statewide (Kilborn, 1991).

The Gainesville intervention is of interest both as an antidote to convenience store robbery and more generally as an example of the opportunity reduction mechanism for curtailing violent crime. A convenience store with two clerks may be a less attractive robbery target than one with a single clerk because of the increased likelihood of victim resistance and the increased chance that the victims will be effective witnesses in the subsequent police investigation. Other tactics for reducing convenience store robbery through opportunity reduction have also been tried. Indeed, five months before Gainesville implemented the two-clerk requirement, an ordinance took effect there that required convenience stores to install security cameras, to train night employees in robbery prevention, to limit cash on hand, and to maintain visibility between the interior of the store and the parking lot (Wilson, 1990)—requirements that previously had been adopted nationwide by the Southland Corporation for its 7-Eleven stores. Opportunity reduction tactics have also been instituted in public transportation and other commercial venues to reduce robbery victimization rates (Cook, 1986). Evidence on the effectiveness of such tactics has practical application and also provides important data for scholars concerned with criminal motivation and cognition.

Evaluating the consequences of the two-clerk rule has proven difficult, for reasons that illustrate the importance of good evaluation practice. The Gainesville Police Department concluded that the rule caused a dramatic reduction in convenience store robbery, basing its conclusion on the fact that the convenience store robbery rate was substantially lower in the months following the two-clerk rule than it had been during the preceding year. Such a simple before-and-after approach to measuring an effect is unreliable and, in the Gainesville case, yielded an erroneous conclusion.

A practitioner, retired police chief Jerry Wilson (1990) provided a more complete evaluation funded by the National Association of Convenience Stores. First, he demonstrated that there had been a sharp spurt in the convenience store robbery rate during fall 1986; this spurt ended in December with the arrest of three men suspected of being responsible for a great many robberies. The two-clerk rule went into effect the following April and had no discernible effect on monthly rates around that time. (There were two robberies each month from January through August). Thus the fact that there were many fewer convenience store robberies in 1987 than 1986 can be more credibly explained by the arrests in December than by the implementation of the two-clerk rule. This conclusion gains support from the fact that the convenience store robbery rate in the surrounding county followed the same temporal pattern as in Gainesville, even though the stores in the county were not subject to the two-clerk requirement.

Thus the conclusion that the two-clerk rule was effective fails when rival hypotheses for the observed pattern are considered.[10] The lesson is that, as in any other enterprise, evaluation can be done well or poorly, and the results may be sensitive to the quality of the work. But while the two-clerk rule did not have the large impact that the Gainesville Police Department claimed for it, there remains a possibility that it had a small deterrent effect. Reliably detecting a small effect (say, 5 or 10%) is very difficult in a city as small as Gainesville. Temporal patterns are difficult to ascertain simply because the numbers are so small. So the ultimate conclusion from the Gainesville story is not that there was no effect, but rather that there was no miracle. A careful evaluation does not rule out the existence of a small effect or the possibility that the rule is worth promulgating. The setting and circumstances of this intervention simply do not allow for a more definite conclusion.

Violence Prevention Curriculum for Adolescents

The development of the *Violence Prevention Curriculum for Adolescents* (Prothrow-Stith, 1987) was motivated by the high rate of intentional violence among youthful acquaintances and a belief that youths could be trained to defuse potentially violent confrontations. Originally developed for use in tenth-grade health classes in Boston high schools, in a series of 10 sessions, it informs participants about their risks for interpersonal violence, teaches them strategies for reducing that risk, and uses videotape both to analyze other violent encounters and to role-play the risk reduction strategies. The developers of the curriculum later adapted it for use in community settings outside the school and launched a comprehensive Violence Prevention Project that involved community-based organizations and mass media campaigns (Prothrow-Stith, 1987). The aim of the program is to change both attitudes and behavior.

In 1987 the Education Development Center, Inc. (EDC) conducted a field-test evaluation of its violence prevention curriculum, with funding from the National Institute of Justice.[11] The results of this evaluation offer only weak support for the claim that this curriculum is effective in reducing violent behavior or victimization. Nevertheless, by the end of 1990, more than 4,000 copies of the curriculum had been sold. While the dissemination of the evaluation results apparently helped stimulate sales and adoptions, the widespread interest in this curriculum is not due to systematic evaluation results so much as other factors: the concern by school administrators that something be done about adolescent violence, the lack of an alternative intervention clearly demonstrated to be effective, and the impressive credentials and visibility of the author, Deborah Prothrow-Stith, a public health professional.

The evaluation of the original curriculum was conducted in six schools across the United States. These schools were recruited primarily from among those that had contacted the EDC concerning the curriculum. In each school one teacher of tenth-grade classes was selected for training, and his or her classes were divided between treatment and control conditions. Participating teachers received one day of training at EDC in teaching the curriculum. The evaluation was primarily based on responses to student questionnaires about attitudes and behaviors, administered before the onset of the program and two months after its completion. A longer-term follow-up was ruled out by the unwillingness of teachers to devote time to administering another questionnaire. Because no posttests were administered in two of the schools, pre-post comparisons were possible for only four schools.

Of the seven questions relating to behavior, for only one did the curriculum appear to make a difference: in all four schools, students who received the curriculum reported having fewer fights during the past week than did those in the comparison classes. It is not clear whether this difference in self-reported behavior was due to real changes in behavior or to changes in the students' attitudes, which caused them to be less willing to admit being in a fight. The evaluators did not make use of official school or police records to validate self-report data.[12]

The results of this evaluation are not persuasive that this approach is helpful in reducing aggressive behavior by high school students. As discussed in Chapter 3, accumulated evidence on the stability of aggressive behavior after middle childhood leaves open the possibility that with suitable changes, a program that applied these principles in the early grades might have shown more success. A more informative evaluation would require more resources. In the absence of clear evidence of effectiveness, it is notable that the curriculum has enjoyed such widespread success and has engendered the more comprehensive community-based program. In any event, the ongoing evaluation of that new, expanded version of the intervention will be of great interest.

Lessons From the Case Studies

These case studies illustrate that successful interventions, sound evaluations, and basic science are mutually supportive but difficult to coordinate and carry out. There is little disagreement with the axiom, "The best way to find out if X affects Y is to manipulate X and measure the change in Y." Unless that is done effectively, neither researchers nor policy makers are entitled to make many definitive statements about what works and what does not.

Yet more is required when Y is violence in homes and communities, and X is a law, police procedure, school curriculum, community-based activity, traditional mode of discipline, or therapeutic intervention. The risk factors discussed in Part II and arrayed in Table 7-1 suggest promising Xs at different levels of description and at different stages in causal chains. But turning those suggestions into workable and effective solutions to violence requires a problem-solving approach that includes designing publicly acceptable interventions, evaluating them, using the results to refine the intervention, and replicating the evaluation. That process can contribute to improved violence control capability while it contributes to scientific understanding of violence. But it takes commitment by policy makers and the research community alike to the principles outlined below.

The Importance of Sound Methodology

Good intentions and a plausible story are not enough to ensure the success of an intervention. The only way to determine if something works is to try it, in a way that lends itself to reliable evaluation. Systematic testing and evaluation are essential to progress in reducing violent behavior.

Evaluation research often depends on existing data systems, and it is limited by the quality of such systems, the breadth of the data collected, and the compatibility with other systems. A particular problem is difficulty of linking data on intentional injuries and other consequences to data on the violent events that cause them.

Randomized controlled field experiments usually have important advantages as an evaluation strategy, yet in some circumstances it is possible to learn a great deal from well-designed "uncontrolled" interventions. Regardless of the basic approach, quality control is as important in evaluation as in other tasks. Seemingly minor methodological flaws in evaluations have occasionally led to advocacy of unnecessary or overly costly interventions and to embarrassment of the advocates; more frequently, they have created uncertainties that led to a misleading conclusion that "nothing works" or that some promising intervention strategy should be abandoned rather than revised and reevaluated.

Long-Term Commitments

Because the predisposing processes relevant to violence work over periods of years, some evaluations will require long-term commitments from implementing agencies, evaluators, and sponsors. Sponsors' commitments of program and project funding must therefore be long term to encourage the best researchers to invest their careers in them. Researchers who join such efforts must make long-term career commitments and maintain them despite publication pressures and the emergence of alternative short-term opportunities—an undertaking that young researchers may find easier as civil servants than in academic settings. And agency administrators who collaborate in problem-solving initiatives must limit their commitments to those they can maintain through budget cuts, changes in political priorities, and other pressures.

Anticipating Mixed Results

Evaluation results are rarely clear-cut. More commonly, an intervention produces the anticipated effect on some outcome measures but not others, or it affects some subjects but not others, or the results are partially obscured by some measurement problem, by some breakdown in implementing the intervention or evaluation, or by some unexpected intervening event.

Such findings should suggest further analyses of the available data, changes in the intervention, or both. The results of reanalyses, while not as conclusive as are the basic results of a randomized experiment, may still provide valuable suggestions for revising the intervention or its implementation, for applying it to a different target population, or for adapting it to some specific subcultural or community context. These suggestions can and should be tested by revising and replicating the evaluation under the different conditions.

Replication

Promising interventions are rarely subjected to more than a few replications before adoption, yet replication is even more critical in evaluation than in the laboratory sciences. Because the effects of most interventions depend on local context, several replications will usually be needed even to distinguish "usually successful" interventions from "usually unsuccessful" ones, a point noted by Reiss and Boruch (1991).

Once replications have established that some intervention works under at least some conditions, more broad-based comparative replications can help to determine what works best in these conditions. Often a comparison of interventions by different professions or control agencies—arrest versus alcohol abuse treatment, for example—is needed. These require more interagency collaboration than is traditional. Because violent events are so diverse, no single institution can expect to prevent more than a small fraction of them. This should be no cause for despair, but rather a call for a broadly diversified strategy of violence control analogous to diversified strategies as pursued in disease control.

Communicating Across Disciplines

Reflecting on its own experience, the panel believes that the difficulty of communication across disciplines and violence control agencies is a major barrier to developing effective interventions. Interdisciplinary communication requires each researcher to invest substantial time and effort in learning one another's vocabularies, in learning how phenomena at different levels of description are measured and classified, and in learning about the fundamental problems and current priorities in other violence-related disciplines. It also requires forums for interdisciplinary exchanges of research findings—something that does not naturally occur in most professional meetings. And it would be facilitated by a clearinghouse in which information could be easily accessed and shared about the current state of the art, disputes, and gaps in knowledge in the many fields concerned with a particular problem in violence research.

Building Science Through Evaluation

Evaluation research has two overlapping but distinct purposes. The first is reactive: to evaluate innovations that have become important because they are receiving consideration for widespread adoption. The second is proactive: to gain knowledge about the effectiveness of various mechanisms for violence control. The reactive agenda is important because of its immediate relevance to ongoing policy decisions. The proactive agenda is important if criminological theory is to be grounded in all available evidence—specifically evidence about relevant causal relationships that cross traditional disciplinary boundaries, particularly between biological and social levels of description. Evaluation evidence that an intervention grounded in some widely accepted theory failed may be the first sign that some such cross-cutting relationship exists.

Evaluation research can be a rich source of evidence to guide theory development, and theory should provide some guidance to policy choices. Innovations in agriculture, medicine, and industry are routinely subjected to testing—sometimes on thousands of subjects over a decade or more—before adoption and dissemination. This practice is much weaker in social interventions, and the results are haphazard policies and a dearth of systematic knowledge.

Basic science, policy development, and evaluation research should not be isolated activities. Rather, they comprise the fundamental triad of a problem-solving approach to violence.

NOTES

1 Deterrence theories differ with respect to their explanations of how people perceive and weigh different sanctions, how alternatives to crime affect choices, the crime types that are most responsive to incentives, and other factors that affect how sanctions influence crimes. Reviews of this literature can be found in Blumstein et al. (1978), Cook (1977), Geerken and Gove (1975), Gibbs (1975), Klepper and Nagin (1989), Paternoster (1987), Tittle (1980), and Zimring and Hawkins (1971).

2 The analysis by Cohen and Canela-Cacho is limited to the post-1975 period because pre-1975 data on individual frequencies of violent offending are not available.

3 Analyzing the criminal careers of a sample of Denver convicts, Petersilia and Greenwood (1978) reported that, if all members of the sample had received one-year terms (i.e., a policy of relatively high certainty of a short sentence), their crimes would have been reduced by 15 percent through incapacitation at a cost of a 50 percent increase in prison population. Mandatory minimum four-year terms only for those with prior convictions (i.e., lower certainty of a long sentence) would have achieved the same crime reduction, but with a 150 percent population increase.

4 For example, Cook and Zarkin (1985) used data on the last nine business cycles to demonstrate that robbery is somewhat countercyclical while criminal homicide is not.

5 Paul Offner describes a life cycle theory of innovations in the welfare reform area. When a reform is being launched, the parties involved are caught up in the excitement and resist research considerations. Administrators are wary of the mysteries of evaluation methods and in any case feel sure of what works and what doesn't. Advocates are by definition convinced that they know what needs to be done; moreover, they are likely to object to experimental designs that require different treatments for similar recipients. Later, when the results almost invariably fall short of heady expectations, research questions are asked concerning costs and benefits (Manski, 1990).

6 This account is informed by a narrative prepared at the panel's request by Lawrence Sherman.

7 An increase in sentence severity may also reduce crime rates through the mechanism of incapacitation. If that were the only effective mechanism, then the observed reduction in crime would occur gradually. For example, if a mandatory sentencing law increased the minimum sentence from one year to three, then there would be no effect on crime during the first year following its implementation. But the evidence suggests an immediate effect, which suggests that the deterrence mechanism was important.

8 It has been pointed out that a shift in public attitudes may have preceded enactment of the new laws, and that the analysis by Loftin et al. could not eliminate the possibility that such a shift, rather than the law, caused the decrease in gun homicides. While that is technically possible, we consider it unlikely that the attitudes of community residents who were contemplating gun homicides coincide with those of the residents whose efforts brought about the new law.

9 A detailed account of this rather unique effort on the part of the police department is given in Goldstein (1990).

10 Wilson (1990) suggests two other rival hypotheses. First is the implementation in November 1986 of the Gainesville ordinance requiring that convenience stores institute various robbery-prevention measures. Second is the possibility that the data on convenience store robberies are affected by the two-clerk rule; some convenience store robbery reports are false, intended to cover up a theft by an employee, and such false reports would be less likely if two clerks were on the premises.

11 This account is based to some extent on a narrative provided at the panel's request by the Education Development Center.

12 School and police records provide incomplete counts of fights, because many fights occur off school grounds and most fights do not lead to arrest. However, these records might have been useful in validating self-reports of some events.

REFERENCES

Berk, Richard A.
1989 What Your Mother Never Told You about Randomized Field Experiments. UCLA Program in Social Statistics Working Paper.

Blumstein, Alfred, Jacqueline Cohen, and Daniel Nagin, eds.
1978 *Deterrence and Incapacitation: Estimating the Effects of Criminal Sanctions on Crime Rates.* Washington, D.C.: National Academy of Sciences.

Boland, Barbara, Paul Mahanna, and Ronald Sones
1992 *The Prosecution of Felony Arrests, 1988.* NCJ-130914. Washington, D.C.: U.S. Government Printing Office.

Cook, Philip J.
1977 Punishment and crime: A critique of current findings concerning the preventive effects of punishment. *Law and Contemporary Problems* 41:164-204.
1980 Research in criminal deterrence: Laying the groundwork for the second decade. In N. Morris and M. Tonry, eds., *Crime and Justice: An Annual Review of Research.* Vol. 2. Chicago: University of Chicago Press.
1986 The demand and supply of criminal opportunities. In M. Tonry and N. Morris, eds., *Crime and Justice: An Annual Review of Research.* Vol. 7. Chicago: University of Chicago Press.

Cook, Philip J., and Gary A. Zarkin
1985 Crime and the business cycle. *Journal of Legal Studies* XIV:115-128.

Cook, Thomas D., and Donald T. Campbell
1979 *Quasi-Experimentation: Design and Analysis Issues for Field Settings.* Boston: Houghton Mifflin.

Coyle, Susan L., Robert F. Boruch, and Charles F. Turner, eds.
1989 *Evaluating AIDS Prevention Programs.* Washington, D.C.: National Academy Press.

Dodge, K.A.
1986 A social information processing model of social competence in children. Pp. 77-125 in M. Perlmutter, ed., *Minnesota Symposium in Child Psychology.* Vol. 18. Hillsdale, N.J.: Erlbaum.

Dunford, Franklyn A., David Huizinga, and Delbert Elliott
1990 The role of arrest in domestic assault: The Omaha police experiment. *Criminology* 28:183-206.

Farrington, David P., Lloyd E. Ohlin, and James Q. Wilson
1986 *Understanding and Controlling Crime: Toward a New Research Strategy*. New York: Springer Verlag.

Geerken, Michael R., and Walter R. Gove
1975 Deterrence: Some theoretical considerations. *Law and Society Review* 9:497-513.

Gibbs, Jack P.
1975 *Crime, Punishment, and Deterrence*. New York: Elsevier.

Goldstein, Herman
1990 *Problem-Oriented Policing*. New York: McGraw-Hill.

Heckman, James J., and V. Joseph Hotz
1989 Choosing among alternative nonexperimental methods for estimating the impact of social programs: The case of manpower training. *Journal of the American Statistical Association* 84(408):862-880.

Hirschel, J. David, Ira W. Hutchison III, Charles W. Dean, Joseph J. Kelley, and Carolyn E. Pesackis
1990 *Charlotte Spouse Assault Replication Project: Final Report*. Washington, D.C.: National Institute of Justice.

Kilborn, Peter T.
1991 Rethinking safety in workplace that lures crime. *New York Times*, April 7, pp. 1, 27.

Klepper, Steven, and Daniel Nagin
1989 The criminal deterrence literature: Implications for research on taxpayer compliance. Pp. 126-155 in J.A. Roth and J.T. Scholz, eds., *Taxpayer Compliance*. Volume 2: *Social Science Perspectives*. Washington, D.C.: National Academy Press.

Langan, Patrick A.
1991 America's soaring prison population. *Science* 251:1568-1573.

Lempert, Richard
1989 Humility is a virtue: On the publicization of policy-relevant research. *Law & Society Review* 23(1):145-161.

Loftin, Colin, and David McDowall
1981 "One with a gun gets you two": Mandatory sentencing and firearms violence in Detroit. *Annals of the American Academy of Political and Social Science* 150:455.

Loftin, Colin, David McDowall, and Brian Wiersema
1991 A Comparative Study of the Preventive Effects of Mandatory Sentencing Laws for Gun Crimes. Unpublished manuscript. College Park, Md.: University of Maryland Institute of Criminal Justice and Criminology.

Manski, Charles F.
1990 Where we are in the evaluation of federal social welfare programs. *Focus* 12(4).

Methvin, Eugene H.
1991 An anti-crime solution: Lock up more criminals. *Washington Post*, October 27, p. C1, C4.

Paternoster, R.
1987 The deterrent effect of the perceived certainty and severity of punishment: A review of the evidence and issues. *Justice Quarterly* 4(2):101-146.

Petersilia, J., and P.W. Greenwood
1978 Mandatory prison sentences: Their projected effects on crime and prison population. *Journal of Criminal Law and Criminology* 69(4):604-615.

Prothrow-Stith, D.
1987 *Violence Prevention Curriculum for Adolescents.* Newton, Mass.: Education Development Center.

Reiss, A.J., Jr., and R. Boruch
1991 The program review team approach and multisite experiments: The spouse assault replication program. Pp. 33-44 in R.S. Turpin and J.M. Sinscare, eds., *Multisite Evaluations.* San Francisco: Jossey Bass.

Sherman, Lawrence
1980 The Specific Deterrent Effects of Arrest for Domestic Violence: A Randomized Field Experiment. Proposal submitted to the National Institute of Justice. Washington, D.C.: Police Foundation.
1992 *Policing Domestic Violence: Experiments and Dilemmas.* New York: Free Press.

Sherman, Lawrence, and Richard A. Berk
1984 The specific deterrent effects of arrest for domestic assault. *American Sociological Review* 49:261-271.

Sherman, Lawrence, and Douglas A. Smith
1991 Interaction Effects of Formal and Informal Social Control for Domestic Violence. Unpublished manuscript. College Park, Md.: University of Maryland.

Tittle, C.R.
1980 *Sanctions and Social Deviance: The Question of Deterrence.* New York: Praeger.

Wilson, Jerry V.
1990 Convenience Store Robberies: The Gainesville, Florida 2-Clerk Law. Washington, D.C.: Crime Control Research Corp.

Zimring, F., and Hawkins, G.
1971 The legal threat as an instrument of social change. *Journal of Social Issues* 27:33.

8

Recommendations

To make progress in the understanding and control of violent behavior, we call for a balanced program of efforts with short-term and long-term payoffs:

(1) problem-solving initiatives of pragmatic, focused, methodologically sound collaborative efforts by policy makers, evaluation researchers, and basic researchers;

(2) modifying and expanding national and local violence measurement systems for diagnosing particular violence problems and measuring the effects of interventions designed to solve them;

(3) programs of relatively small-scale research projects in areas that have been largely neglected by federal violence research sponsors; and

(4) the multicommunity research program described in Chapter 3, which is intended to expand society's capacities to understand and to modify community-, individual-, and biological-level processes that influence individuals' potentials for violent behavior.

The problem-solving initiatives and research programs in neglected areas can fairly quickly make incremental contributions to the understanding and control of violent behavior. The improvement of violence measurement systems and the multicommunity research program, while requiring longer initial investment periods, will lay the groundwork for better diagnosis and understanding of violence and for the design of more effective intervention programs.

PROBLEM-SOLVING INITIATIVES

Available evidence suggests an abundance of promising preventive strategies. As explained in Chapter 7, implementation of these strategies through specific interventions should be an iterative process: diagnosis and intervention design, evaluation involving outcome measures at multiple levels of observation, refining the intervention in light of evaluation results, and replications of the evaluation. Over time, repeated iterations of these steps can expand society's capacity to control violence, and simultaneously contribute knowledge about the processes that cause it. This process should be used in a series of efforts focused on specific components of violence—each of which, although significant, accounts for only a small fraction of all violent events. We call this strategy problem solving in violence.

Six areas seem especially promising for this problem-solving approach. In the next 15 years, sustained collaboration by policy makers, disciplinary researchers, and evaluation researchers in these initiatives could make major cumulative contributions to better control and understanding of specific violence problems.

Recommendation 1: We recommend that sustained problem-solving initiatives be undertaken in six specific areas for which systematic intervention design, evaluation, and replication could contribute to the understanding and control of violence:

(a) **intervening in the biological and psychosocial development of individuals' potentials for violent behavior,** with special attention to preventing brain damage associated with low birthweight and childhood head trauma, cognitive-behavioral techniques for preventing aggressive and violent behavior and inculcating prosocial behavior, and the learning of attitudes that discourage violent sexual behavior;

(b) **modifying places, routine activities, and situations that promote violence,** with special attention to commercial robberies, high-risk situations for sexual violence, and violent events in prisons and schools;

(c) **maximizing the violence reduction effects of police interventions in illegal markets,** using systematic tests and evaluations to discover which disruption tactics for the illegal drug and firearm markets have the greatest violence reduction effects;

(d) modifying the roles of commodities—including firearms, alcohol, and other psychoactive drugs—in inhibiting or promoting violent events or their consequences, with special attention to reducing weapon lethality through public education and technological strategies; ascertaining patterns of firearms acquisition and use by criminals and juveniles; ascertaining and modifying the pharmacological, developmental, and situational processes through which alcohol promotes violent behavior; pharmacologically managing aggressive behavior during opiate withdrawal; ascertaining whether smoking cocaine promotes violence through special pharmacological effects; and reducing drug market violence by reducing demand for illegal psychoactive drugs;

(e) intervening to reduce the potentials for violence in bias crimes, gang activities, and community transitions; and

(f) implementing a comprehensive initiative to reduce partner assault, including risk assessment; experimentation with arrest, less expensive criminal justice interventions, public awareness campaigns, batterers' counseling programs, alcohol abuse treatment for perpetrators, and family services; and further analyses of the relationships between women's shelter availability and assault and homicide rates.

We explain these initiatives more fully in the sections that follow.

Development of Violence Potentials

Five specific elements of biological and psychosocial development discussed in Chapter 3 warrant particular attention in problem-solving initiatives:

- Brain dysfunctions that interfere with language processing or cognition: What is their importance as a risk factor for aggression? How effectively can they be reduced by interventions to prevent substance abuse by pregnant women and to reduce children's exposure to environmental toxins including lead? What is their long-term effect on violent behavior?
- Cognitive-behavioral preventive interventions: What is the comparative effectiveness of the following approaches to reducing childhood aggression in different subpopulations: parent training, school-based antibullying programs, social skills training, cogni-

tive-behavioral interventions that stress the undesirability of aggression and teach nonviolent conflict resolution, and promotion of television programs that encourage prosocial, nonviolent behavior and that appeal to children of diverse cultural backgrounds?

- Prevention of school failure: What are the comparative and cumulative effects of preschool educational enrichment and early-grade interventions, including tutoring by peers or trained high-school students, on early-grade school failure rates? On childhood aggression? On later adolescent and adult violence?
- Development of violent sexual behavior: How important are the following as risk factors: exposure to abnormally high testosterone levels during fetal development, childhood sexual abuse victimization, the learning of tolerant attitudes toward violent acts against women, the development of sexual preferences for violent stimuli, and chronic alcohol use? How do sexual arousal patterns differ between samples of known violent sex offenders and other samples? Are these measures related to any specific neurological, endocrine, or genetic markers?
- Systematic evaluations of preventive and therapeutic interventions for sexual violence: development and testing of early preventive strategies and education about sexual violence; and behavioral therapies such as relapse prevention therapy, assertiveness therapy, and anger management therapy.

Modifying Places and Situations

Even successful developmental interventions will take several years to show effects, and they will prevent only violent acts that have developmental roots. Interventions with a situational perspective should be considered as well in formulating preventive strategies.

For a few people, biological interventions may prevent violent behavior in situations that provoke anxiety but not violent behavior by most individuals. One promising initiative for reducing this problem is the development of anxiolytics that act on the serotonergic system.

Other situations increase the risk of violent behavior for a broad spectrum of individuals. These risks may be more efficiently reduced by modifying characteristics of places and encounters. Based on the discussion in Chapter 3, the following appear to be among the most promising of these:

- Places, routine activities, and encounters: What are the specific risk factors for violent events in high-risk places and encounters, and how can they be effectively modified? By how much are situational risks of violent behavior and victimization increased by alcohol consumption?

- Violence in commercial robberies: What interventions can reduce the numbers of persons who control valuables in exposed locations at night in the course of their employment? Where such situations cannot be eliminated, what modifiable factors can reduce the chances and consequences of violent victimization?
- Situational prevention of sexual violence: How can the harms of sexual violence be most effectively reduced by separating offenders and victims (e.g., by institutionalizing offenders and sheltering victims of partner assaults), by modifying high-risk situations, and by repairing the physical and psychological consequences of victimization? How should prevention of events involving acquaintances and intimates differ from prevention of events involving strangers?
- Violence between custodians and wards: What is the incidence of violent victimizations in schools and prisons? What are the risk factors for violent events in these places? What are the effects of modifying these risk factors?

Illegal Markets

There are plausible reasons to anticipate violent events in illegal drug markets, yet only fragmentary and conflicting evidence exists on how market disruption by law enforcement agencies affects drug market violence levels. The following problem-solving initiatives should therefore receive high priority:

- illegal drug markets (Chapter 4): ascertaining differences in violence[1] patterns for crack houses, "runner-beeper" operations, and open-air drug markets; evaluating the effects on violence of current street-level law enforcement tactics, including possible differential effects in those three types of markets; evaluating the effects of proactive policing on drug-market violence; comparing the effects of centralized and street-level drug law enforcement strategies on violence levels;
- illegal firearm markets (Chapter 6): regular "trace studies" of the distribution channels for firearms acquired by juveniles and used in crimes and tests of interventions for disrupting those channels at the wholesale level; evaluations of intervention programs to enforce existing firearms regulations with street-level tactics currently in use for disrupting illegal drug markets (e.g., "buy-bust" operations).

Other Violence-Related Aspects of Commodities

Beyond their roles in illegal markets, firearms and psychoactive drugs including alcohol influence the chances and consequences of violent events in other ways.

Firearms

Based on the discussion in Chapter 6, the diagnosis and evaluation components of problem-solving initiatives are important respectively in two relationships between firearms and violence.

- Ownership and use: What are the most common patterns of ownership, acquisition, and use of firearms—especially for juveniles and criminals, and for handguns and assault weapons (under alternative definitions)? For what purposes are these weapons acquired and carried? How frequently are gun-owning intended crime victims able to deploy their guns in self-defense and prevent injury or death?
- Reduction of injury and lethality: How do public education and technological interventions intended to reduce firearms injuries and deaths affect the incidence and consequences of violent firearm use?

Alcohol and Other Psychoactive Drugs

Three issues that pertain to the roles of both alcohol and other psychoactive drugs in violent events should receive high priority in problem-solving initiatives:

- Continue developing and refining interventions to prevent adolescents from becoming abusers of alcohol and other psychoactive drugs, and measure the effects on subsequent violent behavior (Chapter 4).
- Use patterns (Chapter 4): What are the most common patterns of psychoactive drug use (including alcohol, and emphasizing use of multiple drugs)? As benchmarks for analyzing causal relationships, what are the profiles of alcohol and other psychoactive drug use by time of day and day of week, for representative samples of different ethnic and socioeconomic subpopulations? What patterns of use—mix of drugs, duration of use, method of administration—are associated with what patterns of violent behavior? How do these risk relationships differ across categories of persons?
- Indirect relationships between psychoactive drugs and violence (Chapters 4 and 5): How is the incidence of violence related

to the use of alcohol or illegal psychoactive drugs, through arguments over debts and family arguments over money, time spent away from home, etc.?

Because alcohol and other psychoactive drugs have somewhat different relationships to violence, certain problem-solving initiatives apply to only one or the other.

Alcohol Problem-solving initiatives at the biological, psychosocial, microsocial, and macrosocial levels may all be useful in reducing alcohol-related violence:

- Mount a program to develop a drug that blocks the aggression-promoting effects of alcohol through various modes of action, for example, on the $GABA_A$/benzodiazepine receptor complex (Chapter 4).
- Develop and evaluate special alcohol-and-violence counseling programs for youth with diagnosed antisocial personality disorder who abuse both alcohol and other psychoactive drugs, whose parents abuse alcohol, and whose behavior brings them under juvenile court or social service agency jurisdiction (Chapter 4).
- For situations that involve drinking alcohol, identify risk factors for violent events and evaluate the violence prevention effects of public information campaigns analogous to "if you drink, don't drive" that encourage people to modify those risk factors (Chapter 4).
- Test the effectiveness of alcohol excise tax increases as a means of reducing violent behavior by adolescent males (Chapter 4).

Other Psychoactive Drugs For most people, the pharmacological effects of illegal psychoactive drugs do not generally promote violent behavior. Two recommended initiatives are concerned with special circumstances in which such effects may occur:

- Test the effectiveness of clonidine and other drugs in managing human aggressive behavior during withdrawal from heroin (Chapter 4).
- Special pharmacological effects of crack (Chapter 4): Does the direct and rapid access of smoked cocaine to the brain promote violent behavior even though powdered cocaine use generally does not?

Illegal psychoactive drugs are related to violence largely through violent crimes committed in the course of purchasing or distribution in illegal markets. Two recommended initiatives are concerned with reducing this violence by reducing demand for illegal drugs:

- Develop pharmacological interventions for reducing users' craving for psychoactive drugs by blocking dopamine and norepinephrine receptor subtypes (Chapter 3).
- For incarcerated psychoactive drug users who are convicted of violent crimes or weapons violations, evaluate the violence-control effects of programs that combine in-prison detoxification and treatment with post release urinalysis and community-based relapse prevention follow-up, using the models of methadone maintenance for heroin users and therapeutic communities such as the "Stay 'N Out" program for users of cocaine and other illegal psychoactive drugs (Chapter 4).

Initiatives at the Social Level

Problem-solving initiatives should be mounted to deal with specific social-level violence problems.

- Violent bias crimes (Chapter 3): Conduct comparison and cross-validation of incidence estimates obtained by police and by community-based organizations; research on the individual- and community-level effects of violent bias crimes; comparison of three strategies to reduce levels and consequences of violent bias crimes: criminal sanctions, identifying risk factors for victimization and educating members of target groups about how to modify them, and interventions to repair the psychological consequences of violent bias crimes victimization.
- Gang-related violence (Chapter 3): Identify risk factors that differentiate violent gangs from other gangs and develop and test interventions to modify those risk factors in violent gangs.
- Community transitions (Chapter 3): Identify the violence risk factors in community transitions (especially economic decline and neighborhood gentrification), and develop and test interventions for modifying those risk factors during transition periods.

A Comprehensive Initiative to Reduce Partner Assault

With the exceptions of arrest in misdemeanor cases and programs for batterers (both of which have generated mixed favorable effects), few of these interventions have been systematically evaluated.

Perhaps more important, there has been no systematic investigation of their comparative effectiveness or of how they might be used together—in part because these interventions are offered by different public authorities and/or community-based organizations. This leads us to recommend a comprehensive initiative against spouse assault, with the following components:

- risk assessment: better estimates in local surveys and the National Crime Survey of the incidence and prevalence of all types of family violence, including attention to cohabiting families; special attention to the incidence of spouse abuse, especially to repeat victimization; tabulations of more information on types of family violence within legal/statistical categories (e.g., disaggregating specific family relationships, capturing sexual assaults on minors);
- case control or randomized experimental studies that follow two groups of families over several years: one group would be exposed to a public awareness and education campaign; another offered an infusion of services including shelter, parenting, vocational assistance, assertiveness training, and day care; these treatments could be provided in communities with different law enforcement policies;
- a jurisdictional comparative analysis of shelter availability with assault and homicide rates;
- evaluation of batterers' programs through experiments using randomized assignment; and
- evaluation of law enforcement and criminal justice interventions including arrest as well as less expensive interventions: (a) restraining orders, (b) police warnings in cases without probable cause, (c) police training coupled with intense public education campaigns, and (d) sanctions varying from mandated courses to work programs.

IMPROVING VIOLENCE MEASUREMENT SYSTEMS

Many questions of fundamental policy and scientific importance cannot be answered today, and emerging violence problems are sometimes slow to be discovered, because of four basic limitations of the systems for gathering information on violence. First, existing systems record only a small slice of all violent behaviors. Second, even for the behaviors covered, they do not provide the data needed to calculate basic conditional probabilities of a violence threat given certain circumstances; of a violent event given a particular kind of threat; or of death, injury, psychological, and financial consequences given the attributes of a violent event.

Third, even if otherwise suitable data are available for social units such as geographic or jurisdictional areas, those units are often too large or heterogeneous to permit precise estimates of empirical relationships or intervention effects. Fourth, the information system categories often mask behavioral diversity: multiple reasons for a homicide, for example, or the chain of events that preceded a firearm injury.

Recommendation 2: The panel recommends that high priority be placed on modifying and expanding relevant statistical information systems to provide the following:

(a) counts and descriptions of violent events that are receiving considerable public attention but are poorly counted by existing measurement systems. These include but are not limited to intrafamily violence; personal victimizations in commercial and organizational robberies; violent bias crimes; and violent events in schools, jails, and prisons;

(b) more comprehensive recording of sexual violence, including incidents involving intimates, incidents of homicide and wounding in which the sexual component may be masked, and more complete descriptions of recorded events;

(c) baseline measurements of conditions and situations that are thought to affect the probability of a violent event (e.g., potentially relevant neurological disorders, arguments between intoxicated husbands and wives, drug transactions, employees handling cash at night in vulnerable locations);

(d) information on the treatment of violence victims in emergency departments, hospitals, and long-term care facilities; links to data on precipitating violent events; and development of these data as a major measurement system;

(e) information on long- and short-term psychological and financial consequences of violent victimization and links to data on violent events;

(f) measurements of violence patterns and trends for small geographic and jurisdictional areas, as baselines for measuring preventive intervention effects; and

(g) information system modifications to record more detailed attributes of violent events and their participants, in order to facilitate more precise studies of risk factors for violence and evaluations of preventive interventions to reduce it.

RESEARCH IN NEGLECTED AREAS

Seven research areas have been largely starved of resources for decades while applicable theory, measurement, and methodology have advanced. As a result, substantial and rapid progress can be expected from relatively small-scale research in the neglected areas.

Recommendation 3: We call for new research programs specifically concerned with the following areas:

(a) nonlaboratory research on the instrumental effects of weapons on the lethality of assaults, robberies, and suicide attempts (Chapter 6) ;

(b) integrated studies of demographic, situational, and spatial risk factors for violent events and violent deaths (Chapter 3);

(c) comparative studies of how developmental processes in ethnically and socioeconomically diverse communities alter the probabilities of developmental sequences that promote or inhibit violent behavior (Chapter 3);

(d) systematic searches for neurobiologic markers for persons with elevated potentials for violent behavior (Chapter 3);

(e) systematic searches for medications that reduce violent behavior without the debilitating side effects of "chemical restraint" (Chapter 3);

(f) integrated studies of the macrosocial, psychosocial, and neurobiologic causes of sexual and other violence among strangers, intimate partners, and family members (Chapters 3 and 5); and

(g) studies of violent behavior by custodians against wards (Chapter 3).

These recommendations are explained more fully in the following pages.

Instrumental Effects of Weapons

We still lack much important basic knowledge about how the choice of weapons influences the lethality of robberies and assaults in actual practice, even though the Centers for Disease Control and the National Institute of Justice now support research on the subject.

Specific issues needing investigation include the lethal effects of weapons in actual use; the effects of street-level and wholesale-level police tactics in enforcing firearms regulations; sources of guns used in crimes; sources of guns illegally carried by minors; organization of the guns-for-drugs trade; the circumstances and frequency of firearm deployment for self-defense and the effect of deployment on victimization consequences; disaggregated measures of weapon availability, ownership patterns and motivation, legitimate uses, and acquisition patterns; and the roles in crime of automatic and semiautomatic rifles and handguns, especially by juveniles.

Demographic, Situational, and Spatial Factors

Many violent events arise from the intersection of demographic, situational, and spatial elements. Much of the relevant research focuses on only one of those levels of analysis at a time. Demographic patterns of violent offending and victimization are well documented. A start was made nearly a decade ago in understanding the situational dynamics of encounters that include violent behavior (Felson and Steadman, 1983). And progress has been made in describing distributions of violent and other crimes across places operationalized as addresses or telephone numbers (Sherman et al., 1989). What is needed is integrated research on how all three kinds of elements—demographic, situational, and spatial—converge to influence individuals' exposure to the risks of victimization in robbery, of sexual and nonsexual assaults, and of death in those events.

Comparative Studies

Similarly, even though racial and socioeconomic differences in violence rates are well documented and evidence supports a number of explanations, many plausible theories remain untested. Analyses of macrosocial influences on violence, including community-level differences in learning environments and access to prenatal and pediatric care, require comparative research on individuals in multiple communities that vary in their composition—variations in ethnic and socioeconomic status mix seem especially important. Similarly, we need to understand how cross-national variation in violence rates is related to other national characteristics.

Biological Markers for Violent Behavior

Although biological markers for an elevated propensity for violent behavior are currently lacking, findings point to several sites in the nervous system where they may eventually be discovered:

- abnormal functioning of the limbic system and temporal lobe of the brain, especially the hypothalamus;
- unusual neural discharge patterns in the temporal lobe; and
- abnormal activity or metabolism of amines, steroids, or peptides that act as neurotransmitters or modulators, especially dopamine; norepinephrine; serotonin; gamma-aminobutyric acid (GABA); monoamine oxidase (MAO); steroid hormones, particularly testosterone; and glucocorticoids.

A common approach to searching for such markers has been psychophysiological research, which explores correlations between aggressive or violent behavior and certain peripheral measures of neurological activity such as heart rate, skin conductance, and evoked potentials. As explained in Chapter 3, these measures are often associated with general arousal levels rather than specific to violent behavior, this approach is likely to identify risk factors specific to violent behavior only through repeated measures linked to records of behavior over time.

More research using the following approaches is needed: observing behavior after pharmacologically blocking or triggering the specific neurobiologic process being tested, and using implanted devices to measure and transmit records of neurophysiological activity by animals during their aggressive and other behaviors in seminatural group settings.

If neurobiologic markers for violent behavior exist, they are more likely to be found if researchers:

- make greater use of general population samples rather than of samples selected on the traditional basis of behavioral or neurological aberrations;
- measure neurochemical activity directly in the brain rather than measuring peripheral levels in hair, saliva, urine, blood, spinal fluid, etc.;
- design studies to distinguish between neurobiologic *causes* and *effects* of violent behavior; and
- search for markers in terms of *responses* to chemical, environmental, or social challenges rather than *resting levels*.

Preventive Pharmacological Interventions

Neurobiologic research has already produced drugs that have proven useful as primary or adjunct therapies for managing certain violent human behaviors in specific populations. These include antiandrogen drugs, beta-blockers, and dopamine receptor antagonists.

Recent findings suggest that two additional promising leads should be followed: use of antianxiety drugs that operate on the $GABA_A$/benzodiazepine receptor complex to inhibit alcohol-related aggression; and use of anxiolytics that act on the serotonergic system to reduce certain aggressive behaviors.

Sexual Violence

Little is known about how potentials for sexual violence develop, how violent sex offenders differ from the general male population in terms of either sexual preferences or socialization toward women, or how the occurrence and recurrence of violent sexual behavior can be prevented. We place particular priority on four sets of research questions:

(1) What are the roles of genetic-environmental interactions, sexual abuse in childhood, the learning of tolerant attitudes toward rape, and chronic alcohol abuse in the development of individual potentials for violent sexual behavior?

(2) What is the role of violent deviant sexual preferences in causing violent sexual acts? How do these preferences differ between samples of known violent sex offenders and other samples? What events produce these violent preferences? What role, if any, does violent pornography play in their development? Are there specific neurological, endocrine, or genetic markers either for them or for an elevated potential to act on them? What subpopulations, if any, would benefit from hormone therapy?

(3) What preventive and educational strategies show promise of reducing sexual violence involving intimates, acquaintances, or strangers?

(4) Several psychosocial interventions—relapse prevention therapy, assertiveness therapy, and anger management therapy—show some promise of changing some individuals' violent deviant sexual preferences, especially when combined with pharmacological interventions that reduce the intensity of the sex drive. Systematic evaluation is needed, involving randomized experiments where

practicable,[2] to assess the effectiveness of these interventions in preventing the recurrence of sexually violent acts.

Improved classification and measurement are essential for making progress on these issues, but they present special problems in the context of sexual violence. Classification systems should be refined and improved to facilitate both better developmental understanding and more effective treatment. In addition, special priority should be placed on improved classification of those who commit violent acts against intimates that do not routinely lead to institutionalization as sex offenders.

Violence Involving Custodians and Wards

Among community institutions, we surveyed violence in only two—prisons and schools. We found a dearth of information on the frequencies, causes, and special consequences of violent events in those settings. We believe that theories and data are similarly lacking on violence in other settings populated by custodians and wards, such as mental hospital staff and patients, caregivers and children, and nursing home staff and patients. One type of violence in this category—violent events involving police and other citizens—has recently become increasingly visible.

Knowledge of situational- and individual-level risk factors in all these settings could be particularly helpful in determining whether changes in personnel selection, training, or organizational accountability can affect levels of violence by custodians. There is also a need for research on the consequences of such incidents, both for the victims and for the surrounding community.

MULTICOMMUNITY LONGITUDINAL STUDIES

There is a need now to lay the basic research groundwork for the next generation of preventive interventions.

Recommendation 4: The panel calls for a new, multicommunity program of developmental studies of aggressive, violent, and antisocial behaviors, intended to improve both causal understanding and preventive interventions at the biological, individual, and social levels.

As described in more detail in Chapter 3, this multicommunity study would include initial assessments, follow-ups, and randomized experiments for two cohorts in each community—a birth cohort and a cohort of 8-year-olds. Here, we first explain more clearly the scientific and policy considerations that call for a longitudinal study of violent and aggressive behaviors. We then discuss the problem of maintaining the long-term support needed for the program.

Scientific Considerations

The methodological advantages of longitudinal panel designs over cross-section approaches for studying the development of delinquent and criminal behavior have been explained in detail elsewhere (Blumstein et al., 1986; Farrington et al., 1986; Tonry et al., 1991). Briefly, they are the ability to observe developmental sequences within individuals (e.g., from low fear response, through aggression, through risk-seeking behaviors, through substance abuse, through violent behavior); the ability to measure the effects of life events that interrupt those sequences; enhanced ability to infer cause-effect relationships by controlling statistically for extraneous variables and establishing time sequences; better information about the accuracy of predictions based on earlier events; enhanced ability to record the forming and breaking of subjects' affiliations with family members, gangs, and other relevant groups; and enhanced ability to record stability or fluctuation over time in individuals' aggressive or violent behavior.

In principle, there has long been no reason why studies combining aggregate and individual-level data could not simultaneously study how the structures and cultures of large and small social units, as well as the dynamics of microsocial encounters, influence individuals' potentials for violent behavior. Useful starts have been made in identifying social-level correlates of both criminal career dimensions and violent victimization risk. But knowledge of correlates is not sufficient for understanding processes. And studies of multilevel processes have rarely been carried out because of the substantial burdens they impose on data collection and on researcher's capacities to competently span the theories and methods of the different disciplines concerned with the different levels. We are calling for a program that would begin to remedy these deficiencies.

Compared with other programs of longitudinal studies, this one would be distinguished by the combination of:

(1) specific emphasis on the relationships between aggressive and violent behavior, including social-level influences on those behaviors;

(2) a multicommunity design to facilitate more extensive study of cultural and biosocial influences, both on developmental sequences and on intervention effects;

(3) neurobiologic measurements that are as specific for relevant hypothesized processes in the brain as is ethically and technically feasible;

(4) designs that facilitate analyses of protective and aggravating conditions and factors in families, peer groups, schools, and communities;

(5) randomized tests of interventions that, on the basis of causal understanding at the social, psychological, and biological levels, show promise of fostering the development of prosocial behavior and inhibiting the development of potentials for violent behavior;

(6) oversampling of high-risk categories and special efforts to minimize attrition by study subjects in those categories; and

(7) cross-validation of official record and self-report versions of violent events.

Policy Considerations

In the face of visible public concern over violence and its consequences, some may view any investment in basic research, such as a longitudinal study, as impractical or not cost-effective. They might opt for spending the same resources on new prison beds. Although criminals sanction will doubtless remain a major violence control tactic, they are not necessarily the most cost-effective approaches to reducing violence levels.

Several risk factors for violence (e.g., poor cognitive capacity, transient neurobiologic conditions, alcohol intoxication) actually inhibit persons from weighing punishment as a possible deterrent to violent behavior. Strategies of selectively longer incarceration terms for convicted persons who have demonstrated elevated potentials for violent behavior will not reduce crime and violence levels without substantial additional increases in prison populations. As explained in Chapter 7, recent experience suggests that if violent crime has been deterred by the threat of incarceration, then it may also have been promoted by other criminogenic factors, some of which arise in the course of individual development. And most fundamentally, criminal sanctions cannot be mobilized until after a violent crime has occurred.

As explained in Chapter 3, some developmentalists argue that a small high-risk group can be identified in early childhood and that early preventive intervention strategies can be devised to reduce the portion of this group that grows up to commit violent acts. Some research has already been done along these lines. But much of this work has generally focused on broader behavioral categories—conduct disorder, aggression, or delinquency, for example. Risk factors for broad categories of behavior tend to overpredict violent behavior, and the implied intervention strategies may be ineffective in preventing rarer forms of violent behavior. A more specifically focused effort is needed to improve understanding and predictive capability both for a predisposition to aggressive behavior, which is usually observable by age 8, and for the aggressive children whose behavior later becomes violent.

Maintaining Support for the Program

In calling for a longitudinal study of aggressive and violent behaviors, we are calling for a substantial long-term resource commitment that offers only a reasonable chance of breakthroughs in the understanding and control of violence. The size of the commitment looks smaller in the context of $10 billion (as of 1989) in ongoing prison construction, or of $10 billion per year for space research. Nevertheless, the program will require a commitment of new funds, and the full potential of returns from the investment will not be realized unless funding continues throughout the entire data collection and analysis period—10 to 11 years for the birth cohort and 12 to 13 years for the 8-year-old cohort.

Ironically, generating and maintaining support for this program may be more difficult than otherwise because relatively few people behave violently. Based on previous longitudinal researchers' experience, Tonry et al. (1991) estimate that about 9 percent of a birth cohort will be arrested for a violent crime before the eighteenth birthday, and that about 36 percent of an early-teen cohort followed for 10 years will report to interviewers that they committed a serious violent act. Given that proportion, a conservative benchmark data collection cost of $500 per year per sample subject would imply a 10-year cost approaching $14,000 per subject who commits a violent offense—a figure that many would consider too high to warrant this project solely as a means of studying violent behavior.

That cost can, of course, be reduced by oversampling from high-risk populations. Moreover, the study will prove cost-effective if the accounting scheme is comprehensive enough, however, because children at greatest risk of aggressive and violent behavior are also at high risk for other problems. Menard et al. report that, of subjects in the National Youth Survey, not only did 36 percent report at least one serious violent offense, but also 87 percent reported general delinquency, 42 percent reported committing index offenses, 94 percent reported illicit alcohol use, 37 percent reported polydrug use, and 24 percent reported mental health problems. In short, even though this study would be the first with a primary focus on violent behavior, it should produce important spin-offs in related areas that are core concerns of agencies in the Office of Justice Programs (a unit of the Department of Justice) and in the Alcohol, Drug Abuse, and Mental Health Administration (a unit of the Department of Health and Human Services). All these areas fall within the basic research mandate of the National Science Foundation. Together, these agencies provide some three-fourths of all federal support for research on violence.

FEDERAL SUPPORT FOR VIOLENCE RESEARCH

These recommendations will require commitments from federal agency sponsors of research on violence. To get a better picture of exactly who they are, the panel conducted a census of all federal agencies thought to be supporting research and program evaluation on violence as of 1989.

The panel was able to account for federal expenditures of $18,080,000 in fiscal 1989. To this amount should be added intramural violence research by 24 full-time equivalent federal employees; with these evaluated at $70,000 each per year,[3] this produces a fiscal 1989 total of $20,231,000 classified by responding agencies as *violence research*.[4]

To some this size of research expenditures may seem large; however, considered in human terms, it amounts to only $3.41 per 1988 violent victimization. This is a tiny fraction of the estimates by Cohen et al. (Volume 4) of the cost per violent event: $54,100 per rape, $19,200 per robbery, and $16,500 per aggravated assault.

As a research topic, violence receives far less support than certain other threats to life. Expenditures on violence research amount to about $31 per year of potential life lost (YPLL) due to violence by age 65. Figure 8-1 compares this amount with research expenditures per YPLL for cancer, heart disease, and AIDS.[5]

This basis of comparison is, if anything, conservative because it fails to compensate for external social costs that may be associated with violent deaths but not with deaths from disease. Such costs include the deterioration of the quality of life and the loss

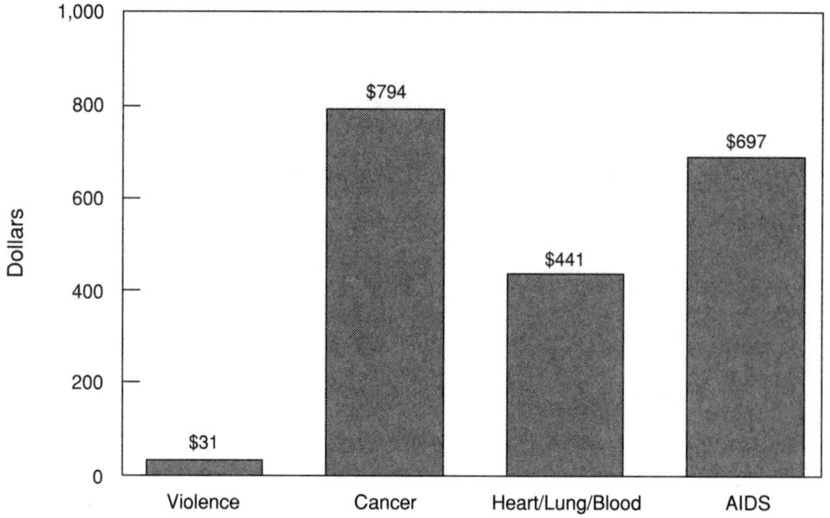

FIGURE 8-1 Research expenditures per year of potential life lost for selected causes of death.

of legitimate economic activity in communities afflicted with high violence levels, and adverse effects that chronic exposure to neighborhood violence might have on children's education and social development.

On this conservative basis of comparison, an increase from the current $20.2 million to $500 million would be needed to bring federal support for violence research into line with federal support for cancer research. Even an increase of that magnitude would bring annual costs for violence research to less than 8 percent of the annual National Institutes of Health budget. It would increase the cost of the societal response to violence—primarily criminal justice system costs—by less than 3 percent (see response cost estimates by Cohen et al. in Volume 4).

Although an increase of this magnitude would be a proportionate response to violence in America, the panel recognizes that such an increase is unlikely in the current federal fiscal climate. Fortunately, 10 percent of that increase would be sufficient to initiate implementation of the recommendations in this report.

Features of the Current Structure

Reflecting the diversity of violent behavior itself, the current structure for federally supported research involves many agencies and fosters tremendous diversity in the topics supported. In all, 22 agencies or units of agencies sponsor more than 60 subcategories of violence research. The topics cover most of the important aspects of the understanding and control of violent behavior.

The agency respondents were asked to characterize the frequencies with which their violence research programs support various disciplines. While there may well be scholars in all the relevant disciplines whose efforts fail to receive the support they deserve, virtually every relevant discipline has a potential home somewhere among the federal violence research programs. Moreover, inspection of the individual agencies' responses suggests that in programs large enough to support several awards each year, most agencies support a reasonable number of different disciplines.

Respondents were asked to characterize the shares of their resources devoted to each of 15 methodologies as zero, minor, or major. Virtually every useful research methodology known to the panel reportedly received a "major" share of the resources of at least one sponsoring agency in fiscal 1989. In that year, however, only three programs devoted major shares of resources to program evaluation.

The panel is especially concerned about two structural problems with federal support for violence research: (1) the ebb and flow of support for violence research—a condition that stems from the position of violence as incidental to most sponsoring agencies' mandates; and (2) the dearth of long-term programmatic objectives and support mechanisms, especially for interdisciplinary violence research.

Violence as an Incidental

For most of the large sponsors of violence research, violence is not a central concern. Rather, violence is considered either in its relationship to some other social problem (e.g., mental illness, drug abuse, alcohol abuse) or as part of some larger mission (e.g., controlling crime, reducing injury). Among the large sponsors of violence research in 1989, for example, violence received only 2 percent of National Institute on Drug Abuse research funds, 1 percent of National Institute on Alcoholism and Alcohol Abuse support, and 17 percent of National Institute of Justice funds. A desirable effect of this position of "violence as an incidental" is the diversity it stimulates. However, it also creates unfortunate distorting effects.

First, when agencies that are focused primarily on related problems such as substance abuse are major sponsors of violence research, funding levels for violence research rise and fall with the tide of funding in the related areas. Were interest in those areas to decline during the 1990s, funding for violence research under the current structure could be expected to fall regardless of either the social costs of violence or the expected social and scientific payoffs.

Second, when individual researchers apply for support for violence research from a program concerned with another field, award decisions tend to be based on investigators' understanding of and attention to the program's primary focus—not their expertise in violent behavior. This raises the possibility that meritorious proposals in terms of contributing to the understanding and control of violence will be overlooked. Over time, proposers' anticipation of this trend may lead to the "slanting" of proposals to overemphasize the related field regardless of its importance as a cause of violence.

Third, over time, violence research proposals come to be judged in terms of classification systems developed for the related fields. For example, in programs governed by psychiatric classification systems such as DSM-III-R, violent behavior is usually grouped with antisocial behavior because "repeated fights or assaults" is one diagnostic indicator for antisocial behavior. Unfortunately, because it is only one of eight such indicators, even an outstanding violence proposal may be rejected as unlikely to make a major contribution to the understanding of antisocial behavior.

Barriers to Sustained Interdisciplinary Commitments

Certain "big science" projects offer the prospect of contributions to the understanding and control not only of violence and its effects on individual victims and communities, but also of such related problems as drug and alcohol abuse and mental illness. Occasional large-scale programs are essential for significantly advancing the understanding and control of violence. Investigations of its causes should sometimes cross traditional academic boundaries, comparative evaluations of preventive interventions should sometimes span the traditional intervention modes of several public agencies, and both kinds of studies sometimes require investigators to follow large samples of individuals for long periods of time.

Unfortunately, interdisciplinary studies that require long-term investments of large-scale financial support currently have no natural home among federal violence research sponsors. When recommendations for longitudinal studies of the development of potentials for crime, delinquency, and prosocial behavior surfaced during the 1980s, no single agency routinely committed sufficient resources for sufficiently long periods, and no agency was in a natural position to organize a consortium of sponsors.

To its credit, the Office of Juvenile Justice and Delinquency Prevention (OJJDP) undertook the Program on Causes and Correlates of Delinquency, which involved longitudinal studies of delinquent development in three sites and a commitment to five years of financial support. The National Science Foundation and other sponsors provided short-term funds to reduce the risk of a hiatus during which the research teams might be dismantled, respondent attrition might increase discontinuously, and the future cooperation of local schools and other data providers might be jeopardized. At this writing, pending reauthorization legislation earmarks funds to continue the program for one additional year, but long-term support is in jeopardy.

In an innovative institutional arrangement, the National Institute of Justice has joined with the health program of the John D. and Catherine T. MacArthur Foundation to launch the Program on Human Development and Criminal Behavior. Creating the consortium and planning required four years of funding. At this writing funding commitments are ensured for the design and pretest phases only. Long-term funding for data collection is still being negotiated.

The experiences of these programs illustrate both the need for a stable organizational framework for underwriting long-term comprehensive research enterprises and the perils of launching such enterprises without long-term commitments.

Recent Promising Developments

Since the panel's survey of fiscal 1989 support, a number of developments have strengthened the federal enterprise in research on violence. Although we have not systematically canvased all respondents, the developments of which we have become aware raise the prospects for positive complementary lines of evolution in violence research and evaluation and point to several programs that could usefully be continued, restored, coordinated, or expanded.

National Institute of Justice

The National Institute of Justice (NIJ), the research arm of the Department of Justice, operated a diverse violence research program through fiscal 1990, which covered such topics as child abuse, partner assault, bias crimes, youth criminality and victimization, homicide and drugs, weapons, and psychiatric aspects of violence. A 1990 reorganization eliminated violence and most other standalone research programs, but violence is an announced program priority for fiscal 1992, and fiscal 1991 funds were awarded for research on such violence topics as police use of excessive force, serial rape, assaults on correctional officers, and less-than-lethal-force weapons. At the 1991 annual meetings of the American Society of Criminology, the institute's director announced the formation of new divisions of research and of evaluation, and plans to form external scientific advisory groups for all program priority areas, including violence. In addition, NIJ is continuing cosponsorship, with the MacArthur Foundation, of the Program on Human Development and Criminal Behavior, a longitudinal study of the development of prosocial, antisocial, and criminal behavior, including an emphasis on aggression and violent behavior.

National Science Foundation

The National Science Foundation (NSF) sponsors basic research through a set of programs defined in terms of academic disciplines. Although no program solicited research proposals specifically on violence, the programs within the Directorate for Biological, Behavioral, and Social Sciences collectively span the range of disciplines that are relevant to violent behavior: law and social science, sociology, anthropology, neural mechanisms of behavior, animal behavior, and behavioral neuroendocrinology. Each program maintains an "open window" for proposals and bases its awards on peer-reviewed comparisons of scientific merit and importance within its discipline.

Because the various NSF program areas operate largely independently, the overall size and composition of its violence research portfolio is determined by a series of award decisions based on scientific merit assessed from specific disciplinary perspectives, rather than by any coordinated assessment of scientific priorities within the field of violence. A proposal for a coordinated initiative on violence research was considered several years ago but was not pursued. Program evaluation or other policy analysis lies outside the NSF mission, except insofar as it has direct scientific relevance.

In late 1991, NSF announced the creation of separate directorates for the biological sciences and for the social, economic, and psychological sciences. The hope has been expressed that, within the latter directorate, research on violent and nonviolent crime will have greater visibility (American Society of Criminology, 1991). It is also important that separation of the directorates does not hinder support of research that reflects an integration of social and neurobiologic perspectives on violent behavior.

Centers for Disease Control

Through its Center for Environmental Health and Injury Control (CEHIC), the Centers for Disease Control (CDC) has begun to sponsor initiatives intended to measure and reduce the public health consequences of violence: primarily intentional injuries and their aggregate consequences for the health care system. As of fiscal 1989, the reference year for the panel's survey, the program was emphasizing the following components: improving the measurement of intentional injuries and deaths, using epidemiological techniques to identify risk factors, establishing measurable objectives for reducing intentional injuries, designing and evaluating strategies for preventing intentional injuries by modifying risk factors, and mobilizing a range of professions, government agencies, and community-based organizations to pursue those strategies.

Since the survey, CDC/CEHIC has completed the development of measurable objectives for reducing interpersonal intentional injury in *Healthy People 2000* (U.S. Department of Health and Human Services, 1991). At this writing, it is in the process of drafting a position paper "Prevention of Violence and Violence Injuries," which sets out strategies for preventing intentional injuries and calls for evaluating interventions that pursue those strategies.

National Institute of Mental Health

At the time of the panel's survey, research on aggressive and violent behavior occurred in three branches of the National Institute of Mental Health: Behavioral Sciences, Neurosciences, and Antisocial and Violent Behavior. Of the three, the latter was the largest, and it sponsored basic research and program evaluations on family violence, on violent behavior by the mentally ill, and on the psychological consequences of violent victimization. At various times, that program supported longitudinal research, with its need for long-term support. During the 1980s, the branch rarely funded research on social-level causes of violent behavior.

During 1990, the unit was renamed the Violence and Traumatic Stress Research Branch, and its annual budget was nearly doubled, to $15.1 million. The reorganized program is divided into four research areas, which relate to (1) the causes, prevention, and treatment of perpetrators of interpersonal violence, with special note of family violence, violence against minorities, and homicide; (2) the victims of violence, especially the psychological consequences of victimization; (3) mentally disordered offenders and the violent mentally ill; and (4) victims of disaster, combat, community violence, and terrorism. In fiscal 1991, the program funded 90 research grants and 10 research training grants in these areas.

Facilitating the Needed Work

The problem facing policy makers is how to preserve diversity while achieving the following objectives:

(1) facilitating more basic research on individual animal and human subjects and on organizations, situations, communities, and societies, specifically designed to add to scientific understanding of violent behavior and violent events;

(2) integrating basic research more fully with the design, evaluation, and refinement of interventions to prevent the occurrence or recurrence of violence or to reduce and repair the physical, psychological, and other harms of violence to individual victims and community institutions;

(3) fostering more interdisciplinary basic research into prosocial as well as aggressive and violent behavior, and evaluating a broader range of violence prevention interventions;

(4) facilitating long-term commitments to research and evaluation efforts that could require a decade or more;

(5) augmenting intellectual capacity through programs of predoctoral and postdoctoral fellowships;

(6) calling attention to violence problems that are receiving insufficient, or *insufficiently comprehensive*, attention, and stimulating or providing support needed to fill such emerging gaps; and

(7) maintaining and disseminating information—about ongoing research projects, new promising leads, and newly available findings and data—to all the diverse communities concerned with violence.

NOTES

1 To avoid repetitiveness, we are here using the term *violence* as shorthand to refer to a set of measures, including rates of violent events, of injuries due to violence, and of deaths due to violence.

2 We are aware of only one randomized experimental evaluation of a treatment program for violent sex offenders that involves follow-up outside an institutional setting. The Sex Offender Treatment and Evaluation Project, mandated and funded by the California state legislature, involved random assignment of volunteers to a relapse prevention program during the last 18-30 months of their prison terms. By 1989, 98 treatment and control subjects had been released to the community and are still being followed up. Since the intervention did not shorten participants' incarceration terms and provided treatment that was not otherwise available, the study did not increase danger to the community. Preliminary findings suggest that the relapse prevention program had some success (Miner et al., 1990).

3 The figure assumes an average professional salary of $50,000, plus a 40 percent allowance for fringe benefits and administrative costs.

4 Not included in these research expenditures are the expenditures for collection and production of violence statistics. These would include prorated shares of the costs for victimizations in the 1988 National Crime Survey (NCS, $7,000,000), for crimes reported to the police in the 1989 Uniform Crime Reports (UCR, $4,500,000), and for deaths in the 1989 national mortality statistics of the United States ($6,800,000). Prorating each program's costs proportionally to the fraction of incidents reported that would be classified as violent under the panel's definition produces a total estimate of $1,753,000 for violence statistics—$1,160,000 in NCS costs, $520,000 in UCR costs, and $73,000 in national mortality statistics costs.

5 Research expenditures for cancer; for heart, lung, and blood disease; and for AIDS are the 1989 actual budget authority figures reported in Public Health Service (1990), respectively, for the National Cancer Institute, for the National Heart, Lung, and Blood Institute (both excluding AIDS), and for AIDS research. Unlike our estimates for violence research, these figures include agency program administration costs; however, they exclude research expenditures elsewhere in the National Institutes of Health that are pertinent to their respective foci.

REFERENCES

American Society of Criminology
1991 McCord testifies before NSF. *The Criminologist* 16(6):1,3.

Blumstein, A., J. Cohen, J.A. Roth, and C. Visher, eds.
1986 *Criminal Careers and "Career Criminals."* Washington, D.C.: National Academy Press.

Farrington, David P., Lloyd E. Ohlin, and James Q. Wilson
1986 *Understanding and Controlling Crime: Toward a New Research Strategy*. New York: Springer-Verlag.

Felson, R.B., and H.J. Steadman
1983 Situational factors in disputes leading to criminal violence. *Criminology* 21(1, February):59-74.

Miner, M.H., J.K. Marques, D.M. Day, and C. Nelson
1990 Impact of relapse prevention in treating sex offenders: Preliminary findings. *Annals of Sex Research* 3:165-185.

Public Health Service
1990 Justification of Appropriation Estimates for Committee on Appropriations, Fiscal Year 1992, Volume III. Washington, D.C.: Public Health Service.

Sherman, L.W., P.R. Gartin, and M.E. Buerger
1989 Hot spots of predatory crime: Routine activities and the criminology of place. *Criminology* 27:27-55.

Tonry, M., L.E. Ohlin, and D.P. Farrington
1991 *Human Development and Criminal Behavior: New Ways of Advancing Knowledge*. New York: Springer-Verlag.

U.S. Department of Health and Human Services
1991 *Healthy People 2000*. Washington, D.C.: U.S. Government Printing Office.

Appendixes

A

The Development of an Individual Potential for Violence

This appendix does not purport to be a state-of-the-art review of individual-level influences on the development of violent behavior; that would require a book rather than a comparatively short paper. It aims to summarize briefly some of the most important findings and theories, but more especially to identify key issues and questions that are unresolved and to recommend ways of resolving them. The recent book edited by Pepler and Rubin (1991) provides more extensive information about findings and theories.

The likelihood of someone's committing a violent act depends on many different factors. Biological, individual, family, peer, school, and community factors may influence the development of an individual potential for violence. Whether the potential becomes manifest as a violent act depends on the interaction between this violence potential and immediate situational factors, such as the consumption of alcohol and the presence of a victim. The focus in this appendix is on factors that influence the development of a person with a high potential for violence in different situations. The emphasis is especially on individual-level factors, such as temperament, IQ, and impulsivity, although other factors (family, peer, and school) that influence the development of a potential for violence are also discussed.

Nonmanipulable individual factors such as sex and ethnic origin are not discussed, except insofar as they interact with other factors. It seems probable that the greater likelihood of males and blacks to commit violent offenses might be explained by reference to some of the other factors discussed here. Most of the developmental research on aggression and violence has been carried out with males.

Many facts about the development of violence are so well known and well replicated that they hardly need to be reviewed here. In particular, it is clear that aggressive children tend to become violent teenagers and violent adults. In other words, there is significant continuity over time between childhood aggression and adult violence. For example, Farrington (1991b) showed that aggressive children at ages 8-10 and 12-14 (rated by teachers) tended to have later convictions for violence and to be violent at age 32 (according to their self-reports). These kinds of results make it plausible to postulate that the ordering of people on some underlying construct of individual difference such as violence potential is tolerably consistent over time. However, it is also true that people change and that it is important to investigate how and why they change.

These results also mean that knowledge gained about the correlates, predictors, and causes of childhood aggression is relevant to the explanation of teenage and adult violence. Many factors present early in life (such as childhood temperament or family influences) may predict adult violence essentially because they influence the development of childhood aggression and because childhood aggression tends to develop into adult violence. The predictors and correlates of childhood aggression and adult violence are so well known and well replicated that they are not reviewed in detail here. For example, Farrington (1989) showed that they include individual-level factors such as low IQ, low school attainment, high impulsivity, and poor concentration and family factors such as low family income, large family size, convicted parents, harsh discipline, poor supervision, and separations from parents.

This appendix begins by discussing some important conceptual issues that need to be resolved, focusing on questions rather than answers. It then briefly summarizes key results, theories, and interventions before concluding with some recommended research priorities.

CONCEPTUAL ISSUES

Are there specific subtypes of violence that need to be explained by different theories? An important issue is whether violence should be treated as a homogeneous or heterogeneous category.

Our preference is for heterogeneity, but in discussing development we usually refer to violence in general. The focus of the panel is on intentional physical assault. Within this context, the most important type of violence that has been studied in developmental research is assault (including wounding), and most of our knowledge is essentially about this phenomenon. Robbery has also been studied quite extensively. The distinction between assault and robbery mirrors that commonly drawn between angry or hostile (emotional) aggression and instrumental violence (e.g., Berkowitz, 1978).

Although we focus on the development of a potential for violence rather than the violent act, it is important to recognize the existence of subtypes of violent acts, such as sexual and nonsexual violence. There has been less developmental research on homicide due to its rarity in community samples (for an example, see Solway et al., 1981). It is unclear whether homicide is qualitatively or quantitatively different from assault and wounding (see below). There has been a great deal of research in recent years on violence to spouses/cohabitants and children, but comparatively little of it has focused on the development of the offender.

To what extent is violence merely one element of a more general syndrome of antisocial behavior? Information about violence is usually obtained from studies of offending in general. There are relatively few studies specifically on violence (e.g., Miller et al., 1982; Hamparian et al., 1978). Generally, violent offenders tend also to commit nonviolent crimes (see the section below on violent crimes in criminal careers). That is, offenders are versatile rather than specialized. Furthermore, there may be a general syndrome of "antisocial personality," which persists from childhood to adulthood and is characterized (in addition to psychopathic traits) by a wide variety of antisocial acts of which violence is one type (Farrington, 1991a). The psychiatric categories of childhood conduct disorder and adult antisocial personality disorder both contain indicators of aggression and violence (American Psychiatric Association, 1987).

There has been quite a lot of developmental research on the categories of psychopathy and antisocial personality disorder (e.g., McCord and McCord, 1956; Robins, 1991). It is important to note that while psychopaths commit a disproportionate number of violent offenses, not all psychopaths are violent and, conversely, not all violent offenders are psychopaths (Hare, 1981). Features of psychopathy include lack of remorse and guilt, callousness and lack of empathy, egocentricity, impulsivity, early antisocial behavior, and the commission of repeated and varied types of criminal acts (Hare, 1981). Psychopaths are unusually persistent offenders, continuing to offend at a high level until age 40 (Hare et al., 1988). Psychopathy has also been investigated extensively at the biological level, including genetic (Baker, 1986), hormonal (Virkkunen, 1987), psychophysiological (Hare, 1978), and neuropsychological (Raine and Venables, in press) factors.

What are the manifestations of violence potential at different ages, and are they part of a developmental sequence? As already mentioned, there is continuity between indicators of childhood aggression and adult violence, suggesting persistence of an underlying construct that is here labeled violence potential. This construct may have different manifestations at different ages. It is important to attend to both homotypic continuity, in which violent behavior per se is preserved, and heterotypic continuity, in which early violence in the teenage years is replaced in adulthood with a different form of behavior that is not obviously violent. Such transformations are common in both psychological and biological development (for a useful discussion of concepts of developmental continuity, see Kagan, 1980).

It is important to investigate sequences of onsets of different kinds of offenses and deviant (e.g., aggressive) behaviors, and to determine the probability of one behavior's following another and the average time interval between onsets. This information should be the starting point in trying to answer questions about why one behavior follows another.

Conceptually there are three main reasons for developmental sequences. First, different acts may be different behavioral manifestations of the same underlying construct at different ages (e.g., an antisocial tendency manifests itself first in shoplifting, later in burglary, and later still in the abuse of spouses and children) but with no facilitating effect of an earlier act on a later one. Second, different acts may be different behavioral manifestations of the same or similar constructs at different ages and also part of a developmental sequence, in which one act is a stepping stone to or facilitates another act (e.g., smoking cigarettes tends to lead to marijuana use—Kandel and Faust, 1975). Third, different acts may be indicators of different constructs and part of a causal sequence, in which changes in an indicator of one construct cause changes in an indicator of a different construct (e.g., school failure leads to truancy).

The first of these ideas can be distinguished empirically from the second and third. If acts in a sequence are all different behavioral manifestations of the same construct (like symptoms of an illness), then preventing or changing an early act in the sequence will not necessarily affect the probability of later acts unless there is some change in the underlying construct. However, with developmental and causal sequences, changing an early act in the sequence will affect the probability of later acts. It is harder to distinguish the second and third ideas empirically, as the key distinction between them is conceptual.

Some key issues are as follows: How can an underlying theoretical construct such as violence potential best be operationally defined and measured at different ages? Does it have different manifestations at different ages, and if so what are they (e.g., cruelty to animals at age 6, assaults on classmates at age 12, wounding at age 19)? What are the most common developmental stepping-stone sequences that include adult violence? For example, does hyperactivity at age 4 lead to conduct disorder at age 8, and then to adolescent aggression and adult violence? How can we establish the existence of such sequences, and distinguish them from causal sequences and from different manifestations of the same underlying construct?

To what extent is violence potential consistent over time? A key question is: What constructs underlie aggressive and violent behavior, and how general or specific should they be? Should we assume that all persons can be ordered on a dimension of violence potential at a given age, or that they can be ordered on a more general dimension such as antisocial personality or "potential for antisocial behavior"? Alternatively, violence could be viewed as a categorical variable, with violent people differing qualitatively rather than quantitatively from nonviolent individuals.

It is important to investigate how violence and violence potential vary with age. Studies show that the most violent people at one age tend also to be the most violent at another. Hence (provided that this does not entirely reflect consistency in the environment), there seems to be consistency in the relative ordering of individuals on the underlying dimension of potential for violence, as already mentioned. However, absolute levels of violence (or violence potential) may vary considerably with age, for example, decreasing markedly after the teens and early twenties. It is important to explain both relative stability and absolute change (Farrington, 1990).

Many projects show significant stability and continuity for aggressive behavior after ages 7-8. In all, 16 separate studies with lags ranging from 6 months to 21 years have reported stability coefficients for aggression ranging from .36 to .95 (Olweus, 1979). Similarly, Huesmann et al. (1984) reported a stability coefficient of .46 between ratings of peer-nominated aggression at age 8 and criminal offenses at age 30. Furthermore, such stability in aggression appears to be consistent across cultures (Eron and Huesmann, 1987). Eron and Huesmann (1990) suggest that such strong stability is a product of continuity of both constitutional and environmental factors. The reasons for the strong stability need to be investigated in more detail.

There is important continuity between juvenile and adult violence, as shown for example in the follow-up by Hamparian et al. (1985). In other words, violent behavior that begins before the eighteenth birthday tends to continue after it.

Are extreme forms of violence (e.g., homicide) different in degree or in kind from other forms of violence? Generally, all types of violence tend to be interrelated in the sense that people who commit one type have a relatively high probability of also committing other types. Again, this is in conformity with the idea of an underlying violence potential.

However, this is perhaps least true of homicide. Some homicides are committed by people with a history of violence, but others are committed by relatively nonviolent people under extreme stress or provocation (see the distinction between undercontrolled and overcontrolled individuals, e.g., Megargee, 1973). Hence, homicide in some cases seems an extreme point on a continuum of violence and in other cases seems qualitatively different from other (less serious) types of violence.

This notion is consistent with the view that violence, like any complex behavior, has multiple and heterogeneous etiologies, and that there is no unitary type of person who is violent. Just as psychiatric categories such as depression and schizophrenia are heterogeneous rather than unitary concepts, violence also is likely to be heterogeneous, if not more so. If this is the case, then an important goal of future research should be to delineate subtypes of violence that may have different etiologies.

We propose to focus more on the development of an individual potential for violence than on the occurrence of the violent act. Generally, violence arises out of an interaction between persons and situations. Some people are consistently more likely to be violent than others in many different situations (just as some situations or environments are consistently more likely than others to elicit violence from many different persons). While characteristic forms and amounts of aggression change dramatically with age (Eron et al., 1983), the aggressiveness of an individual relative to the rest of the population may remain fairly stable. For example, a child who is at the top of the distribution for aggression at age 8 is likely to be near the top of the distribution 20 years later. The focus here is on the violent persons indicated by these cross-situational and cross-time consistencies.

Are the results obtained by studying within-individual differences in violence over time different from those obtained by studying between-individual differences in violence? The prevalence and correlates of aggression and violence at different ages can be studied either within individuals (using longitudinal data) or between individuals (using cross-sectional data). Key issues are the following: How can we explain within-individual changes over age in violence and violence potential, as well as between-individual variations at different ages? How do biological, individual, family, peer, school, and community factors influence within-individual changes and between-individual variations in violence and violence potential? Existing criminological theories are not very useful because they typically focus only on between-individual variations in the teenage years, and they lack a concern with either development or violence. In any case, there is a need for basic developmental information that might inform future theories.

INFLUENCES ON VIOLENCE

It should be noted at the outset that no one influence in isolation is likely to account for the development of a potential for violence, except perhaps in some special cases. It is possible, for example, that to produce a violent adult, one needs, at a minimum, a child born with a particular temperamental profile, living in a particular family constellation, in a disadvantaged neighborhood, exposed to models of aggression and patterns of reinforcement of aggressive behavior, having a particular school experience, having a particular set of peer relations, and also experiencing certain chance events that permit the actualization of violent behavior. Furthermore, it must be remembered that the influences listed below must be viewed within the context of other (biological and social) influences. In particular, factors such as sex hormones, endocrinological factors, psychophysiological factors, and drugs and alcohol might all be expected to interact in complex ways with individual influences.

We know that future adult violence can be predicted, to a statistically significant degree, on the basis of childhood or adolescent factors (Farrington, 1989). Generally, predictive analyses focus on the additive or interactive effects of factors, while causal analyses focus on their independent effects. However, there is a great need for more detailed research on how predictability varies with the ages at which the predictors and outcomes are measured. Specific childhood indicators of aggression include temper tantrums in infancy, physical aggression toward peers and siblings, cruelty to animals, disobedience, quarreling, and disruptiveness in class; prechildhood predictors include pregnancy and birth complications.

Prenatal/Perinatal Factors

Several studies have reported a relation between prenatal/perinatal factors and later violence. Litt (1971) found that perinatal trauma was predictive of impulsive criminal law offenses in a cohort of nearly 2,000 consecutive births in Denmark. Lewis et al. (1979) similarly found that aggressive, incarcerated delinquents were more likely to have sustained perinatal trauma than less aggressive, nonincarcerated delinquents. Mungas (1983) reported a significant relation between violence and perinatal factors within a group of psychiatric patients.

While these studies have indicated a main effect of perinatal factors, one study suggests that prenatal/perinatal factors may interact with social factors in increasing the risk for later violence. Mednick and Kandel (1988) found that minor physical anomalies (an indicator of first-trimester pregnancy complications) were predictive of the number of violent offenses at age 21, but only in children raised in unstable, nonintact homes. Minor physical anomalies have also been found to be elevated in hyperactivity, which itself is related to later delinquency and aggression (Fogel et al., 1985). Similarly, perinatal difficulties have been found to be predictive of aggressiveness (bullying and fighting) at age 18 but, again, this was true only for those raised in unstable home environments.

While these data suggest that a link may exist between pregnancy/birth complications and later violence, there has been almost no research on the pathways by which prenatal and perinatal disturbances might lead to violence. It is possible that obstetric complications may result in damage to brain mechanisms that act to inhibit violent behavior (e.g., the prefrontal cortex). Alternatively, violence may be a by-product of impulsivity, hyperactivity, or cognitive deficits that are themselves produced by damage to the central nervous system resulting from these complications. Possible interactions between pregnancy/birth complications and the early rearing environment are of potential importance, since they suggest that a stable early home environment may protect a child from the negative effects of these complications. For example, it has been observed that being raised in a stable home protects a child from the cognitive deficits otherwise associated with prematurity (Drillien, 1964). These data are at present limited, and confirmation and extension of preliminary studies are required in order to uncover the possible mechanisms by which pregnancy and birth complications may lead to the development of later violence, as well as to establish further the interaction of these complications with social and cognitive factors. In particular, experimental studies that provide greater prenatal care to mothers at risk for pregnancy and birth complications would help to test whether there is a causal connection between such complications and later violence.

An interesting feature of these preliminary findings is that the effect of pregnancy and birth complications is relatively specific to later violence. Such complications do not, for example, appear to be predictive of nonviolent criminal behavior (Mednick and Kandel, 1988). This is of some importance since (as noted earlier) there is relatively little research on factors that selectively predict violence as opposed to nonviolent crime or crime in general.

Temperament

Early temperament may well constitute a risk factor for later aggressive and violent behavior. When confronted with unfamiliar situations (e.g., encounters with unfamiliar children and adults), some children ages 20-30 months tend to be shy, vigilant, and restrained ("inhibited"), whereas others tend to be sociable, spontaneous, and relatively fearless in their behavior ("uninhibited") (Kagan, 1989). Approximately 30 percent of children of this age can be classified into either inhibited or uninhibited categories. These temperamental differences at 21 months are relatively stable, with 75 percent of children being similarly classified as inhibited or uninhibited at 7.5 years. In addition, children exhibiting the most extreme forms of behavior at age 21 months are the most likely to be similarly classified at age 7.5 years. These two temperamental "types" have been found to differ in physiological terms. Inhibited children have higher and more stable heart rates than uninhibited children (Reznick et al., 1986) and show greater heart rate acceleration during cognitive testing. A global physiological index of arousal made up of eight measures including heart rate, pupil dilation, norepinephrine, cortisol, and vocal tension correlated significantly with inhibition at age 21 months ($r = .70$) and at age 7.5 years ($r = .64$), with the uninhibited children being more underaroused.

The significance of this research for violence lies in the possibility that a fearless, uninhibited, early temperament may be a risk factor for later aggression and violence, especially in children with low socioeconomic status, whereas fearfulness may act as a protective factor against aggression. Temperament may explain why only a proportion of children from high-risk homes and neighborhoods develop antisocial or violent behavior (Kagan, 1991). The fact that fearless young children have been found to have low heart rates is consistent with findings of low heart rates in undersocialized children ages 7-15 with aggressive conduct disorder (Raine and Jones, 1987), with the demonstration that persons convicted of violence tend to have low heart rates (Farrington, 1987; Wadsworth, 1976), and with the fact that low heart rate is thought to reflect a factor of fearlessness (Raine and Jones, 1987).

Prospective longitudinal research and cross-sectional studies measuring early temperament in conjunction with measures of physiological arousal and aggression/violence across the life span are required to establish how far early temperament and underarousal are predisposing factors for later aggression and violence. The ability of measures of temperament and heart rate taken as early as 20 months to relate to later violence in adolescence and adulthood is clearly an important topic to be addressed. Although such factors in isolation may not be expected to be strong predictors of violence, in conjunction with other early family and cognitive measures, the degree of prediction may be considerable. The speculation by Kagan (1989) that physiological differences between shy and fearless children may reflect differential thresholds of limbic structures such as the amygdala and hypothalamus is in agreement with research implicating limbic structures in aggression in both animals and humans. Testing in violent and nonviolent subjects using positron emission tomography (PET) techniques could yield important results.

Individual Factors

Violent offenders tend to have certain personality features as children. In particular, they are high on hyperactivity-impulsivity-attention deficit, tend to be restless and lacking concentration, take risks, show a poor ability to defer gratification, and have low empathy (e.g., Farrington, 1989). They also tend to have particularly low IQ scores (more so than other types of offenders).

Physical child abusers have been found to have low self-esteem, a negative self-concept, feelings of inadequacy and inferiority, and an external locus of control (Milner, 1986, 1990). They also have psychopathological personality characteristics, higher trait anxiety and trait anger scores, higher neuroticism scores, and elevations on psychopathic, mania, paranoia, and schizophrenia scales of the Minnesota Multiphasic Personality Index (Milner, 1986).

One longitudinal study indicated that although IQ at age 8 predicts aggression at age 30, IQ is no longer a significant predictor after the effects of aggression at age 8 are removed (Huesmann and Eron, 1984). It is possible that low IQ at an early age contributes to the early adoption of aggressive behavior, and that once such behavior is firmly established its further development into adult violence is relatively unaffected by low intellectual functioning (Huesmann and Eron, 1984).

Family

As already mentioned, violent offenders tend to have experienced poor parental childrearing methods, poor supervision, and separations from their parents when they were children (Farrington, 1991b). In addition, they tend disproportionally to come from low-income, large-sized families in poor housing in deprived, inner-city, high-crime areas. (This appendix does not discuss community influences on crime.)

Recent research has focused on the link between being a victim of physical abuse and neglect as a child and later violent offending. Although it is commonly assumed that individuals who experience physical abuse as children grow up to become violent adults, there are surprisingly few sound empirical data to support this assumption. Widom (1989a), in a critical review of seven different areas of research that bear on this question concluded that most studies were methodologically weak. Her main criticisms include overreliance on self-report and retrospective data, inadequate documentation of child abuse, weak sampling techniques, and infrequent use of control groups.

The soundest study conducted to date on physical abuse of children employed a large matched (case control) cohort design to study the effects of different forms of early abuse (defined by court reports) on later crime and violence (Widom, 1989b). In comparison to controls, abused and neglected children had a significantly greater number of arrests for violence as adults. These effects held for males but not for females, and for blacks but not for whites. Neglect in childhood without violence was just as likely to lead to an arrest for violence in adulthood as was physical abuse in childhood.

Although these findings are consistent with a causal relation between early abuse and later violence, further research is required to rule out other possibilities. It is possible, for example, that the experience of early abuse does not itself cause adult violence. It may be that parental abuse is a response to the child's aggressive behavior, since Eron et al. (1991) found that the best predictor of adult aggression was the extent of childhood aggression, regardless of parental behavior. Furthermore, parents who physically abuse their children may pass on to their children a genetic or biological predisposition to violence that is responsible for the later violence seen in these children (DiLalla and Gottesman, 1991; Widom, 1991). An important issue is whether causal effects are immediate or delayed. For example, we know that abused children tend significantly to become violent adults. Is this an example of a long-delayed "sleeper effect," or is it mediated by a chain of shorter-term causes and effects? If so, what are they?

As already mentioned, numerous studies show that violent offenders tend to come from certain types of family backgrounds. In particular, they tend to have been subjected to physical punishment, they tend to have alcoholic or criminal parents, and they tend to have disharmonious parents who are likely to separate or divorce. Physical child abusers also tend to have parents who lack warmth, are rejecting and hostile, and use reinforcement in unpredictable ways (Milner, 1990) and are less likely to report having had a caring adult/friend in their childhood (Milner et al., 1990). These features of parents may act as mediators between physical abuse in childhood and adult criminal violence.

Each year, 30 percent of female homicide victims are killed by their husbands or boyfriends (Federal Bureau of Investigation, 1982), and over a million abused women seek medical help for their injuries (Stark and Flitcraft, 1982). Most of the research on the etiology of spouse abuse has focused on intrapersonal as opposed to interpersonal or sociocultural factors. This research suggests that wife batterers have witnessed abuse in their own families of origin, have low self-esteem, tend to abuse alcohol, and have low assertiveness (Margolin et al., 1988). These factors, however, also characterize nonviolent criminals, and research is needed to understand the factors that may possibly link experience with early child abuse with later wife abuse. Unfortunately, research into the etiology of wife battering has involved women from small, nonrepresentative samples residing temporarily in shelters. Margolin et al. (1988) have recommended that future research in this area should (a) be directed at nonclinical and noncriminal samples, (b) focus on the development of typologies with a view towards intervention, (c) be developed to test theories of wife battering, and (d) aim to assess what factors predict such violence in a longitudinal context.

Beginning around age 5 or 6, children identify with their parents and with ethnic and class groups. By identification we refer to children's beliefs that they share the psychological properties of the persons or groups with whom they are identified. This universal process is an important part of psychoanalytic theory. It was also recognized by commentators on human nature writing long before Freud was born. Because of identification, children who live with parents who possess undesirable qualities (unemployed, unfair, unjust) will believe that some of these properties also belong to them. As a result, they will establish a conception of themselves as undesirable or as incapable of obtaining desired goals. Such a state is likely to create psychological conditions for later aggressive behavior. One reason why race may be associated with violence in our culture is that black children who live in poverty may identify both with the undesirable qualities of being poor as well as with their ethnic group, which they perceive to be the target of hostility by the white majority. These identifications may be part of the explanation why black children are disproportionally at risk for aggressive behavior.

Peer and School Factors

Coie et al. (1991) has argued that aggressiveness was the single most important reason for a child to be rejected by peers, pointing to the fact that 30-40 percent of socially rejected children were highly aggressive. It is uncertain, however, to what extent peer influences are important in the development of violent offending, and whether rejection by peers causes aggressive behavior, whether aggression causes social rejection, or both. There is some evidence in favor of aggression's causing rejection, which supports Coie's argument (Huesmann and Eron, 1986). However, if rejection causes aggression, then interventions aimed at improving children's social relations with their peers might lead to reductions in aggressive behavior.

Olweus (1991) has estimated that 9 percent of schoolchildren in Norway and Sweden are regular victims of bullying, while 7-8 percent of children engage in bullying. It is believed that four factors contribute to the development of bullying behavior in school: (a) lack of warmth and involvement by the primary caretaker, (b) permissiveness regarding aggressive behavior by the caretaker, (c) the use of physical punishments and violent emotional outbursts as childrearing methods, and (d) an "active and hot-headed" temperamental predisposition in the child (Olweus, 1980). It might be expected that school bullying would predict adult violence, but there appears to be little hard evidence for this at the present time. However, the finding that children who at age 8 are rated by their peers as being aggressive in school have significantly more indications of antisocial aggression as adults than other children would support this expectation (Eron and Huesmann, 1990).

A statistical survey of school crime between 1975 and 1977 indicated that 156 out of 1,000 secondary school students reported having been assaulted. While 42 percent of the student assaults and 11 percent of the student robberies resulted in injury, most injuries were relatively minor (U.S. Department of Health, Education, and Welfare, 1978), and in the past weapons have been infrequently used in such assaults and robberies (McDermott and Hindelang, 1981). Only 1 in 20 student and teacher victimizations resulted in an injury (McDermott and Hindelang, 1981). Spatial characteristics of schools can influence violence in that (a) relatively high numbers of individuals occupy a limited amount of space, (b) the capacity to avoid confrontations is somewhat reduced, (c) the imposition of behavioral routines and conformity may contribute to feelings of anger, resentment, and rejection, and (d) poor design features may facilitate the commission of violent acts. These features of schools suggest possible interventions for reducing school violence (e.g., enhancement of environmental design, promoting student participation in rule enforcement), but to date such suggestions have been largely impressionistic and anecdotal.

Violent offenders tend to have a history of school failure, including low intelligence, poor attainment, and truancy (Farrington, 1991b).

Effects of Television Violence

Most reviews of the literature (e.g., Heath et al., 1989) conclude that exposure to television violence encourages aggressive behavior by children and adults. Even reviews restricted to naturalistic field experiments on aggression, which should have the highest internal and external validity, reach the same conclusion (e.g., Wood et al., 1991). However, there are some differences in interpretation and numerous methodological problems, for example those brought out in the debate between Friedrich-Cofer and Huston (1986) and Freedman (1986). The effects of television violence on aggression may be short term (e.g., activation, arousal, disinhibition, contagion) or long term (e.g., changes in behavior, attitudes, or values), but most research focuses on short-term effects.

An extensive meta-analysis prepared for the panel by Comstock and Paik (1990) covered 188 studies and 1,126 comparisons between 1957 and 1990. They found that the average effect size (in this case, a correlation) was .31. This effect is quite substantial. For example, in a 2 by 2 table, it might correspond to 51 percent of those exposed to television violence showing aggressive behavior, in comparison with only 20 percent of a control (nonexposed) group (Farrington and Loeber, 1989). Laboratory experiments (.40) showed higher average effect sizes than field experiments (.27) or surveys (.19), and effect sizes were greater for physical violence (.23) and robbery (.28) than for criminal violence (.10). Overall, the vast majority of studies, whatever their methodology, showed that exposure to television violence resulted in increased aggressive behavior, both contemporaneously and over time.

Life Transitions

It is important to investigate whether key life events or transitions influence within-individual changes in violence or violence potential over time, such as puberty, moving home or changing schools, graduating from school or dropping out, starting a job or becoming unemployed, getting married, having a child, and so on. Most of these influences have been studied with respect to offending in general rather than specifically to violent offending.

The onset and velocity of puberty vary considerably in females and in males, although it is more common to consider these changes in the course of female than male development because of their more dramatic bodily changes. The variation is such that a substantial number of children can be classified as either early or late maturers. In measuring the behavior of young adolescents it is essential to note that the biological changes accompanying puberty are confounded with psychological changes and adjustments in schooling, given the customary switch from elementary to junior high school that occurs around age 13. Early maturation is generally thought to be a disadvantage in girls (e.g., they may be attracted to older males, older males find them attractive), while it appears to be an advantage in boys (e.g., the increase in muscle mass and coordination contributes to athletic skill). Magnusson et al. (1986) found that girls with an earlier age of menarche committed more antisocial acts than other girls, as a function of having older friends.

During and after puberty an association between increased levels of testosterone and aggressive behavior in males has been demonstrated (Olweus, 1987). Much aggressive behavior typically has its origin in the period prior to the onset of puberty, making it unlikely that rising hormone levels at puberty have a causal influence on onset. Hormone levels are more likely to be related to the frequency or intensity of aggression. It is not clear how variations in gonadal hormones are affected by changes in the social environment, nor is the interaction between gonadal and adrenal sex hormones well understood. In fostering a developmental approach to the study of early determinants of aggressive and violent behavior, these areas are ripe for investigation.

Protective Factors

It is important to investigate how protective factors interact with other influences at the individual level that encourage the development of violence, as well as with influences at the biological and social levels. There are two main definitions of protective factors (see, e.g., Farrington et al., 1988). A protective factor may be merely the opposite end of the continuum to a risk factor. For example, just as low IQ is regarded as a risk factor, high IQ can be regarded as a protective factor. Alternatively, a protective factor may be a variable that interacts with a risk factor to minimize its effect. For example, if low IQ predicted violence among low-income families but not among high-income families, high income might be protecting children from the effects of low IQ.

There have been several studies focusing on why children at risk of offending do not become offenders, and on what the protective factors are. Rutter and Giller (1983) reported that certain life events (e.g., changes in peer group, leaving school, moving away from home, marriage) are associated with reductions in delinquency and crime. Research by Farrington et al. (1988) indicates that the main protective factors seemed to be shyness, nervousness, or social isolation. In other words, the vulnerable boys from typically criminogenic backgrounds who did not become offenders tended to be socially withdrawn and isolated in childhood (and indeed later in adulthood as well).

Such findings are consistent with the possibility that a shy, fearful temperament in early life may represent a protective factor for later aggression (Kagan, 1989). However, research by McCord (1987) suggests that childhood aggressiveness coupled with shyness was more likely to be followed by crime than aggressiveness without shyness, and similar results were obtained by Kellam et al. (1983). Huesmann and Eron (1988) found that aggressive children at age 8 who did not commit later crimes by age 30 differed from the aggressive 8-year-olds who accumulated criminal records in having a higher IQ and in having parents who regularly attended religious services; these were the only two group discriminators after controlling for occupation, income, family size, and geographic residence (Huesmann and Eron, 1988). Other identified protective factors include being firstborn and coming from smaller families characterized by low discord (Werner and Smith, 1982).

VIOLENT CRIMES IN CRIMINAL CAREERS

It is important to investigate how far the "criminal career perspective" (Blumstein et al., 1986) might be useful in explaining the development of criminal violence. This perspective focuses on such concepts as onset, continuation, and desistance; specialization and versatility; escalation in seriousness; and frequency of offending by active offenders. It is important to determine the relationship among these concepts. For example, do those who commit criminal violence at a relatively early age tend to commit violent offenses at high rates and tend to have long careers of violence?

Most studies of violence are based on official records of arrests or convictions, which suggest that violence is a relatively uncommon event. However, self-reports of offending show that physical assault is quite prevalent. For example, Farrington (1989) reported that only 12 percent of the inner-city males he studied were convicted of violent offenses between ages 10 and 32, but as many as 37 percent were involved in physical assaults between ages 27 and 32, when violence was decreasing.

Very few projects permit the investigation of the occurrence of violent crimes in criminal careers. Generally, self-report studies with general population samples (e.g., Elliott et al., 1989) are unsuitable, for two main reasons. First, the prevalence of unambiguously violent crimes (as opposed to "gang fights") is very low, possibly because many of the most violent people in the population are not included in the samples interviewed. Second, information about the time ordering of different types of offenses is not collected in such studies. It would be desirable in future self-report studies of offending to collect time ordering information about unambiguously serious offenses, which are rare; it would be impractical to collect such data about all self-reported offenses.

Self-report or official record studies with retrospectively defined offender samples (e.g., Miller et al., 1982) are also unsuitable, because of the difficulty of reconstructing the criminal careers of any given birth cohort. This leaves prospective cohort studies with official record information about offending as the most suitable for studying violent crimes in criminal careers, but unfortunately many of these studies (e.g., Wolfgang et al., 1972) stop at the eighteenth birthday, before the peak of violent offending in the young adult years (18-25). All results, of course, are greatly affected by the age of truncation of the study, and there is the continuing problem in U.S. studies of linking juvenile and adult records. Also, the sample sizes in many studies are inadequate to investigate violent offending, because of its low prevalence (especially outside the United States).

In his detailed review of knowledge about violent criminal careers, Weiner (1989:Table 2.1) listed 44 relevant studies. However, only three American data sets could provide minimally adequate information about violent crimes in criminal careers: (1) the 506 Cambridge-Somerville (Boston) males born about 1928 and followed up to age 45 by McCord (1980), (2) the 975 Philadelphia males born in 1945 and followed up to age 30 by Wolfgang et al. (1987), and (3) the 633 continuously resident Racine children born in 1942 and followed up to age 32 by Shannon (1988). In addition, four foreign data sets could provide minimally adequate data: (1) the 411 London males born mostly in 1953 and followed up to age 32 by Farrington (1991b), (2) the 710 Swedish males born about 1955 and followed up to age 30 by Stattin et al. (1989), (3) the 15,117 Stockholm children born in 1953 and followed up to age 25-26 by Wikstrom (1985), and (4) the 28,879 Copenhagen males born in 1944-1947 and followed up to age 27-30 by Moffitt et al. (1989). The lack of adequate data about violent crimes in criminal careers makes it easier to raise questions than to answer them.

The main violent crimes that have been studied are homicide, forcible rape, robbery, and assault. It would be desirable to study different types of violent crimes in criminal careers, but this is very difficult. For example, it would be desirable to know how different types of violent crimes are interrelated and whether, for example, homicide offenders have a significant tendency also to commit forcible rape, robbery, or assault. The most suitable data set for answering this question is that collected by Miller et al. (1982), but they do not seem to have addressed it. It would be desirable to know whether these violent crimes were typically committed in a certain order or at certain ages, but available data limit this review to violent crimes in general rather than different types of violent crimes. Some key questions follow:

(1) What proportion of crimes in criminal careers are violent? Is it safe to conclude that only a small proportion are violent? For example, only 12 percent of offenses leading to conviction in the London cohort (85 of 683) were violent, as were only 5 percent of offenses recorded by the police in the Stockholm cohort (1,290 out of 23,774). The 633 Racine children yielded only 21 assaults and 7 robberies, so that only 1 percent of their offenses were violent felonies; only 9 percent of the Philadelphia crimes involved injury.

(2) What proportion of offenders include a violent crime in their criminal careers? These percentages, of course, are higher than those in question 1, but it is still safe to conclude that only a minority of offenders include a violent offense in their criminal careers. For example, only 33 percent of convicted males in the London cohort (50 of 153) were convicted of violence, representing 12 percent of all cohort males. In the Stockholm cohort, 21 percent of recorded offenders were recorded for violence (591 of 2,837), representing 4 percent of the cohort; and in the Copenhagen cohort, 7 percent of recorded offenders were recorded for violence (735 of 10,918), representing 3 percent of the cohort. Even in the Cambridge-Somerville study, only 14 percent of the cohort (69 of 506), or 18 percent of the offenders, were convicted of violent crimes up to age 45.

(3) How many violent crimes are committed by violent offenders? Studies outside the United States show that the majority of officially recorded violent offenders are recorded for only one violent offense. This was true, for example, of 72 percent of the Stockholm violent offenders, 76 percent of the Copenhagen vio-

lent offenders, and 70 percent of the London violent offenders. However, in the Miller et al. (1982) study in Ohio, the violent arrestees included 20 percent arrested 5 or more times for violence and 53 percent arrested 2-4 times for violence, so the same conclusion may not hold in the United States.

(4) How many nonviolent crimes are committed by violent offenders? Is it safe to conclude that violent offenders commit more nonviolent crimes than violent crimes? In the London cohort, the 50 violent offenders were convicted of 85 violent crimes (average 1.7) and 263 nonviolent crimes (average 5.3), so that only 24 percent of their crimes were violent. Nearly all of these violent offenders (43 of 50) were also convicted for nonviolent crimes. Similarly, 86 percent of the recorded violent offenders in the Stockholm cohort (510 of 591) were also recorded for nonviolent crimes. In the Miller et al. study in Ohio, the violent offenders committed twice as many nonviolent crimes as violent crimes (8,368 as opposed to 4,163).

(5) Are violent offenders merely frequent offenders? In other words, does the probability of committing a violent crime increase in direct proportion to the number of crimes committed? In the London cohort, this seemed to be true. Since 12.4 percent of all offenses were violent, it might be expected that 12.4 percent of the 49 cohort males who were convicted of only one offense would be convicted for violence, and the actual figure of 6 was close to the chance expectation of 6.1. Similarly, it might be expected that 23.3 percent of the 30 males who committed two offenses would commit at least one violent offense ($1 - [.876]^2$), and the actual figure of 8 was close to the chance expectation of 7.0. Overall, the actual proportion of all offenders who were violent (33%) was not significantly different from the chance expectation (36%) assuming that violent and nonviolent offenses were committed at random. If there had been any specialization in violent offending, there would have been significantly fewer violent offenders than chance expectation, and they would have each committed more violent offenses on average than expected. These and other results led Farrington (1991b) to conclude that violent offenders were essentially frequent offenders. Similar conclusions were drawn by Miller et al. (1982) in Ohio and by Wikstrom (1985) in Stockholm.

(6) Is there specialization in violent offending? While there is a high degree of generality in violent offending, there also appears to be some degree of specialization. For example, controlling for the number of offenses committed before and after the first vio-

lent or property offense, Moffitt et al. (1989) in the Copenhagen cohort concluded that a first-time violent offender was 1.9 times as likely to commit a violent act among his future offenses as a first-time property offender. It is likely that the degree of specialization in violent offending is greater at adult ages than at juvenile ages.

(7) What is the average age of commission of violent as opposed to nonviolent offenses? Generally, violent crimes are committed at a later age than most types of nonviolent crimes. In the London longitudinal study, violent crimes had the second-highest median age of commission (20) after fraud: higher than the more common burglaries or thefts (17). Violent crimes had a significantly higher age of commission than nonviolent ones, when comparisons were restricted to the 43 men with both violent and nonviolent offenses (31 committed violent crimes at higher ages, 12 committed nonviolent ones at higher ages).

(8) What is the average age of onset of violent as opposed to nonviolent offenses? In the London study, violent crimes had a higher average age of onset than nonviolent ones, when comparisons were restricted to the 43 men with both violent and nonviolent offenses (35 violent higher, 6 nonviolent higher, 2 equal). It was the case for only 7 of the 153 convicted men that their first offense was a violent crime, making it impossible to determine whether the percentage of onsets that were violent changed with age.

(9) What is the average serial number of violent as opposed to nonviolent offenses in criminal careers? In the London study, the average serial number of violent offenses was higher than for nonviolent offenses, when comparisons were restricted to the 43 men with both types of offenses (27 violent higher, 11 nonviolent higher, 5 equal). In other words, violent offenses tended to be committed relatively late in criminal careers.

(10) What is the relation between juvenile violent offending and adult violent offending? Do the majority of juvenile violent offenders go on to commit violent offenses as adults and, conversely, were the majority of adult violent offenders previously convicted of violence as juveniles? In the London study, the majority of juvenile violent offenders did go on to commit adult violent offenses (7 of 10, with the other 3 committing adult nonviolent offenses). However, only a minority of adult violent offenders (7 of 47) were juvenile violent offenders. Of the remaining 40, 20 had juvenile nonviolent offenses and 20 had no juvenile offenses.

(11) How useful are criminal career concepts such as career length and individual offending frequency as applied to violence? What is the probability of committing an $(n + 1)$th violent offense after committing an nth violent offense, and what is the average street time until the next violent offense? In the majority of studies in which the majority of violent offenders commit only one violent offense, ideas about careers of violence are not likely to be very useful. They could be useful in a study such as Miller et al. (1982), although this was not a prospective cohort study. In most projects, the main thrust of the research has to be to investigate the occurrence of odd violent offenses during a predominantly nonviolent criminal career. For example, it would be useful to investigate if violent offenses tended to follow certain types or sequences of nonviolent offenses. However, attempts to identify "violent career criminals" in most studies are doomed to failure.

THEORIES

This section briefly summarizes several theories that are particularly important to understanding of the development of violence and aggression. Several of these theories are complementary (e.g., social learning theory and cognitive-behavioral theory) and should not be viewed as mutually exclusive. Although the focus in this appendix is on developmental theories, it would also be interesting to investigate to what extent other theories (e.g., the rational choice theory of Clarke and Cornish, 1985) explain violent behavior.

Frustration-Aggression Theory

Frustration-aggression theory represents the first comprehensive theory of aggression that assigned a prominent role to learning (Eron, 1990). The basic principle underlying frustration-aggression theory is that, when people become frustrated (e.g., when their goals are thwarted), they become aggressive (Dollard et al., 1939). This theory fostered a great deal of empirical research testing hypotheses generated by it. One basic premise of the model, that frustration is a necessary facilitator of aggression, has been seriously questioned by a number of researchers (Eron, 1990). Other demonstrated weaknesses in this theory led to the development of research that placed a greater emphasis on external environmental cues as elicitors of aggression than on motivational or drive factors (Bandura, 1973).

Social Learning Theory

Bandura (1973) proposed that aggressive behavior is learned and maintained through environmental experiences. He argued that aggression can be learned vicariously by watching (modeling), and that it can be inhibited if punishment succeeds in building up an association between aggression and anxiety (in which the anxiety might be interpreted as "guilt" or "conscience"). According to this theory, the maintenance of aggressive behavior is usually subject to the principles of reinforcement, so that behaviors that are reinforced will be repeated. Although research testing this social learning theory of aggression has generated mixed results, it has received some degree of empirical support (e.g., Eron, 1987).

Cognitive-Behavioral Theories

A cognitive perspective on aggression holds that aggressive behavior is a product of angry, aggressive thoughts. In this framework, interventions aimed at changing the occurrence of such thoughts would be expected to alleviate aggressive behavior. Huesmann and Eron (1989) have developed a cognitive model of the development of aggression that argues that such behavior is to a great extent controlled by programs or "scripts" learned during the child's early development. Such scripts suggest what events are about to occur, how the person should react to these events, and what the outcome will be. These scripts are retrieved from memory in response to appropriate environmental cues and are used to guide behavior. Under this model, a repeatedly aggressive child is one who consistently retrieves and employs aggressive scripts. The child's cognitive processes are also thought to be influenced by the parent's own cognitive processes, in that parents who view the world as hostile may reinforce their child's view of the world as hostile. Huesmann and Eron (1989) argue that aggressive behavior is stable because the scripts for aggression are themselves stable, due to the process of repeated rehearsal, whether through fantasizing, observation, or actual behavior.

Dodge (1986) has developed an influential social information processing model of aggression. This model lays out a sequence of five cognitive operations involved in the development of aggressive behavior: (1) encoding, (2) interpretation, (3) response search, (4) response decision, and (5) enactment. Aggressive children appear to use fewer environmental cues to mediate behavior (Dodge and Newman, 1981) and tend to interpret the behavior of a peer as more hostile (Dodge, 1980). They are also less capable of generating potential responses to conflict situations (Richard and Dodge, 1982) and are more likely to select passive and aggressive responses (Dodge, 1986). Interventions aimed at increasing the aggressive child's social information processing capabilities would, according to this model, have a significant effect in reducing levels of aggression.

Dodge (1991) has recently drawn a distinction between reactive and proactive aggression, which is similar to Berkowitz's earlier distinction (1983) between emotional and instrumental aggression. This suggests that, while some aggressive children are troubling to others and use aggression in a proactive way to meet their goals (proactive aggression), others react in an angry, volatile manner and are troubled by others (reactive aggression). This distinction is supported by similar distinctions made by ethologists and psychobiologists between "affective aggression," characterized by a high degree of autonomic arousal, and "hot-blooded" frenzied anger and between "instrumental aggression" characterized by low autonomic arousal and a cold-blooded, reward-seeking form of aggression. This two-factor model has received some support from factor-analytic studies (Dodge, 1991). While reactive aggressives at a young age are disliked by their peers, proactive aggressives are not necessarily disliked (Dodge and Coie, 1987). Proactive aggressives are also viewed as having leadership qualities and a better sense of humor than reactive aggressives (Dodge and Coie, 1987). Dodge (1991) speculated that these two forms of aggression have different neural substrates, have deficits in different stages of social information processing, and have different etiologies and developmental courses.

RESEARCH PRIORITIES

Key Questions

Important questions about the development of an individual potential for violence should be addressed:

(1) Do male and black persons have a higher potential for violence than others and, if so, why?
(2) To what extent do potentially violent people tend to seek out violent situations?
(3) What are the developmental sequences linking violent offenses with other types of offenses and with childhood aggression?
(4) How do individual, family, and school factors interact to

produce aggressive children and violent adults?

(5) What are the factors that protect aggressive children from becoming violent adults, and what factors facilitate desistance from violent offending?

(6) What are the effects of juvenile and criminal justice sanctions on violent offending?

(7) Are there subtypes of aggression and violence (e.g., reactive and proactive aggression) that have distinct etiologies and are responsive to different forms of intervention?

(8) Through what routes (e.g., temperament, cognitive deficits, social skills deficits) may pregnancy and birth complications lead to later violence, and how are these obstetric factors mediated by family and other environmental factors?

(9) What factors contribute to the manifestation of fearful versus fearless early temperaments, and do early temperamental factors predispose children to later violent adult behavior?

(10) What is the role of physical discipline in contributing to the development of violence?

(11) Can reliable and valid indices of violence be developed?

(12) What differences are there between people who commit violent acts and those who commit more general delinquent, criminal, or antisocial acts?

Research Methods

A variety of different research designs are useful in tackling these questions. For example, in investigating cross-situational consistency in violent behavior, short-term intensive longitudinal studies, with frequent data collection, would be useful. In studying factors that might inhibit aggressive children from becoming violent adults, intervention techniques such as skills training and sanctions should be evaluated in randomized experiments including follow-up periods. Prospective longitudinal studies would be needed to investigate developmental sequences from childhood aggression to adult violence. However, for rare acts such as homicide, retrospective or case control studies would be needed.

Violence is a complex and multifaceted form of behavior. It is likely that there are no simple explanations of violence. It is essential that longitudinal research into violence should include measures of a wide range of variables, including biological, behavioral, social, and cognitive factors. Technological innovations are permitting deeper probing into questions of human biology, and the possibilities of breakthroughs in those areas are ever-present.

Such research has implications for the interaction between influences at the individual level and biological influences.

Longitudinal research does not necessarily have to extend from birth to adulthood. An "accelerated longitudinal design" could be used, in which a few overlapping age cohorts are followed up for a few years each (Tonry et al., 1991). Many correlates and predictors of violence have already been identified in past research. However, the precise ways in which they are linked to violence (e.g., through developmental or causal sequences) is not clear. In future research, frequent data collection is needed to track within-individual developmental sequences over time. Data from several different sources are needed (e.g., biological, individual, family, peers, school, community) to study the major causal influences on development and their interactive and independent effects. Special efforts should be made to investigate how the individual potential interacts with the environment to produce violent events.

Very few studies begin with a sample of aggressive children and investigate possible protective factors influencing why some of them do not become violent adults. Such studies, however, would be capable of providing important insights regarding factors involved in desistance from violence.

One valuable strategy for the future would be to combine longitudinal research studies of violence with experimental interventions, since such studies are capable of providing information on both the natural history and the course of development of violence together with causal effects of intervention methods (Farrington, 1988). A study by Huesmann et al. (1983) included an intervention with a subsample of subjects who were part of a larger longitudinal research design. The intervention was successful in reducing the aggression of the children receiving the treatment over a three-year period. In this continuing investigation the subjects who participated in the intervention at ages 8 to 10 will be reexamined to determine if the reduction in aggression has persisted over 15 years.

In order to establish the effects of interventions on violence, subjects would ideally be assigned at random to intervention programs. It would also be desirable to conduct such studies in large cities, where the problem of violence is most acute. A good official record system, a competent research team, a large sample size, and methods to minimize attrition would be important prerequisites for such a study. Research on the success of interventions not only has important practical and policy implications but also provides important clues about causal effects, and it is to this research that we now turn.

INTERVENTIONS

PRENATAL, PERINATAL, AND POSTNATAL HEALTH CARE

The link between prenatal/perinatal complications and later violence suggests that interventions to reduce violence could be targeted on the prenatal/perinatal period. However, there appear to be no published studies reporting the effects of such early interventions on later violence.

One possible intervention would be to provide prenatal and postnatal health care to an experimental group of mothers (e.g., as in the Infant Health and Development Program directed by J. Brooks-Gunn) and investigate its long-term effectiveness in reducing violence in comparison with a control group. Mothers in the experimental group could be provided with intensive antenatal care, including more frequent home visits by health professionals; education on diet, smoking, and alcohol during pregnancy; and earlier hospitalization to facilitate trouble-free delivery of the baby. Social support provided by midwives during pregnancy to socially disadvantaged mothers with a history of low-birthweight babies has been found to be effective in raising birthweight (Oakley et al., 1990).

Postnatal interventions could be targeted on those within the experimental group who experienced perinatal complications in spite of the intervention. Low-birthweight and premature babies are more likely to experience speech and language disorders, neuromotor abnormalities (e.g., balance and coordination problems), perceptual problems, and visuo-spatial problems. These problems have themselves been implicated in the development of crime and violence (e.g., Moffitt, 1990). Early assessment for such difficulties in the target group coupled with interventions aimed to treat these conditions at an early age could be implemented. Low-birthweight babies are also more likely to suffer intellectual deficits than normal-birthweight babies. Consequently, intervention focused on this group could take the form of a preschool intellectual enrichment program.

These prenatal and postnatal interventions could be carried out on an unselected group of mothers and their offspring. Alternatively, they could be targeted on a group of mothers who are deemed to be "at risk" for pregnancy and birth complications or who are thought to be more likely to have violent offspring on the basis of demographic and social characteristics or on the basis of crime and violence in the child's father. Another possibility is that experimental groups of both high-risk and low-risk mothers could be included to assess the effects of possible interactions between prenatal and perinatal complications and social variables. Since socioeconomic disadvantage increases the risk of school failure in low-birthweight children, it might be expected that interventions would be most effective in socially disadvantaged families.

Although it would take many years to evaluate the ultimate effect of such a health care program on violent adult behavior, initial assessments of success could be made relatively early in life. For example, the effects of this intervention on early temperamental antecedents of aggression could be assessed at age 20-30 months. Ratings of aggressive play behavior could be made at 3-4 years of age, while aggressive behavior in the home and school could be assessed by parents, teachers, and peers in early childhood. By adolescence, it would also be possible to assess self-reported violent behavior and to collect school data and public records. An important advantage of such an intervention is that it would be expected to result in a wide range of health benefits to the individual in addition to any effects on criminal behavior and violence.

Social Learning and Cognitive-Behavioral Interventions

Many studies have been carried out using variants of cognitive-behavioral therapy and interpersonal social skills training with aggressive children, as well as parent training and family therapy (for examples, see the reviews in Crowell et al., 1987; Keith, 1984). Behavioral management interventions based on social learning theory aim to alter the contingencies between responses and reinforcement, since aggression is viewed as inadvertently reinforced or modeled. Several interventions based on this theory are discussed below.

Television Violence

Since research indicates that television violence viewing in childhood predicts adult violence (Eron, 1987), interventions have been conducted to mitigate the possible effects of television violence on aggression. These either attempt to change the child's attitudes about television violence and the appropriateness of aggressive behavior (e.g., Huesmann et al., 1983) or use parent training to help control the child's viewing habits (e.g., Singer and Singer, 1981).

Studies have attempted to increase prosocial behavior in children by encouraging children to watch television programs that emphasize the prosocial behavior of the characters (Eron, 1986; Eron and Huesmann, 1984). Although these interventions have received some success in the short term, no long-term effects have been demonstrated. Furthermore, the observed effects have been confined to the laboratory and have focused almost exclusively on children from preschool ages to age 10 (Eron, 1986).

Some intervention strategies appear to be more successful than others. For example, interventions that work directly with children (e.g., Huesmann et al., 1983) appear to be more successful than interventions that approach the child's behavior indirectly (e.g., Singer and Singer's attempt to alter the child's behavior by intervening with the parent). Future interventions in this area might therefore usefully focus on changing the child's attitudes about television violence and the appropriateness of aggressive behavior using direct methods.

Cognitive/Behavioral Interventions

A major difficulty facing all intervention programs is that aggressive behavioral strategies may be well learned early in the child's life and in consequence may be relatively intractable. Nevertheless, programs that have combined cognitive and behavioral approaches have proved to be the most effective forms of intervention and may be particularly effective with those children at risk of developing aggressive and violent behavior (Eron, 1986). However, Eron has argued that, for such programs to work, they must both emphasize the undesirability of aggressive behavior and also provide the child with alternative problem-solving behaviors.

The success of interventions based on social-cognitive theory may be a function of the context in which the program is administered. For example, Guerra (1990) reported different success for two interventions. The first program aimed to develop social problem-solving skills, change beliefs about aggression, change attitudes toward television, and foster prosocial behavior in black and Hispanic aggressive schoolchildren with low socioeconomic status in the second to fourth grades. It was based on the social information processing theory of Dodge (1986). The intervention program produced no short-term behavioral change in this sample. However, an intervention also based on a social-cognitive training program for seriously aggressive, incarcerated 15- to 18-year-old delinquents resulted in posttreatment reductions in antisocial behavior. The facts that the latter population was older and that the study was conducted in an environment in which there were major incentives to reduce antisocial behavior represent contextual factors that may have led to a more successful outcome (Guerra, 1990). It may be of some value therefore for future intervention programs to pay attention to the role such contextual factors might play in mediating the success or failure of the intervention.

It is common for many cognitive-behavioral intervention projects to show a short-term reductive effect on childhood aggression. However, there are few such studies with large samples, an experimental design, and a long-term follow-up to investigate possible effects on adult violence. Furthermore, most interventions have been carried out on nonclinical samples; research is needed to assess more fully whether success generalizes to more severely disturbed populations of aggressive children (Kendall et al., 1991).

Social Skills Training

A number of studies have demonstrated that social skills training can have effects in changing aggressive behavior in children. Specific aspects of social skills training that appear to be particularly effective in altering behavior include social relations training, prohibition of aggression, anger control, and cognitive-behavioral problem solving (Pepler et al., 1991). Furthermore, some evidence exists to support the notion that social skills training can be generalized to other settings, and that the benefits of such training can be maintained over time (Kazdin, 1988).

One example of a social skills intervention that has demonstrated some moderate behavioral improvements extending over time is the Earlscourt Social Skills Group Program (Pepler et al., 1991). This program, based on social learning theory and cognitive-behavioral theory, is an experiential program designed to improve the self-control and social skills of aggressive children ages 6-12. Eight basic social skills are taught in group sessions conducted twice a week for a period of 12-15 weeks: "problem solving," "know your feelings," "listening," "following instructions," "joining in," "using self-control," "responding to teasing," and "keeping out of fights." The program makes use of a wide number of behavioral techniques, including positive reinforcement, behavioral rehearsal, generalization, and training parents in child management skills. Social-cognitive techniques include enhancing problem-solving skills, increasing awareness of feelings, and promoting thinking aloud to assist self-monitoring. Children in this social skills group showed significant improvements in externalizing behavior problems (including aggression) as rated by teachers relative to a control group on the Achenbach Child Behavior Checklist, and these improvements were maintained over a three-month follow-up period.

Although cognitive social skills programs have been generally effective, most of these have shown improvements in cognitive abilities in a laboratory setting rather than in antisocial behavior, and the extent of change has often been small (Kazdin, 1988). Clear delineation of the target sample, use of stringent selection criteria, and identification of subtypes on whom different varieties of cognitive social skills interventions work best, are further areas that future intervention studies should address (Kazdin, 1988).

Jones and Offord (1989) reported some initial evidence of effectiveness in their PALS (Participate and Learn Skills) community project. This skill development program was offered to an experimental group of all children ages 5 to 15 in a publicly supported housing complex in Ottawa, Ontario for a period of 32 months. A control housing complex had available only minimal recreational services provided by the city department. The PALS project sponsored 40 programs in 25 skill areas. Many of these programs were sports-based, but they also included guitar, ballet, baton, scouting, and other nonsports activities.

During the 32 months of the intervention, police charges against the juveniles at the experimental site were less than one-quarter of those at the control site, and in addition there was a marked reduction in security violations in the experimental compared with the control housing complex. There were also improvements in school behavior and self-esteem in the experimental group, but these changes were not statistically significant. A cost-benefit analysis showed that the potential savings in terms of reduced vandalism, police time, and fire costs greatly exceeded the costs of the program. Two important questions concerning this program remain unanswered: (1) Do such skills interventions have any long-term effects on levels of antisocial behavior? (2) Do they have specific effects on violence in particular? If these questions can be answered affirmatively, consideration should be given to the inclusion of skills training in intervention programs for violent behavior in children.

A recent study by Tremblay et al. (1991) combined social skills training with other interventions in 7-year-old boys selected for disruptiveness and low socioeconomic status. Disruptive boys were randomly allocated to an experimental group receiving interventions, an "observation" group who received no intervention but who completed questionnaires and took part in observational studies, and a control group. Treatment for the boys consisted of social skills training (e.g., instructions on what to do when angry or when teased), training in fantasy play focused on prosocial alternatives to the expression of anger, and training on critical television watching. This treatment was combined with parent training consisting of monitoring the child's behavior, use of positive reinforcement, and family crisis management. Outcome measures (ratings by teachers, mothers, peers, and self-reported delinquency) were taken on three occasions following completion of the two-year program for a period of 27 months.

No positive long-term treatment effects were observed for teacher, mother, or peer ratings. For self-reported delinquency however, treated boys reported reductions in fighting and stealing. Furthermore, fewer treated boys had to attend special educational classes or were held back in school. The fact that reductions in fighting were not immediately observed but did emerge at the longest follow-up period suggests that some intervention effects may take time to work through. Again, a replication and long-term follow-up of the effects of this multimodal intervention on adult violence are required in order fully to assess the benefits of this type of intervention.

Parent Training

Since poor parental childrearing techniques predict delinquency (Farrington and West, 1990), intervention programs that attempt to train parents may play a general role in reducing delinquency and may also result in some reduction in later violent offending.

Patterson (1980; Paterson et al., 1982) viewed violence as in part a coercive act by the child to gain attention from the parent or as a mechanism to reduce frustration. In a parent intervention program aimed at families with delinquent and predelinquent children, parents were trained in effective childrearing methods, such as noticing what a child was doing, monitoring behavior over long periods, clearly stating house rules, making rewards and punishments contingent on behavior, and negotiating disagreements so that conflicts and crises did not escalate. Similarly, children were taught that coercive behavior would not be tolerated and would be met with time-out (isolation) procedures. Patterson's treatment program has been shown to be effective in reducing antisocial child behavior over short periods in small-scale studies, and consequently such programs may warrant inclusion in any future intervention strategy for violence.

Parent training programs have been evaluated in hundreds of outcome studies (Kazdin, 1985) and have been shown to be effective in reducing aggression and conduct disorder in children. As Kazdin (1988) points out, however, brief interventions tend to show fewer benefits, and families characterized by marital discord show fewer treatment gains, while children from families of low socioeconomic status are less likely to maintain these advantages over time. These limitations are not trivial, since aggressive children who are destined to become violent adults are more likely to come from socially disadvantaged backgrounds. Future parent training intervention programs must attempt to address these issues in addition to demonstrating the long-term effectiveness of these programs.

Intervention programs that combine parent training with teacher training may be particularly beneficial because they tackle aggressive behavior in two crucial social settings. Hawkins et al. (1991) conducted such a program based on a social developmental model integrating social control theory with social learning theory (Hawkins and Weis, 1985). First-grade children in eight public elementary schools were subjects, with teacher ratings of antisocial and aggressive behaviors (assessed using the Achenbach Child Behavior Checklist) used as short-term outcome measures taken at the end of the second grade. Parent training consisted of the use of appropriate rewards and punishments, consistent discipline, use of effective communication skills, and skills to involve children in family activities. Teacher training consisted of proactive classroom management methods, cognitive social skills training, and interactive teaching methods. Boys who received exposure to these interventions were found to have lower scores on aggressive behavior and externalizing behavior problems than controls. Girls in the experimental group showed reductions in self-destructive behavior and depression, but no differences in aggression were observed. Importantly, the effectiveness of this dual intervention in reducing aggression in white males was not replicated in black males.

Two important questions are raised by this study. The first is whether combining parent and teacher intervention programs will be more successful than single interventions in the long term. The second is whether the types of intervention programs developed for white children are appropriate for black children; it may be that special programs need to be developed to suit the affective and cognitive styles of black children. Future intervention studies in this area must clearly pay close attention to the issue of race differences both in levels of aggressive behavior and in intervention effectiveness.

School-Based Interventions

Intellectual Enrichment

Farrington and West (1990) have argued that school failure is an important predictor of later offending, and that preschool intellectual enrichment programs show some evidence of reductions in both school failure and later offending. For example, Berrueta-Clement et al. (1984) reported that children who received a preschool intellectual enrichment program were less likely to be arrested or charged, more likely to graduate from high school, and more likely to be employed at age 19 than controls. Future school-based interventions could usefully incorporate preschool intellectual enrichment programs, particularly targeted on those who are at risk for later crime and violence. U.S. Public Law 99-457 mandates the states to provide similar programs for at-risk children ages 3-5 (Short et al., 1990).

Because school failure is a consistent predictor (or correlate) of violent behavior, it may be useful to target children who are at risk of school failure by virtue of living in high-risk neighborhoods. One possible intervention would be to select neighborhoods with high rates of both school failure and delinquency and to test every 4-year-old boy with a battery that assesses knowledge of the alphabet and of numbers and short-term memory. The administration of such a battery would require 45 minutes. About 15 percent of the children tested might show minimal knowledge of the alphabet and numbers and a poor short-term memory; these children are at risk for early school failure. The intervention would be run during the kindergarten year, perhaps by high school seniors who see the children once a day, five days a week, for the academic year. Some communities (Oakland, California, and San Antonio, Texas) have reduced the rate of school failure in this way. However, they did not assess the effects on conduct disorder, although it is quite conceivable that this intervention might lead to a reduction in antisocial behavior and later violence.

Social Relations

The notion that social rejection may predispose children to aggression has led to school-based interventions aimed at increasing the quality of children's social relations with their peers. Coie et al. (1991) report a school-based intervention made up of social problem solving, positive play training, group entry skill training, and dealing effectively with strong negative feelings. Although aggressive-rejected children showed some improvements, few statistically significant differences were observed. Nevertheless, consideration could be given to developing school-based violence prevention programs, aimed specifically at children in elementary and junior high school grades, together with community-based child development centers that provide family support and educational preparation for preschool children.

Bullying

A national intervention campaign against bullying was initiated in Norway in 1983. The program emphasized positive involvement from teachers and parents, setting firm limits on unacceptable behavior, and the use of nonhostile, noncorporal sanctions on rule violations. Not only did bullying decrease by 50 percent over the course of two years, but thefts, vandalism, and truancy rates were also reduced, while student satisfaction with school life increased. Effects were the same for both boys and girls, and aggressive bullying behavior was not found to be displaced to other situations outside the confines of the school (Olweus, 1991). An important question concerns whether the success of this type of intervention in Scandinavia would generalize to aggressive behavior in U.S. schools. This program is currently being tested in Canada, England, and the Netherlands.

Strategies and Issues in the Implementation of Intervention Programs

Research on the prevention of aggressive and violent behavior needs to acknowledge the multiple causes and systems involved in the development of such behavior. Previous interventions based on single variables or sets of variables have met with limited success, and a more successful strategy for preventing later violence might involve simultaneously targeting the individual and other areas such as school, peers, and family factors that are amenable to change (Guerra, 1990). The different elements of a global intervention package might interact to produce a disproportionate effect.

An important issue in intervention research is what individual form of treatment is best able to alter aggressive behavior in children. One way of addressing this is to conduct studies that compare several forms of experimental interventions. It has been argued that single modality treatments are less effective in reducing antisocial behavior than multimodal treatment approaches (Kazdin, 1988). It is desirable to establish not only the effectiveness of a multimodal intervention package but also which individual aspects of the package are responsible for behavioral improvement. Hence, it is recommended that wherever possible multimodal treatment evaluations be complemented by analyses of which components of the package are most effective, and that the types of treatments that are packaged together are carefully chosen and conceptually justified with respect to the target problem at hand.

Many intervention researchers have failed to base their intervention strategies on clearly developed theoretical models of aggression; consequently, the outcomes of these studies have not been encouraging (Coie et al., 1991). It is recommended that future interventions be developed from a sound theoretical basis in order that intervention studies can inform theories of violent behavior.

Farrington and West (1990) have found that the worst offenders in their longitudinal study tended to come from the poorest families with the worst housing. For example, low family income measured at age 8-10 was found to be the best predictor of general social failure at age 32. These findings suggest that one useful strategy may be to target economic resources to the very poorest families in interventions aimed at reducing levels of crime and violence.

The notion that childhood aggression may be differentiated into proactive and reactive types (Dodge, 1991) has implications for intervention. Dodge (1991) argued that most intervention approaches are implemented without regard for the type of aggressive behavior under scrutiny, and that different types of aggression are likely to respond differently to different types of intervention. Reactive aggressives who overattribute hostility to others in provocative situations may respond best to treatment aimed at training them to understand better others' thoughts and feelings. Proactively aggressive children may respond more favorably to consistent punishment of aggressive behavior and reinforcement of nonaggressive responses; this latter group may also have a better prognosis than the former group. Three intervention programs cited by Dodge (1991) as being particularly suitable for differential implementation with these two types of aggressive children include social problem-solving skills training (Spivack and Shure, 1974), anger-control training (Lochman and Curry, 1986), and parent training (Patterson et al., 1982). In a similar fashion, Kendall et al. (1991) have argued that conduct disordered children with lower levels of hostility and aggression are especially likely to benefit from cognitive-behavioral therapy.

Research on sequences and on prediction might help in identifying when and how it might be best to intervene to prevent the development of adult violence. For example, interventions might be targeted just before key developmental transitions (e.g., from less serious aggression to more serious violence) or when the correlation between the predictor and the outcome is still relatively low (indicating malleability). A related issue concerns at what age interventions may be most successfully imposed.

There is some evidence that interventions conducted early in the developmental process are more effective than later interventions (Hawkins et al., 1988), although some exceptions have been noted (Guerra, 1990). From a cost-benefit perspective, it may be better to intervene at a later developmental stage, when one can be more sure that the targeted group represents those with a high likelihood of going on to become violent adults. Some data by Farrington and Hawkins (1991) indicate that childhood events are more important than teenage behavior in predicting the persistence of offending in the twenties, and they speculate that early prevention may have a greater potential than later criminal justice measures for reducing adult crime. Prediction studies that can push back the age at which adult violence can be predicted are clearly important, in that they will help determine at what developmental stage interventions may be most profitably conducted.

Ideas about intervention possibilities can also be obtained by studying aggressive children who do not become violent adults, and seeking to identify factors that protect them from making the progression. Similarly, most violent offenders desist from violent offending in their twenties, but there has been little research investigating the factors that foster such desistance. Some of it may involve switching to other kinds of activities. For example, aggressive juveniles tend to be unemployed and to be heavy drinkers in their twenties, even though their aggressive behavior has declined (Farrington, 1991b).

Attention should also be paid to intervening with those children who possess multiple predisposing factors for later aggression and violence. For example, one intervention that may be of value consists of studying children ages 4-5 with uninhibited (fearless) temperaments who are also at risk of early school failure. The combination of a young child who is minimally anxious and is about to fail a major life task puts that child at high risk for the development of antisocial behavior. Intervention with such children before school entrance could be of great value.

Policy Issues

The results of intervention research have important implications for public policy. The likely effects of large-scale policy changes should be evaluated beforehand in small-scale experiments. Some policy questions that are likely to arise in connection with the development of an individual potential for violence are as follows:

(1) Should aggressive children be identified at an early age (under 10) and given ameliorative intervention programs such as focusing on skills training, anger control (Novaco), and parent training (Patterson et al., 1991)?

(2) Should pregnant women who are at risk for pregnancy and birth complications be provided with better antenatal services in order to reduce the probability of violence by their children in later life?

(3) Should more widespread programs be introduced, targeted on all children rather than those identified as aggressive? For example, the Olweus antibullying campaign is a wide-ranging program, and so is the attempt to convey prosocial values through prosocial models (e.g., Mr. Rogers).

REFERENCES

American Psychiatric Association

1987 *Diagnostic and Statistical Manual of Mental Disorders* (3rd ed., revised). Washington, D.C.: American Psychiatric Association.

Baker, L.A.

1986 Estimating genetic correlations among discordant phenotypes: An analysis of criminal convictions and psychiatric hospital diagnoses in Danish adoptees. *Behavior Genetics* 16:127-142.

Bandura, A.
1973 *Aggression: A Social Learning Analysis.* Englewood Cliffs, N.J.: Prentice-Hall.
Berkowitz, L.
1978 Is criminal violence normative behavior? *Journal of Research in Crime and Delinquency* 15:148-161.
1983 Aversively stimulated aggression: Some parallels and differences in research with animals and humans. *American Psychologist* 38:1135-1144.
Berrueta-Clement, J.R., L.J. Schweinhart, W.S. Barnett, A.S. Epstein, and D.P. Weikart
1984 *Changed Lives.* Ypsilanti, Mich.: High/Scope.
Blumstein, A., J. Cohen, J.A. Roth, and C.A. Visher, eds.
1986 *Criminal Careers and "Career Criminals."* Washington, D.C.: National Academy Press.
Clarke, R.V., and D.B. Cornish
1985 Modelling offenders' decisions. Pp. 147-185 in M. Tonry and N. Morris, eds., *Crime and Justice.* Vol. 6. Chicago: University of Chicago Press.
Coie, J.D., M. Underwood, and J.E. Lochman
1991 Programmatic intervention with aggressive children in the school setting. Pp. 389-410 in D.J. Pepler and K.H. Rubin, eds., *The Development and Treatment of Childhood Aggression.* Hillsdale, N.J.: Erlbaum.
Comstock, G., and H. Paik
1990 The Effects of Television Violence on Aggressive Behavior: A Meta-Analysis. Unpublished report to the National Academy of Sciences Panel on the Understanding and Control of Violent Behavior, Washington, DC.
Crowell, D.H., I.M. Evans, and C.R. O'Donnell, eds.
1987 *Childhood Aggression and Violence.* New York: Plenum.
DiLalla, L.F., and I.I. Gottesman
1991 Biological and genetic contributors to violence—Widom's untold tale. *Psychological Bulletin* 109:125-129.
Dodge, K.A.
1980 Social cognition and children's aggressive behavior. *Child Development* 51:162-170.
1986 A social information processing model of social competence in children. Pp. 77-125 in M. Perlmutter, ed., *Minnesota Symposium in Child Psychology.* Vol. 18. Hillsdale, N.J.: Erlbaum.
1991 The structure and function of reactive and proactive aggression. Pp. 201-218 in D.J. Pepler and K.H. Rubin, eds., *The Development and Treatment of Childhood Aggression.* Hillsdale, N.J.: Erlbaum.
Dodge, K.A., and J.D. Coie
1987 Social information processing factors in reactive and proactive

aggression in children's peer groups. *Journal of Personality and Social Psychology* 53:1146-1158.

Dodge, K.A., and J.P. Newman
1981 Biased decision-making processes in aggressive boys. *Journal of Abnormal Psychology* 90:375-379.

Dollard, J., L.W. Doob, N.E. Miller, O.H. Mowrer, and R.R. Sears
1939 *Frustration and Aggression.* New Haven: Yale University Press.

Drillien, C.M.
1964 *The Growth and Development of the Premature Infant.* Baltimore: Williams and Wilkins.

Elliott, D.S., D. Huizinga, and S. Menard
1989 *Multiple Problem Youth.* New York: Springer-Verlag.

Eron, L.D.
1986 Interventions to mitigate the psychological effects of media violence on aggressive behavior. *Journal of Social Issues* 42:155-169.
1987 The development of aggressive behavior from the perspective of a developing behaviorism. *American Psychologist* 42:435-442.
1990 Understanding aggression. Presidential address to the World Meeting of ISRA, Banff, Alberta, June 12.

Eron, L.D., and L.R. Huesmann
1984 The relation of prosocial behavior to the development of aggression and psychopathology. *Aggressive Behavior* 10:201-212.
1987 The stability of aggressive behavior in cross-national comparisons. Pp. 207-218 in C. Kagitcibasi, ed., *Growth and Progress in Cross-Cultural Psychology.* Lisse, Holland: Swets and Zeitlinger.
1990 The stability of aggressive behavior—Even unto the third generation. Pp. 147-156 in M. Lewis and S.M. Miller, eds., *Handbook of Developmental Psychopathology.* New York: Plenum Press.

Eron, L.D., L.R. Huesmann, P. Brice, P. Fischer, and R. Mermelstein
1983 Age trends in the development of aggression, sextyping, and related television habits. *Developmental Psychology* 19:71-77.

Eron, L.D., L.R. Huesmann, and A. Zelli
1991 The role of parental variables in the learning of aggression. Pp. 169-188 in D. Pepler and K.H. Rubin, eds., *The Development and Treatment of Childhood Aggression.* Hillsdale, N.J.: Erlbaum.

Farrington, D.P.
1987 Implications of biological findings for criminological research. Pp. 42-64 in S.A. Mednick, T.E. Moffitt, and S.E. Stack, eds., *The Causes of Crime: New Biological Approaches.* Cambridge: Cambridge University Press.
1988 Advancing knowledge about delinquency and crime: The need for a coordinated program of longitudinal research. *Behavioral Sciences and the Law* 6:307-331.
1989 Early predictors of adolescent aggression and adult violence. *Violence and Victims* 4:79-100.

1990 Age, period, cohort, and offending. Pp. 51-75 in D.M. Gottfredson and R.V. Clarke, eds., *Policy and Theory in Criminal Justice*. Aldershot, England: Avebury.

1991a Antisocial personality from childhood to adulthood. *The Psychologist* 4.

1991b Childhood aggression and adult violence: Early precursors and later-life outcomes. Pp. 5-29 in D.J. Pepler and K.H. Rubin, eds., *The Development and Treatment of Childhood Aggression*. Hillsdale, N.J.: Erlbaum.

Farrington, D.P., and J.D. Hawkins

1991 Predicting participation, early onset, and later persistence in officially recorded offending. *Criminal Behavior and Mental Health* 1:1-33.

Farrington, D.P., and R. Loeber

1989 RIOC (Relative Improvement Over Chance) and phi as measures of predictive efficiency and strength of association in 2X2 tables. *Journal of Quantitative Criminology* 5:201-213.

Farrington, D.P., and D.J. West

1990 The Cambridge study in delinquent development: A long-term follow-up study of 411 London males. Pp. 115-138 in H.J. Kerner and G. Kaiser, eds., *Criminality: Personality, Behavior, and Life History*. Berlin: Springer-Verlag.

Farrington, D.P., B. Gallagher, L. Morley, R.J. St. Leger, and D.J. West

1988 Are there any successful men from criminogenic backgrounds? *Psychiatry* 51:116-130.

Federal Bureau of Investigation

1982 *Uniform Crime Reports*. Washington, D.C.: U.S. Department of Justice.

Fogel, C.A., S.A. Mednick, and N. Michelson

1985 Hyperactive behavior and minor physical anomalies. *Acta Psychiatrica Scandinavica* 72:551-556.

Freedman, J.L.

1986 Television violence and aggression: A rejoinder. *Psychological Bulletin* 100:372-378.

Friedrich-Cofer, L., and A.C. Huston

1986 Television violence and aggression: The debate continues. *Psychological Bulletin* 100:364-371.

Guerra, N.

1990 Social cognitive approaches to the prevention of antisocial behavior in children. Paper presented at the Workshop on Hostility and Sociability, Warsaw, Poland (September).

Hamparian, D.M., R. Schuster, S. Dinitz, and J.P. Conrad

1978 *The Violent Few*. Lexington, Mass.: Heath.

Hamparian, D.M., J.M. Davis, J.M. Jacobson, and R.E. McGraw

1985 *The Young Criminal Years of the Violent Few*. Washington, D.C.: National Institute for Juvenile Justice and Delinquency Prevention.

Hare, R.D.
1978 Electrodermal and cardiovascular correlates of psychopathy. Pp. 107-144 in R.D. Hare and D. Schalling, eds., *Psychopathic Behavior: Approaches to Research.* New York: Wiley.
1981 Psychopathy and violence. In J.R. Hays, K. Roberts, and K. Solway, eds., *Violence and the Violent Individual.* New York: Spectrum.

Hare, R.D., L.M. McPherson, and A.E. Forth
1988 Male psychopaths and their criminal careers. *Journal of Consulting and Clinical Psychology* 56:710-714.

Hawkins, J.D., and J.G. Weis
1985 The social development model: An integrated approach to delinquency prevention. *Journal of Primary Prevention* 6:73-97.

Hawkins, J.D., J.M. Jenson, R.F. Catalano, and D.M. Lishner
1988 Delinquency and drug abuse: Implications for social services. *Social Service Review* 258-284.

Hawkins, J.D., E. Von Cleve, and R.F. Catalano
1991 Reducing early childhood aggression. *Journal of the American Academy of Child and Adolescent Psychiatry.*

Heath, L., L.B. Bresolin, and R.C. Rinaldi
1989 Effects of media violence on children. *Archives of General Psychiatry* 46:376-379.

Huesmann, L.R., and L.D. Eron
1984 Cognitive processes and the persistence of aggressive behavior. *Aggressive Behavior* 10:243-251.
1986 *Television and the Aggressive Child: A Cross-Cultural Comparison.* Hillsdale, N.J.: Erlbaum.
1988 Early predictors of criminality. Paper presented at XXIV International Congress of Psychology, Sydney, Australia.
1989 Individual differences and the trait of aggression. *European Journal of Personality* 3:95-106.

Huesmann, L.R., L.D. Eron, R. Klein, P. Brice, and P. Fischer
1983 Mitigating the imitation of aggressive behaviors by changing children's attitudes about media violence. *Journal of Personality and Social Psychology* 44:899-910.

Huesmann, L.R., L.D. Eron, M.M. Lefkowitz, and L.O. Walder
1984 The stability of aggression over time and generations. *Developmental Psychology* 20:1120-1134.

Jones, M.B., and D.R. Offord
1989 Reduction of antisocial behavior in poor children by non-school skill-development. *Journal of Child Psychology and Psychiatry* 30:737-750.

Kagan, J.
1980 Perspectives on continuity. In O.G. Brim and J. Kagan, eds., *Constancy and Change in Human Development.* Cambridge, Mass.: Harvard University Press.

1989 Temperamental contributions to social behavior. *American Psychologist* 44:668-674.

1991 The adolescent at risk. Paper presented at a conference "Adolescents at Risk," Cornell University Medical College, New York, February.

Kandel, D.B., and R. Faust

1975 Sequence and stages in patterns of adolescent drug use. *Archives of General Psychiatry* 32:923-932.

Kazdin, A.E.

1985 *Treatment of Antisocial Behavior in Children and Adolescents.* Homewood, Ill.: Dorsey Press.

1988 Treatment of antisocial behavior in children: Current status and future directions. *Psychological Bulletin* 102:187-203.

Keith, C.R., ed.

1984 *The Aggressive Adolescent.* New York: Free Press.

Kellam, S.G., C.H. Brown, B.R. Rubin, and M.E. Ensminger

1983 Paths leading to teenage psychiatric symptoms and substance use. In S.B. Guze, F.J. Earls, and J.E. Barratt, eds., *Childhood Psychopathology and Development.* New York: Raven Press.

Kendall, P.C., K.R. Ronan, and J. Epps

1991 Aggression in children/adolescents: Cognitive-behavioral treatment perspectives. Pp. 341-360 in D.J. Pepler and K.H. Rubin, eds., *The Development and Treatment of Childhood Aggression.* Hillsdale, N.J.: Erlbaum.

Lewis, D.P., S.S. Shanok, J.H. Pincus, and G.H. Glaser

1979 Violent juvenile delinquents. *Journal of the American Academy of Child Psychiatry* 18:307-319.

Litt, S.M.

1971 Perinatal complications and criminality. Doctoral dissertation, University of Michigan.

Lochman, J.E., and J.F. Curry

1982 Effects of social problem-solving training and self-instruction with aggressive boys. *Journal of Clinical Child Psychology* 15:159-164.

Magnusson, D., H. Stattin, and V.L. Allen

1986 Differential maturation among girls and its relations to social adjustment: A longitudinal perspective. Pp. 135-172 in P.B. Baltes, D.L. Featherman, and R.M. Lerner, eds., *Life-Span Development and Behavior.* Hillsdale, N.J.: Erlbaum.

Margolin, G., L. Gorin-Sibner, and L. Gleberman

1988 Wife battering. In V.B. Van Hasselt, R.L. Morrison, A.S. Bellack, and M. Hersen, eds., *Handbook of Family Violence.* New York: Plenum.

McCord, J.

1980 Patterns of deviance. Pp. 157-167 in S.B. Sells, R. Crandall, M. Roff, J.S. Strauss, and W. Pollin, eds., *Human Functioning in Longitudinal Perspective.* Baltimore, Md.: Williams and Wilkins.

1987 Aggression and shyness as predictors of problems. Paper presented at the Biennial Meeting of the Society for Research in Child Development, Baltimore.

McCord, W., and J. McCord

1956 *Psychopathy and Delinquency.* New York: Grune and Stratton.

McDermott, N.J., and M.J. Hindelang

1981 *Juvenile Criminal Behavior in the United States.* Washington, D.C.: U.S. Government Printing Office.

Mednick, S.A., and E. Kandel

1988 Genetic and perinatal factors in violence. Pp. 121-134 in S.A. Mednick and T. Moffitt, eds., *Biological Contributions to Crime Causation.* Holland: Martinus Nijhoff.

Megargee, E.I.

1973 Recent research on overcontrolled and undercontrolled personality patterns among violent offenders. *Social Symposium* 9:37-50.

Miller, S.J., S.D. Dinitz, and J.P. Conrad

1982 *Careers of the Violent.* Lexington, Mass.: Lexington Books.

Milner, J.S.

1986 *The Child Abuse Potential Inventory: Manual.* 2nd ed. Webster, N.C.: Psytec Corporation.

1990 Perpetrator and familial characteristics in physical and sexual child abuse cases. Department of Psychology, Northern Illinois University.

Milner, J.S., K.R. Robertson, and D.L. Rogers

1990 Childhood history of abuse and child abuse potential. *Journal of Family Violence* 5:15-34.

Moffitt, T.E.

1990 The neuropsychology of juvenile delinquency: A critical review. Pp. 99-169 in M. Tonry and N. Morris, eds., *Crime and Justice,* Vol. 12. Chicago: University of Chicago Press.

Moffitt, T.E., S.A. Mednick, and W.F. Gabrielli

1989 Predicting careers of criminal violence: Descriptive data and dispositional factors. In D.A. Brizer and M. Crowner, eds., *Current Approaches to the Prediction of Violence.* Washington, D.C.: American Psychiatric Press.

Mungas, D.

1983 An empirical analysis of specific syndromes of violent behavior. *Journal of Nervous and Mental Diseases* 171:354-361.

Oakley, A., L. Rajan, and A. Grant

1990 Social support and pregnancy outcome. *British Journal of Obstetrics and Gynaecology* 97:155-162.

Olweus, D.

1979 Stability of aggressive reaction patterns in males: A review. *Psychological Bulletin* 86:852-875.

1980 Familial and temperamental determinants of aggressive behavior in adolescent boys: A causal analysis. *Developmental Psychology* 16:644-660.

1987 In S.A. Mednick, T.E. Moffitt, and S.A. Stack, eds., *The Causes of Crime: New Biological Approaches.* Cambridge, England: Cambridge University Press.

1991 Bully/victim problems among schoolchildren: Basic facts and effects of a school based intervention program. Pp. 411-448 in D.J. Pepler and K.H. Rubin, eds., *The Development and Treatment of Childhood Aggression.* Hillsdale, N.J.: Erlbaum.

Patterson, G.R.

1980 Children who steal. Pp. 73-90 in T. Hirschi and M. Gottfredson, eds., *Understanding Crime.* Beverly Hills, Calif.: Sage Publications.

1986 Performance models for antisocial boys. *American Psychologist* 41:432-444.

Patterson, G.R., P. Chamberlain, and J.B. Reid

1982 A comparative evaluation of a parent training program. *Behavior Therapy* 13:638-650.

Patterson, G.R., D. Capaldi, and L. Bank

1991 An early starter model for predicting delinquency. Pp. 139-168 in D.J. Pepler and K.H. Rubin, eds., *The Development and Treatment of Childhood Aggression.* Hillsdale, N.J.: Erlbaum.

Pepler, D.J., and K.H. Rubin, eds.

1991 *The Development and Treatment of Childhood Aggression.* Hillsdale, N.J.: Erlbaum.

Pepler, D.J., G. King, and W. Byrd

1991 A social-cognitively based social skills training program for aggressive children. Pp. 361-379 in D.J. Pepler and K.H. Rubin, eds., *The Development and Treatment of Childhood Aggression.* Hillsdale, N.J.: Erlbaum.

Raine, A., and F. Jones

1987 Attention, autonomic arousal, and personality in behaviorally disordered children. *Journal of Abnormal Child Psychology* 15:583-599.

Raine, A., and P. Venables

In press Antisocial behavior: Evolution, genetics, neuropsychology, and psychophysiology. In A. Gale and M. Eysenck, eds., *Handbook of Individual Differences.* Chichester: Wiley.

Reznick, J.S., J. Kagan, N. Snidman, M. Gersten, K. Baak, and A. Rosenberg

1986 Inhibited and uninhibited children: A follow-up study. *Child Development* 57:660-680.

Richard, B.A., and K.A. Dodge

1982 Social maladjustment and problem solving in school aged children. *Journal of Consulting and Clinical Psychology* 50:226-233.

Robins, L.N.
1991 Antisocial personality. Pp. 259-290 in L.N. Robins and D. Regier, eds., *Psychiatric Disorder in America.* New York: Macmillan/Free Press.

Rutter, M., and H. Giller
1983 *Juvenile Delinquency: Trends and Perspectives.* Harmondsworth: Penguin.

Shannon, L.W.
1988 *Criminal Career Continuity.* New York: Human Sciences Press.

Short, R.J., R.J. Simeonsson, and G.S. Huntington
1990 Early intervention: Implications of Public Law 99-457 for professional child psychology. *Professional Psychology* 21:88-93.

Singer, J.L., and D.G. Singer
1981 *Television, Imagination, and Aggression: A Study of Pre-Schoolers.* Hillsdale, N.J.: Erlbaum.

Solway, K.S., L. Richardson, J.R. Hays, and V.H. Elcon
1981 Adolescent murderers. Pp. 193-209 in J.R. Hays, T.K. Roberts, and K.S. Solway, eds., *Violence and the Violent Individual.* Jamaica, N.Y.: Spectrum.

Spivack, G., and M.B. Shure
1974 *Social Adjustment of Young Children: A Cognitive Approach to Solving Real-Life Problems.* San Francisco, Calif.: Jossey-Bass.

Stark, E., and A. Flitcraft
1982 Medical therapy as repression: The case of the battered woman. *Health and Medicine* 1:29-32.

Stattin, H., D. Magnusson, and H. Reichel
1989 Criminal activity at different ages: A study based on a Swedish longitudinal research population. *British Journal of Criminology* 29:368-385.

Tonry, M., L.E. Ohlin, and D.P. Farrington
1991 *Human Development and Criminal Behavior.* New York: Springer-Verlag.

Tremblay, R.E., J. McCord, H. Boileau, P. Charlebois, C. Cagnon, M. LeBlanc, and S. Larivee
1991 Can disruptive boys be helped to become competent? *Psychiatry.*

U.S. Department of Health, Education, and Welfare
1978 *Violent Schools - Safe Schools.* Washington, D.C.: National Institute of Education.

Virkkunen, M.
1987 Metabolic dysfunctions among habitually violent offenders: Reactive hypoglycemia and cholesterol levels. In S.A. Mednick, T.E. Moffitt, and S. Stack, eds., *The Causes of Crime: New Biological Approaches.* New York: Cambridge.

Wadsworth, M.E.J.
1976 Delinquency, pulse rate and early emotional deprivation. *British Journal of Criminology* 16:245-256.

Weiner, N.A.
1989 Violent criminal careers and "violent career criminals": An overview of the research literature. Pp. 35-138 in N.A. Weiner and M.E. Wolfgang, eds., *Violent Crime, Violent Criminals*. Newbury Park, Calif.: Sage Publications.

Werner, E.E., and R.S. Smith
1982 *Vulnerable but Invincible*. New York: McGraw-Hill.

Widom, C.S.
1989a Does violence beget violence? A critical examination of the literature. *Psychological Bulletin* 106:3-28.
1989b The cycle of violence. *Science* 244:160-166.
1991 A tail on an untold tale: Response to "Biological and genetic contributors to violence—Widom's untold tale." *Psychological Bulletin* 109:130-132.

Wikstrom, P.O.
1985 *Everyday Violence in Contemporary Sweden*. Stockholm: National Council for Crime Prevention.

Wolfgang, M.E., R.M. Figlio, and T. Sellin
1972 *Delinquency in a Birth Cohort*. Chicago: University of Chicago Press.

Wolfgang, M.E., T.P. Thornberry, and R.M. Figlio
1987 *From Boy to Man, From Delinquency to Crime*. Chicago: University of Chicago Press.

Wood, W., F.Y. Wong, and J.G. Chachere
1991 Effects of media violence on viewers' aggression in unconstrained social interaction. *Psychological Bulletin* 109:371-383.

B

Measuring and Counting Violent Crimes and Their Consequences

People often ask, "How much crime is there?" "How many violent crimes are committed each day, month, or year in the United States?" as if these questions admitted of some reasonably precise answer. They do not, and perhaps they cannot, because of the institutional nature of counting.

Any counting system involves some valuative institutional processing of people's observations and reports of what they perceive as events. Any set of crime statistics, therefore, is not based on some objectively observable universe of behavior. Rather, violent crime statistics are based on the events that are defined, captured, and processed as such by some institutional means of collecting and counting crimes (Biderman and Reiss, 1967). There is consequently no single way to define, classify, and measure the domain of violent behavior or its subset of behavior that constitutes violent crimes. Rather, there are a multiplicity of ways of doing so, each of which has its own counting and classification errors.

The institutional nature of counting requires that we have multiple means of counting, each of which compensates for some of the errors in classification and counting in the others. At best, however, a national system of crime counts produces multiple and divergent estimates for which only some errors in measurement are estimated. As we probe the undercounted domain of violent crime, it is apparent that current institutional means of counting and accounting do not cover satisfactorily the kinds of violent behavior that are required for its understanding, and that the domain of violent crime is not covered by any current institutional means of counting. New means of counting are not easily compared with existing systems, because each has its own rules for selecting, classifying, and counting crime events.

The example of parental assault of children illustrates some of the problems. If we try to estimate how many and how frequently parents assault their children, neither Uniform Crime Reports (UCR) nor the National Crime Survey (NCS) can currently supply accurate information. Both systems rely primarily on family members for their information. At present they rarely receive information on parental assaults on children, but if either were to attempt a systematic count of parental assaults, they would encounter substantial underreporting. Reports to police involve self-incrimination for the assaulting parent(s), making it unlikely that the violence would be reported in single-parent families or in families in which both parents are assaultive. Likewise, the parent who does not commit the violence may fail to report the incident because of intimidation or the fear that it will jeopardize the family economy or unity. In addition, there are problems of separating peer and sibling assaults from parental assaults and of assault from accidental injury—formidable problems to accurate classification and counting of such events. And counts of parental assault obtained by means independent of the UCR and NCS estimates are not merged with them to obtain a more comprehensive estimate of assaults.

The current institutional system of acquiring information on physical assaults by parents relies primarily on reporting by professionals who have contact with children. The school and the medical clinic or office are the main places for these contacts by physicians, nurses, and teachers. Preschool children are the least likely to be observed by professionals. Their contacts with medical personnel and social workers are sporadic. Nonmedical professionals, moreover, rely on superficial visual examination, which risks missing evidence of sexual assault, for example.

The observational injury data supplied by teachers or medical personnel do not provide information to indicate if the injury is the result of violent behavior, if the behavior constituted a criminal act by a parent, or even whether a parent is the source of the injury. Establishing these facts requires investigation by others, an investigation that generally must rely on home visits and testimony either by parent and child or by persons in a position to observe the family's behavior. Moreover, many of these observations of injury are investigated and institutionally processed through social rather than police service organizations. Hence, their criminal status remains undetermined. Although this loosely structured system increases the chances of detecting, counting, and processing injuries of children as the result of violent behavior, the status of many remains indeterminate and only the most serious cases are detected and processed as violent crimes. Any system for counting parental physical assaults that respects parental rights, is loosely structured around professionals' contact with children, and relies on visual evidence that must be verified by still others is likely to encounter serious problems of misclassification and underreporting.

SOCIAL CONSTRUCTIONS OF VIOLENT BEHAVIOR AND VIOLENT CRIMES

It is no simple matter to determine which violent behaviors are to be regarded as violent crimes for purposes of measurement and counting. What constitutes a violent crime is the result of societal determinations of what is violent behavior and which violent behavior is violent crime. Social constructions of violent behavior are dynamic and change both temporally and organizationally. Social constructions of violent behavior that are institutionalized in the criminal law as violent crimes can be institutionalized differently in other systems, such as state systems that process behavior or crimes and their accounting systems (e.g., family courts or mental health systems). Whether violent acts will be institutionally processed as crimes depends on the processing of events by legal agents empowered to make decisions to arrest, charge, prosecute, and adjudicate criminal matters. Not all social constructions of violent behavior and violent crime are formal; they emerge from informal processes as well.

The domain of violent behavior includes some behaviors that are not legally and institutionally processed as violent crimes. That is, not all violent behavior is socially construed as criminal. The physical punishment of children, for example, may be regarded as discipline rather than as violent behavior on the part of the disciplinarian. Similarly, most violence in competitive contact sports such as ice hockey is regarded as acceptable. Only rarely does intentionally inflicted harm in sports fall within the sphere of violent crime, even when it results in death. Perhaps the most highly institutionalized acceptance of violent behavior in a sport is the prize fight.

What constitutes an incident of violent behavior or violent crime is sometimes subject to the discretion of decision makers. Some types of violent behavior that laws have recently criminalized lie at the margin of institutional processing as violent crime—date rape is an example. Other forms of coerced sexual behavior may lie outside the criminal law, as is currently the case in most states with marital rape. Recording of assaults involving custodians and their wards, in prisons and mental hospitals, for example, is often discretionary and fragmentary.

Domestic Assaults

The significant changes in the last 40 years in the role of women in society have influenced social constructions of domestic assault. Historically, the police dealt with reported domestic assaults on women as crimes only if the bodily injury was serious enough to qualify as an aggravated or felony assault. As a consequence of some major tort liability suits against police departments and the results of the experiments in Minneapolis (described in Chapter 7) concluding that arrest was a deterrent to repeated domestic assault (Sherman and Cohn, 1989), there has been a substantial change in their reporting.

Eleven states now mandate arrest in all cases of domestic assaults—misdemeanor as well as felony. Mandatory arrest policies appear to affect the determination of the threshold between a simple (misdemeanor) assault and an aggravated (felony) assault. Most important, however, mandatory arrest substantially increases the official reporting of domestic violence as it reduces police discretion to make threshold decisions. In the state of Connecticut, for example, the official reporting of domestic assaults more than doubled following the passage of a mandatory arrest law.

Unfortunately, we cannot determine just how much of the recent rise in the assault rate nationwide to attribute to an increase in domestic violence reporting. Our systems of national reporting do not adequately classify and count repeat incidents of domestic violence by the same and different offenders. It seems reasonable to conclude, nevertheless, that changes in the social construction of domestic violence and police response to such violence account for some of the increase in the reported number of assaults and domestic assaults.

Bias Crimes

Another recent change in social construction involves bias crimes. A minority of states have enacted bias crime legislation; among the first to do so were Maryland, Pennsylvania, and Connecticut.

The Hate Crimes Statistics Act of 1990 mandates development of a national reporting system for bias crimes.

Statistics on bias crimes committed in 1990 or earlier are available from only a few of the police reporting agencies in UCR. The statistics that are available are collected by national organizations such as the National Gay and Lesbian Task Force Policy Institute and B'nai B'rith. The U.S. Department of Justice also collects information on grand jury indictments and convictions involving the criminal violation of the civil rights of ethnic minorities. The Civil Rights Division of the department collects information on complaints against police. The National Gay and Lesbian Task Force Policy Institute has collected information on statistics from gay service organizations in six major metropolitan areas and reports a substantial increase from 1989 to 1990 in these metropolitan areas. Just how much of this increase is due to a greater awareness and willingness of victims to report their victimization is undetermined because the information is not available. What is clear is that the Federal Bureau of Investigation, the U.S. Attorneys, and local police departments have shown increased willingness to bring indictments and prosecute bias crimes under federal civil rights statutes.

Sexual Assaults

The social construction of sexual assaults has undergone considerable change in part as a result of efforts by the women's and gay rights social and political movements. Two effects are particularly noteworthy: the redefinition of rape and other sexual assaults and the redefinition of their reporting. Although the effects of the redefinition of rape and its reporting to the police are still being assessed, it appears that our society's conception of rape has changed in several respects. First, social movements have been reasonably successful in removing the social stigma surrounding the reporting of rape. Of special importance is the emphasis now placed on ensuring that women who have been assaulted will be treated with dignity and sensitivity by law enforcement officials. Whenever possible, initial investigations of sexual crimes against women that require the victim's cooperation are handled by female police officers. Social support groups now aid women during this process to prevent their being socially stigmatized during or after its reporting.

The second major change involves what constitutes a reportable sexual assault. There now is a concept of date rape and of the moral obligation to report all coerced as well as completed nonconsenting sexual intercourse as rape regardless of the victim's relationship to the offender. In years past, few rapes or attempted rapes that occurred on a date were reported because of the youth of the women involved and the social stigma occasioned through its reporting. Women are now more likely to define themselves as victims when coerced into sexual intercourse while on a date. With this change has also come a redefinition of the necessity for equal consent to sexual relations and a redefinition of coercion. This redefinition of what constitutes rape or sexual assault undoubtedly has a greater impact on self-report surveys of sexual assault victimizations than on incidents of rape reported to the police. A number of surveys report a substantial prevalence rate of rape by an acquaintance or friend. The stigmatization of males who report being victims of sexual assault is also attenuating—leading to increased reporting of male rape in the National Crime Survey.

Some states also have forged a redefinition of rape at law. Historically, the law of evidence for conviction on a charge of rape required two independent sources of evidence that it had occurred. Typically, this required some evidence of coerced penetration or the recovery of semen, procedures often experienced as degrading by the victim. Now some states require only the sworn testimony of the victim for conviction, providing there is no evidence to impeach that testimony; the victim's moral integrity is ordinarily not permitted as grounds for impeachment. The nature of these changes is to redefine what behavior comprises rape, to ensure that the victim will be treated with respect when reporting the rape, and to encourage greater victim reporting by reducing the stigma of victimization.

Assaults on Children

With a growing concern for child abuse and neglect, there is increased reporting of simple and aggravated assaults of children. Special attention has been given to child sexual abuse (Bolton et al., 1989). Substantial changes in its reporting as well as redefinition of permissible behavior toward children are under way. Other major changes are affecting the status of children as victim witnesses. Recent case law, for example, now permits children who are victims of sexual and other forms of abuse to testify under certain circumstances without having to submit to cross-examination or to give testimony in the presence of the accused.

Systemic Influences: Drug Markets

Systemic changes in recent decades appear to have affected the composition and volume of violent crime in ways that raise new counting and classification problems. The most noteworthy of these is the growth of illegal drug markets and the population of drug users. The growth of drug markets is well documented, although it is difficult to estimate the size of local markets (Johnson et al., 1990). The violent crime of armed robbery has increased with the demand for drugs in a cash market. Robbery and burglary have become the principal means of meeting this individual demand for drugs. Of the two, robbery is preferable in that it provides ready cash for their purchase (Cromwell et al., 1991; Rengert and Wasilchick, 1989). The increase in armed robbery may also have increased the felony murder rate somewhat.[1]

A second major systemic change is in the territorial organization of drug markets. There has been a proliferation of small illegal drug markets, often organized around a particular illegal drug. Until recently, illegal markets were controlled by a syndicated structure that used violence only sparingly to control the size and scope of its market. Normally the markets were stabilized by explicit or tacit agreements with other syndicates; violence was used only occasionally, when such agreements broke down. Traditionally illegal market syndicates had less need for violence to control their territory because they could co-opt and corrupt the police to permit their operations.

These syndicate conditions do not prevail in current urban drug markets. The marketing of at least some drugs requires different ethnic and national connections and a local territorial base, so that small syndicates have arisen around these connections. The marketing of drugs is somewhat disorganized, then, because it is fragmented and lacks central coordination. The presence of valuable drugs and large amounts of cash is an incentive for robberies in and around drug markets, but practice varies about whether to classify these events as robberies or drug related. Similarly, violence is a principal means for opening new markets, expanding the scope of existing local markets, and defending a small local market against encroachment from other entrepreneurs. That violence is armed, often with high-calibre weapons that are particularly deadly. In drive-by shootings to disrupt a local market, discharges from a automatic weapons injure or kill some bystanders (Sherman et al., 1989), but because such victimizations are not premeditated, their classification as crimes, or perhaps as accidents, is problematic.

MEASURING AND COUNTING VIOLENT CRIMES

Statistics about violent crimes and their victims are usually reported in terms of incidents—specific criminal acts or behaviors involving one of more victims in a single event. An offense is specific behavior that is legally prohibited; the major violent offenses are homicide, rape, robbery, and assault. The perpetrator of the offense is the offender; if more than one is involved in an offense, they are co-offenders. The victim of an offense can be a person, a household, an organization, or the public—but only persons are regarded as victims of violent crimes.

The newspaper accounts of homicides in New York City that began this report illustrate some of the complexities involved in counting crime incidents. A single event or situation may result in several different types of violent crime. Heriberto Altreche, the son who beat his mother and sister, was arrested for an assault for punching his sister and, depending on the results of the autopsy, may also be held liable for the homicide of his mother. In the shootings at the Bedford Park Christmas party, the 34-year-old man was a homicide victim, and the 28-year-old man wounded in the shooting was undoubtedly a victim of an aggravated assault. An unreported number of other people were also shot at the party but fled before police arrived. Similarly, the number of offenders in a single incident can also vary. Two men dressed in black clothing and hoods were involved in the killing of Mr. Rodriguez, but neither will contribute to statistics on murder arrests unless police have evidence as to which one or both fired the fatal shot.

A crime incident can also be described in terms of the place and circumstances of its occurrence and the consequences to offenders or victims, such as injury or arrest. When the incident includes more than a single victim or offender, not all offenders may have committed the same offense and not all victims may have experienced the same victimizations—all of which can be separate counts.

This variation in the complexity of crime incidents is the basis for differences in crime counts among classification and counting systems for violent crimes.

Four Different Systems

The counting of violent behavior in our society is organized around four independent systems, each with its own constructions of which violent behavior is to be measured and counted as violent crime.

(1) Violent crimes reported to law enforcement agents and their investigation are the basis of the Uniform Crime Reports system of classifying and counting crimes.

(2) Deaths from violent causes processed by medical examiner's offices, which also report the cause of death, are the basis of the National Center for Health Statistics (NCHS) death registration system.

(3) Sample surveys of a population to secure information for some interval of time on criminal victimizations are the basis for the National Crime Survey system of classifying and counting crime; some information can also be obtained from specialized sample surveys such as the Survey of Occupational Injuries and Illnesses and the National Hospital Discharge Survey, but these ordinarily are not used for counting crime incidents.

(4) Information systems infer violent crime from the consequences of violent behavior; the most common are injury surveillance systems based on reports of persons seeking compensation for injury or seeking treatment in emergency and other facilities.

These are all voluntary reporting systems, and only the first three compile national statistics. None of them is developed solely for the purpose of counting violent crime, and none is developed to measure and count all forms of violent behavior. Only the UCR and the NCS are organized exclusively around measuring and counting crimes and some of their consequences, and each has classification and counting rules that limit what is counted as a crime of violence. Information on homicides derives primarily from the UCR system and the Office of Vital Statistics reports on deaths. None of these systems covers *all* forms of violent crime, although UCR has the most comprehensive coverage. As summarized in Chapter 2, differences among the systems derive primarily from the population covered, the means for collecting information, and the rules for classifying and counting behavior.

The UCR system traditionally classified and counted crime occurrences or events in terms of only the most serious offense committed in an incident and arrests of offenders within the incident.[2] The Federal Bureau of Investigation is moving to a system in which at least the larger police agencies will use a National Incident Based Reporting System (NIBRS) that will classify and count all offenses, offenders, and victims in incidents and their surrounding circumstances.

The National Crime Survey counts victimizations from crime and their circumstances with the minimal information victims can report about their offenders. One of the reasons for developing the National Crime Survey was that a great many violent crimes are not reported to the police, and hence a substantial proportion of violent crimes are not measured and counted in UCR. The NCS provides another institutional means for measuring and counting violent crime by securing reports of victimizations from a national sample survey of households and their members who are age 12 and older.

Consider classification and counting for an incident in which an offender attempts an armed robbery of two victims, shooting both as they flee, killing one, and subsequently being arrested. The UCR would count this as a murder under its hierarchical rule of counting the most serious offense; the offense would be cleared by the arrest; a Supplemental Homicide Report would be filed on the victim's being killed in a felony homicide—the robbery. There would be no reporting of the assault on the second victim nor of the attempted robbery of the two victims—information that will now be reported as part of the NIBRS. The NCS would obtain information on the incident only from the surviving victim and count an attempted robbery and an aggravated assault for the surviving victim, weighting the robbery by one-half for the presence of a second victim. There would be no count of the homicide.

Reconciling UCR and NCS Counts

As we illustrate in Chapter 2, when the trends for NCS and UCR are compared, they produce divergent results. In recent years this difference has generated considerable discussion in the popular media, Congress, and research literature (see Blumstein et al., 1991; Jencks, 1991).

One reason offered for the difference between the two data series—essentially no change in NCS offenses while UCR offenses have increased, especially during the 1980s—is that the rate at which victims report crimes to the police has increased. Yet NCS data on victim reporting rates to the police have been remarkably stable, remaining between 50 and 60 percent for robbery and aggravated assault throughout the period 1973 to 1989 (Jencks, 1991). Moreover, reporting rates are not a factor in accounting for year-to-year variations in UCR crime counts (Blumstein et al., 1991).

Jencks (1991:103) offers a more cogent explanation for the difference between NCS and UCR trends: "[T]he police are recording more of the violence that citizens report to them. In 1973, for example, citizens reported about 861,000 aggravated assaults to the police. The police recorded only 421,000. By 1988 citizens said they reported 940,000 aggravated assaults to the police, and the police recorded 910,000. The same pattern recurs for robbery and rape."

The stark increase from 49 to 97 percent of victim-reported assaults being recorded by the police provides compelling evidence that changes in police recording practices account for differences between NCS and UCR trends. It is possible that changes in citizen willingness to report crimes to the police might account for some of the observed difference, but it seems unlikely that such changes would fit the observed pattern in reporting. The same distinctive upward trend in police recording rates characterizes violent and property crimes alike. The trends for the various crime types, however, suggest the need for caution in relying entirely on the police recording hypothesis. By 1989, police recording rates—calculated from the ratio of UCR crime counts to NCS counts of offenses reported to the police—exceeded 100 percent. For burglary, the recording rate has continued to rise steadily from 100 percent since 1981, and the recording rate for rape is highly variable and often well above 100 percent.

If police crime counts are indeed becoming more accurate through more complete recording of citizen-reported offenses, then the trend in recent years for UCR crime counts to exceed NCS counts of reported crimes raises the possibility of crime undercounts by the NCS. Victimization of populations that are typically underrepresented in NCS samples—especially transient, homeless, and offender populations, all of whom are at substantially greater risk of violence—may be an important factor in NCS crime undercounts. The extent to which these special populations have increased over time or become more difficult to survey would contribute to an absence of upward trends in NCS counts of violent crimes.

Information About Offenders and Offending

The current systems of collecting information on violent crimes provide substantially more information on the violent crime incidents and their victims than they do on offenders and their patterns of offending. Both UCR and NCS provide only limited information on offenders. The only other major source of information on offenders is the National Prisoner Statistics.

UCR currently provides information only on arrested offenders, and it is limited. Information is provided on ethnic status, age, and sex of arrestees and the most serious crime for which arrested. Until the incident-based NIBRS reporting system is fully implemented, ethnic status-sex-age distributions cannot be obtained. Moreover, the *same* offender may be arrested more than once in a given year, so that it is impossible to calculate prevalence rates for arrest or to determine the characteristics of an offender population. The information available amounts to a population of arrests and the characteristics of persons arrested. Arrest counts are available by size and type of jurisdiction and place, but this is an extremely limited data base. The NIBRS system will provide considerably more information on arrested persons, such as whether or not they were armed or had drugs in their possession. It remains unclear how soon it will be possible to calculate national rates based on that information.

The Supplementary Homicide Report provides somewhat more information on persons arrested for homicide and permits a determination of the characteristics of multiple offenders in homicides. The information is quite limited and incomplete on both the homicide and the offender. For example, the relationship of the offender and victim was unknown in one-third of all homicides (Federal Bureau of Investigation, 1989:13). Even the circumstances of the murder were not reported for 22 percent of all murders in 1988 (Federal Bureau of Investigation, 1990:14).

NCS provides only a limited amount of information on offenders, and it is based on the victims' unverified descriptions of their offenders. Information is solicited on the number of offenders in the incident; their ethnic status, sex, and age; and whether or not the offender is known to the victim and if so what the relationship is. When there is more than one offender, the information is sought on their aggregate composition by ethnic status, age, and sex (or for example the age of the oldest and youngest offender). Information is also sought on whether any was believed to be drinking or on drugs. There are no validation studies that permit an assessment of the accuracy of victim accounts of offenders for the NCS.

Considerably more information could be obtained for offenders convicted of violent crimes, but there are few national tabulations for uniquely identified individuals. National prisoner statistics are also limited to major type of violent crime for which incarcerated and ethnic status, sex, and age characteristics of inmates. These characteristics of offenders can be obtained by jurisdiction and size of place from which committed.

There are no national statistics on the criminal careers of persons who commit violent crimes. Available knowledge is derived from studies of special incarcerated populations or by tracing the careers of cohorts of arrested offenders using the arrest records available through state and federal identification bureaus. Some information on criminal careers also is available from small-scale longitudinal follow-ups of cohorts sampled from the general population (e.g., Elliott et al., 1989) or from self-report studies of juveniles.

The dearth of information on violent crimes in offenders' careers is a severe limitation on developing an understanding of violent criminal activity and of interventions to prevent its occurrence. One way to develop that information is investigation based on longitudinal studies of cohorts who are followed from birth to the middle years, as we describe in Chapter 3.

BARRIERS TO OBTAINING COMPLETE INFORMATION

Measuring the Risk of Violent Victimization

Two questions are often asked: What are my chances of becoming the victim of a rape, a robbery, or an assault? Are there ways to alter my behavior to lower my chances of being a victim? To answer them and indeed to understand the nature of violent behavior and its consequences, it is necessary that one understand how changes in conditions surrounding the violent behavior affect its occurrence.

To understand a robbery murder—such as that of Mr. Waldermarian recounted at the beginning of this book—implies understanding a chain of events, each of which could change the outcome. These are referred to statistically as *conditional probabilities*, the probability associated with a given condition, such as being in a particular place or situation. The chain of conditional probabilities for the robbery murder would include the chances of being approached in a given place and situation by a robber and, if approached, by one who is armed with a gun. Given the robbery attempt, what is the likelihood that one will be shot by the robber and then, if shot, that one will be injured? Moreover, given the injury, what is the likelihood that it will be life-threatening and, if life-threatening, that it will result in death—the fate of Mr. Waldermarian?

Looked at from the perspective of the effectiveness of interventions, to know that some intervention reduces robbery murder levels implies that it reduces at least one conditional probability in the chain without causing offsetting increases in the others.

For example, interventions that reduced the supply of guns in the population would reduce the chance that an injury kills the victim, one of the conditional probabilities in the chain. It would reduce the number of robbery murders provided there are not offsetting conditions that would increase other chances of a fatal injury during a robbery, such as more frequent victim resistance.

One of the barriers to assessing the risk of violent behavior for ordinary citizens, of testing hypotheses about violent behaviors, or of verifying claims about preventive interventions is that one lacks the data needed to calculate the necessary conditional probabilities. Clearly most of that information is lacking for calculating the conditional probabilities for robbery murder, for at least three reasons:

(1) *Lack of denominators for rate calculations*: One can often ascertain many elements of circumstances surrounding an event such as an attempted robbery (e.g., Mr. Waldermarian was in the driveway of his house on Christmas Eve carrying Christmas presents). Unless one knows how many other men in similar situations were *not* victims of attempted robberies, one cannot calculate the first conditional probability in the chain or know how important time and location are as risk factors. One can assemble information on theoretically relevant circumstances from police or prosecutors' records, but it is different because these data are not routinely tabulated in statistical reports.

(2) *Probabilities are usually unavailable for the population at risk*: Two of the succeeding conditional probabilities—of being approached by two men attempting robbery and of a gunshot injury—could be obtained from victimization surveys, but only for surviving victims. One cannot tell from victimization data if victims who die are somehow different from those who live. Police data potentially can provide information on those who report attempts to rob with a shotgun and of how many homicides are deaths from shotgun wounds, but we would lack information on how many people are wounded by shotguns in attempts to rob, since it is possible that, despite the legal obligation to report, some of these would not be reported to the police or require emergency treatment and the hierarchy rules result in underreporting.

(3) *Inability to link data from different sources*: The last probability, of death given the injury, is well established for many epidemiological injury categories, but that information cannot be linked to the rest of the chain without data that distinguish violent from unintentional injuries.

Progress in understanding violent crime is severely hampered by the lack of information to calculate conditional probabilities. This is a severe limitation not only for understanding causal chains leading to violent crimes and their outcomes but also, as noted above, for our capacity to assess the effect of interventions to reduce violent crime. Such assessments depend substantially on securing information on the base for a rate that is integral to the calculation of a conditional probability.

Discretionary Decisions

After a crime incident occurs, the initial decisions whether to report and what to report are made by the immediate participants, far removed from the government agencies with official responsibility for classifying and counting crimes. Police agencies must depend on the discretionary decisions of victims or witnesses of violent crimes. Unless they call, an incident that might qualify as a violent crime will not be accessioned in official police statistics. The police likewise have thresholds for determining what constitutes a violent crime. Although governed by the criminal law, police officers have discretion whether to classify and record incidents reported to them by citizens. What constitutes a violent crime, then, will vary among legal jurisdictions, depending on citizen and police construction of events and the decisions they make regarding them.

As we said, the NCS was developed to address the problem that many violent crimes are not reported to the police. However, as a sample survey of people reporting victimizations to interviewers, it too depends on discretion: people's willingness to be interviewed and to respond to the survey questions as they understand them. Despite an estimated compliance rate of about 96 percent of all eligible housing units participating in the 1988 survey (Bureau of Justice Statistics, 1990:120), there are reasons to conclude there is a sample selection bias in the NCS. That is, respondents at high risk of violent behavior—as both victims and offenders—are underrepresented, for example, young unemployed black males and homeless people. The age limitation on the NCS results in underestimates of assaults against minors by family members and peers, as well as underestimation of strong-arm and even armed robberies against those under age 12. Some, but by no means even a majority, of those offenses will be counted by UCR because adults report them to the police.

In classifying and counting the information from respondents, the NCS survey organization follows a particular procedure to determine which of the behavioral incidents are to be considered violent crimes; this procedure substitutes for the discretionary decisions of citizens and the police. The NCS uses an algorithm to classify violent and other crimes based on the answers to individual survey questions. For example, the NCS has not asked respondents whether they were victims of a completed or attempted forcible rape. Rather, individuals are first asked screen questions; if they respond to one or more indicating they were a victim of force or threat to use force, they are asked for information on a crime incident form (Bureau of Justice Statistics, 1990:Appendix II). That form asks more specific questions about the nature of the threat or attack. If the victim describes the attack or describes the injury in terms of a sexual assault that the interviewer considers forcible rape, the interviewer then exercises discretion to code it as "tried to rape" or "raped." The procedure thus depends on victims' associative recall when asked more general questions about threats and attacks on the person or on the nature of injuries.[3]

Similarly, the NCS does not ask direct questions about family violence, although it provides estimates by special tabulation of the family relationship between the victim and the offender, the location of the victimization, and other information considered relevant to classifying victims of intrafamily assaults. This procedure does not include partner or cohabitant assaults in the estimate. By contrast, the current UCR classification procedure depends on both the discretionary decision of officers when taking a report and the subsequent review of that classification by trained staff. The new UCR incident-based reporting system will more closely resemble that of the NCS, in that officer responses to individual items about the incident will enable classification by algorithm. Also, the NCS is entirely dependent on the victim as the source of information, whereas police departments derive their information from a variety of sources. Witnesses and others bring violent crimes to the attention of the police that victims would fail to report; this is especially the case for reporting assaults.

A substantial number of incidents of violent crime are reported neither to the police nor to survey interviewers. Some information on the nature of such events can be gleaned from reverse-record check studies[4] conducted by the NCS in Washington, D.C. (Bureau of the Census, 1970a), Baltimore, Md. (Bureau of the Census, 1970b), and San Jose, Calif. (National Institute of Law Enforcement and Criminal Justice, 1972). These studies concluded that in each city a substantial proportion of the rapes and attempted rapes, robberies, and assaults that occurred were not reported to the police; the NCS survey also failed to capture a sizable proportion of the violent crimes that were reported to the police. In San Jose, for example, just under half (48 percent) of all aggravated assaults included in the police case report subsample were reported by victims to survey interviewers. At the same time, only somewhat more than half of all persons who reported an aggravated assault to the survey interviewers said they reported it to the police. Each method of data collection thus fails to collect information on a substantial proportion of victims counted by the other, although overall the survey method captures more victims.

Reporting Crimes to the Police

Relatively little is known about how citizens decide to mobilize the police to deal with violent crimes. Recent work on domestic violence provides evidence that a sizable fraction of battered women do not call the police. Fear of retaliation from spouses is one of the more commonly stated reasons for calling a shelter rather than the police. There is likewise little information on why victims of violence do not report their victimization to survey interviewers. Again, what little information is available concerns domestic violence. In design interviews for the NCS, some of the men and women respondents indicated that they did not regard simple assaults at home, at work, or in bars to be crimes, suggesting that cultural constructions of men's and women's roles may account for failure to report these incidents either to the police or to victim interviewers.

The main source of information on citizens' mobilization of the police when they are victimized by a violent crime is the NCS, which determines whether each victimization reported to the survey interviewer was also reported to the police,[5] and if so why. For a victimization that was not reported to the police, the victim is queried as to the reasons. More than one reason may be given by a victim for each victimization so that there are more reasons given than there are victimizations. In 1988, for the estimated 5,909,570 violent victimizations, a total of 5,938,390 reasons were given for reporting (Bureau of Justice Statistics, 1990:Table 102) or not reporting (Bureau of Justice Statistics, 1990:Table 103) the victimization to the police. Fewer reasons apparently were given on the average for reported victimizations than for those not reported.[6]

Roughly 1 in 10 victims says that he or she reported the victimization to the police because "it was a crime" (Bureau of Justice Statistics, 1990:Table 102). The other reasons given for reporting vary with the type of violent victimization. For aggravated or simple assault, the main reason given for reporting 2 in every 10 victimizations is to prevent the offender from further violence toward the victim. These victimizations appear to be largely assaults in which the victim and offender are in a continuing relationship, primarily domestic assaults for female victims and acquaintance assaults for male victims. Evidence for this is also found in the fact that only about 5 percent of the reasons given for reporting assault victimizations to the police were to catch or find the offender. Another 1 in 10 assault victimizations is reported to the police because the victim hoped this offender would be prevented from committing a similar crime against any citizen; for an additional 1 in 10, the reason is to punish the offender.

In about one-fourth of all completed robbery victimizations (Bureau of Justice Statistics, 1990:Table 102), the reason expressed for reporting was to seek the recovery of property. When recovery of property is not a motive, victims of attempted robbery are most likely to respond that they called because it was a crime. The number of rape victims is insufficient to do a reliable analysis of their reasons for calling the police, but the pattern that emerges is one of reporting in the hope the police will catch the offender, who will then be punished or prevented from further offending—reasons given for more than half of all rape victimizations. Few injured victims state that they called the police because they needed help due to a violence-related injury—perhaps because in most cases victims are still ambulatory and can seek medical help on their own.

A variety of reasons are also given for *not* reporting victimizations to the police (Bureau of Justice Statistics, 1990:Table 103). In roughly 1 in 10 of the victimizations, the reason expressed for not reporting to the police was that it was reported to some other official. This reason seems to be offered more often for victimizations that include an injury. The two most frequently given reasons for not reporting a violent victimization to the police are that the matter was private or personal and that the offender was not successful in an attempted crime or that property was recovered in a completed property crime.[7] That it was a private or personal matter is more likely to be the reason given for not reporting assault than for rape or robbery victimizations. Fear of reprisal is given for more than 10 percent of all completed robbery and rape victimizations. Fear of reprisal is given as a reason for not reporting in fewer than 5 percent of the assault victimizations.

For crimes not reported to the police, there are not only more reasons given but also much greater diversity. For 17 percent of such victimizations in 1988, some reason other than the 12 adopted by the NCS was given (Bureau of Justice Statistics, 1990:Table 103). Some other reason was given for not reporting 4 in 10 rape victimizations and for one-fifth of all completed violent crimes. There is apparently no simple explanation for not reporting violent crimes to the police from the perspective of their victims, and a sizable minority give more than one reason for not reporting.

A minority of victims give reasons indicating they regard their victimization as lacking the seriousness worthy of police mobilization. In about 5 percent of all violent victimizations, the reason given is that the crime was not important enough to merit police attention; for almost 7 percent the reason was that the police would not want to be bothered. For another 6 percent, the reason was a lack of proof. For 3 percent, the reason given was that reporting is too time-consuming or inconvenient. Although these percentages are not additive because a victim could give more than one reason, perhaps as many as one-fifth of all victimizations are not reported to the police because citizens do not regard the incidents as worthy of police resources.

Whether or not a crime is reported to the police also depends on the status of victims and offenders, the degree of violence in the event, and the consequences of violence:

- Victims are more likely to report each type of violent crime if the crime is completed, is a serious assault on the person, and involves injury (Bureau of Justice Statistics, 1990:Table 92). By way of example, 8 of every 10 completed robberies with injury from a serious assault were reported to the police in 1988, compared with fewer than 4 of every 8 simple assaults attempted without a weapon.
- Females are, with few exceptions, somewhat more likely to report their violent victimizations to the police than are males (Bureau of Justice Statistics, 1990:Table 94).
- Blacks who recount violent victimizations to NCS interviewers are more likely than whites to state that they reported the incidents to the police (Bureau of Justice Statistics, 1990:Table 95).
- Persons ages 12 to 19 are less likely to report their violent victimizations to the police, except that females in this age group

are more likely to report their victimization by rape than are older females (Bureau of Justice Statistics, 1990: Table 97).

Other Barriers

There are other reasons why crime counts differ depending on the institutional means of classifying and counting. The police information used in the UCR system to classify crimes is collected quite close in time to the event, and the information is secured from interviews not only with the victims but also from other informants, some of whom were witnesses to the event. The NCS relies solely on self-reports by persons who consider that they were victimized by an offender or offenders. Reporting depends entirely on recall of victimizations over the previous six-month period, which entails substantial inaccuracy in the recall and dating of events (Skogan, 1990).

As Chapter 2 discusses, a major barrier to accurately estimating violent crime incidents is that, when three or more crime victimizations are similar if not identical, victims often are unable to recall the details of each incident so that they can be separately classified, or they cannot provide an accurate count of the number of such incidents. These are designated *series incidents* by the NCS. Because their number cannot be precisely measured, their count is excluded from NCS reports of victimizations and its estimates of incidents.[8]

The NCS provides some information on the effect this error has on estimates of crime. Table B-1 presents 1988 NCS counts for victimizations not in series, series victimizations, and the combined total, counting each series victimization as only a single victimization, based on the victim's report of the most recent one. In comparing the total combined count with the official count based on victimizations not in series, it is apparent that excluding violent series crimes from the count of violent victimizations underestimates the amount of violent crime. Even when counting a series victimization as a single additional victimization, the 1988 violent victimization count is underestimated by 9.2 percent. Multiplying each series incident by 3 would add an additional 1,638,690 violent crime victimizations to the 1988 count, resulting in an estimated increase of 27.7 percent.

What is most evident from the table is that series victimizations are in the aggregate less serious crimes than are victimizations not in series. This is evident in a number of ways. Proportionately, more of the violent series victimizations are attempted

TABLE B-1 Crimes of Violence, 1988: Number and Percent Distributions of Series and Nonseries Victimizations by Type of Violent Crime

Type of crime	Total Victimizations		Series Victimizations		Victimizations not in series	
	Number	Percentage	Number	Percentage	Number	Percentage
Crimes of violence	6,455,800	100.0	546,230	100.0	5,909,570	100.0
Completed	2,338,690	36.2	158,700	29.1	2,179,980	36.9
Attempted	4,117,100	63.8	387,520	70.9	3,729,580	63.1
Rape	137,350	2.1	9,970	1.8[a]	127,370	2.2
Completed	65,550	1.0	0	0.0[a]	65,550	1.1
Attempted	71,790	1.1	9,970	1.8[a]	61,810	1.1
Robbery	1,111,160	17.2	63,150	11.6	1,048,000	17.7
Completed	730,870	11.3	46,610	8.5	684,260	11.6
With injury	275,250	4.3	12,380	2.3[a]	262,870	4.5
From serious assault	133,920	2.1	3,820	0.7[a]	130,090	2.2
From minor assault	141,320	2.2	8,550	1.6[a]	132,770	2.3
Without injury	455,620	7.0	34,220	6.2	421,390	7.1
Attempted	380,280	5.9	16,540	3.1	363,730	6.1
With injury	118,540	1.8	8,260	1.5	110,270	1.8
From serious assault	56,850	0.9	6,360	1.2[a]	50,490	0.8
From minor assault	61,680	0.9	1,900	0.3[a]	59,780	1.0
Without injury	261,740	4.1	8,280	1.6[a]	253,450	4.3
Assault	5,207,290	80.7	473,090	86.6	4,734,190	80.1
Aggravated	1,842,100	28.6	100,710	18.4	1,741,380	29.5
Completed with injury	610,720	9.5	40,130	7.4	570,580	9.7
Attempted with weapon	1,231,380	19.1	60,580	11.0	1,170,800	19.8
Simple	3,365,180	52.1	372,370	68.2	2,992,800	50.6
Completed with injury	931,540	14.3	71,950	13.2	859,580	14.5
Attempted without weapon	2,433,640	37.8	300,410	55.0	2,133,220	36.1

[a]Estimate is based on about 10 or fewer sample cases and should not be considered reliable.

rather than completed crimes of violence. Series victimizations are less often the more serious crimes of rape, robbery, and aggravated assault. Likewise, proportionately fewer of the series victimizations are reported with injury. It is also noteworthy that simple assaults are overrepresented among series victimizations compared with those not in series. This provides some additional evidence that the self-report victim survey is more likely to record the less serious crimes of violence—those that are less likely to be reported to the police.

Even adding series victimizations as a single incident to the total count is still an underestimate, since a sizable number of victims estimate four or more incidents in their series. Loftin and MacKenzie (1990) estimated the effect of multiplying each series incident by the victim's estimate of the number of separate incidents in the series for 1987 incident-level data. The vast majority of incidents had a frequency of less than 10, but the distribution extends to 150 incidents in a series. High-frequency series victimizations have a considerable impact on the estimate when each series crime is weighted by the victim's estimate of the number of incidents in a series. Loftin and MacKenzie found that weighting by victim estimates of the number of victimizations in a series increased the estimated frequency of victimization 10 times over the estimate that excludes series victimizations. By this estimate, repeat victimization of a relatively small number of the total victims—the series victims—accounts for the bulk of victimizations in the weighted estimated rate.

Loftin and MacKenzie caution against uncritical acceptance of a victim's estimate of the number of incidents in a series. They draw attention to the fact that response errors are necessarily large for series crimes because information is not collected for separate victimizations (incidents). Also, violent series crimes with high frequency are extremely rare, yet they have a substantial impact on the overall rate. Investigation of repeat victimization over time provides a third reason for caution. Multiple incidents reported as either series or nonseries victimizations persist for only short periods of time in the NCS population of victims. It seems likely that the sharp fall in repeat victims, especially of series victims, from one six-month interview to the next is an artifact of the survey procedure that does not measure repeat and continuing victimization adequately (Reiss, 1981:48).

STATISTICAL AND OTHER COMPENSATING MECHANISMS

Just how seriously the national violent crime rate is underestimated given the fact that each of the two main methods misses a substantial proportion of victims captured by the other cannot be estimated precisely at the present time. Using a capture-recapture statistical model of estimation for the 1980 NCS data on aggravated assault and the data on aggravated assault reporting from the San Jose reverse-record check study, Reiss estimated that the estimated 1980 crude aggravated assault victimization rate using multiple capture was almost twice as high as that estimated by the NCS and over three times that estimated from police case reports (Reiss, 1985:166-167). These are crude estimates and should be regarded as illustrative of the problems faced in estimating the magnitude of violent crime rather than as definitive estimates.

Although it is clear that each method fails to capture the whole picture, the magnitude of the loss from any one method in estimating the national violent crime rate is difficult to ascertain. There are a number of reasons for this conclusion. Multiple capture methods require that individuals or events be uniquely identified for accurate estimates, as that is the only reliable means of determining whether they are capturing the same events or individuals. There are significant institutional barriers to unique identification of individuals, particularly by government agencies such as the Bureau of the Census, which closely guards individual identity. Moreover, to increase the accuracy of matching, each information system would need to be redesigned, since it is no simple matter to achieve unique identity matching of either individuals or incidents. Unique identity of crime incidents reported by two or more systems is even more difficult to determine. The accuracy of any system of multiple capture would be enhanced by the use of dual frame or multiple frame sample selection, which again would require major institutional changes in data collection.

It is useful at this point to note the substantial number of data collection systems, not currently taken advantage of, that acquire information on violent crimes. Use of that information could substantially increase our ability to estimate the nature of violent behaviors, including violent crimes, and their consequences. Emergency medical services are a major potential source of information on violent behavior and its consequent injuries. A number of studies in the United States and abroad provide evidence that emergency medical treatment services process a substantial number of victims of violent crime that are not reported to the police. A study of characteristics of victims of self-reported assaults admitted to St. Vincent's General Hospital Accident and Emergency Center in Sydney, Australia, reported that 57 percent of the 60 percent of self-reported victims of assault who consented to be interviewed did not intend to report their assault to the police (Cuthbert et al., 1991:138, 143). In one northeastern Ohio county where rates for the victims of police assault incidents were compared with the rate for assaults known to hospital emergency departments, the emergency medical services incidence rates for assault with physical injury (including forcible rape) were nearly four times the rates reported in UCR (Barnachik et al., 1983).

NOTES

1 A felony murder is one committed during the course of committing any felony. Armed robbery is a felony. There is some evidence that persons who are under the influence of drugs and/or are young inexperienced robbers are more likely to fire their weapon during an armed robbery, resulting in a deadly assault.

2 An exception is the UCR Supplementary Homicide Report, in which age, race, sex, ethnic status, and relationship are reported for victims and known offenders.

3 The Redesign Phase III of the National Crime Survey currently being implemented has added a screen question directly inquiring about "any rape, attempted rape, or other type of sexual attack" as well as a further probe about "incidents involving forced or unwanted sexual acts (that) are often difficult to talk about." Respondents who acknowledge such attacks are asked specific questions about them on the Crime Incident Report (Forms NCS 1X and 2X, OMB no. 1121-0111).

4 A reverse-record check study basically compares two methods of data collection by embedding a sample of those subject to one method of data collection on a population of events within a probability sample of individuals subject to the same event who are then exposed to a second method of data collection on the same population of events. These reverse-record check studies embedded a sample of victims of rape, robbery, and assault whose victimization was known to the police of the city within a probability sample of the households of that city in which all members were interviewed.

5 The term *reporting* to the police rather than *calling* the police is used for a number of reasons but primarily because the victim is not always the person who called the police. Additionally, some victimizations are reported in person rather than by calling the police.

6 The total number of reasons for reporting is substantially less than the total reported victimizations (compare Bureau of Justice Statistics, 1990:Tables 92 and 102). That discrepancy may be the result of error in tabulation or reporting.

7 Unfortunately, the NCS combines the reasons of "offender unsuc-

cessful in the attempted crime" and "property recovered" for completed crimes. These would seem to be related to the type of violent victimization with the former reason more commonly given for rape and assault and the latter for robbery victimizations.

8 Table B-1 reproduces statistics on 1988 series victimizations published in a methodological appendix by the Bureau of Justice Statistics (BJS). The series counts for forcible rape illustrate the BJS dilemma. Ignoring series rape victimizations undercounts completed plus attempted rapes by at least 8 percent and probably far more. Yet, because the sample sizes for series rapes are too small to obtain valid counts, BJS might, by including these data in the body of its report, create a misimpression that only about 1 in 10,000 series rape attempts are successful. Placing the table in a methodological appendix discourages such misinterpretations while helping researchers to make adjustments to estimates based on their criteria.

REFERENCES

Barnachik, J.I., B.F. Chatterjee, Y.E. Greene, E.M. Michenzi, and D. Fife

1983 Northwestern Ohio trauma study: I. Magnitude of the problem. *American Journal of Public Health* 73:746-751.

Biderman, Albert D., and Albert J. Reiss, Jr.

1967 On exploring the "dark figure" of crime. *Annals of the American Academy of Political and Social Sciences* 374:1-15.

Blumstein, Alfred, J. Cohen, and R. Rosenfeld

1991 Trend and deviation in crime rates: A comparison of UCR and NCS data for burglary and robbery. *Criminology* 29:237-263.

Bolton, Frank, L. Morris, and A. MacEachron

1989 *Males at Risk: The Other Side of Child Sexual Abuse.* Newbury Park, Calif.: Sage Publications.

Bureau of the Census

1970a Victim recall: Pretest household survey of victims of crime. Washington, D.C. (mimeo).

1970b Household surveys of victims of crime: Second pretest. Baltimore, Md. (mimeo).

Bureau of Justice Statistics

1990 *Criminal Victimization in the United States, 1988.* A National Crime Survey Report, December 1990, NCJ-122024.

Cromwell, Paul F., J.N. Olson, and D'aunn W. Avery.

1991 *Breaking and Entering: An Ethnographic Analysis of Burglary.* Newbury Park, Calif.: Sage Publications.

Cuthbert, Marjorie, Frances Lovejoy, and Gordian Fulde

1991 Investigation of the incidence and analysis of cases of alleged violence reporting to St. Vincent's Hospital. In Duncan Chappell, Peter Grabosky, and Heather Strang, eds. *Australian Violence: Contemporary Perspectives.* Canberra, Australia: Australian Institute of Criminology.

Elliott, D.S., D. Huizinga, and S. Menard
1989 *Multiple Problem Youth.* New York: Springer-Verlag.

Federal Bureau of Investigation
1989 *Uniform Crime Reports: Crime in the United States, 1988.* Washington, D.C.: U.S. Government Printing Office.
1990 *Uniform Crime Reports: Crime in the United States, 1989.* Washington, D.C.: U.S. Government Printing Office.

Jencks, Christopher
1991 Is the underclass growing? In Christopher Jencks and P. Peterson, eds., *The Urban Underclass.* Washington, D.C.: Brookings.

Johnson, Bruce D., T. Williams, K. Dei, and H. Sanabria
1990 *Drug Abuse in the Inner City: Impact on Hard-Drug Users and the Community.* In Michael Tonry and J.Q. Wilson, eds. *Drugs and Crime.* Chicago: University of Chicago Press.

Loftin, Colin, and Ellen J. MacKenzie
1990 Building National Estimates of Violent Victimization. Draft paper presented at the Symposium on the Understanding and Control of Violent Behavior. Destin, Fla. April 1-4.

National Institute of Law Enforcement and Criminal Justice
1972 San Jose Method Test of Known Crime Victims. Statistics Technical Report 1, Statistics Division. Washington, D.C.: U.S. Government Printing Office.

Reiss, Albert J., Jr.
1981 Measuring repeat victimization in the National Crime Survey and the special case of series victimization. *Social Statistics Section Proceedings of the American Statistical Association* 41-50.
1985 Some failures in designing data collection that distort results. Pp. 161-177 in Leigh Burstein, Howard E. Freeman, and Peter H. Rossi, eds., *Collecting Evaluation Data: Problems and Solutions.* Beverly Hills, Calif.: Sage Publications.

Rengert, George, and J. Wasilchick
1989 *Space, Time, and Crime: Ethnographic Insights into Residential Burglary.* Report to the National Institute of Justice, Temple University.

Sherman, Lawrence W., and Ellen G. Cohn
1989 The impact of research on legal policy: The Minneapolis domestic violence experiment. *Law and Society* 23:117-144.

Sherman, L.W., L. Steele, D. Laufersweiler, N. Hoffer, and S.A. Julian
1989 Stray bullets and "mushrooms": Random shootings of bystanders in four cities, 1977-1988. *Journal of Quantitative Criminology* 5(4):297-316.

Skogan, W.G
1990 Criminal victimization. Pp. 7-22 in A. Lurigic and G.G. Skogan, eds., *Crime Victims.* Newbury Park, Calif.: Sage Publications.

C
Panel Biographies

ALBERT J. REISS, JR. (Chair) is the William Graham Sumner professor of sociology at the Institution for Social and Policy Studies and a lecturer in law at Yale University. He has served as a consultant to the President's Commission on Law Enforcement and the Administration of Justice (1966-1967), the National Advisory Commission on Civil Disorders (1967-1968), and the National Commission for the Protection of Human Subjects in Biomedical and Behavioral Research (1976). Under presidential appointment, he served as a member of the National Advisory Commission on Juvenile Justice and Delinquency Prevention (1975-1978). He is a past president of the American Society of Criminology and is currently serving as president of the International Society of Criminology. He is a fellow of the American Academy of Arts and Sciences, the American Statistical Association, and the American Society of Criminology. He has authored or edited 12 books including *Social Characteristics of Urban and Rural Communities* (1950, with O. Duncan), *The Police and the Public* (1971), *Indicators of Crime and Criminal Justice: Quantitative Studies* (1980, with S. Fienberg), and *Communities and Crime* (1986, with M. Tonry). He received a Ph.D. degree in sociology from the University of Chicago, an L.L.D. (honoris causa) degree from the City University of New York, and a Docteur Honoris Causa from the Université de Montréal.

DAVID P. FARRINGTON (Vice Chair) is professor of psychological criminology at Cambridge University, where he has been on the staff since 1969. His major research interest is in the longitudinal study of delinquency and crime, and he is director of the Cambridge Study in Delinquent Development, a prospective longitudinal survey of over 400 London males from age 8 to 32. He is also co-principal investigator of the Pittsburgh Youth Survey, a prospective longitudinal study of over 1,500 Pittsburgh males from age 7 to 17. In addition to over 120 published papers on criminological and psychological topics, he has published 11 books, one of which (*Understanding and Controlling Crime*, 1986) won the prize for distinguished scholarship of the American Sociological Association Criminology Section. He is president of the British Society of Criminology, a member of the National Research Council's Committee on Law and Justice, a member of the advisory boards of the U.S. National Archive of Criminal Justice Data and the U.S. National Juvenile Court Data Archive, joint editor of the Springer-Verlag book series on Research in Criminology, and a member of the editorial boards of several journals. He has been a member of the National Research Council's Panel on Criminal Career Research, a member of the national Parole Board for England and Wales, and chair of the Division of Criminological and Legal Psychology of the British Psychological Society. He is a fellow of the British Psychological Society and the American Society of Criminology. He received B.A., M.A., and Ph.D. degrees in psychology from Cambridge University, and the Sellin-Glueck Award of the American Society of Criminology (in 1984) for international contributions to criminology.

ELIJAH ANDERSON is the Charles and William L. Day professor of the social sciences at the University of Pennsylvania. An expert on the sociology of black America, he is the author of the widely regarded sociological work, *A Place on the Corner: A Study of Black Street Corner Men* (1978) and numerous articles on the black experience, including "Of Old Heads and Young Boys: Notes on the Urban Black Experience" (1986), commissioned by the National Research Council's Committee on the Status of Black Americans, and "Sex Codes and Family Life Among Inner-City Youth" (1989). For his recently published ethnographic study, *Streetwise: Race, Class and Change in an Urban Community* (1990), he was honored with the Robert E. Park Award of the American Sociological Association. He has also won the Lindback Award for Distinguished Teaching at Penn. He is associate director of Penn's Center for Urban Ethnography and associate editor of *Qualitative Sociology*. Other topics with which he concerns himself are the social psychology of organizations, field methods of social research, social interaction, and social organization. He received a B.A. degree from Indiana University, an M.A. degree from the University of Chicago, and a Ph.D. degree from Northwestern University, where he was a Ford Foundation Fellow.

GREGORY CAREY is assistant professor of psychology at the Department of Psychology, and faculty fellow, Institute for Behavioral Genetics, University of Colorado, Boulder. His research and publications are in the area of quantitative methods in the study of the genetics of behavior with a special emphasis on the development of and genetic architecture behind antisocial behavior, alcohol abuse, and drug abuse in teenagers. He received a B.A. degree from Duquesne University, an M.A. degree from the Graduate Faculty, New School for Social Research, and a Ph.D. degree from the University of Minnesota, Minneapolis.

JACQUELINE COHEN is associate director of the Urban Systems Institute and senior research scientist in the H. John Heinz III School of Public Policy and Management, Carnegie Mellon University. Her research concerns quantitative methods (including econometrics and stochastic processes), criminal careers, and incapacitation. She is a member of the American Society of Criminology, the Law and Society Association, the American Sociological Association, and the Academy of Criminal Justice Sciences. She received B.S. and M.A. degrees from the University of Pittsburgh and a Ph.D. degree in urban and public affairs from Carnegie Mellon University.

PHILIP J. COOK is professor of public policy and economics at Duke University. His main research interests encompass criminal justice policy, public health regulation, and public finance. He has written extensively on alcohol control measures and on the technology of personal violence. His most recent book is *Selling Hope: State Lotteries in America* (with Charles T. Clotfelter). Cook received a B.A. degree from the University of Michigan (1968), and a Ph.D. degree in economics from the University of California, Berkeley (1973). From 1985 to 1989 he served as director of Duke's Institute of Policy Sciences.

FELTON EARLS is professor of human behavior and development at the Harvard School of Public Health and professor of child psychiatry at the Harvard Medical School. He is also director of the Program on Human Development and Criminal Behavior, which is supported by the MacArthur Foundation and the National Institute of Justice, and director of the Developmental Epidemiology Research Unit at the Judge Baker Children's Center. He chaired the advisory panel to the Office of Technology Assessment of the U.S. Congress that produced the three volume study, *Adolescent Health,* and more recently has chaired the Violence Prevention Panel at the Centers for Disease Control as part of their project on Setting the National Agenda for Injury Control in the 1990s. His research has focused primarily on cultural and social determinants of conduct problems and substance use in children and adolescents and is currently concerned with how these elements interact to produce violence and crime.

LEONARD D. ERON is professor of psychology and emeritus research professor of the social sciences in psychology at the University of Illinois at Chicago. His major research interest has been in the development of aggression in children. He has conducted two major longitudinal studies: one over 22 years and one in its twelfth year, which is presently being conducted in four countries—the United States, Finland, Israel, and Poland. Currently he is also engaged in a large-scale preventive intervention in the public schools of Chicago and Aurora, Illinois. He is on the editorial board of the Guggenheim Review of Violence, Aggression, and Dominance and is chair of the Commission on Youth and Violence of the American Psychological Association. In 1980 he received the APA Award for Distinguished Professional Contributions to Knowledge. He was editor of the *Journal of Abnormal Psychology* from 1973 to 1980 and is author or coauthor of seven books including *Learning of Aggression in Children* (1971), *Growing Up to Be Violent* (1977), and *Television and the Aggressive Child* (1981). He received a B.S. degree from the City College of New York, an M.A. degree in psychology from Columbia University, and a Ph.D. degree in psychology from the University of Wisconsin.

LUCY FRIEDMAN is the founding director of Victim Services, a not-for-profit organization begun in 1978. Through hotlines, schools, police precincts, courts, and community offices throughout New York City, Victim Services helps over 100,000 victims each year, providing practical services, counseling, peer support groups, and advocacy. Victim Services operates specialized services for battered women, families of homicide victims, child sexual assault, and elder abuse victims. As a longtime advocate for victim rights, Dr. Friedman has written on various aspects of crime, its impact on victims and their families, and its treatment in the criminal justice system. Before founding Victim Services, she was an associate director at the Vera Institute of Justice. She received a B.A. degree from Bryn Mawr College and a Ph.D. degree in social psychology from Columbia University.

TED ROBERT GURR, who formerly taught at Princeton and Northwestern Universities and the University of Colorado, has been professor of government and politics at the University of Maryland since 1989, and distinguished scholar of the University's Center for International Development and Conflict Management. Political conflict and violence have been the main foci of his research, including *Why Men Rebel* (recipient of the Woodrow Wilson Prize for best book in political science of 1970), *Violence in America: Historical and Comparative Perspectives* (with Hugh Davis Graham, 1969, 1979), and *Minorities at Risk: Dynamics and Outcomes of Ethnopolitical Conflict* (forthcoming from the United States Institute of Peace). He also has analyzed long-run trends in violent crime and the evolution of criminal justice systems, including *The Politics of Crime and Conflict: A Comparative History of Four Cities* (with Peter N. Grabosky and Richard C. Hula, 1977) and *Violence in America: The History of Crime* (1989). He has held offices in the American Political Science Association (APSA) and the International Studies Association, and in 1991 was given a Lifetime Achievement Award by the APSA's Conflict Processes Section. He received a B.A. degree in psychology from Reed College and a Ph.D. degree in government and politics from New York University.

JEROME KAGAN is professor of psychology at Harvard University and has been in this position since 1964. His research involves the study of cognitive and emotional development in children with a special emphasis on sources of temperamental variation in children. He has been awarded the Distinguished Scientific Award by the American Psychological Association and also by the Society for Research in Child Development. He was a Kenneth Craik scholar at Cambridge University, Phi Beta Kappa Travelling Scholar, and recipient of the Wilbur Cross Medal from Yale University. He received a B.S. degree in biology from Rutgers University, and a Ph.D. degree in psychology from Yale University.

ARTHUR KELLERMANN is medical director of the Emergency Department at the Regional Medical Center at Memphis and is associate professor of internal medicine and preventive medicine at the University of Tennessee, Memphis. His major research interests include emergency department technology assessment, provision of health services to the poor, and the epidemiology of fatal and nonfatal firearm injuries in the United States. He is a member of the Society for Academic Emergency Medicine, the American College of Emergency Physicians, and the American Public Health Association. A former Robert Wood Johnson Clinical Scholar, he received a B.S. degree from Rhodes College, an M.D. degree from Emory University, and an M.P.H. degree from the University of Washington. He is board certified in both internal medicine and emergency medicine.

RON LANGEVIN is director of Juniper Associates Psychological Services and associate professor of psychiatry at the University of Toronto. His major research interest concerns sexual and violent offenders. He has examined both etiology and treatment of these problems from a psychobiological perspective. He is author of *Sexual Strands: Understanding and Treating Sexual Anomalies in Men* (1983) and editor of *Erotic Preference, Gender Identity and Aggression in Men* (1985) and *Sex Offenders and Their Victims* (1990). He is a member of the International Academy for Sex Research and a board member of the Association for the Treatment of Sexual Abusers (ATSA). He is editor of the ATSA journal, the *Annals of Sex Research*. He received a B.A. degree from McGill University in Montreal and a Ph.D. degree in psychology from the University of Toronto.

COLIN LOFTIN is professor of criminology in the Institute of Criminal Justice and Criminology and director of the Violence Research Group at the University of Maryland at College Park. His research concerns crime statistics and the causes and consequences of violence. It has focused on monitoring the character and distribution of violence, understanding violence as social processes that extend beyond individual action, examining population risk factors for criminal violence, and evaluating violence prevention strategies. He received B.A., M.A., and Ph.D. degrees in sociology from the University of North Carolina at Chapel Hill.

KLAUS A. MICZEK directs the psychopharmacology laboratory at Tufts University where he serves as professor of psychology. He has authored some 80 research articles, 25 reviews and edited half a dozen volumes on psychopharmacological research in various animal preparations on the topics of brain mechanisms of aggression, anxiety, and social stress. He has served since 1983 on research review committees for the National Institute on Drug

Abuse, National Institute on Mental Health, and National Institute on Alcoholism and Alcohol Abuse. He is currently the coordinating editor of *Psychopharmacology* and serves on the editorial board of several other journals in this area. He is the current president of the Behavioral Pharmacology Society, past president of the Division of Psychopharmacology, and the past chair of the Committee on Animals in Research and Ethics of the American Psychology Association. He is a fellow or member of 10 scientific societies. He was originally educated in Berlin, Germany, and received a Ph.D. degree in biopsychology from the University of Chicago.

MARK H. MOORE is the Guggenheim professor of criminal justice policy and management at the John F. Kennedy School of Government, Harvard University. His major research interests lie in the fields of criminal justice policy, public management, and governmental ethics. Within the field of criminal justice, he has concentrated on the control of "criminogenic commodities" such as drugs, guns, and alcohol; on "dangerous offenders"; and on juvenile justice. He is the author or editor of six books including *Buy and Bust: The Effective Regulation of an Illicit Market in Heroin*; *Dangerous Offenders: Elusive Targets of Justice*; *From Children to Citizens: The Mandate for Juvenile Justice*; and *Beyond 911: A New Era for Policing*. He also chaired the National Research Council's Panel on Alternative Policies for the Prevention of Alcohol Abuse and Alcoholism and is coeditor of its report entitled *Alcohol and Public Policy: Beyond the Shadow of Prohibition*. He has also been a member of the National Committee for Injury Prevention and Control and led a national "Executive Session" at Harvard on the future of policing. He received a B.A. degree from Yale University and M.P.P. and Ph.D. degrees in public policy from Harvard University.

JEFFREY A. ROTH, study director for the panel, is currently research director for the Law and Public Policy Area of Abt Associates, Inc. He previously served as study director for National Research Council panels on research on criminal careers and on taxpayer compliance. Before joining the NRC staff, he served as senior economic analyst at the Institute for Law and Social Research and as director of legal studies at Westat, Inc. His previous publications concern pretrial release decision making, taxpayer compliance, and mentally disordered offenders. His current research interests include violence and the evaluation of drug treatment programs. He received B.A., M.A., and Ph.D. degrees in economics from Michigan State University.

JAMES F. SHORT, JR. is professor of sociology and senior research associate at the Social and Economic Sciences Research Center, Washington State University. He was director of research (with Marvin E. Wolfgang) of the National Commission on the Causes and Prevention of Violence (1968-1969) and a consultant to the President's Commission on Law Enforcement and the Administration of Justice (1966-1967). He is past president of the American Sociological Association and editor of the American Sociological Review. A recipient of the Edwin H. Sutherland Award of the American Society of Criminology, the Paul W. Tappan Award of the Western Society of Criminology, and the Bruce Smith Award of the Academy of Criminal Justice Sciences, Short is a fellow of the American Society of Criminology and has been a Guggenheim fellow and a fellow at the Center for Advanced Study in Behavioral Sciences (Stanford), the Centre for Socio-Legal Studies and Wolfson College (Oxford), and the Institute of Criminology and Kings College (Cambridge), and a resident fellow at the Rockefeller Center in Bellagio. He received the 1990 Distinguished Contribution Award of the Section on Environment and Technology (American Sociological Association). His books include *Suicide and Homicide: Some Economic, Sociological and Psychological Aspects of Aggression* (with A. Henry), *Group Process and Gang Delinquency* (with F. Strodtbeck), and *Delinquency and Society.* He has edited several volumes, including *The State of Sociology: Problems and Prospects, The Social Fabric: Dimensions and Issues*, and *Organizations, Uncertainties, and Risks* (with Lee Clarke). He received a B.A. degree and an honorary D.Sc. from Denison University and M.A. and Ph.D. degrees in sociology from the University of Chicago.

LLOYD STREET is associate professor of human service studies at the College of Human Ecology, Cornell University. His research and teaching interests include race and crime, human service delivery, and program planning. Publications that reflect these interests include *The Transient Slum* (with Phil Brown), *Background for Planning* (with E. Fruedenberg), and *Race, Crime and Community* (in press). He received B.A., M.A., and Ph.D. degrees in sociology and a post master's certificate in community organization research from the University of California, Berkeley.

FRANKLIN E. ZIMRING is William G. Simon professor of law and director of the Earl Warren Legal Institute at the University of California at Berkeley. His major research interest is the empirical study of law and legal institutions, with special emphasis on criminal violence. He is author or coauthor of *The Changing Legal World of Adolescence* (1982), *Capital Punishment and the American Agenda* (1987), *The Scale of Imprisonment* (1991), and *The Search for Rational Drug Control* (1992). He received a B.A. degree in 1963 from Wayne State University and a J.D. degree in 1967 from the University of Chicago, where he served on the law faculty from 1967 to 1985. He is a member of the American Academy of Arts and Sciences.

Index

A

B

D

E

F

I

N

O

P

R

S

T

U

V

W